Woman to Woman

A collection of Christian articles
by women for women.

Compiled and

GW00586655

Sylvia P

Quotations are taken from the *New International Version*, unless otherwise stated, although some are the author's own.

ISBN 1 902859 29 4

Printed in England.
First published in 2002.

The Open Bible Trust
Bethany, Tresta,
Shetland, ZE2 9LT, GB.

Bible Search Publications Inc.
13927 Dallas Court,
Rosemount, MN 55068, USA.

About the Editor

Sylvia Penny was born in Bexleyheath, Kent, in 1956. She was educated at Harriet Costello School and Queen Mary's College, Basingstoke, before studying accountancy at Oxford Polytechnic, now Oxford Brooke University. She qualified as a Chartered Accountant and practised in the profession in England for a number of years before going to America with her husband. There she became a homemaker and a pastor's wife, leading adult Sunday School as well as Junior Church. She returned to England, and to chartered accountancy, in 1999 and lives with her husband and two teenage children in Berkshire.

Other works written by Sylvia Penny include:
Resurrection! When? (Written with Michael Penny)
Theories of Creation
Forgiveness
Lying

Contents

Woman to Woman 4

Preface

This book is made up of different articles which first appeared in *Search*, the bi-monthly magazine sent out by the *Open Bible Trust*. They are written by women, for women.

These articles cover a large variety of different topics, ranging from studies of women in Scripture, to how Christian women should live their lives today: from the Apostle Paul's attitude towards women, to contemporary views on modern-day issues.

My prayer is that you may find them interesting and helpful, and enjoy reading them as much as I have enjoyed compiling and editing them.

Sylvia Penny

Notes

Part 1
Women in Scripture

Old Testament Women

1. Reflections of Miriam
Sylvia Penny

It is hot, here at Kadesh. I feel I could rest for ever under the cool shade of these trees, looking at the water. Life isn't so hectic now. There seems time, time to remember and reflect.

How long ago it seems since I was a young girl, standing among the reeds on the banks of the Nile and looking at the water. My baby brother was floating gently on it in a little papyrus basket. I so much wanted to know what would happen to him. My mother was heart-broken that he was to die. I remember tears coming to my eyes as I thought of him being tipped into the water and gone, for ever. We had only had him a brief three months, but he was such a lovely baby. We couldn't bear the thought of losing him.

I remember standing there in the reeds, crying. Then Pharaoh's daughter herself came down to the Nile to bathe. I held my breath as I heard her ask one of her slaves to fetch the little basket. One glance told her it was a Hebrew baby, but she just gazed at him and smiled wistfully.

He cried and she must have felt sorry for him. At this, without thinking of the consequences, I jumped up and ran to her as fast as I could. I asked whether she would like me to get a Hebrew woman to nurse the baby. She said yes! I couldn't believe how easy it was.

I remember running back to my mother - I could run in those days. I was full of elation, telling her to come quickly. I laugh now at the thought of it, as I did then, remembering Pharaoh's daughter asking my mother to look after her own baby boy -and saying she would pay her to do so!

So we had our little baby back until he was weaned. We were so thankful that day. The Lord had smiled on us. Little Moses (as he was later called by Pharaoh's daughter) had been saved.

When I think of who that baby grew into, I wonder if Pharaoh's daughter ever regretted that day. But now I realise that the Lord already had a great purpose for him, even when he was a tiny baby. Mind you, he never thought of himself as great. Not in the least. I have never known such a humble person. It used to irritate me, but not any more. Nothing irritates me any longer. All I want is to lie down and have some peace and quiet. I have gone beyond my years of determination and ambition.

Dear Moses! He was so meek. He even had to ask the Lord to use our elder brother, Aaron, as his spokesman. He didn't think he would be able to find the right words himself.

He certainly had the right actions though. I will never forget that incredible night when he stretched out his hand over the sea and the waves parted. We all crossed on dry land. We were amazed. Stunned. But when we got to the other side, didn't we rejoice! We danced for joy, and I could dance in those days. I took a tambourine and all the women followed me with theirs. We sang and danced for hours.

Sing to the Lord, for he is highly exalted. The horse and its rider he has hurled into the sea.

What a long time ago that seems now. So much has happened since. It was such a good start to the new life, and yet, somehow things seemed to go wrong after that. They never did reach that high pitch of rejoicing and thankfulness again. There was always something somebody was complaining about, or others were grumbling at. No meat! No cucumbers! Some even wanted to go back to Egypt.

How angry the Lord must have been with us at times. He was with me once. I remember it so well. I suppose it was my fault really, looking back on it. I started to grumble against Moses and complain about his wife, and got Aaron to agree with me.

I remember thinking that what we said should hold as much weight as what Moses said. After all, I was a prophetess and Aaron a priest. But Moses was just as humble as ever and wouldn't take the bait. That was when the dreadful thing happened. The Lord came down in a pillar of cloud and asked us why we had not been afraid to speak against his servant Moses. When the cloud lifted, I was covered in leprosy from head to foot. I shudder even now as I remember that moment. It was the worst in my life. I spent the next seven days outside the camp before my skin cleared and I was finally allowed back in. I never challenged Moses' authority again after that.

Yes! I have had a full life. An exciting one. But now all I long for is peace and quiet. I feel I could stay here at Kadesh for ever, resting in the shade of these trees, looking at the water.

2. Rahab
Hazel Stephens

Hebrews 11 offers us a list of God's servants in the Old Testament who displayed great faith. In this group we have such well known names as Abraham, Moses, Jacob and David yet a rather surprising inclusion is that of the Gentile prostitute Rahab (11:31). This in itself is remarkable, but the New Testament does not stop there. James describes her as righteous, and offers her as an example of actions arising from faith, (James 2:25), and Matthew includes her in our Lord's genealogy (Matthew 1:5).

Joshua 2

Let us turn to Joshua 2 to find the account of Rahab's actions of great faith.

After forty years of wandering in the wilderness, because of their unbelief, the time had come for Israel to enter the Promised Land. Joshua secretly sent two spies to investigate the land, especially Jericho. On their arrival it was the prostitute Rahab who gave them shelter. This evidently came to the attention of the king and he sent messengers to Rahab to demand the surrender of the spies.

The woman's life was at stake but nevertheless she protected the two Israelites and supplied the king's men with false information which sent the pursuers on the wrong trail. After the king's men went out of Jericho, the spies made their escape, but before going, Rahab requested a token that she and her family would be spared from the coming destruction. Notice how she put her family before herself.

The Scarlet Token

She said that terror had fallen on the inhabitants of Jericho, including herself. They had heard of Israel's dealings with Sihon and Og, kings of the Amorites. She feared for her family's life because she recognised that the Lord was with the Israelites and knew that Jericho was doomed.

The spies granted her request and told her that the token required would be the scarlet cord by which she was to help them escape.

Rahab was to tie the cord to her window, and when the Israelites came, her family would be safe under its protection. The only condition imposed was that they were to stay in the house. If they went into the streets, their death would be their own responsibility.

Notice here the ministry of type and shadow. Just as all were protected by the blood on the lintel and doorposts at the Passover, and just as we are protected by the blood of the Lord Jesus Christ on Calvary, so too was Rahab and her family protected by the scarlet cord.

The fulfilment of this is found in Joshua 6. Every living thing in the city of Jericho - men and women, young and old, cattle and sheep and donkeys - was destroyed, (v 21). Only Rahab and her family were saved, (vs 22,23). This was not a mere temporary reprieve either, for she continued to live with the Israelites, (v 25).

Rahab's Faith

Rahab was a prostitute in Jericho, but her conversion completely changed her way of life. She married among the Israelites and was used by God to exhibit His grace and forgiveness to all repentant sinners. She is included in our Lord's genealogy together with Ruth the Moabitess, (Matthew 1:5), the only two Gentiles in the genealogy. This shows that while the Lord Jesus Christ was sent only to the lost sheep of the house of Israel in the first instance, (Matthew 15:24), there was room for those with true abiding faith, whether Jew or Gentile.

Rahab's faith was not just a passive acceptance of salvation. She was not content to stand by and see others perish. She was intent on saving others. In James 2:25 it is confirmed that she was justified by her works, when she hid the spies. However, in Hebrews 11, it is clear that from her initial faith in the token of the scarlet cord, the sign of her salvation, she continued in faith to the end of her life and will gain great reward for a life faithful to God.

Rahab and Us

Should we not be more like Rahab? We should not be content with our own salvation but be willing to help others to find the truth, the way and the life. We should put behind us all our sins, whatever they be, and start life afresh in the path that the Lord has marked out for us, and continue until the end. Then, when we are called to account, like the servants in the parable, we may hear the commendation, "Well done, thou good and faithful servant" (Matthew 25:21, *KJV*), and not the upbraiding words, "Thou wicked and slothful servant" (Matthew 25:26).

3. Hannah

Sylvia Penny

Many of the great and famous characters of the Bible were the result of miraculous births, and many were born of seemingly barren women. Sarah gave birth to Isaac in her old age. Rebecca gave birth to Jacob and Esau after being barren for twenty years. Rachel gave birth to Joseph, but only after her rival, Leah, had borne Jacob six sons. Of course, the greatest miraculous birth was that of the Lord Jesus, being born to a virgin, Mary.

However, a story which is less well known than these, but which runs along similar lines, is that of Hannah and her son Samuel, who became the great prophet.

Hannah and Peninnah

Hannah was one of Elkanah's two wives, a situation which inevitably caused upset and tension, and whilst Peninnah had several children, Hannah had none.

To make matters worse, Peninnah provoked Hannah year after year, especially when they made the yearly trip to Shiloh to make sacrifices to the Lord. Hannah ended up in tears, unable to eat, but her husband did not seem to understand her plight. He implied that he, himself, should be worth more than ten sons to her!

However, for a Jewish woman to be barren was considered a reproach, and added to that, Hannah was one of two wives, the other having had many children. Obviously she felt deeply about this, more than Elkanah could imagine.

One year, when they were all in Shiloh, Hannah could bear it no longer. She went to the house of the Lord and prayed:

"O Lord Almighty, if you will only look upon your servant's misery and remember me, and not forget your servant but give her a son, then I will give him to the Lord for all the days of his life, and no razor will ever be used on his head." (1 Samuel 1:11)

Hannah, Eli and Samuel

Eli the priest was sitting nearby. He saw Hannah's lips move but heard no voice, as she was praying in her heart. He concluded that she must be drunk and told her to get rid of her wine. Hannah told him he was wrong and that she had been praying in great anguish and grief. At this Eli changed his attitude and said:

> "Go in peace, and may the God of Israel grant you what you have asked of him." (1 Samuel 1:17)

The result was that a baby boy was born some time later. Hannah named him Samuel, "because I asked the Lord for him" (1 Samuel 1:20).

After Samuel had been weaned and while he was still a young boy, Hannah took him to the house of the Lord at Shiloh. There she left him with Eli so that his whole life could be given over to the Lord. He had answered her prayer and now Hannah faithfully kept her part of the bargain.

From then on she saw her son but once a year, when they made their annual visit for the sacrifice. For each occasion she made Samuel a new little robe which she gave to him.

Eli, however, recognised the personal sacrifice which Hannah made and blessed Elkanah and Hannah. He asked the Lord to give them more children in place of Samuel, the one who had been given back to the Lord. The situation ended happily with the Lord answering this request, and Hannah having a further three sons and two daughters.

What can we learn from Hannah?

So what can we learn from this sad story with a happy ending? Hannah's attitude towards the various people with whom she had contact is worth contemplating.

Hannah and Penninah

There was Peninnah, her rival. How would we act towards someone who constantly provoked us on purpose, hurting us at our weakest spot, especially if that person shared our husband's affection and if it was someone from whom we could never escape? I think most of us would turn in the end and repay like with like, retaliating in whatever way we could. But not Hannah! She bore this year after year. Her only reactions were passive ones, weeping and not eating.

We can compare Hannah's situation to that of Sarah, Abraham's wife. When Sarah had failed to have children for many, many years, she gave her maidservant, Hagar, to Abraham, in order to build a family through her. But once Ishmael had been born, Hagar despised Sarah whose reaction was to ill-treat Hagar so badly that she fled into the desert, preferring to die there than to submit to any further violence from Sarah.

We can also compare Hannah with Rachel who, when she found she could not bear children, became jealous of her sister Leah. In Hannah's case, however, there was neither ill-treatment nor jealously of Peninnah.

Hannah and Elkanah

Then there is her husband, Elkanah. Although he loved Hannah (1 Samuel 1:5), it seems he did not love her enough to have only her for a wife, unless he had been tricked into his union with Peninnah as Jacob had been with Leah - but there is no mention of this. Nor did Elkanah seem to realise how much misery her barrenness caused Hannah. He did not seem to notice that Peninnah's taunts made her so depressed. His view was that having him as a husband should be as good as having ten sons. In a society where failure to produce children was considered a great disgrace, he showed a remarkable lack of feeling.

What was Hannah's attitude towards her husband? Despite everything, she did not reproach her husband or point out how insensitive he was. Instead she turned to the Lord in prayer. In all this she sets many good examples, teaching us all important lessons.

Nothing can be gained from pointing out the failings of another, whereas turning to the Lord opens many possibilities. Criticism is negative; prayer is positive.

Hannah and Eli

And what about Eli, the priest? He mistakenly accused Hannah of being drunk and told her to get rid of the wine. This throws much light on the corruption of that time. It suggests that there was much drunkenness, even among women, which was carried even into the temple.

Hannah had been wrongly accused, but her reaction was not one of anger or indignation. It was one of explanation, quietly telling Eli that she was greatly troubled, full of anguish and grief.

If only we could remember Hannah! It is seldom worth getting angry when we are wrongly accused. A few quiet words of explanation can achieve so much more. Hannah's quiet words resulted in Eli praying to the God of Israel, asking that he would grant whatever she asked and so, in the course of time, Samuel was born.

Hannah and the Lord

Lastly, there was the Lord. In her misery she prayed for a child and promised to give him back to the Lord if He granted her request. He answered that prayer and she did not forget her promise.

When Samuel had been weaned, she took him back to Eli at the temple and left him there to serve the Lord for the rest of his life. What a sacrifice this must have been for her, almost as great as that of Abraham being told to offer Isaac back to God in sacrifice.

Samuel was her only child and she did not know that she would have further children. Yet her attitude was not one of regret, it was one full of thankfulness and praise.

Hannah's prayer, in 1 Samuel 2:1-10 is full of rejoicing, despite the fact that she was parting with her only son and would not see him again for a year. In fact her prayer had very little to do with her son, the gift she had been given. It had much more to do with the Giver. So often, for us, the reverse is true. The gift is remembered, but the Giver forgotten.

Hannah and Mary

Hannah's prayer is not unlike the song of Mary in Luke 1:46-55 which Mary uttered in response to Elizabeth's greeting. Many of the phrases used are very similar. Both women were overcome with joyfulness, and for good reason. Hannah was the mother of Samuel who as a child "continued to grow in stature and in favour with the Lord and with men" (1 Samuel 2:26). Mary became the mother of Jesus Who as a child "grew in wisdom and stature, and in favour with God and men" (Luke 2:52).

There are a number of similarities between these two women and, perhaps, it was for the certain finer qualities which they possessed that they became the mothers of such great men: Hannah the mother of Samuel and Mary the mother of our Saviour.

When I was a child, one of my favourite books told the story of Hannah, and Samuel, the child in the temple. Now I am a wife and a mother with children of my own, I find Hannah's life is so full of good examples for us to follow, and is such a touching chapter of human experiences, that it has once again become a favourite of mine.

4. Prophetesses
Sylvia Penny

Vine's *Expository Dictionary* explains that:

> Prophecy is not necessarily, nor even primarily, fore-telling. It is the declaration of that which cannot be known by natural means, Matthew 26:68, it is the forth-telling of the will of God, whether with reference to the past, the present, or the future.

It goes on to say that:

> The prophet was one upon whom the Spirit of God rested, Numbers 11:17-29, one to whom and through whom God speaks, Numbers 12:2.

Therefore a prophet or prophetess did not necessarily predict what was to happen in the future. Rather, they were a mouthpiece for God, and let people know what He wanted them to know.

Although the gift of prophecy is predominantly given to men in the Bible, women were not excluded altogether. There are a number of prophetesses mentioned throughout scripture, the most prominent of which is Deborah. There are no scriptures that preclude women from prophesying, and in fact several which refer to them doing just that.

1 Corinthians 11:5 makes it quite clear that women, as well as men, were expected to prophesy - "And every women who prays or prophesies with her head uncovered dishonours her head". Whether this should be expected of men and women in this dispensation however is another matter, prophecy being one of the gifts of the Spirit for that time (1 Corinthians 12:10).

Joel 2:28 talks about future conditions in Israel, a time in the future after Christ has returned. Although there was a partial fulfilment of this during the Acts period, the years just after Christ ascended, the complete fulfilment awaits the days after His second coming.

> And afterwards, I will pour out my Spirit on all people. Your sons and daughters will prophesy.

Here, again, is a reference to women prophesying, along with the men. This verse is repeated by Peter in Acts 2:17 in his famous speech at

Pentecost. The three main women referred to as prophetesses in the Old Testament are Miriam, Deborah and Huldah.

Miriam

Miriam does not appear to have a great role to play as a prophetess. However, she is referred to as one in Exodus 15:20. "Then Miriam the prophetess, Aaron's sister, took a tambourine in her hand, and all the women followed her, with tambourines and dancing."

Whether her position as a prophetess is merely because she was Moses' and Aaron's sister, or whether it was in her own right, is hard to tell. However, in this verse she does lead the women to praise God, and verse 21 gives the words of her song - "Sing to the Lord, for he is highly exalted. The horse and its rider he has hurled into the sea." This is the refrain of Moses' song which is given in Exodus 15:1-18, which again is a song of praise to God. Micah 6:4 also refers to Miriam's role as a leader of the people - "I sent Moses to lead you, also Aaron and Miriam."

However, the other main reference to Miriam is in Numbers 12 where she is struck with leprosy for daring to talk against Moses. Although it is both she and Aaron who oppose Moses, it is only Miriam who is struck with leprosy. It seems that she must have been the instigator of the complaints against Moses, or else it seems a little unfair that she was singled out to suffer in this way, and not Aaron too.

Deborah

The story of Deborah is given in Judges 4 and 5, and she appears nowhere else in scripture. However, she was an important person at that time and was the leader of Israel. Judges 4:4,5 says:

> Deborah, a prophetess, the wife of Lappidoth, was leading Israel at that time. She held court under the Palm of Deborah between Ramah and Bethel in the hill country of Ephraim, and the Israelites came to her to have their disputes decided.

Her main achievement was leading the Israelites into victory against Jabin, the king of Canaan, after which the land "had peace for forty years" (Judges 5:31). Her presence gave security to the Israelites and to their military leader Barak. "Barak said to her, 'If you go with me, I will go; but if you don't go with me, I won't go'" (Judges 4:8).

However, because Barak did not have the utmost faith in the Lord that he would win a victory, Deborah prophesied that "the honour will not be yours, for the Lord will hand Sisera (the commander of Jabin's army) over to a woman" (Judges 4:9). Subsequently this came true. All of Sisera's troops died by the sword, leaving only Sisera himself. He sought refuge in the tent of woman called Jael, who, after he had fallen asleep, promptly killed him by driving a tent peg through his temple.

Huldah

Huldah the prophetess is mentioned in 2 Kings 22:14 and in 2 Chronicles 34:22, both of which record the same prophecy. She lived at the same time as Josiah who was one of the few good kings of Judah. Although she prophesied a future disaster for Judah, she also prophesied that Josiah would be buried in peace and would not see the disaster which God was to bring. He was to escape the disaster because "your heart was responsive and you humbled yourself before the Lord when you heard what I have spoken against this place and its people" (2 Kings 22:19).

It is interesting to note that despite the fact that both Jeremiah and Zephaniah were both actively prophesying at this time, it is a woman who was chosen by God to prophesy on this occasion.

Noadiah and Isaiah's wife

There are two further women mentioned as being prophetesses in the Old Testament. Noadiah is named in Nehemiah 6:14: "remember also the prophetess Noadiah and the rest of the prophets who have been trying to intimidate me." She is included in a group of false prophets who seemed united in opposition to Nehemiah. Such false prophetesses are condemned by Ezekiel in Ezekiel 13:17-23 which describes some of their ways of deception in detail. They "prophesy out of their own imagination".

Isaiah 8:3 merely refers to his wife in passing, and presumably she is referred to as a prophetess simply because she was married to a prophet. "Then I went to the prophetess, and she conceived and gave birth to a son."

Prophetesses in the New Testament

The remaining prophetesses referred to in Scripture are in the New Testament. Anna the prophetess is mentioned in Luke 2:36-38. When she met Mary and Joseph in the temple with Jesus at the time of His presentation to the Lord "she gave thanks to God and spoke about the child to all who were looking forward to the redemption of Jerusalem" (Luke 2:38).

Acts 21:9 refers to the four unmarried daughters of Philip the evangelist, all of whom prophesied. However, no details are given of any of their prophecies. These had the gift of prophecy referred to in 1 Corinthians 12:10, and were subject to the rules of 1 Corinthians 11:5.

Lastly, Revelation 2:20 refers to "Jezebel, who calls herself a prophetess." However, only a few verses describing her behaviour need to be read to realise why only she would call herself a prophetess.

Pilate's wife

Although she is not referred to as a prophetess, perhaps Matthew 27:19 should be included here:

> While Pilate was sitting on the judge's seat, his wife sent him this message: "Don't have anything to do with that innocent man, for I have suffered a great deal today in a dream because of him."

It seems likely that the fact of Christ's innocence was revealed by the Lord to her. However, unlike the prophetesses of scripture she did not proclaim her message publicly, but notified her husband privately as a warning to him. Also, unlike the named prophetesses of scripture, she was a Gentile. Pilate, however, was then left with no excuse for letting the execution go ahead.

Conclusion

Although women are greatly outnumbered by men as prophets in the Scriptures, it can be seen that there are a number of significant exceptions. The greatest of these was Deborah, but the others had their place too. And it seems that in Israel, at some time in the future, after Christ has returned, once again men and women will prophesy together as foretold by Joel.

5. *Five Women*
Sylvia Penny

If you're like me, when you come to a long list of names in the Bible you quickly skip to the next meaningful verse! This is especially true of genealogies which appear both boring and unpronounceable!

Having said that, however, I thought it might be interesting to look at the genealogy in Matthew 1:1-16. It is unusual, and contrary to Jewish custom in that it lists five women, including two Gentiles and two adulteresses. Most commentaries point out that their inclusion shows the great condescension of Christ in taking on human nature. Who were these five women?

Tamar (Genesis 38)

Tamar's story is described in one brief chapter. Having read it, one wonders why such a person was included by Matthew. After all, no mention is made of Sarah, or Rebecca, or Rachel, who were seemingly far more worthy than Tamar.

Although Tamar's actions cannot be condoned, they can be understood. Judah, her father-in-law, promised to give his third son, Shelah, to her as a husband when he was old enough. Shelah was to take the place of his older two brothers, in accordance with the Law of Moses, for they had been her first and second husbands before their deaths.

Judah, however, broke his promise and so Tamar devised her own scheme whereby she could have a child and avenge herself at the same time. Rather than condemning Tamar, Judah recognised that "She is more righteous than I, since I wouldn't give her to my son Shelah" (Genesis 38:26).

Tamar is also mentioned in Ruth 4:12, where the elders, speaking to Boaz, said "Through the offspring the Lord gives you by this young woman (Ruth), may your family be like that of Perez, whom Tamar bore to Judah." So despite a seemingly bad start, Perez and his family turned out to be worthy people, examples to subsequent generations. The Lord is gracious in whom He uses to carry out His will and purpose.

Rahab (Joshua 2 and 6)

The first thing we are told about Rahab is that she was a prostitute. She was also a member of a wicked and doomed race. Yet she, like Tamar, is included in the genealogy of Christ. Despite her ignominious origins she was later considered righteous and faithful because of what she did for the Lord. There are two further references to Rahab in the New Testament; one refers to her faith and the other to her righteousness.

Hebrews 11:31 says, "By faith the prostitute Rahab, because she welcomed the spies, was not killed with those who were disobedient." Here, she is listed with many of the great characters of the Old Testament: Abraham, Isaac, Jacob and Moses, who all lived by faith.

Scripture does not gloss over the faults of its characters. Rather it gives the plain facts, showing them as they were. Yet these people served the Lord despite their deficiencies.

James 2:25 says, "In the same way, was not even Rahab the prostitute considered righteous for what she did when she gave lodging to the spies and sent them off in a different direction?" Here Rahab is used as an example of how faith should result in good deeds. She believed the Lord was the true God and this affected how she acted.

In Joshua 6:25 we are told that Rahab and her family were saved from destruction and started new lives among the Israelites.

In Matthew's genealogy we see she married Salmon and became the mother of Boaz, and so the mother-in-law of Ruth. Despite the fact that Rahab changed her ways, it still seems strange that a one-time prostitute should be listed among the great people of God in Hebrews 11, and named in the genealogy of the Lord Himself. Yet these very facts provide more evidence of God's grace and forgiveness. It also shows that, unlike us, He looks on the hearts of people and knows those who are truly repentant for their actions.

Rahab's repentance and subsequent life were acceptable to Him and she was rewarded. She and her family escaped death, and she also has a special place both in Scripture, being included in Christ's genealogy, and in God's plan, being amongst the heroes of Hebrews 11.

Ruth (Ruth 1 - 4)

Like Rahab, Ruth was a Gentile. The first piece of information we are given about Ruth is that she was a Moabite woman who married an Israelite, the son of Elimelech and Naomi. Although marriage with Canaanite wives was forbidden to Jewish men (see Deuteronomy 7:3) marriage to Moabite women was permitted. There were certain restrictions on Moabite men entering the congregation of Jehovah (see Deuteronomy 23:3) but otherwise it appears that Moabites were free to become proselytes if they so wished.

The second piece of information we gather about Ruth is that she wished to do just this. Both Naomi's husband and her two sons (one being Ruth's husband) died in the country of Moab, and Naomi was left by herself with her two daughters-in-law, Orpah and Ruth. With persuasion Orpah decided to stay in Moab, but Ruth insisted on staying with Naomi and returning with her to Bethlehem. Ruth said to Naomi:

> "Don't urge me to leave you or to turn back from you. Where you go
> I will go, and where you stay I will stay. Your people will be my
> people and your God my God. Where you die I will die, and there I
> will be buried. May the Lord deal with me, be it ever so severely, if
> anything but death separates you and me." (Ruth 1:16,17)

Although Ruth was a Gentile, she desired to become a Jew and live with them and worship the one true God. The book of Ruth tells the story of how she met Boaz in Bethlehem, and how they eventually married, had children, and so became part of the line of ancestors of the Lord Jesus. She is a further example of how the Lord is gracious. He uses her in His plan and purpose despite the fact she was originally a Gentile.

Bathsheba (2 Samuel 11 - 12)

Unlike the other four women in Matthew's genealogy, Bathsheba is not mentioned by name. Instead she is referred to as "Uriah's wife". This is the only reference to her in the New Testament.

The first reference to her in Scripture is in 2 Samuel 11:2 where David is recorded as seeing a beautiful woman bathing while on the roof of his palace. The next verse names her as Bathsheba "the daughter of Eliam and the wife of Uriah the Hittite."

Scripture emphasises from beginning to end that she was another man's wife and that David should never have taken her. Her beauty seems to be the source of his desire. His sin of adultery (2 Samuel 11:4-5) is followed by an attempted cover up (2 Samuel 11:6-13) and finally by murder (2 Samuel 11:14-17).

After a time of mourning for her murdered husband, Bathsheba became David's wife, but 2 Samuel 11:27 says "the thing David had done displeased the Lord." Throughout this episode there is little indication that any blame for what happened was attributed to Bathsheba. The Bible is explicit and makes little attempt to cover up the failings of its characters. Thus the lack of any such condemning details in Bathsheba's case indicates that she was indeed free from guilt. The fact remains, however, that she was an adulteress, willing or not.

Mary

Mary is the fifth and last woman mentioned in Matthew's genealogy. She stands in direct contrast to the other four in that both her life and her pedigree were impeccable. She was a virgin and she was a Jew.

Conclusion

Tamar, Rahab, Ruth and Bathsheba had all experienced prior marriages, or sexual relationships, before marrying the men by which they produced the children destined to be ancestors of the Lord. Tamar and Bathsheba had also committed adultery, and Rahab fornication. Rahab and Ruth were both Gentiles.

Having looked at these women, it is difficult to understand why they were picked out to be mentioned above others who, humanly speaking, were more worthy to be included, such as Sarah, Rebecca and Rachel, for example. However, maybe one reason is to show the lowliness of our Saviour in that His lineage was composed of human beings with many failings. If He had waited for pure and spotless people to be His human ancestors, He would never have come to save us.

6. Hagar, literally and figuratively
Sylvia Penny

There are fourteen references to Hagar in the Bible. Twelve occur in four passages in Genesis (16:1-15, 21:8-20, 21:12-18 and 25:12-18) and the other two in Galatians 4:21-31.

Genesis 16:1-15

We are introduced to Hagar in Genesis 16:1. She is the Egyptian maidservant of Sarah, Abraham's wife. God had promised Abraham a son, but Sarah was unable to have children. She decided that perhaps God's promise to her and Abraham could be brought about through Hagar. So she gave Hagar to her husband, thinking that she would build a family through her, as in accordance with the law of that time any children of a maidservant and her master would belong to the mistress.

However, all this turned to Sarah's disadvantage. When Hagar discovered she was pregnant, she started to despise her mistress. In return, Sarah mistreated Hagar, who fled into the desert to escape her. While she was there, the angel of the Lord visited her and told her to go back to Sarah and submit to her. The angel also promised Hagar that her descendants would be too numerous to count and continued:

> You are now with child and you will have a son. You shall name him Ishmael, for the Lord has heard of your misery. He will be a wild donkey of a man; his hand will be against everyone and everyone's hand against him, and he will live in hostility towards all his brothers. (Genesis 16:11-12)

So Hagar returned to Abraham and Sarah, and Ishmael was born when Abraham was eighty-six years old.

Genesis 21:8-20

This passage refers to the time just after Sarah had given birth to Isaac, the child promised by God. Ishmael, who would have been about sixteen at the time, adopted a mocking attitude towards Sarah, possibly through jealousy of Isaac. As a result Sarah told Abraham to get rid of both Hagar and Ishmael. She said that Ishmael would never share in the inheritance with Isaac, her own son.

Although Abraham was distressed about this, no doubt because Ishmael was his son also, the Lord told him not to be and to do what Sarah wanted. The Lord also told Abraham that because Ishmael was his son, He, the Lord, would make him into a great nation. Such is the grace of God. Despite Sarah's lack of faith, which resulted in the birth of Ishmael, God graciously promised this other son, the son of a slave-woman, that he would be the father of twelve rulers and be the start of a great nation (Genesis 17:20).

Genesis 25:12-18

So Abraham sent Hagar and Ishmael out into the desert, but the Lord preserved them, according to His promise. Hagar found an Egyptian wife for Ishmael and Genesis 25:12-18 records the names of his twelve sons. It also states that they lived in hostility towards all their brothers. All this was in accordance with what the Lord had said.

One point of interest is in Genesis 28:8-9. When Esau realised how displeased his father, Isaac, was with his Caananite wives, he went to Ishmael and married one of his daughters, Mahaleth. This was, perhaps, an attempt to please Isaac.

Thus Hagar, despite being only an Egyptian slave-woman, was allowed by God to be the mother of another great nation. All this was a result of her association with Abraham which came about because of Sarah's lack of faith.

Galatians 4:21-31

The remaining two references to Hagar are in the New Testament and occur in Galatians 4:21-31. This is a figurative passage which is an allegory based on Hagar and Sarah.

Paul uses this method in an attempt to show the Galatian Gentile Christians their position in Christ. They were to consider themselves free from the Law of Moses and not slaves in bondage to it. They should look upon themselves as Isaac, the child of a free woman, not as Ishmael, the child of a slave-woman.

In this passage there is a strong distinction between Hagar and Ishmael, on the one hand, and Sarah and Isaac on the other. Ishmael was the son of a slave woman, born in the ordinary way, according to the law of nature. Isaac was the son of a free woman, born as a result of God's promise, according to God's grace.

Paul was concerned that some Jewish Christian Judaizers were insisting that Gentile Christians had to be circumcised and obey the Law in order to secure their salvation. To illustrate the two opposing principles of law and grace, Paul used Hagar and Sarah as figures of two distinct and different covenants.

Hagar illustrates the covenant given from Mount Sinai, a covenant which resulted in slavery with the people in bondage to the Law. Interestingly, the Arabic name for Mount Sinai is, in fact, Hagar. Paul stated also that Hagar corresponded to the present city of Jerusalem, the centre for the Mosaic Law, because she was in slavery.

Sarah, the free woman, illustrates the covenant of promise, a symbol of grace, and is linked with the Jerusalem that is above and which is free. Sarah, then, stood for freedom, as opposed to slavery to the Law; a covenant of grace, as opposed to one of law.

It was through the grace of God that Isaac was born, a result of God's promise to Abraham. The Galatian Gentile Christians were like Isaac, the children of promise, the children of grace. They were the children of a free woman and thus not slaves, not in bondage to the Law.

However, just as Ishmael, the son born in the ordinary way, persecuted Isaac, the son born by the power of the spirit, so did the Judaizers persecute the Gentile Christians. This prompted Paul to quote the very words of Genesis 21:10. "Get rid of the slave woman and her son, for the slave woman's son will never share in the inheritance with the free woman's son." These words, which Sarah used to Abraham, Paul quoted to the Galatians, who should have had nothing to do with those who were insisting they should be circumcised and obey the Law. Gentiles were never required to keep the Jewish Law but rather were to enjoy and revel in the grace which comes through Jesus Christ. They should have seen that their faith in Him was sufficient, and of course the same is true of us today.

New Testament Women

7. Martha
Sylvia Penny

There are three references to Martha of Bethany in Scripture, the same three references as for her sister Mary. However, Martha is shown to be a very different sort of person to Mary.

There is far more of what Martha said recorded during these three events than Mary. In fact, only one sentence of Mary's is recorded. Perhaps Martha was the more dominant personality, being the elder sister, the one in charge of the home, the one who was spokeswoman, and the one who also appears to be far more practical, and much less emotional.

Martha was the one who is recorded as opening her home for the Lord in Luke 10:38-42. She was practical. She realised the needs of the Lord and His disciples, and that they needed a place to stay and food to eat. She was very concerned for their welfare, in fact so much so that she was totally distracted by all the preparations which she felt had to be made on their arrival. Her heart was obviously in the right place but she didn't recognise the fact that external things do not matter as much as internal things. She was put out by the fact that the Lord did not seem to be very concerned that Mary was not helping her to do the necessary work. The Lord did not condemn Martha for her actions, but merely defended Mary's actions and compared them to Martha's. In the Lord's opinion, Mary had chosen the better course of action in listening to Him. He told Martha that she was worried and upset about many things, whereas there was only one thing she really needed to worry herself about. The Lord was concerned with Martha's order of priorities. He knew Martha's mind, and that the daily chores and physical necessities of living filled more of her mind and time than was necessary. It was not her practical outworking which was wrong - it was the importance which she attached to this which was wrong. We can learn an important lesson from Martha by the way in which the Lord dealt with her as compared to Mary. It is more important to get to know the Lord Jesus Christ than to be troubled with the things of this world. However, it is also important that there should be a practical outworking once this relationship with the Lord has been established.

In John 11:1-46, where the death and resurrection of Lazarus is recorded, again Martha is shown to be far more practical than Mary. Mary's emotion meant that she was in no fit state to listen to the Lord's words of comfort regarding resurrection. He directed these comments to Martha only, as she was in greater control of herself than Mary, and therefore was of far more practical use.

When Martha heard that the Lord was coming to Bethany she went out to meet Him, whereas Mary stayed at home. Martha said the same as Mary did later, that if the Lord had been there Lazarus would not have died. However, she expanded this and said she knew that even now God would give Him whatever He asked. She obviously had great faith in the Lord, and it even appears that she may have believed He had the power to raise Lazarus from the dead even then. Perhaps since His last visit to her home she had taken His words to heart and concerned herself more with Him and His teachings than she had before.

The Lord told her Lazarus would rise again and she displayed her knowledge of Scripture by saying she knew he would rise again at the last day. She also said she believed the Lord Jesus was the Christ, the Son of God, Who was to come into the world as prophesied. Martha was a true believer, and knew exactly Who the Lord was. She gave Him His rightful place, and knew His teachings. Perhaps by this time she had managed to readjust her priorities, and had given the Lord the first place in her life.

Martha went to get Mary when the Lord asked to see her. When they all went to the tomb, the Lord asked them to roll away the stone. Again, it was Martha who spoke up, and with her usual practicality she said that there would be a bad odour as Lazarus had already been in the tomb for four days. Although she had stated previously that she believed God would give the Lord whatever He asked, she probably could not comprehend how this would be achieved. In her own experience she knew what state a dead body would be in after four days, and only when the Lord said to her that if she believed she would see the glory of God, was the stone rolled away and Lazarus walked out. There is no record as to Martha's reaction at receiving her dead brother back to life, alive and well, but one imagines that true to her nature she would be very practical and down to earth and go and find him some food and clothes and water to wash.

The last reference to Martha is in John 12:1-3, where a special dinner was held in the Lord's honour in her home. Possibly Martha arranged this in gratitude for what He had done, and she is recorded as serving at the table. So again in this last reference to Martha her practicality is referred to. Martha's way of showing her thankfulness was to give the Lord a special dinner and to serve it herself.

8. *The Anointings of Jesus*
Sylvia Penny

There is an account of Jesus being anointed in each of the four gospels. Each time it is performed by a woman, using an expensive perfume, and each time it is disapproved of by the men present, apart from the Lord Himself, who commends each woman for her action.

However, it is easy to confuse the separate accounts as many aspects are very similar. Two occur in the house of a man named Simon. Two refer to His feet being anointed, and then wiped by the woman's hair. Three refer to the Passover being close at hand, three refer to the Lord's burial, and in all of them the Lord defends the woman against the surrounding men's criticisms. Interestingly, only one of the accounts names the woman involved. It is in John's account, and her name is Mary, the sister of Martha and Lazarus.

A number of people have attributed the other three passages to assorted Marys, although there is nothing in these narratives to support this. Dwelling on certain similarities between the passages, and ignoring the differences, has led some to this conclusion.

The First Anointing

Chronologically, the first anointing mentioned in the gospels is referred to in Luke 7:36-50. Simon the Pharisee invited Jesus to have dinner at his house. While they were eating, an unnamed woman arrived bringing an alabaster jar of perfume with her. She stood behind the Lord at His feet weeping, and wet them with her tears. Then she wiped them with her hair, kissed them, and poured perfume over them.

Privately, Simon disapproved, as she was a well known sinner, a prostitute, and he thought Jesus should know better than to let her touch Him. However, Jesus defended her. He pointed out to Simon that he had not given Him water to wash His feet, (a common courtesy), nor given Him a kiss, (a sign of greeting), nor put oil on His head (which was then a sign of honour). This woman had done all these things. Her many sins had been forgiven and therefore she loved the Lord very much.

There is nothing in this passage to identify this woman with Mary Magdalene, who is first named in the next chapter of Luke (Luke 8:2), although perhaps some link the two simply because the one narrative follows the other. Mary Magdalene was cured of seven demons, and maybe some interpret that as her having lived an exceptionally immoral life, although there is nothing either to support or negate this view.

Others think this may have been Mary of Bethany on an earlier occasion, before she was saved, simply because the actions are so similar. However, wherever Mary of Bethany (Martha's sister) is named, her character is unquestionable, and there is never a hint of an immoral past. It seems unnecessary to cast this slur upon her character by identifying the two.

Another theory, which again though unsubstantiated may have some credence, is that this woman may be the same one as the woman taken in adultery in John 8:1-11. This woman was brought to the Lord by the teachers of the Law and the Pharisees, as she had been caught in the act of adultery. They rightly pointed out to the Lord that the Law of Moses commanded that people caught in such a way were to be stoned. However, He replied that the person without sin should throw the first stone, and so they all left. When only the woman remained, the Lord told her "Go now and leave your life of sin" (John 8:11). It would be nice to think this is the same woman that subsequently came to Jesus to anoint Him and to whom He finally said "Your faith has saved you; go in peace" (Luke 7:50).

The Second Anointing

The second anointing is referred to in John 12:1-8. This time Mary of Bethany is clearly named as being the woman involved. Verse one makes it clear it was six days before the Passover, and that Jesus arrived at Lazarus' house where a dinner was given in His honour.

Mary took a pint of pure nard, an expensive perfume, and poured it on Jesus' feet, and wiped His feet with her hair. On this occasion Judas Iscariot objected, as he said the perfume was worth a year's wages and could have been sold to give money to the poor. His real reason, however, was that he was a thief and would have liked some of the money for himself.

The Lord defended Mary's action and said, "Leave her alone. It was intended that she should save this perfume for the day of my burial.

You will always have the poor among you, but you will not always have me" (John 12:7-8).

It is interesting to speculate whether Mary realised the significance of her action at the time, or whether it was just performed spontaneously, out of her love for the Lord. No reason is given for her action, and Jesus does not indicate that she had any. He just answers Judas' objection by explaining why the perfume would have been kept rather than sold, even if she had not poured it out in such a manner.

However, after Jesus had mentioned the perfume in the context of His burial, it is possible that Mary then understood fully what He meant. In Mark 16:1 it says, "When the Sabbath was over, Mary Magdalene, Mary the mother of James, and Salome bought spices so that they might go to anoint Jesus' body." There is no mention of Mary of Bethany. Similarly in Luke 23:55-56; it is the women from Galilee who followed Joseph, found out where the tomb was, and went home to prepare spices and perfumes to anoint His body after the Sabbath. Again, there is no mention of Mary of Bethany.

Possibly she was the only one among all the disciples that fully believed and understood that as Jesus was the life and the resurrection, He must rise from the dead. If that were so, there would be no need for the spices and perfumes after His death, as He would be risen. Whether she realised this before she anointed His living body, or after she had done so, can be debated, but perhaps before He died on the cross she, alone, believed unwaveringly that He would rise on the third day, just as He had said.

The Third Anointing

The third anointing is referred to in both Matthew 26:1-13 and Mark 14:1-9. In these passages, the woman is again unnamed. Both passages say clearly that the Passover was now only two days away, and that Jesus was, on this occasion, in the house of Simon the Leper, albeit still in Bethany.

In order to harmonise these passages with the one in John, some think that Martha's husband may have been Simon the Leper, but this seems to be unlikely and unnecessary. Also, this event is described as happening only two days before the Passover, rather than six. It seems far more probable that this is, in fact, a later anointing, and it is possible that this woman, having heard about Mary's action, wished to do a similar thing.

This time the perfume was in an alabaster jar which the woman broke and then poured the perfume over the Lord's head, rather than His feet. This time it was some of the disciples, rather than just Judas, who were indignant. They said it was a waste as it could have been sold and the money given to the poor. Yet again the Lord defended the woman. This time He said, "When she poured this perfume on my body, she did it to prepare me for burial. I tell you the truth, wherever this gospel is preached throughout the world, what she has done will also be told, in memory of her" (Matthew 26:12,13).

Here, it seems that the Lord almost suggested that this woman understood what she was doing. With Mary he merely said that it was intended she should save the perfume for the day of His burial. With this woman He said she actually did it to prepare Him for burial, as if she knew there would be no further opportunity. If this woman had heard of Mary's action, and heard of the Lord's defence of her, then rather than waiting until it was too late, like Mary Magdalene and the other women of Galilee, she chose to anoint Him while she still could. If so, then no wonder the Lord chose to perpetuate the memory of her action throughout the world and throughout time. What she did showed supreme faith in the resurrection, and as such was worthy of remembrance throughout the following ages.

Conclusion

So, whether we believe that all of the anointings were by women called Mary, and that they all took place in the house of someone called Simon, or whether we believe there were only two rather than three, or whether it was the head or the feet, or both, that were anointed .... all such contentions pale into insignificance when the main messages of forgiveness and salvation (the first anointing), and Christ's resurrection from the dead (the second and third anointings) are accepted and believed.

9. *Mary Magdalene*
Sylvia Penny

One of the most wonderful things we can think about at Easter is the resurrection of our Lord and Saviour, Jesus Christ. "For," says Paul, in 1 Corinthians 15:14, "if Christ has not been raised, our preaching is useless and so is your faith."

It is recorded in Mark 16:9, "When Jesus rose early on the first day of the week, he appeared first to Mary Magdalene, out of whom he had driven seven demons." Mary Magdalene was the first person to witness this wonderful event and later that same day, when Jesus appeared to the eleven, "He rebuked them for their lack of faith and their stubborn refusal to believe those who had seen him after he had risen" (Mark 16:14).

What a privilege Mary Magdalene had! Why would our great God and Saviour appear first to an insignificant woman like her? There is little said about her in the scriptures, except for her role at the resurrection.

Demon possessed

She is first mentioned in Luke 8:1-3:

> The Twelve were with him, and also some women who had been cured of evil spirits and diseases: Mary (called Magdalene) from whom seven demons had come out; Joanna the wife of Chuza, the manager of Herod's household; Susanna; and many others. These women were helping to support them out of their own means.

Her life before meeting the Lord, and after, must have been dramatically different. There are no details given as to what her life was like when she was demon-possessed, but she may have been similar to the two men in the Gadarene region who "were so violent that no-one could pass that way" (Matthew 8:28); or the man who was blind and mute in Matthew 12:22; or the boy with a demon of whom his father said, "He has seizures and is suffering greatly. He often falls into the fire or into the water" (Matthew 17:15).

However, after her healing, she travelled around Galilee with several other women supporting the Lord and His disciples out of her own money.

The cross

Nothing more is said of her until the Lord was dying on the cross. Then, in each of the four gospels, either by name or by inclusion in the group of women there, she is mentioned again.

> Many women were there, watching from a distance. They had followed Jesus from Galilee to care for His needs. Among them were Mary Magdalene, Mary the mother of James and Joses, and the mother of Zebedee's sons. (Matthew 27:55-56)

The accounts in Mark 15:40, Luke 23:49 and John 19:25 are all similar. Again, the only details given about her are that she came from Galilee, and helped to care for the Lord's needs. Presumably she had been faithful from the time she met Jesus and had ended up following Him to the cross along with the other women.

The burial

Next came the burial of the Lord. Usually the bodies of criminals and those who were crucified were thrown onto the rubbish heap just outside Jerusalem. They would not have been given a decent burial. However, Joseph of Arimathea, a rich and prominent member of the Jewish Council, asked for the body of Jesus for burial.

Each of the gospels records how he placed it in his own new tomb, and rolled a stone over the entrance. Matthew, Mark and Luke also record that various of the women at the cross witnessed this burial. Matthew 27:61 says, "Mary Magdalene and the other Mary were sitting there opposite the tomb." Mark 15:47 says "Mary Magdalene and Mary the mother of Joses saw where he was laid." Luke 23:55 says "The women who had come with Jesus from Galilee followed Joseph and saw the tomb and how his body was laid in it." John does not mention the women at the burial.

The women must have been concerned to know where His body was so that they could anoint His body with spices and perfumes later, as was the custom. They could not do so straight away for, as Luke records, "the Sabbath was about to begin" (Luke 23:54), and so "they went home and prepared spices and perfumes. But they rested on the Sabbath in obedience to the commandment" (Luke 23:56).

The resurrection

The last mention of Mary Magdalene is at the resurrection of the Lord. It is the most detailed reference to her by far and it makes you wonder why she was singled out by the Lord for this enormous privilege. She was the first to see His resurrected body. Maybe her enthusiasm and zeal for the Lord was rewarded in this special way. The scriptures do not tell us why He appeared to her first. They just tell us that He did.

Of the many events detailed in the four gospels, sometimes in slightly different ways or orders, the details of events given for that first morning after the Lord's resurrection appear to be some of the most confusing and hard to reconcile one with another. Perhaps it is more important to keep in mind the main thrust of these passages, the fact that Christ did indeed rise from the dead, and because of this we can all look forward to the day when we will be resurrected too; "For as in Adam all die, so in Christ all will be made alive" (1 Corinthians 15:22).

However, it is also in these passages that we find out more about the person of Mary Magdalene. The order of the events may be problematical, but the fact that they happened is beyond a doubt. A possible scenario is given below.

Resurrection morning

There are five different accounts of what happened on the resurrection morning, if the two separate narratives given in Mark are included. Mark 16:9 says, "When Jesus rose early on the first day of the week, he appeared first to Mary Magdalene, out of whom he had driven seven demons." The narrative in John's gospel, chapter 20, gives the details of this encounter, and it appears that what is recorded in verses 1-17 must have happened prior to those events recorded in the other three gospels.

John 20:1 says, "Early on the first day of the week, while it was still dark, Mary Magdalene went to the tomb and saw that the stone had been removed from the entrance." As it was still dark, presumably she went before sunrise, which means that her visit must have been before that recorded in Mark 16:2, which says some women went "just after sunrise".

Although Mark 16:1 mentions Mary Magdalene by name, this is only in a list of the women who bought the spices. Verse 2 need not necessarily include her in this particular group of women, especially as she had already visited the tomb, found it empty, and subsequently met the risen Lord. She would then hardly have found it necessary to go back to anoint a body which she knew was not there! Also in Mark 16:3 these women were debating "Who will roll the stone away from the entrance of the tomb?" Mary Magdalene had already seen the stone had been rolled away, and is therefore unlikely to have been among these women.

Dawn or dusk?

Matthew 28:1-4 says:

> After the Sabbath, at dawn on the first day of the week, Mary Magdalene and the other Mary went to look at the tomb. There was a violent earthquake, for an angel of the Lord came down from heaven and, going to the tomb, rolled back the stone and sat on it. His appearance was like lightning, and his clothes were white as snow. The guards were so afraid of him that they shook and became like dead men.

The word translated "dawn" can also be translated "dusk". If dusk is meant then there are few problems reconciling this passage with the other gospels. The Sabbath would have been over at around 6 p.m. on Saturday evening, just about dusk. Mary Magdalene and the other Mary went to see the tomb again. After they had gone, the events of verses 2 to 4 would have happened, and the remaining verses are almost identical with those in Mark 16:6-8.

There may have been a gap of a few hours between the earthquake and the angel talking to the women in Matthew 28:5. Although the narrative reads continuously, if verse 5 were altered slightly to read, "That same angel was the one who later said to the women ....", it would make the actual course of events clearer. However, if verse 1 is translated as "dawn" it is difficult to see how this fits into the narratives of any of the other gospels.

Eager and anxious

The picture I see of Mary Magdalene is one of an eager and anxious woman, wanting to do something, but unable to. She visited the tomb at the burial, she purchased spices and perfumes, prepared them, and then had to rest on the Sabbath. However, directly the Sabbath was over, at dusk, she visited the tomb again with Mary. It was getting dark, the stone was still rolled in front of the tomb, and so they went home for the night. However, maybe she did not sleep well that night, as she was up before dawn, and went again to the tomb while it was still dark. She is the one who was most urgent, and the most anxious of all of them, to see the Lord's body again. John 20:2 says:

> So she came running to Simon Peter and the other disciple, the one Jesus loved, and said, "They have taken the Lord out of the tomb, and we don't know where they have put him!"

After all her pent up feelings, her anxiety, her hopes, she must have been emotionally overcome when she found the tomb was empty. No wonder she went running immediately to the disciples. Having gone and looked in the tomb, Peter and John then returned to their homes, "but Mary stood outside the tomb crying" (John 20:11).

Peter and John were little comfort to Mary. No conversation is recorded and verse 9 adds, "They still did not understand from Scripture that Jesus had to rise from the dead". They seemingly offered no explanations of their own to Mary, and just went home, leaving her still standing there. As Mary wept, she bent over to look in the tomb and this time she saw two angels in there. Unlike the guards, who "were so afraid of him that they shook and became like dead men," Mary displayed no fear. They asked her, "Woman, why are you crying?" "They have taken my Lord away," she said, "and I don't know where they have put him" (John 20:13).

Overcome with emotion

Maybe she was so overcome with emotion by this time that she had no time to feel afraid of the angels, or maybe the angels appeared differently to her than the one did to the Roman guards. Whatever the reason for her lack of fear, she was single-minded in wanting to know where her Lord's body had been taken. Then she turned around and saw Jesus, although she did not recognise Him at first. "Woman," he said, why are you crying? Who is it you are looking for?" Thinking he was the gardener, she said, "Sir, if you have carried him away, tell me where you have put him, and I will get him" (John 20:15).

It seems that in His resurrection body Jesus could disguise or reveal Himself at will, however He wished. Certainly Mary neither recognised His face nor His voice. Also, He asked her two questions He already knew the answers to. Maybe He did this to put her at ease, and so as not to startle her. By this time she must have been desperate, and perhaps she looked on this stranger as her last hope. Then Jesus said to her, "Mary" (John 20:16).

The first fruits

Jesus only had to say this one word in His old voice for her to recognise Him instantly. She turned and tried to hold on to Him and cried out "Rabboni', which means "Teacher". Imagine how Mary must have felt at this moment in time. Bewildered, elated, and overcome with joy. No wonder her instinct was to throw herself towards Him in relief and amazement, but Jesus said:

> "Do not hold on to me, for I have not yet returned to the Father. Go instead to my brothers and tell them, 'I am returning to my Father and your Father, to my God and your God'" (John 20:17).

In Matthew some of the women, having been to the tomb, also met Jesus and clasped His feet. On this occasion He did not tell them to let go. On the earlier occasion, with Mary Magdalene, He explained that He had not yet returned to the Father. He was possibly referring to the wave-offering of the firstfruits of Leviticus 23:11, where, the day after the Sabbath, the priest had to wave a sheaf before the Lord. Jesus was to fulfil the wave-offering by presenting Himself before the Father, and before He did this, for some reason, He could not be touched.

Mary Magdalene went to the disciples with the news. "I have seen the Lord!" And she told them that He had said these things to her (John 20:18). The account in Mark supplements this by saying: "When they heard that Jesus was alive and that she had seen him, they did not believe it" (Mark 16:11). What a strong and determined woman Mary Magdalene must have been! Not only did she get no comfort from Peter and John, but later all she got was the disciples' disbelief. Not until the Lord Himself appeared to the eleven that evening did they believe.

Later Jesus appeared to the Eleven as they were eating. He rebuked them for their lack of faith and their stubborn refusal to believe those who had seen Him after He had risen (Mark 16:14).

Conclusion

That completes all the Scriptures have to say about Mary Magdalene. She comes over as a woman strong in faith and conviction. She used her worldly resources to support the Lord and His disciples. She was not afraid to follow Him to the cross and beyond. She seemed to have more resolve and determination after His death than any of the other women, and perhaps that is why she ended up being the first person to whom the Lord appeared. Although no more is said about her, one imagines her to have been present with the 120 in Jerusalem after Christ's ascension (Acts 1:14-15), and to have been faithful to the end of her life.

10. The Third Day (Mary Magdalene)
Sylvia Penny

Mary stood outside the tomb She wept quietly. Many thoughts rushed through her head, crowding her mind and tugging for her attention But there was one that continually returned, time and time again. Jesus was dead. He was gone for ever.

It seemed such a short time ago that she had first met Him, and now it was all over. He had been killed, crucified on a cross. It had all happened so quickly, three days ago. Three days! Why did that sound significant? Mary couldn't remember, and she couldn't concentrate, as that thought was pushed out by another one.

When Mary first met Jesus

She cast her mind back to that happy day, over two summers ago, when she had first met the Teacher. Until then her life had been a complete misery. She had been in continual torment and torture from demons. What a wretch she had been. Then, on a hot and sultry day, He had calmly walked up to her and commanded the demons to come out of her. At last she was free! She still remembered her own amazement and the startled reaction of the people around, and yet He had remained peaceful and serene, with a small, quiet smile on His calming face. Now, she would never see that face again, nor that smile.

Mary helped Jesus

She had joined the group of other women who followed Him and His chosen disciples wherever they went, helping them in whatever way they could. She had stayed close to Him. Since that time He had been everything, but now He was gone, dead!

Mary listened to Jesus

She had often listened to Him, but had found it difficult to understand what He taught. Sometimes she asked Peter or John whether they could explain, but often they could not. They had told her of the time when He had been in the Temple at Passover. He had driven everyone out with a whip, and when asked for a miraculous sign to prove His authority He had replied, "Destroy this temple, and I will raise it again in three days." What had He meant? Mary wondered. Surely He could not build such a place single-handed, and certainly not in three days! Perhaps He had been joking. Build it again in three days, three days!

Three days and three nights

She remembered another time when He had been asked to show the people a miraculous sign. He had refused and this time said, "A wicked and adulterous generation asks for a miraculous sign! But none will be given it except the sign of the prophet Jonah. For as Jonah was three days and three nights in the belly of the huge fish, so the Son of Man will be three days and three nights in the heart of the earth."

She didn't understand this "sign of the prophet Jonah" and had asked Peter and John. They didn't know and hadn't been able to explain what He meant. She still remembered His words, and the three days and three nights. She knew what three days and three nights meant, but all this about Jonah and the heart of the earth! However, despite not understanding much of what He had taught, she had been content just to be near Him and to help Him and His followers whenever she could.

Arrested and crucified

She tried to think of other things He had said, of other times He had mentioned three days, but then her mind clouded over as she recalled that dreadful day when she awoke to find that He had been arrested. Then He had been crucified, that same day. It had all happened so swiftly. But she hadn't been able to stay away. Along with many other women she had been there until the bitter end. She had watched it all. She had seen His mother there, with a far away look in her eyes, as if she was thinking about things which had been said or done years ago.

The tomb

Now a new day was about to dawn. She had been unable to sleep and while it was still dark she made her way to the tomb, His tomb. When she got there the stone at the entrance had been rolled away. The tomb was open. It was empty!

All was confusion and chaos in her mind. What was going on? Not only had He been killed, now someone had taken His body. This was the final straw. In desperation she ran back and found Peter and John, sobbing as she told them the news. They had come back with her to the tomb but they couldn't explain what had happened and they were unable to comfort her. They had returned and wanted her to come, but she refused, staying there on her own.

The angels

"Gone! Gone!" was the only thought that ran through her head as the tears ran freely down her face. She looked into the tomb again, as if to check, and then she looked again. There were two men in white, sitting where His body had been. "Woman, why are you crying?" they asked. Mary replied as best she could that the body of her Lord had been taken away and that she didn't know where it was. But she was puzzled and confused.

The gardener

She turned away from them when she got no answer and saw another man. He asked her, "Woman, why are you crying? Who is it you are looking for?" Through her tears Mary took Him to be the gardener and asked Him if He had taken the body, and where He had placed it. She looked away, not expecting any helpful answer, but then, through the noise of her sobs, she heard one word, spoken softly, gently: "Mary." She turned towards Him. Her eyes sharpened. The tears dried. Her mouth opened. "Teacher!" she cried with a broken voice.

The Lord Jesus

She gazed at Him. She moved towards Him. Overcome with emotion she reached towards Him with arms outstretched, but He took a pace backwards and putting up a hand said, "Do not hold on to me, for I have not yet returned to the Father." Then He told her to go and tell His brothers.

Raised on the third day

Mary turned and ran. As she made her way to the disciples her elated emotions gave way to a deep feeling of pure joy. Then, suddenly, her mind cleared. She was thinking clearly at last. She remembered what He had said when they had been in Galilee together, "The Son of Man must be delivered into the hands of sinful men, be crucified, and on the third day be raised again." The third day! The third day! There it was again. The third day and her Lord was alive again. The third day! Why hadn't she remembered those words before?

11. Mary, the Mother of Jesus
Sylvia Penny

Susan and John had been married for about three years when they decided that it was the right time to start a family. John had a good job and had just been promoted. They had been fortunate enough to raise a mortgage to buy their own home, and it was pretty well furnished.

Yes! They would be able to afford their first child. Yes! They could afford all the essential items needed for a new baby. The list seemed endless; cot and carrycot, car seat and bouncing cradle seat; pram and buggy; baby sling and Moses basket, not to mention the bedding, clothing and toiletries required.

*****

The angel said to her, "Do not be afraid, Mary, you have found favour with God. You will be with child and give birth to a son, and you are to give him the name Jesus..." "How will this be," Mary asked the angel, "since I am a virgin?" The angel answered, "The Holy Spirit will come upon you, and the power of the Most High will overshadow you." "I am the Lord's servant," Mary answered, "May it be to me as you have said." (Luke 1:30-38)

What a contrast! Mary would have been barely twenty when she received this astounding message from God. Mary had no say in the matter. She was told by the angel what was going to happen. She had no husband, no home set up in readiness - just an eagerness to do what God wanted.

*****

After a few months Susan found, sure enough, that she was pregnant. Once it had been confirmed by the doctor, and the early weeks of morning sickness had passed, she began happily telling all their friends, relatives and anyone else who might be interested.

There were so many appointments to make—with the hospital, the doctor, the midwife. There were blood tests and urine tests and, most exciting of all, an ultra sound scan where she would actually see the baby for the first time, growing steadily in her womb. All the changes in her body were amazing, but everything was under control. She was in the hands of the professionals.

*****

At that time Mary got ready and hurried to a town in the hill country of Judah, where she entered Zechariah's home and greeted Elizabeth ... Mary stayed with Elizabeth for about three months and then returned home. (Luke 1:39,40,56)

It is most likely that it was during this period of time that Mary conceived the child. She was safely chaperoned throughout that period by Elizabeth and Zechariah who could testify to Mary's integrity and purity. However, understandably, Joseph, Mary's husband-to-be, wanted to divorce her. (Divorce was necessary for engaged couples at that time.)

This is how the birth of Jesus Christ came about: His mother Mary was pledged to be married to Joseph, but before they came together, she was found to be with child through the Holy Spirit. Because Joseph her husband was a righteous man and did not want to expose her to public disgrace, he had in mind to divorce her quietly. (Matthew 1:18-19)

Not for Mary the exciting time of telling friends and relatives the good news. She had to keep everything quiet. Even her betrothed husband had it in mind to leave her. It must have been a lonely and difficult time for her.

Her main happiness must have come from her deep faith, and in her sure conviction that what the angel had told her would come to pass. However, her problems must have eased considerably once the angel had appeared to Joseph and explained to him just what had happened to Mary. After that he took her home with him as his wife, but he had no union with her until after the birth of the Lord Jesus.

There was no modern technology for Mary; no tests or scans; no regular check ups with the midwife, or visits to the doctors. She and Joseph were on their own.

*****

The scan had pin-pointed the date at which Susan would have the baby. The time was drawing near. Everything was ready. Her place was booked at the local maternity hospital, and she would stay in for a week, to learn to look after the new baby. She would be taught to feed the baby and have help changing, bathing and generally caring for the baby.

She was asked what pain relief she would like during labour; gas and air, Pethidine or epidural. She had been to the ante-natal and relaxation classes which taught her just what was going to happen and how to cope with it. She had seen videos. She felt at ease, fully prepared.

*****

In those days Caesar Augustus issued a decree that a census should be taken of the entire Roman world . . . And everyone went to his own town. (Luke 2:1-3)

Mary had no such preparation, no such assurance, no such certainty about what was to happen. When the decree came from Caesar, stating that everyone was to return to their home town, she knew that she would have to undertake that journey while she was still pregnant. From Nazareth to Bethlehem would take ten days on a donkey. No smooth running comfortable car to a modern hospital. No prospect of any help with the delivery. No after birth care. She was a long way from home, and had to face having her first child on her own, in a crowded town with few, if any, resources.

*****

With the pain relief given by the gas and air Susan suffered very little from labour pains and gave birth to a healthy, bouncing baby boy. Everything was done efficiently and swiftly, with clinical cleanliness. After it was over, Susan relaxed in a warm, disinfected bath and the baby was wiped clean, wrapped in snowy white sheets, surrounded by a blue cellular blanket and placed carefully in a hospital cot.

Friends and relatives came to visit. The presents for the baby mounted up, and both Susan and John felt the euphoria of being first-time parents. It was wonderful!

*****

> While they were in Bethlehem, the time came for the baby to be born, and she gave birth to her first-born, a son. She wrapped him in strips of cloth and placed him in a manger, because there was no room for them in the inn. (Luke 2:6-7)

We are not told what Mary suffered in giving birth. We are just told, baldly, that a son was born. There was no room for them in the inn so Mary must have had her first child in a stable.

There was no pain relief, no sterilised equipment, no doctors, no nurses, just a dark and dirty stable, shared with animals.

There were no snowy white sheets, blue blankets and clean cot for her baby, just strips of cloth and a manger of hay in which to lay Him.

There were no admiring friends, no relatives calling in with presents. There were just shepherds, who had been told by the angel that Christ the Saviour had been born, and that they would find him in Bethlehem, in a manger, wrapped in strips of cloth.

> And Mary treasured up all these things and pondered them in her heart. (Luke 2:19)

*****

How different were Mary's and Susan's experiences of pregnancy and childbirth. How different were things then, compared to things today. Perhaps next Christmas we should spare a thought for Mary, and ponder a little more on just what she went through to give birth to God's Son, our Saviour, the Lord Jesus Christ.

12. Mary's Story (Mother of Jesus)
Sylvia Penny

Mary sat back in her chair by the window and closed her eyes. Her Son had finally gone. He had been taken back into heaven, with the promise that one day He would return. John had just returned from the mount of Olives with the other ten of Jesus' special friends. He told her all that had happened, and now they had to wait for the Holy Spirit to come.

Dear John! The one that Jesus chose to look after her, when He could no longer do so Himself. She reflected on how He had always been so concerned about her. Even while He was dying on the cross, He had been thinking of *her* future welfare.

She thought back over the past three years and the many people He had helped, the many things He had said, and the many miracles He had performed. All those miracles! And yet so few believed in Him. Even her other sons, His own brothers, had been sceptical until now.

But she had always believed in Him. She had not needed the last three years to know Who He was. She had her own special three years to remember. Three years filled with wonderful miracles that only she and Joseph knew of. And since Joseph had died, she wondered whether she should tell others of those special events that happened over thirty years ago.

The first miracle

It all started so suddenly when she was just a young girl in Nazareth. She was carrying out her daily tasks as usual when, suddenly, a man appeared and spoke to her. As a young girl, and alone, her first reaction was to feel frightened and vulnerable, but his words calmed her. She would never forget those words:

"Greetings, you who are highly favoured! The Lord is with you."

Those words troubled her and she wondered what they meant, and why he had come, and what he was leading up to. Then he said:

"Do not be afraid, Mary, you have found favour with God. You will be with child and give birth to a son, and you are to give him the name Jesus. He will be great and will be called the Son of the Most High. The Lord God will give him the throne of his father David, and he will reign over the house of Jacob forever; his kingdom will never end."

That was the first miracle.

She soon realised this man was none other than a special messenger from God, an angel. She felt so small and humble in the light of his wonderful words. All she could think of was how she could become a mother as she was a virgin. He replied:

"The Holy Sprit will come upon you, and the power of the Most High will overshadow you. So the holy one to be born will be called the Son of God. Even Elizabeth your relative is going to have a child in her old age, and she who was said to be barren is in her sixth month. For nothing is impossible with God."

Mary smiled to herself as she sat in her chair and thought back to that one and only occasion in her life when she had been visited by an angel. When the angel left her she felt strangely elated. She thought first of herself, and then of dear old Elizabeth, who had been longing for a child for so many years. Who would have thought it? Her first idea was to rush to Judea to visit Elizabeth, and tell her the news. Then she thought of Joseph too. They were engaged to be married. She had to explain to him that she was going to become pregnant through the working of God's Holy Spirit. Would he believe her? Would he even believe she had been visited by an angel? She decided to visit Elizabeth first and seek her advice as to what she should do, and so left for Judea without delay.

The second miracle

She remembered how she had only just enough time to greet Elizabeth before Elizabeth almost shouted out to her:

"Blessed are you among women, and blessed is the child you will bear! But why am I so favoured, that the mother of my Lord should come to me?"

That was the second miracle, just a few short days after the first. There was no way that Elizabeth could have known what had been revealed to Mary, except through God Himself.

Mary was filled with praise for God, filled with a feeling of her own humility, and filled with awe at the way God uplifted the humble yet brought down the proud. Somehow the words had come flowing from her lips without effort, and Elizabeth sat there watching her, and listening and understanding. What a help and comfort Elizabeth was during those three months Mary stayed with her.

The third miracle

Mary was sure in her heart that it was then, during those three months, that the wonderful miracle of conception occurred. After that she went home to Nazareth.

The fourth miracle

Mary remembered her first meeting with Joseph after her return. She had talked to Elizabeth about what she would say, but she was still hesitant and unsure of herself, uncertain of what his reaction would be. Although he was a good man, a man who loved God, upright and honourable, he just could not accept that this special and wonderful miracle could have happened as Mary had said. He did not want her made a public disgrace and took the only compromise that was open. He told her that he would break their engagement quietly. How her heart sank, and how sad she felt.

Then the fourth miracle happened! Joseph had a wonderful dream in which the angel of the Lord explained everything that had happened, and soon after that they were married.

Mary sat upright in her chair as she remembered jogging along on the back of a donkey on her way from Nazareth to Bethlehem. That was an uncomfortable journey, and she was glad to arrive. Caesar Augustus decreed that everyone was to return to their home towns in order for a census to be taken, and that meant Bethlehem for her and Joseph. They settled in an inn, but when the time came for the baby to be born, there was no privacy. Jesus was born in a stable, and laid in a manger.

Mary remembered that night as if it were yesterday. She looked down at His tiny body, at how small and helpless He was, and wondered at the immense responsibility God had laid upon her and Joseph's shoulders. Here indeed was the Son of God, hers to love and cherish and care for. She studied that little face repeatedly, and watched every fleeting expression with awe and wonder. What a unique privilege she had over every other woman; over every other person. She alone had seen both the birth and the death of her Lord and Saviour, Jesus.

The fifth miracle

But while she was smiling down at His tiny face, she remembered being suddenly disturbed. Some shepherds entered the stable. At first she thought it was a mistake, but when she heard their story, she realised that another miracle had taken place. An angel of the Lord had appeared to them, and told them of the birth of Jesus, and how they could find Him. Then a great company of the heavenly host had appeared with the angel, praising God.

When the shepherds finally left, Mary sat quietly with her thoughts, trying to make sense of everything that had happened. It seemed to her that God was miraculously letting many people know of Jesus' wonderful birth. It was not an event that she and Joseph were to share alone, but one in which many people were to be involved. She wondered who would be next.

She had not had to wait long. When she and Joseph took Jesus to the temple in Jerusalem to consecrate Him to the Lord, a devout old man called Simeon came into the temple courts and met them there. He took Jesus in his arms and praised God for letting him see this tiny baby. He had been promised by God that he would not die until he had seen the Christ with his own eyes. Mary remembered how this old man looked at her little baby with such reverence and awe, and remembered the surge of love she felt for her firstborn son.

As if this had not been enough, moments later an old woman approached them. She was a prophetess called Anna, and she prophesied to those around, giving thanks to God for Mary's baby. Mary finally left the temple together with Joseph, feeling uplifted and almost exhilarated with all that had happened. Everything had been so wonderful in those first days and weeks after Jesus' birth. And then it was time to settle down to the tasks of day to day living in Bethlehem. She soon got used to being a young mother, and Joseph was a devoted husband, and a helping, caring father.

The sixth miracle

The months went by, and Mary enjoyed her busy life in Bethlehem among her and Joseph's relatives. The miracles surrounding Jesus' birth became happy memories for her, and ones which she often recalled and thought about afresh.

Then one evening, she had some unexpected visitors. Jesus was following her about the house, clutching on to her robe with his little fists, and trying to talk to her with the few words He knew. She opened the door and there a group of foreign and learned looking men confronted her. Through the open door she noticed a strange and unfamiliar glow, and when she looked closer it seemed like a bright and shining light had settled just above her house.

Her mind quickly flickered back to the angel Gabriel's visit to her, to the shepherds in the stable, and somehow she knew this visit was something to do with them. She welcomed her strange visitors and was overawed when they presented little Jesus first with gold, then with incense, and lastly with myrrh. Instead of running away and hiding, He stood there silently, gravely, watching them. Those majestic men bowed down and worshipped her small child, and somehow He seemed to understand.

Mary sat back and relaxed in her chair. Looking back all those years she felt sure that Jesus understood the visit from the wise men, despite being such a young child at the time. When they left, Jesus pointed out of the doorway at the bright and shining light which was fading fast. All He said was, "Star, ...gone!"

The seventh miracle

What a lifetime away that seemed now. And then, their tranquil life was shattered. Joseph was visited by another angel in a dream and warned that Herod planned to kill the child. They were to escape to Egypt as quickly as possible. She was anxious and frightened. They packed and left that very night, with only the belongings they could carry on the back of a donkey. How different that ride was to the one from Nazareth, when she had been full of expectancy and hope. Now they were fleeing for their lives, with no idea of when they would return.

She remembered their time in Egypt. It seemed so long and difficult. They did not see any family or friends, and were cut off from all they knew. But Jesus was a never ending source of comfort and joy to them. He amused them when they felt down, and kept Mary busy looking after Him. She always wondered whether the special feelings she had for Him were because He was her firstborn son, or because she knew that He was the Son of God and her Saviour.

The eighth, and last, miracle

After what seemed such a long, long time, Joseph had another dream in which an angel told them to take Jesus back to Israel as Herod was dead. What thankfulness she felt! How eagerly she packed once more, to return. They were going home at last.

They arrived in Bethlehem to discover that Archelaus was now reigning in Judea instead of Herod his father. They heard of the terrible slaughter that had taken place shortly after their escape to Egypt, and discovered that in all Bethlehem there were no boys surviving of Jesus' age. Mary and Joseph were afraid to stay there, and so they journeyed north, back to the district of Galilee, and settled down to live in Nazareth where they had first met. And there they stayed.

Mary sighed. The angel which appeared to Joseph in Egypt had been the last miraculous event she remembered before Jesus began His ministry just over three years ago. But she remembered all those wonderful events as if they had happened yesterday. She would never forget them. She had treasured them in her heart for many years.

Maybe soon she would tell someone all about those memories. They would make such a wonderful story, which now she wanted to share with others. Why should she keep them to herself any more? The time was right for people to hear about the birth of the Saviour.

13. Reflections of Priscilla
Sylvia Penny

Timothy has just been to see us. He had another letter from Paul from his prison in Rome. He sent us his greetings. He always seems to be thinking of others rather than himself. What an incredible person he is! How privileged we are to have known him. How I hate to think that soon he is to be executed. It reminds me of the time (what a long time ago that seems now) that we nearly lost our own lives, but I'd do the same again, given half the chance. And it was even longer ago than that when we first met Paul, nearly twenty years ago now.

It was spring, and Claudius had ordered all us Jews out of Rome, and so Aquila and I had to leave. We went to live in Corinth, and it was here that we met Paul. He was on his way from Athens, and I suppose because we were tentmakers, the same as he was, he decided to stay and work with us. He stayed with us for over a year and a half, and what a wonderful time of blessing that was for us. He used to teach in the synagogue and at the house of Titius Justus, and of course, we had our own house meeting too. The fellowship was certainly good in those days.

At Ephesus

I think it was about the time when Nero took over from Claudius that we sailed to Ephesus with Paul. He was on his way to Syria, but he stopped with us a short time, just long enough to visit the Jews in the synagogue and have a few discussions with them. Then he left, but he promised us he would come back if it was the Lord's will. We made our home in Ephesus, started another house meeting, and settled down.

It was shortly after Paul left that we first met Apollos. He came from Alexandria, and was certainly well versed in the Scriptures. It was a joy to be with him and talk to him about the Lord and the Word of God. We had him back to our home and discussed the Scriptures with him, and he was very keen to learn more and more of the Lord, and everything we had been taught by Paul. Later he wanted to travel to Corinth, and as we knew many of the brothers there we wrote to them introducing Apollos and asking them to welcome him among them. We knew they would, as he was so keen for the Lord and such a bold speaker.

After a while Paul did return to us in Ephesus and again we had a marvellous time of blessing and fellowship with him for over two years. He began by speaking in the synagogue but when the people turned against him he left, and conducted discussions at the lecture hall of Tyrannus instead. His fame spread far and wide, throughout the whole province of Asia and many people turned to the Lord. Even Paul's handkerchief used to heal people in those days. What a wonderful time that was! Now Timothy tells us Paul has left Trophimus at Miletus sick, and Timothy himself always seems to have something wrong with him. Time was that Paul could have sent his apron and cured them, but those days are gone now.

He wrote a letter to the believers we had left behind in Corinth, to help and encourage them in his absence. He intended to travel to see them as soon as he could. And I remember just after that when many of the sorcerers came out into the open and burned all their evil scrolls in public. They were worth a fortune too! What a testimony that was to the Lord and the way He had worked in the hearts of those people.

Back to Rome

It was shortly after, that Paul started talking about leaving and going back to Jerusalem, and then on to Rome to visit the believers there. Aquila and I decided to go back to Rome to live, as by this time Claudius' decree had lapsed, and we longed to return to our home and see all the people we had known there.

So we packed up and left for Rome and Paul left too. A few months later we heard from him, as he sent a letter from Corinth to all us believers in Rome. He was so encouraging, and getting the letter was the next best thing to seeing him. He promised to come to Rome and visit us, and we so looked forward to that time. Little did we think that it would be as a prisoner that he would come. What a lot seemed to happen in that four or five years in between.

So Paul came to Rome. We were overjoyed to see him again, although it was with sadness too, because he was a prisoner. His attitude however was still so positive, so enthusiastic for the Lord. He testified to the great comfort and support that the Lord can give in times of testing which inspired us all. Still, many of the leaders of the Jews just couldn't seem to bring themselves to believe the wonderful message that the Lord Jesus was the Messiah.

The Change

After that, there was a change in what Paul taught. He stressed the unity of all believers much more strongly. He emphasised the fact that to God there was now no difference between us Jews and the Gentiles, that we were all on a total equality in the eyes of God.

His teaching was just as strong and sure as ever, he was the same Paul we had always known, but there was a change in his message after the Jewish leaders in Rome had turned their back on his message. Things for us Jews were never the same again. Paul told us that the ordinances had been set aside by God and that none of our ceremonies mattered any more. He no longer spoke of the nearness of the Lord's return but taught about being blessed in heavenly places.

That was about five or six years ago now. He was released for a time, but now they have got him again, and this time it seems like the end. Nero is becoming more and more of a tyrant and seems to have a special grudge against us Christians.

Times have changed. Many seem to have fallen away under this persecution. Even we had to move from Rome again to get away from the centre of the trouble. There doesn't seem to be many of us left now. But at least Timothy is here with us. That is some consolation. He is our link with Paul. We have been praying so hard for him in these times of darkness. I wonder how it will all end?

Note: References to Priscilla are:
AD 52 Acts 18:2,3,18,19,26
AD 57 1 Corinthians 16:19
AD 58 Romans 16:3
AD 68 2 Timothy 4:19
(The dates are taken from *The Companion Bible*: Appendix 180)

Part 2
Christian Living

14. Hospitality
Carolyn Mansell

It is often said that in any marriage it is the woman who is the home-maker. If this is true, it surely means that the wife has primary responsibility for hospitality. In 1 Timothy 5:10 this is one of the good deeds for which a woman must be well known if she is to be added to the list of widows.

A number of years ago, when we moved from London to the Isle of Man, we had many opportunities both to give and receive hospitality. As with so many other aspects of the Christian walk, giving hospitality proved to have a reward in this life as well as the next. What a joy for us to have been able to share many happy hours of fellowship with the friends who made the long journey, sometimes across a stormy Irish Sea, to come and see us in our home. That really helped us realise the meaning of hospitality, which is more than just providing a bed and breakfast service. It is a practical example of love where you truly care for a person's needs. That was made easy for us, as the friends who came to stay were all Christians with whom we could share so much.

However, it is interesting to note that the word translated "hospitality" in the New Testament is really "the love of strangers". This was the sort of hospitality the Lord spoke of in the parable of the Good Samaritan. Those who shared in the same faith as the injured traveller passed him by, and it was a Samaritan who showed the true hospitality in caring for the needs of a stranger.

We have plenty of opportunities to show hospitality in this way, but we often don't recognise them. Often the sort of people who need our hospitality go unnoticed by us, or perhaps are not the easiest folk to get on with. For example, a rather awkward elderly next-door neighbour, who subsequently died, seemed to look after herself fairly well. However, she still needed her shopping requirements each week and welcomed a visit now and again. 1 Peter 4:9 tells us that this hospitality must be offered without grumbling, which is not always easy.

Give me a faithful heart, likeness to Thee,
That each departing day henceforth may see,
Some work of love begun, some deed of kindness done,
Some wanderer sought and won. Something for Thee.
(*Something for Jesus* - third verse of hymn by Robert Lowry)

15. A Living Temple
Hazel Stephens

Present your bodies, a living sacrifice, holy, acceptable unto God,
which is your reasonable service. (Romans 12:1, *KJV*)

The above verse is an achievement we should aim for as we grow in
grace and knowledge. However have we seriously thought about the
pitfalls marring our witness and service which the world can bring upon
us, even without our being aware of them?

We all know the obvious ones like swearing, drunkenness,
fornication and the like as these are plainly banned in Scripture,
(Ephesians 4:29; 5:4; Romans 13:13, Galatians 5:21), not to mention the
vices still frowned upon by Christian and non-Christian alike. But what
about the little pitfalls? The ones plainly visible, but not thought of very
much because they are always with us in some shape or form?

Clothes

The wardrobe of clothes, full to bursting, all high fashion once, but now
left forlorn! The outside world will see such a dress conscious Christian
as one who keeps up with fashion, and consequently it is assumed that
they have "nothing better to do with their money than spend it on
clothes." At the other extreme, there is wearing clothes until they are
threadbare, and the reaction to this is "they're too stingy to pay out
money for a dress."

These two extremes are easily fallen into, and it is not until it is
shown to us, often by the reaction of non-Christians, that we can see
how our witness can be affected.

The Scriptures show that a woman should be modestly dressed (1
Timothy 2:9), which does not necessarily mean covered from neck to
foot and shoulder to wrist which, in some outfits, can be more
provocative than the skimpiest dress! We should dress neatly, in well-
fitting clothes, not so classic that we show up as being ten years or more
out of date, but neither so with-it that our clothes attract more attention
than our witness.

Health

The Scriptures inform us that our bodies are temples of the Holy Spirit (1 Corinthians 3:16; 6:19) and that we are to glorify God in our bodies (6:20). Ought we not, therefore, to take extreme care of such temples? Surely this will include not doing anything to excess, particularly overeating, drinking, smoking and many other habits which can have a harmful effect on our health.

Enjoying our Christian life is always a good witness, but how often do we see in front of us only the things which trouble us, and not the glorious truths which should lift our hearts with joy? More often than not we tend to see the trials of this world with a clarity which cannot be avoided, but our gaze should be extended beyond the immediate, to see the joys of Christ shining through, showing that all things here are temporal and have only a fleeting hold on each of us.

Witness

It is easy to be a silent giver and to sit back on our laurels, but the trouble with this method of service is that it is not visible. At times we shirk from making an open statement, whether by word or action, in an attempt not to offend friends or neighbours. Sometimes, indeed, it can be so silent a witness that no one notices that we are different. Then comes the shaft: "I didn't know you were a Christian!"

> The gift of God is eternal life through Jesus Christ our Lord, (Romans 6:23, *KJV*).

Should we not respond to this blessed gift by refraining from giving ourselves over to the trials of this world and to overcoming them with joy and hope and faith? Shouldn't we respond by refusing to give others cause for criticism and leading them on to see our inner peace which comes only from our God and Saviour? This, then, may enable the Holy Spirit to use us as a more effectual witness, and to some people, be more effectual than all the preaching, (e.g. 1 Peter 3:1,2).

The Remedy

How are we to avoid these pitfalls which can so easily mar our Christian service? If we look after our appearance and health, ensuring neither is detrimental to our witness and walk, then surely through the study of the Scriptures and prayer our spirit will grow in accordance with His wishes; a living sacrifice, holy, acceptable unto God.

16. Our Ambitions
Mary McLean

Do you, like me, have difficulty in reconciling your own ambitions or desires with what God may intend for you? Are you sometimes discouraged when you meet others who are so confident that God has revealed some sort of cut and dried plan for their lives? If so, perhaps the contemplation of Psalm 37:4 may be of help.

> Delight thyself in the Lord, and He shall give thee the desires of thine heart. (*KJV*)

It first came to my attention at a time when I was particularly concerned about my future and the achieving of a specific desire that I had at that time. This verse seemed to hit me right between the eyes in that wonderful way that just occasionally does happen to prove that the Bible is, indeed, a living word.

Thinking about my situation, I began to realise I was putting things back to front, being only concerned with self-fulfilment and seeking my own security, and looking to the Lord as a means of achieving this end. Slowly, it dawned upon me that if my relationship with the Lord was such that I delighted in Him, then He Himself would become my heart's desire.

This is not to say that God is not concerned about the details of our lives or that, as we are sometimes tempted to think, His plans must be a negation of our hopes. No! He is interested in our jobs, our homes, families and friends. But above all, it is our knowledge of His person that is of prime importance. As Paul puts it in Philippians 3:8-10, it is the excellency of the knowledge of Christ and the power of His resurrection which makes all our own ambitions or achievements refuse in comparison.

Perhaps our lives would be more fruitful if we learnt the secret of resting in the Lord, learning of Him, rather than constantly worrying about the keeping of some sort of divine timetable that we think He has set for us to keep.

17. Don't Hurry
Penny Richardson

There was a man who was followed by a car with lights that kept winking at him. The car pulled him over and a man in a uniform, who took his job seriously, gave him a copy of a form which he wrote out. This form had to be taken to the municipal traffic court, for a rule had been broken. The man had been hurrying.

Be still, and know that I am God

There is one verse in the Psalms which the Lord brings to mind whenever I get caught in a whirlwind of rushing here and there. It is Psalm 46:10a: "Be still and know that I am God". The impact of each part of that phrase is powerful.

Be - just be!

Be still - cease your efforts! The Hebrew word *raphah*, still, means to abate, to cease, to idle, to let alone. In other words relax somewhere by yourself and be still. Ensure that there are no distractions and let the Lord's presence be felt. Quiet the heart! Don't let pressures come in and disturb the stillness. Don't think of that long list of things which have to be done. All that can be done later. Any irritants are disturbing factors, so give them over to the Lord in prayer and let your heart, your mind, your soul, be still.

Be still and know that I am God. The Hebrew word for know is *yada* and can mean observation, care, recognition, acknowledge, comprehend, declare, discover. It is not enough to stop and be quiet and to let all the distractions fade away for a moment. We are to know who God is. He is God Almighty. He is in charge of all creation and we have a part in His plan.

The Butterfly

In *Zorba the Greek*, Nikow Kazantakis relates a very simple but poignant event that shaped much of his thinking on the use of time.

I remembered one morning when I discovered a cocoon in the bark of a tree, just as the butterfly was making a hole in its case and preparing to come out. I waited a while, but it was too long appearing and I was impatient. I bent over it and breathed on it to warm it. I warmed it as quickly as I could and the miracle began to happen before my eyes, faster than life. The case opened. The butterfly started slowly crawling out and I shall never forget my horror when I saw how its wings were folded back and crumpled, the wretched butterfly tried with its whole trembling body to unfold them.

Bending over it I tried to help it with my breath, in vain. It needed to be hatched out patiently. And the unfolding of the wings should be a gradual process in the sun. Now it was too late. My breath had forced the butterfly to appear all crumpled before its time. It struggled desperately and a few seconds later died in the palm of my hand.

That little body is, I do believe, the greatest weight I have on my conscience. For I realised today that it is a mortal sin to violate the great laws of nature. We should not hurry. We should not be impatient. But we should confidently obey the eternal rhythm. If only that little butterfly could always flutter before me to show me the way.

The Simple Things

Our world seems intoxicated with hustle and bustle, rush and dash. Many times the hurricane of hurry catches us unawares and we are inundated with things we feel we must do, and we are upset if they are not done. But stop …! Look! Are they really that important?

The simple things of life really bring contentment to our lives. The simple delights of earth, the wind against our faces, savoury aromas in our nostrils, moist grass beneath our feet, the fragrance and beauty of flowers, a child in our arms, a smile from a friend or a loved one (Hansel, *When I relax I Feel Guilty*).

The New Testament tells us of Christ's love, a love beyond measure. It tells of our hope, a hope beyond reason. It tells us of a lifestyle, a peace, a love and a joy that can be ours each day. That is contentment, and we should take time to experience it.

18. *Fullness of Joy*
Janet Horobin

With almost his last breath, Paul tells Timothy that all Scripture is useful for teaching, rebuking, correcting and training in righteousness, (2 Timothy 3:16). One has only to think of the Psalms, and the help and inspiration they have been to many believers, to know the truth of those words. Consider, for instance, Psalm 16:8,9:

> I have set the Lord always before me. Because he is at my right hand, I shall not be shaken. Therefore my heart is glad and my tongue rejoices; my body also will rest secure.

The Psalm shows David's hope of resurrection and life everlasting. The above words were spoken by David about his Lord, but David was a man who had made many mistakes. However, he had accepted the Lordship of God into his life and so he was able to look forward to fullness of joy in God's presence, (Psalm 16:11).

The Lord of our lives

But we have to ask, where do we stand? Have we accepted the Lordship of God in our lives! Do we know something of that Christian joy now? Are we confidently looking forward to fullness of joy when our hope is realised?

One small word stands out in verse 8. David is able to say, "I have set the Lord always before me." He did not write "I have set the Lord sometimes before me." Perhaps that is the key to why he can say, "Therefore my heart is glad" (Psalm 16:9).

Always

Let us look through the Scriptures to see what other things we should always do to make our hearts glad.

> Let your conversation be always full of grace, seasoned with salt. (Colossians 4:6)

That is a very tall order for a start! When men meet together they talk football, rugby, cars, politics. But is seems more difficult for women to keep their conversation from slipping into exaggerations and rumour, even gossip about other people. This is probably because many women are at home for a good part of the day. They are alone, or with young children. Therefore, when they do meet a friend socially they may feel that they have to make all their news sound exciting and interesting, so it is easy for exaggerations and distortions to creep in.

Yes, women have a wider scope for ungracious speech than men, so we must be on our guard. Notice that this verse says we should be seasoned with salt. Salt makes people thirsty to hear more, and it is a wonderful challenge, but we must ask ourselves whether people want to hear more of our conversation because it is salty or because it is spicy.

Pray always

Ephesians 6:18 tells us to pray always. There's an old saying which states that "A woman's work is never done" so when are we going to find the time to be always praying? Our day just isn't long enough! There's too much to do! But maybe these words don't mean praying at set times, on our knees. Maybe they say more about our relationship with God. It should be such that we are in tune with Him, anytime and at all times, in any situation in which we may find ourselves. Wherever we may be, we can pray to Him.

Nehemiah was in a difficult situation, and we read in Nehemiah 2:4,5 that he recognised his need and said a prayer, possibly the shortest prayer possible, but he was given the courage straightaway to answer the king. That is the closeness we should be experiencing with our Lord, able to talk to Him and call on Him at anytime, with but a moment's notice.

But our weakness is to pray only when we are in trouble, when someone is ill, when we've a lot at stake, or an important decision has to be made. Christ said, "I am with you always" and if we realise this, our Christian living and witness will be much more effective.

Give thanks always

The next thought leads on from this one: "give thanks always for all things" (Ephesians 5:20). This, surely, is a logical extension of always praying. There are so many things we forget to give thanks for. There are millions starving yet, we forget to give thanks before each meal. Do we remember to thank Him for our measure of good health? Do we remember to thank Him for those close to us who love and support us - our husbands, our parents, our children, and our friends?

With so many social benefits given to us in this society, we accept many gifts as a right. Let us never forget the most important gift this world has ever received - the One who gave everything. He gave Himself. He kept nothing back.

Rejoice always

People who have received the wonderful gift of salvation and eternal life should surely then be thankful and understand how Paul could write, "Rejoice in the Lord always," (Philippians 4:4). Christians should be happy, with a joy coming from the heart and a contented life.

Paul was able to say that in whatever state he found himself, he could be content. So many people seek that inner peace that can surround our hearts and minds. Many would love to know the reality of it. Paul was able to speak with confidence. He found out that we are able to rejoice in the Lord always because of the unchanging nature of God's love to each one of us.

Always or sometimes?

Now the Lord Jesus Christ said, "I always do what pleases the Father" (John 8:29). This verse is very similar, to the one we started with, in Psalm 16:8, and here again we will probably have to substitute the word "sometimes" for "always". For us, then, it would read, "I sometimes do what pleases the Father" but we must remember that there is a power available to us which can enable us to always please Him.

> He is able to do immeasurably more than all we ask or imagine, according to His power that is at work within us. (Ephesians 3:20)

Paul prayed that the Ephesians would get to know that power, (Ephesians 1:19-20), and it may take us years to fully submit our lives to it. However, if in those years we are growing spiritually then we shall be getting to know more of God's plan for this world and His purpose for our lives. Then, perhaps, we shall be able to say, "I try, with His power, to always do what pleases the Father."

Always be prepared to answer

Now lastly, and perhaps most importantly, we have another "always" in 1 Peter 3:15.

> Always be prepared to give an answer to everyone who asks you to give the reason for the hope that you have.

Many religions have wonderful traditions and offer glorious prospects after death. However, it is only Christianity which has a sure and certain hope, a resurrection from the dead to eternal life. This has been clearly demonstrated by the Lord Jesus Christ Himself. Thus it is such a wasted opportunity if we are unable to explain the reasons why our faith is so personal and precious. So what is our hope?

Ephesians 2:4-9 tells us that Christ is seated at the right hand of God in the heavenly realms. But it also states that we are to be there, to be there with Him. He has gone to prepare a place for each one who trusts and believes in Him and who is saved to everlasting life. We may not fully understand what it will be like there. We may not appreciate all the spiritual blessings that await us there, but we can have the faith to believe what God says.

I once heard it said that "faith starts with an experiment and ends with an experience". That is the faith that so many people need today.

Always! Always! Always!

So we have considered some of the "always" of Scripture and perhaps they link together and provide us with practical help for our daily living. We have had gracious speech, praying, rejoicing, giving thanks, and knowing for certain what is our hope. These are just some of the "always" and they are a challenge to us. Also, hopefully, they provide a few pointers which could lead us on to really experience the fullness of joy which is found only in Christ Jesus, our Saviour and our Lord.

19. Rules for Life
Penny Richardson

Some rules are easily recognised and acknowledged by all believers in Christ. Consider, for example, the rules given in Colossians 3:18-21.

1) Wives, submit to your husbands, as is fitting (to attain to, be proper, convenient) in the Lord.
2) Husbands, love your wives and do not be harsh with them.
3) Children, obey your parents in everything, for this pleases the Lord.
4) Fathers, do not embitter your children, or they will become discouraged.

These are the rules for every household, and if they are taken to heart and applied, the harmony that results between husband and wife and between parents and children is wonderful. This is what God intended for us - happiness and contentment. There are other rules, or guidelines, that I would like to discuss. They aren't so clear as those quoted from the above verses but they are worth reviewing.

Live Here and Now

People have a tendency to cherish their dreams but rarely act to make them happen. Anticipation fills their lives as they look to the future for happiness. God's life is within us now. God has given us everything we need to be happy now. Certainly Paul was aware of this.

Let the peace of Christ rule in your hearts and be thankful. (Colossians 3:15)

I have learnt to be content whatever the circumstances. (Philippians 4:11)

But godliness with contentment is great gain (1 Timothy 6:6)

And God is able to make all grace abound in you, so that in all things at all times, having all that you need, you will abound in every good work. (2 Corinthians 9:8)

The Greek word for "content" is *autarkes* from *autos* and *arkeo*. It means be enough, suffice, be sufficient. Webster's dictionary defines content as "being satisfied, easy in mind" and the Oxford dictionary says "satisfied with what one has." Let us realise that the peace and happiness we seek must begin with an unadorned acceptance of who we are, what we are and where we are, now. The fact is that we are in Christ and we are complete in Him. Can we accept that?

Don't take yourself too seriously

For everyone who makes himself important will become insignificant, while the man who makes himself insignificant, will find himself important. (Luke 14:11)

Following this statement the Lord Jesus gave an illustration aimed at certain people who were confident of their own goodness and who looked down on others.

Two men went up to the temple to pray, one was a Pharisee, the other a tax collector. The Pharisee stood and prayed like this with himself. "Oh, God, I do thank thee that I am not like the rest of mankind, greedy, dishonest, impure, or even like that tax collector over there. I fast twice every week: I give away a tenth part of all my income." But the tax collector stood in a distant corner, scarcely daring to look up to heaven, and with a gesture of despair, said, "God, have mercy on a sinner like me." I assure you that he was the man who went home justified in God's sight rather than the other one. For everyone who sets himself up as somebody will become a nobody. And the man who makes himself a nobody will become a somebody. (Luke 18:10-14)

The result of taking ourselves too seriously can be that we become pretentious or defensive in our behaviour. One might work five times harder than is necessary, in order to continuously prove oneself to the world. In doing that one can forget to laugh, and one can especially forget to laugh at oneself.

The problems which arise from taking ourselves too seriously are countless. Afraid to fail, we no longer do anything different. Afraid that someone will see the real person behind the facade, we no longer share. Afraid that we will appear vulnerable, we no longer ask for help. The end product of taking ourselves too seriously is that we find it impossible to be fully human and fully alive. Let us recognise our weakness and failings, let us recognise that we are sinners but let us recognise what we are in Christ and that we can do all things through Christ who strengthens us (Philippians 4:13).

Be Grateful

Someone once said, "Success is getting what you want. Happiness is wanting what you get." The Bible expresses a similar idea, albeit it in a different way in 1 Thessalonians 5:18.

> Give thanks in all circumstances, for this is God's will for you in Christ Jesus.

The point is that the essence of happiness and peace lies in gratitude.

> Delight yourselves in the Lord; yes, find joy in him at all times . . . tell God every detail of your needs in earnest and thankful prayer. And the peace of God, which transcends human understanding, will keep constant guard over your hearts and minds as they rest in Christ Jesus. (Philippians 4:4-7)

Two things should be noted here. First, that gratitude is not an option for a Christian, it should be there at all times. Second, gratitude is a source of peace. We may not understand how this process works but we are never required to understand any process before we may use it. Thus the greatest ground-rule for peace and contentment is insistent, consistent and persistent gratitude. We must practice and learn to be diligent in our giving of thanks. Gratitude is not only expressed in words. Gratitude can be expressed by hard work, by patience, by laughter, by creativity, by the certainty of our love, by the depth of our hope and by the quality of our peace. There is no substitute for gratitude. It is a sure way to spiritual health.

Conclusion

So live here and now. Don't take yourself too seriously, and be grateful

20. Contentment
Sylvia Penny

"If we are a Christian we should be content." No doubt you have heard this, or something similar, said many times, but do you agree with such statements? Are you always content? If you are like most of us your answer will be "No!". So, have you ever considered how to achieve it? Or wondered if it is even possible?

A snapshot of contentment

When this came up again recently I sat back and thought through what makes me content. Immediately a picture came into my mind of sitting comfortably in a big arm chair, being well fed and feeling pleasantly warm. The atmosphere was quiet and peaceful, with a view through the window of rolling countryside, trees, bushes and grass. I was happy in the knowledge of being loved by family members, of having good friends and of having a well-defined purpose in life. A beautiful snapshot of what I considered the state of contentment to be like.

However, it was also pretty obvious that I did not enjoy these circumstances very often, if at all! So is my picture one of Christian contentment? If not, what is Christian contentment and how do we achieve it? Is it a God given gift? Or do we have to work to attain it ourselves?

Definition of contentment

Vine's *Expository Dictionary* defines contentment as follows:

> to be sufficient, to be possessed of sufficient strength, to be strong, to be enough for a thing ... to be satisfied ... adequate, needing no assistance ... satisfaction with what one has.

There are only four passages in the New Testament which refer to contentment, and these are in harmony with the above definition. They all imply that no matter what possessions we have, even if they are only a few in comparison with other people, we should be content with them.

(1) The secret of being content

Probably the best known passage is Philippians 4:11-13, in which Paul says:

> I am not saying this because I am in need, for I have learned to be content whatever the circumstances. I know what it is to be in need, and I know what it is to have plenty. I have learned the secret of being content in any and every situation, whether well fed or hungry, whether living in plenty or in want. I can do everything through him who gives me strength.

Here Paul links contentment with circumstances. However, he does not say it is a result of favourable circumstances, but rather that he is content whatever his circumstances, good or bad.

2 Corinthians 11:23-29 catalogues some of the disasters which Paul underwent. In Philippians he writes that despite all these, or as a result of them perhaps, he learned the secret of contentment. For Paul then, contentment was something that he learned as a result of going through exceptionally difficult experiences. Interestingly Paul refers to this as a secret, as if it is something not easily gained. Yes! it is easy enough to be content when things are going well for us, as in my "snapshot of contentment', but it is not easy to be content in each and every situation, good or bad.

Acts 5:41 describes the apostles as rejoicing because they had been counted worthy of suffering for Christ. They had been flogged. Unless they were masochists, this attitude of mind, this rejoicing in the face of affliction, must have been a learned response, an attitude developed as a result of realising the great sacrifice the Lord had made for them on the cross. It also must have been a result of the Holy Spirit working directly in their lives.

(2) Godliness with contentment is great gain

Another passage written by Paul referring to contentment is in 1 Timothy 6:6-8:

> But Godliness with contentment is great gain. For we brought nothing into the world, and we can take nothing out of it. But if we have food and clothing we will he content with that.

Earlier Paul refers to people who think that godliness will lead to financial gain. Paul contrasts the attitude of those who are out for what they can get financially to those who are content with what they have. However, he does imply that we do have something by the way of food and clothing to be content with. It is hard to be content without the basics of life.

(3) Be content with what you have

Hebrews 13:5 repeats the same thought:

> Keep your lives free from the love of money and be content with what you have, because God has said, "Never will I leave you; never will I forsake you."

Again Paul contrasts loving money with being content with what we have. However, nowhere does he say that others should be content whatever their circumstances, content even if they are hungry and in need. In Philippians it appears he is referring only to himself.

(4) Be content with your pay

The fourth and last passage in the New Testament referring to contentment is Luke 3:14 where John the Baptist told the soldier to "Be content with your pay." Again, it is very much a contentment with material things.

Conclusion on Christian contentment

So, can we achieve Christian contentment? I think the answer is "yes", if it is accepted that this refers to being satisfied with what we have materially. If our aim is not financial gain or the acquisition of possessions, but rather Godliness with contentment, Christians can achieve this and it will be a "great gain" for them.

However, what Paul is talking about in Philippians seems to go far beyond this. Not only was he content when he had enough to eat and had clothes to wear, he was also content when he was hungry and cold. He had learned to he content whatever his circumstances. It is doubtful if many of us Christians from the affluent, comfortable, industrialised world will ever achieve such a state.

21. Peace of Mind
Sylvia Penny

In my previous article on Contentment I referred to Paul having learned to be content whatever his circumstances; whether in need or in plenty, whether well fed or hungry (Philippians 4:11-12). To be like this, to be above the needs of the body, seems to be different from the physical state of contentment. Perhaps Paul had learned not only the art of being content, but had also achieved an inner peace. But what is peace?

Definition of Peace

Vine's *Expository Dictionary* defines peace as:

(a) harmonious relationships between men,
(b) between nations
(c) friendliness
(d) freedom from molestation
(e) order, in the State; in the churches
(f) the harmonised relationships between God and man, accomplished through the gospel
(g) the sense of rest and contentment consequent thereon.

The majority of references to peace in the New Testament are examples of (a) to (f) listed above. The "inner peace" or peace of mind referred to in (g) does not occur very frequently, but it is this one that may give us an insight into the state of mind which Paul achieved.

Peace is a fruit of the Spirit

Galatians 5:22,23 lists the fruit of the Spirit as "love, joy, peace, patience, kindness, goodness, faithfulness, gentleness and self-control". Interestingly the list does not include contentment, which furthers the argument that this is not so much a spiritual quality, but rather a physical state, a frame of mind, which helps us cope whatever our circumstances. However, peace is included in the list. Maybe this spiritual fruit embraces all the varieties of peace listed by Vine and therefore would include "inner peace" or "peace of mind".

As we grow in the Spirit we should, as a result, display more and more of these fruits, and possess more of these qualities. It is a process which includes both ourselves and God. He will work through us and in us, as we allow Him to. This is in accordance with what Paul says in Philippians "I can do everything through Him who gives me strength".

Through Paul's experiences of hardships in his life he learned to lean on the Lord more and more, and allowed Him to work through him so much so that he learned the secret of being content in any and every situation.

Paul often uses the expressions "grace and peace to you" or "the God of peace be with you". Such salutations may give us the idea that the believers he was writing to were to have peace of mind. It was something that Paul very much wished them to have, perhaps as a result of knowing what a comfort it was for himself.

How do we get peace of mind?

We come back to the question as to whether "inner peace" is a gift from God, or whether it is something we can work to attain in our Christian lives.

Colossians 3:15 says "Let the peace of Christ rule in your hearts, since as members of one body you were called to peace". Peace is "of Christ" but we have to allow it to rule in our hearts. This is a two-way process.

John 16:33 says "I have told you these things, so that in me you may have peace. In this world you will have trouble." Again, peace is found "in Christ" and by believing what is said in the Scriptures. It is contrasted with the troubles of the world.

Romans 14:17 says "For the kingdom of God is not a matter of eating and drinking, but of righteousness, peace and joy in the Holy Spirit." Here, peace is found "in the Holy Spirit".

Peace is therefore a spiritual quality found through our relationship with Christ and the Holy Spirit. The way in which we can increase the peace we have is by our own prayers and the prayers of others and by growing in faith.

Paul, in Romans 15:13 prays "May the God of hope fill you with all joy and peace as you trust in him, so that you may overflow with hope by the power of the Holy Spirit."

Again, in 2 Thessalonians 3:16 Paul prays, "Now may the Lord of peace himself give you peace at all times and in every way." As mentioned before, this was something that Paul very much wished every believer to possess.

Paul admits he has no peace of mind

Lastly, Paul explicitly refers to "peace of mind" in 2 Corinthians 2:12-13. "Now when I went to Troas to preach the gospel of Christ and found that the Lord had opened a door for me, I still had no peace of mind, because I did not find my brother Titus there. So I said good-bye to them and went off to Macedonia." Here Paul seems to contradict what he writes in Philippians where he says he has "learned to be content whatever the circumstances". Maybe this is simply explained by the fact that when he wrote Philippians he was several years older and had learned contentment in the intervening period. Years of hardships can teach us a lot. Or maybe, as suggested earlier, contentment is more a physical state, whereas peace of mind a spiritual one. It would be possible to be content without material possessions while still not possessing an "inner peace".

Paul resolves his own lack of "peace of mind" by going to Macedonia where he does meet Titus and is comforted. 2 Corinthians 7:5-6 records "For when we came into Macedonia, this body of ours had no rest, but we were harassed at every turn - conflicts on the outside, fears within. But God, who comforts the downcast, comforted us by the coming of Titus...'

It seems incongruous that Paul should have no peace of mind in Troas, where he had an open door to preach the gospel, whereas in Macedonia, where he was harassed at every turn with conflicts on the outside and fears within, he should be comforted. What made the difference to Paul was the arrival of Titus. This shows how important individuals were to Paul, and particularly to his state of mind. How true this is of us. I return to the 'snapshot of contentment' I gave in my last article (see chapter 20). It included a knowledge of being loved, and having good friends. Christians cannot exist in a vacuum. We need friendship and fellowship and these contribute towards our attaining an inner peace.

Conclusion

To sum up, we should be content with our material possessions and not be covetous of others. Through prayer, faith, friendship, and fellowship, we can change our state of mind. If we have this as our goal and if we allow God to work in our lives, He will work through us enabling us to display further fruit of the Spirit as we grow in Him.

Whether we will ever achieve the heights of Philippians 4:11-13 and be content whatever the circumstances possibly depends on how much suffering and hardship we have to endure. It is clear that we are unlikely ever to go through even a fraction of what Paul did, so perhaps we should not expect to achieve his level of spirituality.

22. Criticism
Sylvia Penny

Why is it so easy for us to point out when another says or does something wrong? Why is it so much harder to compliment them on the good they say or do? Could it be our sinful human nature? Or is it just that people do wrong things at the wrong time most of the time! Of course, we ourselves cannot be included! After all, even if what we do or say doesn't quite come out how we would like, we know in our heart that our motivation is good and true.

Perhaps we should stop and think about this anomaly. If we knew all the facts, and understood the motivations of others, then we are likely to discover that our criticism is unfounded. An example of this is in Judges 8:1 where the Ephraimites criticise Gideon. In the next verse Gideon explains how their criticism is unfounded. In Acts 11:2,3 Peter is criticised by circumcised believers. Peter explains his actions and in verse 18 his critics have no further objections. In both cases it was shown that the critics had no grounds for complaint. What was deficient was their appreciation of all the facts.

Although this might not necessarily be the case, most criticism is negative and potentially damaging to the person it is aimed at. Such criticism achieves nothing except bad feelings, discord, and defensive behaviour. How much better it would be to praise what we see to be a person's strengths. This would encourage good feelings, the desire to deserve such praise, and harmony in our relationships.

In 2 Corinthians 8:20 Paul describes how he takes great pains to avoid any criticism as to how a gift is administered to the churches. He is concerned to "do what is right, not only in the eyes of the Lord but also in the eyes of men." This is ironic, as surely if something is acceptable to God, it should be to men, but Paul points out this is not so. God can look at a person's heart and know the reasons for their actions. We see outwardly, and often our opinion may be coloured by prejudice, selfish concerns, and lack of knowledge.

A good motto is to "do-as-you-would-be-done-by". None of us like to be criticised. None of us like to have our failings pointed out, and especially not on a regular basis. So why should we think that other people will not be upset if we criticise them?

On the other hand, it may be that positive criticism, appraisal, could be useful. This, however, entails a little more thought on our part. We have to go one step beyond what, in our opinion, a person is saying or doing wrong. We have to think of an alternative which would be more acceptable, and suggest that the person consider that idea, or that approach.

There are many places in every-day life where this technique can be applied; from people we have only a passing contact with, to those who we see daily and on an intimate basis.

Neighbours

If our neighbours have an untidy garden which is ruining the look of our own property as well as theirs, criticising them for being lazy and untidy, either to other neighbours or to family and friends, will achieve very little. However, suggesting that they might like to clear it up, and that we would be willing to help them and that we have some spare bulbs and plants, might achieve both a tidier neighbourhood and a closer relationship.

Schoolteachers

If our little boy is being bullied by bigger and tougher boys at school, and the teachers do not seem to do anything about it, complaining to the teacher or headmaster that our child is being bullied and what a bad school it is, is not likely go down well.

However, if we explain the problem, recognising that our own son may have contributed to the situation, and suggest that they discover the culprits and that we would be happy with whatever course of action they deemed desirable, then we may achieve some positive action and have a better relationship with the school should future problems arise.

Ministers

Our church may hold a weekly Bible study on a Thursday evening, but perhaps the minister does not always turn up when we feel he ought. Indeed we might think he should be there regularly. Criticising him to other church members for his lack of commitment, or organisation, will achieve nothing.

On the other hand, if we take the trouble to find out that he often visits an old and sick person that evening, Thursday being the only convenient evening, constructive action can be taken. We could offer to visit instead of the minister, thus freeing him to show more "commitment" to the Bible study.

Employers

"Why don't they pay me what I'm worth?" Asking such questions at work can initiate long, negative, depressing conversations with fellow employees, without achieving one positive result. The main outcome is continued bad feelings about work, resulting in a worse work performance. John the Baptist advised some soldiers in Luke 3:14 to "be content with your pay". How much more should we be content with our pay, especially those of us who live in Western society where our life is one of luxury compared to most other societies, both in the past, and present.

Instead of being critical, would it not be better to have an attitude of thankfulness that we have a job, that the conditions are tolerable, and that we have no worries about food, clothing or shelter? Admittedly our salary will not increase as a result, but perhaps our level of general satisfaction and contentment will.

Work colleagues

Moaning about our work colleagues for complaining all the time, or for never being cheerful, or for being unfriendly, seldom achieves very much, except perhaps isolation and unhappiness. Instead, a positive action such as inviting them to have lunch with us, or supplying them with cakes and cookies on our birthday, may do wonders for increasing morale.

Our own parents

Criticism of parents usually diminishes drastically when we ourselves become parents and realise what a daunting task it can be. However, indirect criticism is levelled at our parents when we claim to others "Well, if I'd only been brought up differently, then I wouldn't be like I am today!" or "Be in the mess I'm in today." Seldom, however, are our achievements and good qualities attributed to our upbringing! These are claimed as something we achieved on our own.

Would it not give great pleasure to our parents to be told that we appreciate what they did for us when we were children? That must be one of the biggest rewards a parent can receive after what can amount to years of selfless giving.

Other parents

It is very easy to point the finger at other parents and criticise them for not disciplining their children properly, or bringing them up as we think they ought. It is much harder to be constructive and offer to look after them while the parents take a much needed break!

It is only when we get close to a family that we begin to realise all the difficulties they have. They are seldom the same as our own, but they are difficulties none-the-less. Criticism only makes things worse for them. Positive help, encouragement, and support can work wonders.

Children

It is easiest of all to criticise children, and particularly our own. They cannot defend themselves, and their very dependence on adults makes them extra vulnerable. Almost anything a child does will not come up to adult standards, so it is possible to continually criticise. The results of this can be devastating.

In contrast, a conscious effort to praise and encourage where it is deserved reap benefits that last a lifetime.

Spouse

This is the person we are closest to and have the most contact with. The one we love the most, and, quite often, the one who receives the most or the worst of our criticism!

When we are living with someone day-in and day-out, we are bound to notice all the little things that they tend to "do wrong".

However, it is also true that we are in the best position to notice all the positive and good things that they do. Why is it easier to notice when something isn't done to our satisfaction, than when it is? Why is it easier to focus on the fact that our husband has not done the washing-up, the vacuuming, the ironing, or whatever it is we would like them to do most, rather than that they have run several errands, picked up the kids for us, and taken the car through the car-wash?

When our loved one always does certain chores every day, then they are invariably taken for granted. However, when they are occasionally omitted for some reason then the criticisms start. Again, why don't we concentrate on being positive, encouraging, and appreciative for all the things they do, rather than being critical for all the things they don't?

Conclusion

Let us be positive, rather than negative. Let us praise, rather than condemn. Let us encourage, rather than demoralise. Let us accept, rather than reject. Let us think, before we speak. In this way we will surely achieve greater harmony in our relationships with others.

> Lord, make us instruments of thy peace.
> Where there is hatred, let us sow love;
> where there is injury, pardon;
> where there is discord, union;
> where there is doubt, faith;
> where there is despair, hope;
> where there is darkness, light;
> where there is sadness, joy.
> (Saint Francis of Assisi; 1181-1226)

23. "He has made everything beautiful in His time"
Rusty Hughes

Staring moodily out of the train window day after day I let my thoughts have full reign. Gradually a picture emerged of myself. I had come to the Lord several years before and this had changed my life. However, the difficult life that I had been forced to lead prior to this had embittered me. I read my Bible and other Christian literature avidly, attended Bible studies and church regularly, and learned as much as I could, but, I had to face facts. I was accumulating head knowledge, was thrilled by it but there was a vacuum inside that no amount of learning could fill, and praying didn't help either. I wore my "mask" bravely whilst I struggled to be free of whatever was binding me. Where, I wondered, was the joy "they" had promised me?

The beginning of realisation came from an unlikely source. A derelict site on the railway embankment by Finsbury Park in North London. The beauty of Hertfordshire went unnoticed by me, but daily I grew more aware of this piece of land. There it was, ugly, littered with old bits of rusty railway track, wire, lumps of brick, choking weeds, brambles and rubbish. "Just like me, Lord," I thought and got strange comfort from that. Then, as winter passed I began to notice that the scruffy bushes became covered with pussy willow followed shortly by pale green leaves. Spring rain washed the grass clean and, suddenly, daffodils! Where had they come from? These were succeeded in turn by lupins of glorious hue and mauve covering of willow herb. Buddleia bushes bloomed, alive with butterflies, and the tangled brambles bore fruit. Lastly, just before the next winter, Russian Vine blossomed in great profusion.

One day my derelict site was fenced off, then teams of workmen began to clear the land. I was disappointed and I asked, "Why?" Clearly the answer came, "Wait." Slowly the land was renewed and eventually in front of my fascinated gaze a beautiful garden emerged for people to walk in with seats to rest upon, and I thought, "He has made everything beautiful in His time". At that point, light glimmered and I thought, He bought my derelict life with His blood, just as the developer bought that land and He is waiting to transform me too.

I believe that Jesus saw hidden beauty in my life and was waiting for me to recognise this before He would begin to refurbish it. I love to picture Him, The Master Builder, picking up the battered bricks of my former life, turning them over in his scarred hands, knocking off the sharp corners, binding them together with the cement of the Holy Spirit; cleaning up the dirty, sharp, rusty wire and forming a protective fence around me, so the enemy finds it harder to encroach; polishing the corroded rails and setting me back on them and then giving me a guidebook and clear signals to follow down the track of my future; giving me hope that even when I do slip (often) my Master Builder will be there to gently put me back on the right track. Life changed for me when hope dawned and joy found a foothold.

How strange, I never knew before
    that flowers grew just that way.
And daffodils nod on their stalks
    as if to greet the day.
The air's alive - it's crisp and clear
    the whole world hums and throbs,
The milkman's bottles chink and thus
    as on his round he plods.

The birds fly forth to greet the dawn
    and bathe in pods of dew -
Their eyes are bright, they burst with song
    it is as if they knew -
My heart is light, my feet have wings
    despite the pouring rain.
A whole new life before me lies -
    for, I am born again.

24. Anger!
Sylvia Penny

In your anger do not sin. Do not let the sun go down while you are still angry, and do not give the devil a foothold (Ephesians 4:26-27)

Although the first part of these verses may be puzzling, the second part is very clear and gives good advice. Although these verses come in the middle of a section which is not specifically addressed to husbands and wives, it has always seemed particularly applicable to married couples. Last thing at night, who is it you are most likely to be angry with if not your husband ... or maybe your children?

When you have all gone your separate ways during the day, the main time for any meaningful interaction is usually in the evening, and often late in the evening. Then it is so easy for serious discussions to become arguments, and arguments to develop into anger. It is then that Paul's advice becomes so useful, if we could but take it and do it. Sometimes it may involve adopting an attitude of humility when we least feel like it, or backing off when we really feel like battling to the finish. So the application of these verses is simple, at least in theory!

But, is Paul referring to this sort of personal outburst of emotional temper, or does he actually mean righteous indignation? Are people actually able to be angry without it being a sin? I wonder if people justify certain outbursts of anger by using this verse, when they feel that their point of view is the correct one, and that they are in the right.

Many parts of Scripture describe the wrath of God, and His anger towards people, and of course by definition this must be righteous anger. Romans 2:8 says:

But for those who are self-seeking and who reject the truth and follow evil, there will be wrath and anger.

Mark 3:4-5 says:

Then Jesus asked them, "Which is lawful on the Sabbath: to do good or to do evil, to save life or to kill?" But they remained silent. He looked round at them in anger and, deeply distressed at their stubborn hearts, said to the man, "Stretch out your hand." He stretched it out, and his hand was completely restored.

God's righteous anger is directed against sin and evil; against people who reject the truth, those who are self-seeking and self-righteous. Can man emulate such righteous anger? Exodus 32:19 says:

When Moses approached the camp and saw the calf and the dancing, his anger burned and he threw the tablets out of his hands, breaking them to pieces at the foot of the mountain.

Moses' anger was kindled for a righteous reason. He was incensed by the idolatry indulged in by his people such a short while after he had been away. But the result of his anger was that he broke the tablets with the writing of God on them. So maybe men can display righteous anger, but the manifestation of that anger may well be their downfall.

Today, it may be possible to feel righteous indignation against the evils in our society, miscarriages of justice and the like. But it is most unlikely that such feelings are the ones referred to by Paul in this verse in Ephesians, as otherwise why would he advise there to be an end to such anger?

No! It seems Paul must be referring to anger as a state of mind here. "In your anger do not sin" is a direct quote of Psalm 4:4 and has the sense of a command. It is assumed that we will be angry at some time or another, and perhaps in itself, that is not a sin. However, there is the utmost danger that it will become sinful if it is not carefully kept in check, and instead of extinguishing it by the end of the day, we harbour resentment and keep the feeling burning alive in us. It has been said that "If we would be angry and not sin, we must be angry at nothing but sin," which is a concise way of saying that it is well nigh impossible to be angry without sinning.

Galatians 5:20 lists the acts of the sinful nature and includes "fits of rage" which refers to emotional outbursts of anger. Ephesians 4:31 says, "Get rid of all bitterness, rage and anger." and Colossians 3:8 says, "But now you must rid yourselves of all such things as these: anger, rage." As such, it seems pretty obvious that anger is an undesirable emotion, no matter what the motivation or apparent justification.

James 1:19,20 is also very clear; "Everyone should be quick to listen, slow to speak and slow to become angry, for man's anger does not bring about the righteous life that God desires." If we are to try to put into practice what God wants us to do, then He shows us "the most excellent way" in 1 Corinthians 13. Verse 5 of this chapter tells us that love "is not rude, it is not self-seeking, it is not easily angered, it keeps no record of wrongs."

In both James and 1 Corinthians it is interesting to note that anger is not completely denied. Rather, we must be slow to anger; not easily angered. It recognises that such an emotion is inevitable at times, but that it should be kept in check, and restrained as much as possible. When we become angry about something, or with someone, we have a choice. Either we can choose to nurture the feeling and add fuel to the fire, or we can attempt to reconcile ourselves to the situation or the person involved. However, let us not take Ephesians 4:26 out of context and use it in self-justification. It is far more useful to remember that "love is not easily angered."

25. *Considering Others*
Sylvia Penny

Each of you should look not only to your own interests, but also to
the interests of others. (Philippians 2:4)

One of the hardest things for us to do, it seems, is to stop thinking of
ourselves, and to consider others first. Every creature has been given a
self-preservation instinct by God, but somehow in man this has gone far
beyond concern for preserving our life. We tend to be naturally self-
seeking, self-centred, and selfish. Without Christ, we would be like the
rich fool in Luke 12:19, who said, "Take life easy; eat, drink and be
merry", and lived exactly as he pleased. But in the next verse God says,
"You fool! This very night your life will be demanded from you. Then
who will get what you have prepared for yourself?" God makes it clear
that no matter what we amass for ourselves in this life, we will not be
able to take it with us after we die. Selfishness in the end is meaningless,
and leads to nothing.

However, we are not only selfish in our actions. It permeates our
whole being, so that our thoughts and words are also coloured with
selfishness. Most of what we think about most of the time is to do with
ourselves, and much of what we say is again all about ourselves. So,
how do we break out of this pattern? As Christians, it is important that
we realise there is a problem to start with, as only then can we try to do
something about it.

Actions

Maybe the easiest place to start is with our actions - what we do. It is
also the most important, as is borne out by Scripture. Scripture
recognises that we are essentially selfish beings. As Philippians 2:21
says "everyone looks out for his own interests". That is why we are told
we should "love your neighbour as yourself" (Luke 10:27). The basic
fact is that we love ourselves.

Then, we are told, try to love others in the same way. How are we
to do this? 1 John 3:18 tells us, "Dear children, let us not love with

words or tongue but with actions and in truth." How do we love with actions? An example is given in James 2:15,16:

> Suppose a brother or sister is without clothes and daily food. If one of you says to him, "Go, I wish you well; keep warm and well fed," but does nothing about his physical needs, what good is it?

It is no good just saying the right things, we also have to do them. There is no point telling someone we love them, if we never do anything for them. Love is proved by action.

> This is how God showed his love among us: He sent his one and only Son into the world that we might live through him. (1 John 4:9)

God's love is shown through His actions. Our love should do likewise. In this way we can partly fulfil what Paul exhorts us to do in Philippians 2:4, quoted at the beginning of this article: "Each of you should look not only to your own interests, but also to the interests of others."

We may wonder how we can help others, when most people in our westernised society have enough clothes, food, and shelter. After all, the quote from James related to a very different society where such basic needs were not always necessarily supplied.

However, I think it's a question of positively searching for the needs of others. People do not necessarily ask others for help in this age when self-sufficiency and independence are considered to be virtues. Many would rather struggle on, coping with many private difficulties rather than ever admit to others that they are in need of help. It is these people we should, as Christians, be alert to, and offer help where we see it is needed. Therefore, first of all, we need to foster a positive interest in others. We will never notice the needs and interests of others, if we are always wrapped up in our own needs and interests. If we are over-involved in our own personal world, just ourselves, and maybe our close family and friends, then we are unlikely to ever reach out to others in need, and touch their lives.

In every church there are many people in need of help. Some may be lonely, others struggling with broken marriages, others with illness or the death of a loved one. Some old people may need physical help, young mothers may need moral support or childcare, and so the list goes on. However, it is our responsibility to find out what these needs are, and try to meet them. In such a way we can begin to break away from a pattern of selfishness, to a pattern of looking to the interests of others. If we do not find any people with needs that we think we can fulfil, then maybe we are just not looking hard enough.

Words

Not only are we often selfish in our actions, we are also self-centred in what we say. How many of our conversations revolve around what we have done recently, where our family has been, and the problems we have just had to cope with. I'm sure many of us have met the person who has asked us, "And how was your holiday this summer?" and proceeded to tell us all about their own! Or we have been asked how we have been keeping, only to be told at length of the other person's recent ailments! Unless we are aware of this happening, how many times have we ourselves been guilty of this way of conversing?

This is not to say that we should therefore never talk about ourselves, or what we have been doing. However, there is a balance. Our conversation should show a genuine interest in the other person, which involves active listening to what they have to say. Active listening means that not only do we listen, but we also make a conscious effort to remember what we have heard. It is all too easy to feign interest and concern during a conversation, only to have forgotten all about it an hour later. We all value those people who remember what we have said to them. Similarly we are of far greater value to those in whom we show a genuine and caring interest.

Many of King Solomon's proverbs are concerned with talking, and what good, or what damage, can result from what we say. Proverbs 12:18 says, "the tongue of the wise brings healing", and Proverbs 15:4 "The tongue that brings healing is a tree of life". We can do a lot of good by what we say, if we can only learn to listen attentively to other people and seek to fulfil their needs. The more we can learn to put ourselves in someone else's shoes, and look at things from their point of view, the less self-centred we will become, and the more caring for others.

Thoughts

This is the hardest area to clear of selfishness. It is as natural as breathing to think about ourselves the majority of the time. Obviously we have to be concerned about where we are going, what we are doing, and all the many things which go to make up our daily lives. However, as Christians, we have a duty to others to fulfil. We are commanded to "love our neighbour as ourselves". If we never even think about our neighbour, it is unlikely we will ever do anything for them. That is one reason why prayer for others is so important. Praying for others is one way in which we can "look ... to the interests of others". By praying regularly for all the people we converse with, for their needs and their problems, we will constantly keep them in mind, so that the next time we see them we should have less trouble remembering what they told us last time. We are also far more likely to think of ways in which we can actively help the people with whom we have contact. If we constantly bring them to mind in our prayers we are far more likely to be prompted into action on their behalf, than if we never think of them until we next see them.

There are many Scriptures which urge us to pray continually, and this is one good reason for doing so - it will alter the way in which we ourselves act. 1 Thessalonians 5:17 says, "pray continually" and 2 Thessalonians 1:11 tells us that Paul prayed all the time, "we constantly pray for you", while in Ephesians 6:18 the apostle says, "And pray in the Spirit on all occasions with all kinds of prayers". If we did this it would help us to play down our own natural selfishness and go some way in enabling us to do as Paul exhorted the Philippians:

Each of you should look not only to your own interests, but also to the interests of others.

Let us try to do this then, in thought, word, and deed.

Part 3
Husbands and Wives

26. *The Wife of Noble Character*
Sylvia Penny

A wife of noble character who can find?
    She is worth far more than rubies.
Her husband has full confidence in her and lacks nothing of value.
    She brings him good, not harm, all the days of her life.
She is clothed with strength and dignity;
    she can laugh at the days to come.
She speaks with wisdom,
    and faithful instruction is on her tongue.
She watches over the affairs of her household
    and does not eat the bread of idleness.
Her children arise and call her blessed;
    her husband also, and he praises her:
Many women do noble things,
    but you surpass them all.
Charm is deceptive, and beauty is fleeting;
    but a woman who fears the Lord is to be praised.
(Proverbs 31:10-12, 25-30)

This passage has always been a favourite of my husband's for as long as I can remember. He pointed it out to me just after we first met. Perhaps he was trying to tell me something!

It certainly is an ideal worth attempting to attain - for surely, if we have confidence in and respect for our partners and other members of our family, this goes a long way towards a happy home and a contented life.

Fear the Lord

I think the key lies in the very last line a woman who fears the Lord is to be praised. If our priorities are right and we put the Lord first, then it may be possible for us to display the other qualities. Fortunately charm and beauty are not included among these, else many of us might have a good excuse to not even start trying to live up to the demands of this passage.

I have omitted verses 13 to 24 as these cover many practical duties which may have been performed by a wife in the community of Solomon's time. Although applications of these can be made, many specific points are not particularly relevant to today's housewife or working mum. Of course, it also means I can avoid having to cover the verse which states that the wife of noble character gets up while it is still dark - one of my weaker points, as any who know me well will verify!

So I have concentrated on the verses where qualities of character are mentioned. These do not depend upon customs, or a way of life, or the part of the world in which we happen to live. They depend largely on our own choice. We can choose the way we act in certain situations and should control what we say, especially to those nearest and dearest to us. It is so easy at the end of a long, tiring day not to live up to this ideal and, usually, those who suffer will be those we least wish to hurt.

All the days of her life

Verse 12 says that she brings her husband good, not harm, all the days of her life. It may be easy to carry this out in the first few months, or even the first few years of a happy marriage. But this verse refers to a lifelong commitment, where many years after discovering that your partner does actually have some faults, your priority is still to give him moral support and to speak well of him, rather than to criticise and make sure everyone is well aware of the weaknesses you have discovered in him.

Verse 25 refers to her being clothed with strength and dignity, and laughing at the days to come. I tend to think that the strength refers to character rather than muscle, as the whole passage is dealing with a wife of noble character. This strength of character is surely necessary if we are to act and speak in the right way, especially towards the people we can too easily take for granted such as our partner and family. It is all too often true that familiarity breeds contempt and we should try to ensure that this does not creep into our closest personal relationships.

Planning and Thinking

We should have no anxiety for the future so that we can laugh at the days to come. This is a practical statement which depends on how prepared we are to ensure a smooth life ahead of us. None of us can bargain for the unexpected problems which crop up now and again, but all of us can prepare for the daily routine which is inevitable. Good forward planning now can save us from much anxiety in the future. Less anxiety in the future means we can free our minds to concentrate on how we act and what we say. This, then, leads on to verse 26 where "she speaks with wisdom, and faithful instruction is on her tongue."

What we say is always so important. Words can never be taken back. Speaking with wisdom invariably involves thinking before we speak, not after. Just because we know our husbands and families better than anyone else does not mean we need not think or control what we say to them. If, whenever we speak, it happens to be the first thing which comes into our heads, then we can hardly expect respect and confidence in return.

Verse 27 is another practical one, referring to keeping the house in order and not being idle. Even today the affairs of the household are more often than not the responsibility of the wife, even if she happens to go out to work as well. In order to carry this out properly I think most women will testify that it would be impossible to be idle at the same time.

Confidence and Praise

So what can we expect in return for being such a perfect wife? The full confidence of our husbands, states verse 11; his praise, says verse 28; and our children calling us blessed. Not many of us would complain at that.

In an ideal world this would be the happy state of affairs within all marriages and family relationships. Surely this is the Lord's ideal, and what He would wish for every one of us. Perhaps we can start the ball rolling by fulfilling our part of the bargain, and coming back to verse 30, realising that:

A woman who fears the Lord is to be praised.

27. Women, Wives & Wisdom
Sylvia Penny

Solomon was the wisest man that has ever lived. When he was a young man the Lord told him that he could have whatever he asked for. So he asked for discernment and the ability to distinguish between right and wrong. The Lord was so pleased with this that He gave him a wise and discerning heart and stated that there would never be anyone else like Solomon, (1 Kings 3.12), except the Lord Himself (Matthew 12:42).

The book of Proverbs is mainly a result of this wisdom and chapters 10 to 29 record many of the wise thoughts and sayings of Solomon - some of them intriguing, some beautiful, some difficult.

Kind-hearted or ruthless?

Even a very brief reading of these proverbs reveals advice which can help us all. There are so many quotable quotes, so many good memory verses. There are a number which are aimed specifically at women, some of which I found quite enlightening, some thought provoking, and some plain amusing.

> A kind hearted woman gains respect, but ruthless men gain only wealth. (Proverbs 11:16)

It is obvious from the way this verse is worded that wealth is considered to have little value compared to respect. What brings us happiness? Is it money and possessions? Or is it to be well thought of by the people who know us? Many people who have won fortunes have testified to the misery it has brought them, and how they wish they had never won.

Many an ambitious person has driven himself to the top in order to earn more money or to achieve a higher status in the eyes of others, only to be destroyed by the effects of stress, a heart attack, a nervous breakdown, a broken marriage.

Kind-heartedness is contrasted with ruthlessness. Kind-heartedness is a selfless quality, one which seeks the well-being of others, and wishes them no harm. Ruthlessness is basically selfish and self-seeking, and not worried about trampling over others to attain its selfish goals. It is not surprising that kind-heartedness gains respect, whereas ruthlessness only achieves wealth.

> Like a gold ring in a pig's snout is a beautiful woman who shows no discretion. (Proverbs 11:22)

This conjures up a vivid and comical picture in my mind; the thought is so incongruous. So, to the Lord's mind, must be the combination of physical beauty and lack of all the finer Christian qualities. To Him there is no point in having physical beauty and yet having no discretion. The beauty is wasted, just as the beauty and value of a gold ring would be wasted if set in a pig's snout. This figure would have an even greater impact upon Jews, for whom the pig was an unclean animal.

Figure and face or .....

So often today, the most important feature of a woman is considered to be her looks, even at the expense of all the other qualities she may possess. It is drummed into us from a very early age by advertising, by the media, by any of the many magazines aimed at women or girls. What matters most is our figure and face!

How many of those same magazines ever contain articles on how to gain discretion, how to act wisely, how to improve our behaviour towards others? But to the Lord these are all-important so, perhaps, our reading should centre more in the pages of the Scriptures than in the latest magazine or colour supplement. All of us are affected and influenced by the material we read.

> A wife of noble character is her husband's crown, but a disgraceful wife is like decay in his bones. (Proverbs 12:4)

Proverbs 31:10-31 describes the qualities of a wife of noble character. Here are twenty-two verses which I imagine would make most wives feel inadequate and acknowledge their limitations. They give us an ideal at which to aim. Such a wife is her husband's crown and, like a crown, precious to him. Note that there is no proviso that the husband should be worthy of such a wife. We should do our best, regardless of his faults.

A disgraceful wife, on the other hand, is like decay in her husband's bones. Instead of building him up, completing and complementing him, she can destroy him, like a disease in his body.

..... character and behaviour?

It would seem that a wife has quite a lot of responsibility on her shoulders. Her behaviour can have a considerable effect on the health and happiness of her husband.

The old saying states that "behind every great man there is a woman". I wonder if the reverse is true. How many unhappy and unsuccessful men have been goaded into that state by their wives?

> The wise woman builds her house, but with her own hands the foolish one tears hers down. (Proverbs 14:1)

This verse reminds me of the parable of the wise and foolish builders, (Matthew 7:24-27). The wise man built his house on the rock, while the foolish man built his on sand. The first house had a firm foundation as the builder put the Lord's words into practice, whereas the second fell down with a crash because although the builder had heard the Lord's words, he had not heeded them. The wise woman is one who listens to what the Lord has to say and attempts to do what He wishes.

Homemaker or home breaker?

A woman is seen very much to be the homemaker, or breaker. It is the woman who is the wife and mother, who creates the atmosphere at home, who keeps the family together, who cares for the needs of its different members and who gives them time.

A wise woman builds up a home where there is contentment, happiness and a feeling of belonging. The foolish one can destroy this harmony, setting one member against another. This verse may also be saying something about the material wealth of the home, where wise and careful housekeeping builds it up, but wastefulness and needless spending on unnecessary and worthless objects and possessions reduces it.

A quarrelsome wife is like a constant dripping on a rainy day; restraining her is like restraining the wind or grasping oil with the hand. (Proverbs 27:15,16)

There are no less than five wise sayings concerning quarrelsome wives! (See also 19:13; 21:9,19 and 25:24.) Clearly Solomon felt it necessary to emphasise this characteristic for some reason, maybe because of his many political marriages. He certainly seems to have strong feelings on the subject. Is it something we women are particularly bad at?

Knitting or nagging?

My husband is very fond of the old saying that "Women either knit or nag", and then follows with the information that I don't knit! Is nagging akin to quarrelling? Perhaps one leads to the other. There are many small things which go to make up our daily living requirements, and most of us have slightly different ideas as to how these little things should be done and by whom. It is easy to slip into nagging, arguing and, ultimately, quarrelling about them. Perhaps we should sit down for some short time each day and think about the things in life which really matter. Then the questions of who is to wash up, who is to make the tea, who left the shoes out, who squeezed the toothpaste in the middle, will pale into insignificance.

To Solomon it seemed better to live elsewhere than with a quarrelsome wife. He considered it an impossible fault to remedy, just as impossible as restraining the wind or grasping oil in the hand. Some issues are not worth arguing about. It is far better for husbands and wives to spend their time building up, encouraging and helping each other, rather than looking for faults and picking quarrels over jobs not done. I wonder how many seeds of divorce have been sown by nagging and bickering, arguing and quarrelling over small things - seeds that grow into trees which push the partner into the arms of another.

He who finds a wife finds what is good and receives favour from the Lord. (Proverbs 18:22)

This verse is rather a good one for us wives to sit back and quote! Although given as an unqualified statement here, we must remember the requirements of the noble wife described in Proverbs 31:10-31. Also proverbs 19:14 states that "a prudent wife is from the Lord". So we cannot sit back and glow in self-satisfaction just because we are someone's wife!

Men look for the wrong things?

In some ways it seems ironic that Solomon who wrote all this good advice "had seven hundred wives of royal birth and three hundred concubines, and his wives led him astray," (1 Kings 11:3). It seems that amongst all those women, not one was what he was looking for, for he wrote that "I found one upright man among a thousand, but not one upright woman among them all" (Ecclesiastes 7:28).

The writer of Proverbs 31:10 asks, almost wistfully, "A wife of noble character who can find?" and one can almost hear Solomon adding, "I can't." Maybe he looked for the wrong things. Maybe he looked for beauty instead of discretion. If he did, no wonder his wives led him astray.

28. *Husbands and Wives*
Sylvia Penny

This article summarises the responses I received to a questionnaire sent out to various women on the subject of the relationship between husbands and wives. It also includes a few of my own observations.

Obedience

The first question was to do with obedience. It asked whether you promised to obey your husband in your marriage service, and to give the reasons for your decision. For those who answered "yes" the main reason was that it was a scriptural principle. However, there were a variety of opinions as to whether there was a specific verse in the Bible which instructed a wife to obey her husband.

In fact, there is no verse which so instructs a wife, but there is an allusion to it in 1 Peter 3:5-6.

> For this is the way the holy women of the past who put their hope in God used to make themselves beautiful. They were submissive to their own husbands, like Sarah, who obeyed Abraham and called him her master.

Those who felt obedience was a scriptural principle all qualified their answer by saying they meant obedience in only some things, not everything. However, they felt there had to be one person with whom a final decision should rest, a captain of a ship, as it were. This would apply only in particular circumstances when a joint decision was necessary. It was also stated that obedience would be given only if the decision was considered to be in accordance with the Lord's will.

Not everyone answered "yes". One reason for not making such a promise was that it was doubted they would be able to keep such a vow, and that it was therefore unwise to make it.

Submission

The next question was on submission. It asked what you understood by the word submit, and what difference there was between submission and obedience.

The Bible does instruct a wife to submit to her husband in a number of places:

Wives, submit to your husbands, as to the Lord. (Ephesians 5:22)

Wives, submit to your husbands, as is fitting in the Lord. (Colossians 3:18)

Wives, in the same way be submissive to your husbands so that, if any of them do not believe the word, they may be won over without words by the behaviour of their wives. (1 Peter 3:1)

People understood submission in a variety of ways, including putting your husband before yourself, yielding, or respectfully giving way to him, and adopting this as a permanent attitude of life. It was not, however, allowing yourself to be dominated by him.

Some felt it was very similar to obedience, whereas others disagreed, stating that obedience is stronger than submission, for it doesn't allow any debate or discussion. However, on reading 1 Peter 3:1 again, it does appear that submission is very much linked with keeping quiet and not arguing.

Some felt that whereas submission is a permanent, general attitude within marriage, obedience was more to do with one-off specific circumstances, to do with decision-making on particular occasions on certain issues.

Husbands as "head'

The next subject was the headship of the husband over the wife. It was asked what you felt the Bible means when it says the husband is head of the wife.

For the husband is head of the wife as Christ is the head of the church, his body, of which he is the Saviour. (Ephesians 5:23)

Now I want you to realise that the head of every man is Christ, and the head of the woman is man, and the head of Christ is God. (1 Corinthians 11:3)

There was virtually unanimous agreement on this. The headship of the husband meant that he had the leadership role and was therefore responsible for his wife's actions and well-being, an example being Adam and Eve in the garden before the fall. Adam was responsible for Eve, and so the Bible tells us that it was through Adam that sin entered the world, not Eve. (Romans 5:12) This ties up with the thought of his being the captain of the ship. His leadership leads to his being responsible.

In the first century, the figure of headship primarily referred to one person supplying the needs of another. They believed that the head supplied all the needs of the body. Thus, Christ was head of the church in that He supplied all the needs of the church, and the husband likewise was head of the wife, because it was his responsibility to supply her needs. In their society, Jewish women did not work outside the home. Their role was home-maker. The husband was the head, in that he provided for his wife and children. In fact, 1 Timothy 5:8 says that the man who did not provide for his family "denied the faith and is worse than an unbeliever."

Thus it seems that the more modern understanding of the figure of headship is primarily that of leadership which leads to responsibility, whereas the first century understanding of headship was primarily that of responsibility, which ultimately led to leadership.

In today's society, where many women contribute to supplying the needs of their families by working outside the home, and where some are the sole bread-winners, perhaps under the first century understanding of the figure of headship they are in fact the head, either jointly with their husband, or in their own right, as they supply the needs of the family.

Respect

The next question concerned respect. It was asked what you understood by the Bible saying a wife should respect her husband, and what was the difference between respect and obedience.

Ephesians 5:33 says "the wife must respect her husband" but this is reciprocated in 1 Peter 3:7 which states "Husbands, in the same way be considerate as you live with your wives, and treat them with respect as the weaker partner." Here the feeling is that respect should be mutual, and that it means taking into consideration one another's feelings. It was thought that whilst respect is mutual, obedience is more one-sided.

Role reversal

It was asked whether you thought it was wrong for a woman to work while her husband stayed at home, and the reasons for your answer.

No-one felt that it was categorically wrong, but that it was considered more proper for a husband to support his wife, unless circumstances forced it to be otherwise.

Another point made was that if a wife did go out to work while the husband stayed at home, it was still right for the husband to be the head and the wife to submit to him. However, as we saw above, it is possible that this is not in accordance with the first century understanding of the figure of headship.

Role reversal is a subject which the Bible does not deal with. Society in those days was so different that the question did not even arise. Sometimes we have to apply biblical principles and use our wisdom and judgment as to what we should and should not do in today's society.

Love

It was asked why you thought the Bible never categorically tells a wife to love her husband, whereas it does tell a man that he should love his wife. This, perhaps, was the most interesting question and also the most controversial one.

> Husbands, love your wives, just as Christ loved the church and gave himself up for her. (Ephesians 5:25)

> Husbands, love your wives and do not be harsh with them. (Colossians 3:19)

In both cases the previous verse tells the wife to submit to her husband.

Titus 2:3-5 refers to women loving their husbands. However, there is no direct exhortation to do so. Rather there are instructions to the older women to:

> train the younger women to love their husbands and children, to be self controlled and pure, to be busy at home, to be kind, and to be subject to their husbands, so that no-one will malign the word of God.

This encompasses a number of practical matters.

Without exception it was felt that it came more naturally to a woman to love her husband, rather than the other way round. She might need training by the older woman for her love to be manifested in the right way, but she did not need a command to love him.

Some felt there may be exceptions to the general rule and that some men may naturally be more loving than some women. However, others felt that men do not love as easily or as unselfishly as women do, and therefore needed to be told to do so.

Another reason suggested for husbands being told to love their wives was that the responsibility for a wife lies with her husband and not the reverse. Thus he is the one who is told to love her.

I must admit I am not sure I agree with the most popular reason, that it is more natural for a woman to love her husband than the reverse. After all, the Bible never specifically tells a man to submit to his wife, and yet the reason for that cannot be because it is more natural for him to do so!

Ephesians 5:21 says "Submit to one another out of reverence for Christ." This is addressed to Christians in general, which therefore includes husbands who are part of this group. So husbands and wives should submit to one another, because they are both Christians. However, when husbands and wives are addressed in particular, it is the wives who are exhorted to submit and husbands who are told to love.

It seems to me that these two balance one another. If a wife submits to her husband, then he is more likely to love her. If a husband loves his wife, then she is more likely to submit to him. Perhaps this is a self-perpetuating circle where the one encourages the other, and so both respect and love are continually increasing, resulting in a harmonious marriage.

Conclusion

In this day and age it is particularly important for us to stop and think about our marriage, to consider what attitudes we have towards our partner, how we think of each other and what our different roles are.

By re-examining our relationship every so often it is possible for us to determine whether we are still living by scriptural principles or whether we have allowed our worldly cares and burdens, desires and aspirations, to affect how we think of each other and the way in which we act towards each other.

May our aim always be to put the Lord Jesus Christ first in our lives and our spouse second. All other relationships will then develop on a sure foundation.

29. Why do Christian marriages break down?
Sylvia Penny

If there were a simple answer to the question "Why do Christian marriages break down?", I suppose there would be no need to ask it in the first place. Yet, alarmingly, the rate at which marriages are breaking down seems to be forever on the increase, and statistical surveys suggest that Christian marriages fare little better than non-Christian ones.

Perhaps if the major cause of marital break-ups was generally known, then couples could take precautionary measures to ensure they don't fall into the same trap. This should be particularly true of Christian couples who have the common desire that their marriage should be "until death us do part" - and would, therefore, be more willing to work at keeping together, and living happily ever after.

Of course, in every break-up there are individual circumstances and particular details which differ from most others. But perhaps there are also some general trends which if determined may make it possible for thoughtful couples to discuss in advance and so avoid or alleviate.

Divorce is easier

Half a century ago divorce was uncommon. What has brought about the change? One simple explanation is that it is far easier to get divorced nowadays, and that there is no longer any stigma attached to being a divorcee, and that it is now an economically viable alternative open to women. None of these was the case fifty years ago.

This is an extremely negative point of view. It presupposes that in days gone by just as many couples would have liked to have got divorced. It suggests that they would have done so if they knew they would be accepted by society afterwards, and if it had been financially viable. Of course, this can never be proved one way or the other.

Women are now more assertive and demanding

In today's society many women are more assertive, more ambitious, more demanding. As such, they pose a threat to both men and the traditional roles and values that men and women have accepted for centuries. Perhaps this threat, whether real or perceived, whether acknowledged consciously or subconsciously, proves too much for some men, who would prefer a more traditional life with a home-based wife.

It is debatable what has created this modern-day image of women, but one contributory factor must be the media: television, videos, films, magazines. James Dobson in *Man to Man about Women* says:

> Never in the history of mankind has there been a comparable force with such power to rewrite social customs and values in so brief a time ... The current campaign is devoted to reconstructing the role of women in America and probably elsewhere. One simple message is dramatised in a thousand ways: if you are at home raising children, you are being cheated, bored, exploited, and wasted as a human being. Why don't you put some meaning in your life and get into the business world like the rest of your sisters. To sell this idea more effectively, women are cast as policewomen, surgeons, newspaper editors, or anything other than wives and mothers.

Concerning the image of women portrayed today, he goes on to say:

> Today's woman is always shown as gorgeous, of course ... exudes self-confidence ... she is virtually omniscient, except for a curious inability to do anything traditionally feminine such as cook, sew, or raise children.

Perhaps this is slightly exaggerated, but surely a constant daily bombardment of what is perceived as the normal marital relationship from the TV set must eventually wear off on the unsuspecting population.

Does this account for the fact that almost as many Christian couples break-up as non-Christian ones? After all, most Christians succumb to watching as much television as other people.

Raising children

A great part of today's new woman involves her going out to work rather than staying at home to run the home, raise the children and be a wife. This automatically means she has less time to do what was, for many centuries, considered a full-time job. As a result many women expect their husbands to pitch in and help out in many ways, including child-rearing, which would have been unheard of and not expected previously.

Men are expected to change and bath their young offspring, read them stories and put them to bed, not on an occasional basis, but on most, if not all, nights. Men are expected to look after toddlers with tantrums for many hours on Saturdays while their wives have a chance to do the shopping and attend to other matters, which they have been unable to do in the week because they have been at work. Even non-working wives have started to expect their husbands to help with the jobs around the house, and expect them to be more involved with the children. This trend is catching and is spreading.

Men helping with the washing up and vacuum-cleaning occasionally is one thing, but one question that needs to be asked is this: should wives expect their husbands to get involved with children, especially young toddlers, on a daily basis? Could this be another contributory factor to marital break-down?

Judging from my own observations it appears that, in general, women are far better adapted to coping with the traumas and tantrums, the inconsistencies and frustrations, involved with raising young children. There are always exceptions to this, of course. However, most people involved in child-care and pre-school, primary and elementary education, and jobs associated with dealing with young children are women. Few men choose to enter such professions.

If men are involved with youngsters, quite often it will be with teenagers. Men seem better able and far happier dealing with teenage boys. In contrast, many women find this group particularly difficult.

Certainly there is no indication in Scripture that Christian men should get involved with rearing young children. Keeping discipline is mentioned, but there is the caution for a father not to be too strict (Ephesians 6:4). And in Jewish homes fathers began to teach their sons the Scriptures when they neared their teens. However, the day to day caring of young children was very much the role of the woman.

Lack of extended family

There is, however, a great disadvantage that many women suffer from today - the lack of the extended family. Even fifty years ago, families were bigger and the population was much less mobile. People were more likely to live in close proximity to their many relatives for the duration of their lives. This meant that women at home with little children had plenty of support from mother and mother-in-law, from sisters and sisters-in-law, from aunts and cousins. There would have been no need to call upon their husbands for any help, to relieve them from some of the stresses and strains of child-rearing. But nowadays, often a woman has no-one to call upon other than her husband! Yet if she does so on a regular basis, it will put a strain on the marriage!!

With many family members all around, the age-old traditional roles could be upheld. As a result, this led to more stability within the marriage with fewer demands upon each partner, and so less strain and greater happiness. Where roles are more clearly defined, and where a wide variety of help is easily available from the extended family, life is easier.

Unfortunately it is impossible to turn back the clock or to reverse the tide which is sweeping through our society. None-the-less, if we are aware of one of the major contributory factors to stress in our relationship, we can be alert to it, discuss it together, and be better able to circumvent it.

It would seem that wives need to recognise that their husbands may find too much child-care too great a strain. However, husbands need to realise that without the extended family they are often the only people their wives can turn to, to relieve them from that demanding task.

If I am right in thinking that women today, Christian ones just as much as non-Christian, expect too much from their husbands and are too demanding, especially in the area of child-care, then perhaps this could be one of the major causes of marital breakdowns. Any person who is pressurised into doing something which they are not very good at, and which they do not enjoy, is quite likely to opt out. In the marriage situation this means the man will up and leave, quite often escaping into the arms of another more sympathetic woman, and not infrequently one who has no children. Indeed, this has been made easier by so many women being in the work force, working alongside men, so that such relationships are far more common. Today, the work place, more than any other, provides opportunities for extra-marital affairs.

Balancing our responsibilities

As Christian women we have to learn to balance our responsibilities. Woman was created to be a helper and we have to learn to be a helper suitable for our husband, being a good companion for him (Genesis 2:18).

We also have to be a good mother and discharge our responsibilities in bringing up our children. Sometimes the two may seem almost incompatible or even impossible without help. However, we should never be one to the exclusion of another. If we are, we run the risk of either ignoring our children or, more commonly, alienating our husbands.

Part 4
Raising Children

30. Aw, go on Mum
Barbara Parsons

When Jim was just eleven
The skateboard craze caught on.
So, coming up to Christmas
Jim got round his dad and mum
For a skateboard and a helmet
And pads for arms and knees.
Then he terrified old ladies
By zipping past at speed!
He practised every evening
Of skateboards, he was king!
It lasted from that Christmas
'Til he got bored in spring!

Next Christmas, it was easy,
'Cos *Rubik's Cube* came in!
Soon Jimmy's friends all practised
To be as fast as him!
But though the *Cube* absorbed him,
Kept him happy hour by hour,
The craze was quickly over.
The *Cube's* forgotten now!

Then, last year, Jimmy pleaded,
He sulked, cajoled and begged,

So Christmas Day found *Astro Wars*
Wrapped up beside his bed!
In three days Jimmy cracked it,
Ten Thousand; standard four!
But *Astro War's* no challenge
Once you've got the highest score!

And now the Christmas Season,
Once more gets into swing,
And Jimmy tells his mum and dad
"Computers are the thing!"

To Jim, Christmas means "getting",
A list of things to buy
Which always *seem* important
But never satisfy.

That's a long way from the stable.
A long, long way to come.
A long way from the Father
Who *gave* the world His Son.
A long way from the wise men
Who sought the infant King.
A long way from poor shepherds
Who had no gift to bring!

We've traded Christ and Christmas,
For things seen on TV,
For gimmicks seen on adverts,
For an annual spending spree.
We're demanding and we're selfish,
Just look what we've become,
A long way from the Father
Who gave the world His Son!

31. Jesus Christ and Father Christmas
Gillian Henry

"Father Christmas and Jesus are best friends." A quote from young Darryl, aged 6, recorded in Nannette Newman's collection of children's sayings entitled *Lots of Love*. Together with this comment was a picture of Father Christmas, sled and all, flying over a collection of suburban homes labelled Bethlehem!

Parental Problems

This statement, together with the picture, illustrates one of the problems faced by Christian parents. Should they tell their children about Father Christmas or not? If they do, will Christian belief and Christmas mythology become associated together in the child's mind so that if they believe both when they are young, will they reject both when they are older?

The Lord Jesus is often most talked about and most real to many people at Christmas time, as is Father Christmas also. They are both associated with winter and gifts, so it is easy to imagine how a child, like Darryl, might combine the two into one overall myth. Then, as the child grows to reject one aspect, Father Christmas, might he not also reject the other - Jesus Christ?

A child in a Christian family will, after all, be taught much that is humanly fantastic and beyond his senses. For example, he is taught that if he prays, God will hear, and that the Lord Jesus rose from the dead and gives us eternal life. However, he may also be taught to write letters to Father Christmas, who will then read them and fill everyone's stocking with presents. How difficult is it for a young child to separate the historical facts of Jesus Christ from the fantasy and fiction of Father Christmas?

Materialism and Lying

The festive Christmas season has become increasingly materialistic and Father Christmas is an integral part of it. There is a possibility that belief in Father Christmas will simply encourage a getting rather than a giving attitude, which is already so prevalent in today's society. Perhaps a better idea would be to ask children what presents they will be giving, rather than what they want, and expect, to receive.

Another problem the Father Christmas myth raises is that many feel that they are simply sanctioning and institutionalising lying if they tell their children that Father Christmas exists, unless they make the pretence very clear.

All year round

However, no child is likely to maintain any Christian belief solely on the basis of the Christmas stories of the shepherds and wise men. The child's ability to distinguish the facts of Jesus Christ from the fantasy of Father Christmas will be aided by his seeing the Lord Jesus as a living reality all year round in the lives of his parents. If Christ is often talked about at home, then children will not have any difficulty with any association with Father Christmas. Will they not naturally leave behind the myth of the fat man in red as they mature?

Lives full of Fantasy

It could be very difficult, if not impossible, to separate children from the myth anyway. Father Christmas is such an integral part of Christmas and he is likely to put in an appearance at parties, playgroups, shops, and so forth. Wouldn't it be confusing and counter-productive to deny children participation in what their friends so obviously believe.

A young child's life is so full of fantasy and make believe anyway. Does the addition of Father Christmas amount to anything more than a harmless and pleasant addition to that stage of life? This myth, after all, does not carry the sinister implications that traditional Halloween celebrations do. If the Lord Jesus Christ has a central place in the family all year round, maybe the annual visit of Father Christmas is insignificant? Or maybe it does encourage materialism, lying, and the exercising of faith and belief in fiction and fantasy? Or maybe it simply doesn't matter at all?

32. Toys
Sylvia Penny

Most of us, whether parents or grandparents, uncles or aunts, will spend some time during the month of December visiting assorted toy shops in order to buy presents for the children in our lives. This raises several immediate questions:

> (1) How much time should we spend hunting for suitable toys?
> (2) How much money should we spend?
> (3) What sort of toys should we buy?
> (4) How many toys should we buy?
> (5) Are toys really necessary for children?
> (6) Are children affected by advertisements for toys?

(1) How much time should we spend?

Toy shops in December are akin to being on the London Underground in rush hour, so maybe the answer to this question is "as little as possible!" However, if you are like me, the temptation to browse around toy shops and toy departments is too great to resist despite the crowds.

The problem is, if you take children with you, you have to be prepared for one of two alternatives. Either they get fed up long before you do, and a conflict situation arises, or else you want to leave before they do, in which case a different conflict situation arises! Therefore, before you go, you have to appreciate you will be in a no-win situation.

Maybe the answer is to go without children, but in most cases this is easier said than done. If it can be achieved, however, you are likely to spend four times the amount of time, and four times the amount of money on the toys. No doubt this time could have been spent more usefully staying at home and playing with the children and their existing toys.

(2) How much money should we spend?

The sums of money spent on children's toys at Christmas time is phenomenal. It is questionable whether children actually appreciate the value of the presents they receive. It is even questionable whether they want many of them. That being the case, we have to ask whether it can be morally right to pour so much money into the coffers of the toy manufacturers when there are so many children in this world deprived of even the basic necessities of life. The answer to this question is obvious, but the solution is not.

Collectively there will never be a solution, but as individual Christians we have the choice as to where our money goes this Christmas. We could choose to spend proportionately less on toys this year and put the savings in our favourite children's charity. The last people to notice such a cut-back would be our children! Even the most discerning child is unlikely to notice that the total value of their presents has been reduced by, say, ten percent!

(3) What sort of toys should we buy?

This question cannot be answered by merely determining the age and sex of the children we are buying for. There is such an incredible variety that the choices appear endless.

We have to decide upon some sort of criteria for determining which we will choose and which we will leave on the shelves. Of course the selection process is further complicated if the children in question happen to be our own, if they happen to be with us on the buying expedition, and if they happen to have strong ideas of what they want.

"Mum! Mum! Mum! Can I have one of these? P-l-e-a-s-e?" is always a difficult question to escape, especially if you are harassed and pushed for time. However, if we are allowed a small say in what our children should have, we are probably most concerned about value for money, durability, educational worth, and other such worthy considerations.

Having recently read *Children at Play* by David Porter, there is a further characteristic of our children's toys which has been brought to my attention - the question of morality. His book tends to cover toys, books and magazines available for children of school age and over, as it is difficult to see how rattles, building blocks and shape sorters could be moral or otherwise. However, he does have a point, particularly for Christian parents who are concerned that their children grow up with Christian values.

Some board games produced for older children are based on either horror or the occult. Some video games contain a sick sense of humour. And some reading materials are filled with warped sexual innuendoes. Thus there is much we have to be aware of in order to protect our children from the baser aspects of this world. Even in seemingly harmless items such as Barbie and Cindy dolls and My Little Pony, David Porter sees a variety of pitfalls, such as the lack of real values in the doll-world where possessions mean everything, and the amorality of the pony-world where the possibility of sinfulness doesn't exist.

He also touches on the problems of war toys and whether our children should be provided with guns and swords. I must admit that when our little boy received a gun for his fourth birthday from one of his friends I had mixed feelings. I was relieved when he didn't like the loud bang from the caps and these were promptly disposed of. The gun now lies unused at the bottom of the toy box. It was never confiscated, just forgotten.

David Porter makes the point that a toy gun can only ever be used as a gun, it being impossible for it to double up as anything else. Thus a child is likely to discard it for a more versatile toy.

Lego can be built into a gun, transformed into a car, then made into a house. I have discovered, as millions of other parents before me have, that toys such as Lego, and its younger version Duplo, have lasting appeal and provide no moral dilemmas.

(4) How many toys should we buy?

If you have children under twelve and your home is anything like ours, it will, in all probability, resemble a small toy shop!

One of my later questions is whether children are affected by advertisements for toys. However, it is a certainty that adults are considerably affected. I know myself that until I have walked into a toy shop, browsed through a catalogue, seen an advertisement on television, I am not aware of what is available. If I had remained blissfully ignorant, the state of our house would not be as it is now, with toys everywhere!

There can be no doubt that today's child has toys vastly in excess of what it needs or even wants. Years ago the choice and availability were simply not there, and neither was the money to buy them. The problem, today, is that although most of us have the time, money and access to fully stocked shops to buy toys galore, should we do so?

How many times have you heard people say that children play more with the wrapping and the boxes than their contents? And how many play happily for hours with water and dirt, sticks and stones, paper and string, without ever needing brightly coloured plastic objects?

Are we teaching our children materialism from an early age? Will they grow up expecting and demanding excesses of material possessions? As Christian parents would we be right to limit our children's toys? As children naturally compare notes with their friends and peers, does it create difficulties for them by making them have less or appear different? It seems there is no easy answer.

(5) Are toys really necessary for children?

As I said earlier, toys, as we know them, were simply not available many years ago. Those generations of children grew up quite adequately without them. Even today, in many parts of the world, the toys of the affluent west are simply not available. Yet the children in those countries grow into adulthood without their aid. The answer is that toys are not really necessary, but they do add variety and interest to a children's world.

It is possible to justify the possessions of a few well-chosen and long-lasting toys as being necessary for a child's development, education and understanding. However, in the main, the vast majority of toys would have to be classed as unnecessary luxuries, so how can we justify the extreme consumerism that all these toys represent?

(6) Are children affected by advertisements for toys?

If the answer to this was "No!" then millions of pounds are wasted annually by the vast number of companies advertising their products on children's television and directing their advertising straight at youngsters.

It is impossible to escape advertisements for toys nowadays. They are on television, in the papers, in magazines, in catalogues and in direct mail. They are in shops, on trains, on buses, on notice-boards. They permeate our whole society and have one sole aim, which is to induce us to buy a product previously unwanted and probably unknown.

Advertising creates a demand where there was none. It stimulates a dissatisfaction which was previously not there. It appeals to our fallen human nature and is, consequently, a great success. And our children are not immune. They are, in all probability, more susceptible to the subtle pressures engaged in advertising. Perhaps we should protect our children from the effects of advertising, but in our society this is well nigh impossible. It is only our awareness that there is a danger in advertising that provides us with some measure of protection against it. Children are unaware that they have a fallen nature, thus they cannot know that it is being appealed to and consequently are ripe for exploitation.

As Christian parents we can attempt to control our children's demands and expectations and try to put them in perspective. However, it would be unrealistic to expect that we can totally negate all the influence of effective and persuasive advertising.

Conclusion

I have raised a number of questions, but provided few answers. It is so difficult in this day and age to strike out alone and act differently from our contemporaries. Christians have automatically got caught up in the materialistic society in which we live and it is difficult for us to separate ourselves from it.

Maybe next Christmas we should think again about where our real values lie and what we most desire for the children in our lives. Are we materialistic, wanting our children to have as much or even more than their peers? Or do the eternal and spiritual values come first, with us wanting our children to appreciate more of the selflessness of the One Who became a Babe at Bethlehem?

33. Coping with Motherhood
Sylvia Penny

5.30 a.m. Baby wakes. Time for her first feed of the day. Caroline stumbles out of bed, half asleep, and prepares for an hour of alternate feeding and winding. She looks down at her baby daughter sucking away furiously.

"Thank you, Lord, for giving me a perfect, healthy, little girl."

Then she returns to a state of semi-stupor, letting the baby get on with it.

6.30 a.m. Baby still unsettled. Will not go back to sleep. Seems to be in pain from bad wind. By this time Caroline is feeling much less thankful for her perfect baby daughter, and much more tired and cross.

"Please, Lord, give me a little more patience, and a bit more stamina to last through. Help me feel more loving, and less resentful of the time slipping by which could have been spent asleep in bed."

7.15 a.m. At last! Baby settled. Caroline gingerly places her back in the carrycot, tiptoes out and rushes back to bed.

"Thank you Lord!"

7.30 a.m. Toddler starts shouting for attention from his cot. "Mum, mum, mum, mum, mummy!" Impossible to ignore this noise, and anyway, he might wake up the baby. Caroline stumbles out of bed again, still tired, but by now is wide awake.

"Give me strength to change his nappy and wash him, Lord, while he is persistently trying to run round and play with his toys."

8.00 a.m. Breakfast time for toddler. An hour of preparation, coaxing, picking up food thrown onto the plastic mat, cleaning and reprimanding. Caroline manages a few mouthfuls of cereal here and there and eats a few soldiers left by the toddler.

"Lord help me not to get cross with him when he throws his food on the floor. I know that I'm tired but that's no excuse to take it out on him."

9.00 a.m. Toddler left to play happily. Caroline upstairs and into a lovely, hot, relaxing bath. The sun streams through the window onto the water. Caroline closes her eyes and imagines herself in an exotic swimming pool on a tropical island.

"Thank you Lord for a lovely comfortable home, for two healthy little children, plenty of food to eat, and few worries. Thank you for all the blessings you've given me in this life. There's so many I take for granted. Help me not to complain too much - especially about being tired."

9.30 a.m. Baby wakes for next feed. Toddler falls off the settee onto his Thomas-the-tank engine and bangs his head. Both cry simultaneously, demanding attention.

"Lord, help me to cope with their screeching together. It's a terrible noise but help me to keep calm, and not get uptight."

Caroline placates the toddler first who recovers instantly, then she feeds the baby and relative peace returns.

10.00 a.m. Never-ending Household chores started. Caroline faces these philosophically - they are all her toddler will allow her to do while he's awake, so she might as well get on with them. She looks ruefully at the pile of magazines and papers she would rather be reading. She knows that if she picks them up, toddler will allow her two minutes reading time, at maximum. She thinks:

"It would be nice to have a couple of hours to sit down and read an article or chapter properly. Can't remember the last time I had the chance to do so."

12.30 p.m. Lunchtime, then toddler to bed for afternoon sleep. He settles down as baby wakes for next feed. "Still no time to myself," Caroline sighs despondently.

> "Lord, help me to learn the lesson to always put others first, myself last. Help me not to begrudge time given for others. Not only my children, and my family, but also my friends, acquaintances, and any others who may need me. It's so easy to think about me first all the time. Certainly these two little children have forced me to act otherwise. Help me not only to do this, but to enjoy it also."

2.00 p.m. Baby settled again. Toddler still asleep. At last. A spare one-and-a-half hours. What can this precious time be spent doing? Dilemma!

> "Please forgive me, Lord, for choosing to go back to bed and sleep, rather than doing a Bible study, or reading one of the pile of articles or booklets I have stored up to look at. Somehow I don't think I'll survive the evening without a bit more sleep."

Feeling a bit conscience stricken, Caroline returns to bed. After all, not all women are lucky enough to have both children sleeping simultaneously in the afternoon - so perhaps she shouldn't waste this precious time given to her.

3.30 p.m. Toddler awakes. Caroline reluctantly emerges from the bedroom, feeling more tired than when she went. Toddler is bright and perky and wants to play.

> "Help me to be enthusiastic and give him my time happily, Lord. After all, he doesn't often get my undivided attention now, since the baby came. Help me to be enthusiastic in everything I do. I like it when others are - so perhaps I should try to be so myself. Help me to be enthusiastic for you too, Lord. Its so easy to forget about you in my day so full of children."

4.30 p.m. Dinner preparation begun. Baby wakes for another feed. Caroline attempts to do both. Five minutes feed, five minutes potato peeling, five minutes feed etc. Screeching and nappy changing in between times. Toddler starts whining for a tower to be built with his bricks.

> "Lord, help me to keep calm. Help me to be organised. Help me to cope with having four things to do at one time. I'm sure there must be hundreds of others who have to cope with far worse than me."

Caroline finds it difficult to imagine who they might be at the moment.

5.30 p.m. Dinner. Baby still unsettled and crying throughout. Must have wind again. Toddler pours half his drink into his lap, and throws his chicken dinner on the floor. Caroline's dinner slowly goes cold while she cleans the toddler up, and attempts to placate the baby. Even a quick prayer is beyond her now. All her attention is taken up in merely coping.

6.30 p.m. Plays with toddler for half-an-hour before getting him ready for bed. Bounces baby in bouncy chair to keep her (relatively) happy. She's always wide awake from her afternoon feed through to bed-time at 10.30 p.m.

> "Thank you, Lord, for such a happy little boy for a son. He's such fun. Help me to appreciate him more and more."

Somehow with only half-an-hour to go before his bedtime, Caroline seems to get renewed strength from somewhere. Could it be the prospect of a toddler-free evening ahead?

7.30 p.m. Toddler safely in bed, blissfully quiet. Baby needs another feed. She seems to need feeding and winding most of the evening. "Still no time," thinks Caroline.

> "Lord, how can Christian mums fit in "quiet times"? How do they find time to study your Word? When do they have time to read about you? Or listen to what others have to say? Am I so unusual? Am I so badly organised? Please help me to find the time. I'm sorry my prayers are so unspiritual too. Help me to pray for others instead of myself all the time. Help me to pray for others, particularly those in my own situation. I can understand their problems so clearly."

8.30 p.m. Baby falls asleep. Most unusual. Caroline uses this rare moment to catch up on the pile of ironing which has mounted over the past week and a half. Then the phone rings.

"Hello, Caroline. It's Margaret. How are you?"

"Not too bad, thanks. How about yourself?"

"Well, it's been a hectic day at the office, and my boss seems just as bad as ever. Deadlines all the time, and no consideration as to whether I want a lunch hour. I couldn't get those chorus books after all. I had to type a massive report for him and stayed in half my lunch hour to do it. I feel shattered now."

"Oh. I am sorry you've had such a bad day."

"Didn't have too good a night either. Dawn chorus woke me up again, and I couldn't get back to sleep for ages. Luckily I did in the end, otherwise I don't know how I'd have coped at work. It's all right for you. At least you're at home all the day and can take it easy. Did you manage to get a rest today?"

"Yes. Would you believe both children slept at the same time this afternoon, so I went back to bed to catch up on lost sleep."

"Wish I could go to bed in the afternoon. Well, I've just done an hour on Sunday School preparation. I've nearly finished it now. How about you?"

"Well, I just don't seem to have had the time. I'll try and fit it in somewhere tomorrow, hopefully. David's not working so he'll be able to keep the children happy while I do it."

"If you want any material, then let me know. If not, I'll see you on Sunday."

"O.K. Thanks. See you then."

"Bye."

"Bye."

9.00 p.m. Caroline continues ironing.

"Lord, please help Margaret to cope with her work situation, and with her boss in particular. Give her the strength to get through the day without feeling shattered at the end of it. Thank you for her work in the Sunday School, and thank you that she offered to help me. I don't know how we'd manage without her now. Lord, although I've not had time to prepare my own Sunday School class, thank you that I can come to you in prayer at any time day or night. Thank you for this marvellous privilege, and teach me to use it more and more, to rely on you more and more, and less and less on myself."

10.30 p.m. Bed-time drink. Wakes baby to change and feed her for the night.

"Lord, thank you for everything you've given me. My home, my friends, and most of all my husband and children. Teach me to appreciate them more and complain less. Thank you for a good day, and help me organise my time well tomorrow. Give us all a good night's rest. Amen."

Caroline winds the baby, settles her and tiptoes out.

11.30 p.m. Time for sleep.

34. Bringing up Children
Gaynor Titterington

Many people would say that children today have a better start in life than at any other time in history. That is proved to be true, in the material sense, when we look at all the nursery items now on the market. Pre-school books, advising parents on the reading and writing techniques employed in schools, provide an invaluable help in the home. But, what about when our children go to school? As a mother of two young children, one of whom started school last year, I am convinced that to bring up children correctly in the eyes of the Lord is proving to be more difficult than ever before.

At school

When a child starts school, he or she is often mixing with children from families completely different from their own. The standards set at home can be very different from what is expected of their contemporaries. As children are so easily influenced by each other, the rebellion against home Christian teachings can soon start.

We read in the newspapers that schools providing a Christian education are few and far between in our multicultural society. My husband and I are fortunate in that our daughter attends a school which is very keen on preserving Christian teachings and standards, so what instruction we give her at home is usually supported by her teachers.

The media

Schools apart, children are perpetually bombarded by the influences and dangers of an ungodly world. Television programmes aimed at children show violence and greed as the norm. Magazines, comics and books tend to portray very little respect for fellow men. All these forms of entertainment can be very influential on our children's thinking.

Strangers

Nowadays, in this age of child abuse, we have to bring to the attention of our children the dangers represented by strangers. We have to make them aware that some adults may wish to harm them! In contrast to when we were children, our offspring have to play with their freedom severely curtailed. This necessary lack of trust in others must have some effect on their outlook on life.

What do we do?

In the face of so much opposition to Christianity in everyday life, what should we do for our children? Ought we to keep them separate as much as possible and give them nothing but our views and opinions? Surely, that is as bad as giving them a free rein. When all is said and done our children have to live with these influences when they grow up. They have to be in a position to cope with everyday situations outside the security of the home.

I feel that we should be able to guide them from the Scriptures at home, teaching them to put their trust in the Lord Jesus. As Paul expresses in Ephesians 6:4:

> Fathers do not exasperate your children; instead bring them up in the training and instruction of the Lord.

As parents it is our duty to do this, so that if our children have a knowledge of the Lord we may, perhaps, be rewarded by their acknowledging Him in later life as Saviour and taking the love of the Lord Jesus into their hearts.

35. *Putting the Lord First*
Sylvia Penny

When people say it is most important to put the Lord first, I feel, sometimes, that this is a little glib, although at face value it is eminently correct. But what exactly do we mean by 'putting the Lord first'? How do we put it into practice?

Does it mean spending a large proportion of our time going to church, attending meetings, studying the Bible, reading Christian books and magazines, praying and the many other things which come flooding into our minds as activities which please the Lord? Or does it mean putting others first, commencing with our immediate family?

Other thoughts about the words 'putting the Lord first' also come to mind. For example, is it used as an excuse to justify our spending time on what we want to do? All of the above mentioned activities are right and proper things to do. The only drawback is that for one reason or another it may not be possible to do them all and so we have to choose which we do: or choose not to do those which we do not want to do!

Mothers and young children

As a married woman with two young children under school age, this choice appears to be fairly restricted. There are so many things one cannot do with very young children that it is a pleasant surprise to find the occasional Christian activity in which they can sensibly be included.

One starting point is the local church. If one is fortunate to live near a church large enough to run a crèche then there are three choices open to you; to attend the services and leave the children in the crèche, to take them into the service with you or not to go to church at all.

It seems to me it depends almost entirely on the child as to which of the three is best. Some babies seem to be born placid, love sleeping in their portable car seats and, if not sleeping, will gurgle happily and beam at anyone within eyeshot. This type of child may be easily left in a crèche and the parents attend the service with an easy mind.

On the other hand the baby which screams whenever placed anywhere but in its mother's arms, that has colic twenty-four hours a day and is never placated by a dummy, is rather difficult to leave in a crèche. If it also happens to be the sort which needs to be walked up and down incessantly, then leaving it in a crèche or taking it into church would not appear the most sensible thing to do. The only choice is to stay at home.

Mothers and toddlers

Moving on a couple of years, the placid baby will now be a happy toddler, playing quietly on the crèche floor with a few toys. It will never have heard of such things as tantrums or experience the delights of being disobedient! It would never enter its head to take a toy from another child or bang it over the head with a nice Christian book!

Again, the parents can participate in the service with an easy mind, knowing that they are raising a well-rounded, loveable child who does what it is told and who is a testimony to their ability as good parents.

On the other hand the screaming, screeching baby has become an aggressive little toddler whose aim in life is to wreak havoc in the cosy crèche, take all the toys off the other children and make enough noise to drown the singing of the entire congregation!

It is rather difficult for the parents of such a child to use the crèche with an easy conscience. Yet taking such a child into the service would prove a disaster, what with running up and down the aisles; hiding in the pulpit, standing at the feet of the minister, falling down the steps and howling at maximum volume. No! There is no choice. It would be best to stay at home.

Mothers and Sunday school

The next stage in the progression is the Sunday school. The same story continues. The one child is welcomed with open arms, praised for its attentiveness and apparent interest in the subject. But the unruly, over-active child who cannot sit still, cannot concentrate and disrupts the whole group is not really the sort of child who is eagerly welcomed by the long-suffering Sunday school teacher. It is easier to keep this child at home. But how many parents have children like the first, the quiet and passive type? And how many have children like the second, the noisy and active type?

A large proportion of parents I suspect would consider their child to be of the second sort, myself included! That being the case could this possibly explain why there is such a lack of people in church between the age of 25 and 40? Their absence may well be nothing to do with not wanting to put the Lord first. It may have much more to do with avoiding embarrassing situations and not wanting to over-stretch the limited facilities of the local church.

To subject either a difficult baby to a crowded and hot crèche or an active toddler to a restricted and claustrophobic space for a whole hour is not in their best interests. How can this be interpreted as doing the right thing, of putting the Lord first? The parents may clock up an hour's attendance at church, but at what cost to the child? Surely its interests should come first, particularly in their early years. I am always being told to make the most of this time as it passes by so very quickly. There will be ample time and opportunities for attending church services, meetings and suchlike in the years to come, so shouldn't we put the children first when they need it most?

Pram services

Some churches put on special services for mothers with small children. These are designed to revolve around the needs of two and three year olds. Here it does not matter if little Johnny decides he wants to use the back pew as a balancing beam, and if he wants to explore the pulpit he can do so without dozens of disapproving eyes watching him.

Such services I feel ought to be greatly encouraged as they cater for just those mothers who feel excluded from the Sunday services. There you are made totally welcome without being totally embarrassed, so you can feel relaxed. I am fortunate to have benefited greatly from such services and my two children have thoroughly enjoyed them.

Mothers and crèches

Other churches may have daytime midweek gatherings for prayer and/or Bible study. Again the crèche facilities may be provided and mothers are encouraged to show an interest and turn up. However, do babies and toddlers actually like these crèches? I am sure that there are some children who love them and positively look forward to the opportunity of thrusting their little personalities on the other children there. But there may be many others who, if they had the choice, would rather be at home with Mummy doing a jig-saw or building a Duplo farm. Having had one child of each sort I can see both the advantages and disadvantages.

With the first type of child one could gaily attend five such meetings a week in the knowledge that the child was thoroughly enjoying itself and getting plenty of stimulation from being with other children of the same age. On the other hand, the second type of child would grow to hate the very look of the outside of the church building as it conjures up ideas of being parted from Mummy, stuck with relative strangers and surrounded by hordes of boisterous children for what, to them, seems to be eternity. The mother of this type of child could not with a good conscience concentrate on the passage being studied or the prayers being offered. It would be better to stay at home, give the child the love and attention it needs and try again in a couple of years.

Baby sitters

Unfortunately judgments are made by well-meaning Christians on the spirituality or otherwise of such young mothers merely on whether or not they attend church on Sunday and turn up to various midweek meetings. However, it may be that putting the Lord first involves putting the family and their needs first.

But there are always the evening meetings. Why not solve the problem by getting a baby-sitter and going to some of these? Again, there is more to this than meets the eye.

Most breast-fed babies like to have their mothers around in the evenings, and especially those who suffer from colic. To leave them with a baby-sitter at this stage would mean trauma all round. The baby would screech for comfort for three solid hours and the fifteen-year-old, well-meaning girl, who was going in for nursery nursing, would be reduced to a tearful wreck and decide to follow a career in banking. The parents would have a guilty conscience for going out and a sleepless night trying to calm the baby down.

But what about when breast-feeding is over? Unfortunately, some children have the habit of being unable to sleep in the evenings. Despite endless stories, nursery rhymes galore, interspersed with a few videos of

Thomas the Tank Engine and Postman Pat, the child finally settles to sleep around midnight with their parents snuggled down beside him, physically exhausted and with frayed patience from their attempts at getting their offspring off to sleep. Such unfortunate parents will have to wait a few years before they can enjoy spiritual activities in the evening again.

The occasional gem of a baby-sitter willing to put up with this sort of evening regularly each week is hard to come by, and impossible to retain. She could be baby-sitting for the people down the road whose children go to bed every night at 7 o'clock and who never wake until the next morning.

Husbands and Wives

Of course parents can attend Church activities separately: one parent goes and the other looks after the children. They do this on a rota basis, so that neither misses out.

Unfortunately if there is a series running it becomes disjointed by being able to attend only half of the meetings. However, it also means that you are deprived of the enjoyment and value of discussing the subjects together afterwards. Also, I feel that the more a married couple do together as a unit, the more they grow together: the less they do together, the less the relationship develops and grows. One going out and one staying in can be detrimental to the marriage, to the parents working in unison as a partnership and to the family as a whole.

Perhaps it would be better to stay at home together, go through the problems of parenting young children together and, in future years, strengthened by the experience of dealing with and overcoming the difficulties of bringing children into this world, start to attend the Sunday services regularly and the midweek meetings with renewed enthusiasm and increased insight. That may be the right way of putting the Lord first.

36. Has God Got Ears?
Sylvia Penny

Think of all the teachers and preachers there are! Think of all the Bible expositors there are! Think how many people are called on to preach the gospel, to teach the Bible, to lead meetings, take studies, lead workshops and guide discussion groups! Think how many difficult and searching questions are thrown at them. What a task they have!

Thankfully I am not called upon to have such a role. Indeed most people have not got the necessary talents. Few have the speaking ability required to get over a message and answer questions clearly and concisely. However, the people called upon to preach and teach are usually given advance warning, are allowed time for preparation, to think around their subject, collect their thoughts and consider what issues might arise. In other words, they can be fully prepared for the occasion.

But what about the many other non-trained teachers who are called upon at a moment's notice to answer the deepest theological questions with no advance warning, no time for preparation and no notes to refer to. Answers have to be short, to the point and, most important, right. I am, of course, referring to mothers.

How many of us have children who, at the drop of a hat and when we least expect it, ask the most difficult and awkward questions? As my eldest is just under four I am sure I still have a long way to go and a lot more to learn. However, I already have this deep-down feeling that I'd better make sure I'm well prepared for what the future has in store.

For a start, what a golden opportunity we have as mothers to explain to our children the basics of our faith before they are old enough to be sceptical, disbelieving and generally unreceptive. Small children are like little sponges, waiting to soak up information, ideas and opinions that pass their way. More and more I feel the responsibility of being a Christian mother, to bring up my children in the knowledge of the Lord, to give them a sound grounding in how they should live their lives, and why they should get to know the Lord Jesus as their Saviour.

So, when it comes to the crunch, can I come up with the goods? Do I have a ready answer for each question? Imagine the following scene:

mother and toddler are sitting on the bed together at night, ready to say thank you prayers to God.

Mother: Now it is time for our thank you prayers.
Child: Can God hear our prayers, Mummy?
Mother: Yes, of course He can.
Child: Has He got ears then?
Mother: No, He hasn't.
Child: How does He hear our prayers then?
Mother: God doesn't need ears to hear us. He's not the same as we are.
Child: What's He like then?
Mother: (Thinks, "Good question!") Well, He is Spirit. He is everywhere.
Child: Can I go to the toilet?
Mother: ("Phew!" feeling of relief at being let off the hook.)

The next evening: same time, same place.

Mother: Now it is time for us to say thank you to God.
Child: Where does God live, Mummy?
Mother: In heaven.
Child: When can we go and see Him?
Mother: Well, after we die, we come alive again and will go to heaven and see Him.
Child: Oh! After I die on a cross like Jesus. Then I can go to heaven.
Mother: NO! No! You won't die on a cross like Jesus, but you will go to heaven like Him.
Child: Can I have my sheet please?

The next week: same time, same place.

Child: Has God got legs, Mummy?
Mother: No dear.
Child: How does He walk then?
Mother: He doesn't. He doesn't need to.
Child: Why doesn't He need to?
Mother: Because God is everywhere. (Thinks: "I've been here before.")

Child: Is heaven everywhere Mummy?
Mother: (Thinks: "He's got me!") Err ... No.
Child: Where is heaven?
Mother: That's where God is. (Thinks: "I'm not doing very well here.")
Child: Can we go swimming tomorrow?
Mother: YES! Yes! (With relief and feeling totally inadequate.)

Conversations like this make you realise just how difficult it is to explain your beliefs in simple, understandable terms. It also makes you realise how easy it is to go round and round in circles without giving a proper answer.

This, I am sure, must be equally true of some of the answers we give to older children who ask more complex and difficult questions. It is so important that we should be prepared and able to give proper and reasoned answers, or reply truthfully that we don't know the answer, but will try and find out. The child will then gain confidence in us and will continue to question and learn to grow in the knowledge of the Lord - and so will we!

37. Discipline
Sylvia Penny

And you have forgotten that word of encouragement that addresses you as sons: "My son, do not make light of the Lord's discipline, and do not lose heart when he rebukes you, because the Lord disciplines those he loves, and he punishes everyone he accepts as a son." Endure hardship as discipline; God is treating you as sons. For what son is not disciplined by his father? If you are not disciplined (and everyone undergoes discipline), then you are illegitimate children and not true sons. Moreover, we have all had human fathers who disciplined us and we respected them for it. How much more should we submit to the Father of our spirits and live! Our fathers disciplined us for a little while as they thought best; but God disciplines us for our good, that we may share in his holiness. No discipline seems pleasant at the time, but painful. Later on, however, it produces a harvest of righteousness and peace for those who have been trained by it. (Hebrews 12:5-11)

Human theories on discipline

Discipline is a subject on which most parents hold fairly strong views, and I am no exception to that rule. However, I have discovered that as the years have gone by those views have altered to accommodate my experiences.

When my two children were under two years old, I had little experience but lots of theories. Now they are both over five years old I have much more experience, but far fewer theories! Having read numerous books on discipline, written from varying angles ranging from suggestions of immediate and severe punishment to "letting them do as they please because they'll grow out of it, won't they?", I have come to the conclusion that there are almost as many theories as there are writers. That being the case, where can we go for guidance?

Discipline in the Bible

Even a quick read through Hebrews 12:5-11 makes it quite clear that discipline is necessary and desirable, not only for children, but also for adults. "God disciplines us for our good, that we may share in his holiness," and discipline "produces a harvest of righteousness."

It seems there are three aspects to discipline; motive, method, and results. Each of these has to be right. When God the Father disciplines, His motive is love. The method may be painful, but the results are for our good, producing in us righteousness and peace. When we discipline our children we should follow these three, using them as our role model.

Proverbs

Hebrews 12:5-6 is a quotation from Proverbs 3:11-12. Proverbs is the book in the Bible which contains most on the subject of discipline. A quick read through the book reveals nearly thirty sayings on the subject, and most of the passages give advice to the person being disciplined, but a few counsel parents who are doing the disciplining.

The very purpose of Proverbs is stated in the first few verses of the book:

> The proverbs of Solomon son of David, King of Israel: for attaining wisdom and discipline; for understanding words of insight; for acquiring a disciplined and prudent life.

Solomon had good authority for writing as he did. We are told in 1 Kings 3:12 that

> I (God) will do what you (Solomon) have asked. I will give you a wise and discerning heart, so that there will never have been anyone like you, nor will there ever be.

So God Himself states that Solomon would be the wisest person ever to live, apart from Christ Himself (Matthew 12:42). What better authority can there be for accepting and following what he has to say on the subject of discipline?

Mothers

Firstly, in the male dominated society of that time, it is perhaps surprising to note that several of Solomon's sayings refer to a child's treatment of his mother, and *vice versa*. Her role of teaching a child is recognised as important, and not something to be scoffed at or despised. Proverbs 1:8 states, "Listen, my son, to your father's instruction and do not forsake your mother's teaching." Proverbs 15:20 says, "A wise son brings joy to his father, but a foolish man despises his mother." And Proverbs 23:22 has, "Listen to your father, who gave you life, and do not despise your mother when she is old."

It is clear that teaching and instructing children in the way they should behave and conduct themselves was not left entirely to fathers. It was the shared responsibility of both parents. But was discipline also a shared responsibility, and what form did it take?

Method

Proverbs 13:24 says, "He who spares the rod hates his son, but he who loves him is careful to discipline him." Proverbs 22:15 has, "Folly is bound up in the heart of a child, but the rod of discipline will drive it far from him." In Proverbs 23:13-14 we read, "Do not withhold discipline from a child; if you punish him with the rod, he will not die. Punish him with the rod and save his soul from death." And, lastly, Proverbs 29:15 states, "The rod of correction imparts wisdom, but a child left to himself disgraces his mother."

These four passages deal clearly with the method of discipline. Despite modern day theories on how children should be brought up, the wisest man who ever lived makes it quite clear that corporal punishment was to be used in disciplining a child. Many books written today by well-meaning child psychologists give lengthy explanations as to why a child should never be struck by any adult, and explain how it can do long-lasting psychological damage. They also claim that it teaches children that violence is acceptable under certain circumstances.

Nowadays, a distinction is usually drawn between discipline, which is positive, and punishment, which is negative. Discipline uses the natural consequences of a child's own actions to teach him. It involves a system of rewards for good behaviour and ignores bad behaviour. The theory is that all children crave attention more than almost anything else, so if they get none for bad behaviour, it will gradually decrease and go away.

Physical punishment, on the other hand, is seen as entirely negative and achieves nothing but resentment and bad feelings, teaching the child that it is acceptable to strike another person. However, as we have already seen in Hebrews 12:11, "No discipline seems pleasant at the time, but painful." The Bible seems to link discipline with some sort of painful experience. Ignoring bad behaviour does not come into the picture at all as "a child left to himself disgraces his mother."

Modern-day theories do not take into account the important fact that every child is born a sinner. The natural tendency for human beings, and particularly children, is to copy bad, rather than good, behaviour, and to consider themselves first, and others second, if at all. If there is a group of a dozen children, one of whom has a tendency to scream piercingly loudly, it is quite likely that several others in the group will copy such a scream. However, if one child in a group of a dozen is consistently helpful at packing up the toys at the end of playtime, how many others copy such behaviour?

It is generally true that bad behaviour is more "catching" than good. Perhaps Solomon with his God-given wisdom observed a few more truths about human nature than some of today's psychologists. Solomon was inspired by God to write Proverbs, and who knows more about the nature of human beings than their Creator?

Unfortunately, Solomon did not give us detailed instructions on how to discipline our children. Nor did he state any exceptions to the rule. Neither did he cover the problems of child abuse, or the problems of dealing with mentally handicapped children. He did not tell us when "the rod" was necessary, and when it was not. As with some other subjects in the Bible, the general principles are laid out clearly, but the individual circumstances for different people are not. We have to use our own, limited, wisdom as parents to apply the generalities. That is what makes it so hard.

Motivation

Strangely, Solomon has little to say on the motivation for parents' discipline of their children. Perhaps it is taken as obvious that the only motivation must be love. What else would sustain parents as they endeavour to produce a reasonable and decent human being out of their offspring? In Proverbs 13:24, quoted above, Solomon goes as far as to say that a parent who "spares the rod hates his son". Parents who refuse to discipline their child can end up producing one who "disgraces his mother". The verse goes on with, "he who loves him is careful to discipline him." This is the only one of Solomon's sayings which explicitly links love with the act of discipline, except for Proverbs 3:11-12, quoted in Hebrews 12, which refers to God's love and discipline.

Results

Most importantly, what should be the results of discipline administered in love? Proverbs 19:18 says, "Discipline your son, for in that there is hope; do not be a willing party to his death." Proverbs 22:6 has, "Train a child in the way he should go, and when he is old he will not turn from it." And Proverbs 29:17 states, "Discipline your son, and he will give you peace; he will bring delight to your soul."

All of these sayings assume a response in the child. If the discipline is effective and the child respects his parents for it, in later years the results may be "peace" and "delight". This is surely something for every parent to aim for. However, this may not always happen, as Solomon makes clear in advice directed to the child himself. "He who heeds discipline shows the way to life, but whoever ignores correction leads others astray" (Proverbs 10:17). "A fool spurns his father's discipline, but whoever heeds correction shows prudence" (Proverbs 15:5).

If the child chooses to ignore correction and spurn discipline, he is described as being a fool. As parents we can never force our children to follow our advice, except when they are very young. However, we can always hope and pray that they will end up "bringing delight to our souls". Just as we have a choice in following our heavenly Father's advice given in the Bible, so our children have a choice in accepting or rejecting ours.

Conclusion

In Solomon's epilogue to Proverbs he describes a wife of noble character, and in Proverbs 31:28 he writes, "Her children arise and call her blessed". Solomon knew what a good wife and mother should be like, but unfortunately among his thousand wives and concubines he never found one to match his ideal (Ecclesiastes 7:28). Perhaps we should follow his advice and contemplate his many sayings, to make us better parents, to help us deal with our children more correctly, and to be more in accordance with God's will.

Part 5
Spiritual Subjects

38. *A God for our Time*
Barbara Parsons

So you think of God
   As a staid old Victorian
With a long list of rules
   And a frown on His brow -
A God for past ages
   A page out of history -
Not a God for our time!
   Not a God for us now!

For this is the age of technology -
   A micro-chip age of genetic discovery!
And we can make babies in test-tubes
   And freeze them!
And fly to the stars
   And step into space!
And religion and church - and God
   Haven't a place
In our time!

And we don't want morals
   To hinder our license -
Yet the pain when a husband or wife go astray
   Is so crushing a blow
It is like a bereavement -
   The death of respect
     In the wake of dismay.
And God, only God
   Can carry the burden

Of hearts that are empty
When love goes away.

Then, science is speechless
When death takes a loved one
And great waves of sorrow
Descend on the soul -
And grief is a chasm
You cannot climb out of
As you sob on your bed in the night
All alone.
And God, only God
Can carry the burden
Of a heart deeply mourning
For the one who has gone.

Can technology answer
The tired and the lonely?
Give hope to a parent
Whose children go wrong?
Or succour the dying?
Or lighten depression?
Restore peace of mind?
Bring back love to a home?

Men have failed!
Only God is sovereign, eternal
Untouched by the years
By which we are confined!
The same yesterday, and today
And forever!
A Friend and a Saviour
A God for our time!

39. *The Cost of Living*
Janet Horobin

The cost of living is often a topic of conversation between women. Every time we go shopping we see rising prices. Everything is going up. But let us stop and consider, our salvation was bought for a price. However, after nearly two thousand years God's charge is still the same, only that we believe in the Lord Jesus Christ. When we discuss the cost of living again, let us remember what it cost Christ to enable us to have eternal life. Everything going up may well be a good motto for us if it means our praise, our thanks, our troubles, all ascending in prayer to God.

In Colossians 3:2 Paul reminds people to set their "mind on things above, not on earthly things." Earthly things or heavenly things? Earthly riches or heavenly riches? These seem to be the choices that Paul is talking about.

Earthly riches usually means money, but that is worthless, until it is exchanged for something, and there are certain temptations which only trouble the rich. In 1 Timothy 6:17 we read:

> Command those who are rich in this present world not to be arrogant nor to put their hope in wealth, which is so uncertain, but to put their hope in God, who richly provides us with everything for our enjoyment.

However rich people can be very useful to God, and what could be better than a rich person who puts God first in everything? First, however, he may have to learn the truth of Jeremiah 9:23,24:

> Let not the rich man boast of his riches, but let him who boasts boast about this: that he understands and knows me, that I am the Lord.

In this materialistic and affluent age there is so much dissatisfaction and complaining but it is not easy to learn to be content. The Lord Jesus stated that "whoever wants to save his life will lose it, but whoever loses his life for me and for the gospel will save it," (Mark 8:35). All too often we want to cling on to what we have but Proverbs 30:8,9 records what should be our prayer concerning earthly riches:

> Keep falsehood and lies from me; give me neither poverty nor riches, but give me only my daily bread. Otherwise, I may have too much and disown you and say, "Who is the Lord?" Or I may become poor and steal, and so dishonour the name of my God.

Here we begin to see right values and our priorities start to fall into place. True earthly riches are not a matter of wealth and possessions but the closeness of friends, the love of our families and our service to the Lord Jesus Christ who must be first in all things.

But what about heavenly riches? The "incomparable riches" as Paul calls them in Ephesians 2:7. This is far too big a subject to discuss here, except to note what is said in two well loved verses. Ephesians 1:7 states that in Christ "we have redemption through his blood, the forgiveness of sins, in accordance with the riches of God's grace." That same wonderful word *riches* is found again in Philippians 4:19. "And my God will meet all your needs according to his glorious riches in Christ Jesus," Surely that promise should give us strength for our daily living because, if you noticed, it said "according to his glorious riches", not just out of His riches.

So where do we stand? We must set our affection on things above, not on things on the earth, but we mustn't stand still in this life and do nothing. Just as athletes in the Olympic Games were chosen to run in a race, and the medal was not theirs unless they reached the tape first, so we are told that we must press on and reach the prize associated with the high calling of God. We have been given the free gift of eternal life, which has been bought with a price, but now we must run the race set before us, endeavouring to win the prize.

So when we next hear about the cost of living, let us remember what it cost Christ to redeem us: His death on the Cross. When we next notice the rising prices, let us notice that God's price never alters; He requires us to believe in the Lord Jesus. When we next talk about everything going up, let us make sure that we are talking about our praise and our prayers.

40. Is Your God Big Enough?
Hazel Stephens

The first positive encounter with God is sought when the awareness of our own sin is seen to separate us from God. Our desire to be made right with God brings each one of us to our knees, and we acknowledge His divine judgement upon our lives. We admit to Him and to ourselves that we can do nothing about the immense gulf of sin that keeps us from Him. This first step is the hardest to make. God seems, at this point, to be a Judge who is never wrong. His decisions are right. There seems no way to cross over to His side.

The bridge

He then points us to His Son, and shows us how, through Him, we can cross the gulf of sin. We need faith in Jesus Christ (John 3:16), so that He can bring us safely over to His side and set our feet on the road towards trust in God. When once we cross the bridge, we see God as merciful and we are filled with gratitude. We get up off our knees and experience His peace and joy.

The path

We never forget the blessings we receive when we realise that Jesus Christ died and rose again for us. But what do we do next? Do we start along the path ahead of us? Or do we sit down, thinking that our journey is at an end? Unless we go down the path, we will miss getting to know God in a much more personal way than we would otherwise. As Psalm 16:11 says:

> You have made known to me the path of life; you will fill me with joy in your presence, with eternal pleasures at your right hand.

God will remain a distant figure, and we will never experience the love of God in a real sense, unless we are prepared to walk along the path to meet him.

The journey

However, the path is not wide, straight and well lit. It is narrow, winding and dark. As we tread it, we will fall, experience loss and pain and, sometimes, consider whether the end of the journey will compensate for the troubles we experience. We need help to travel the path and we are given the Bible for our light (Psalm 119:105) and for our guidance (2 Timothy 3:16). When we start to walk, we find help at our side, and are led along the path. The further we go, the more we learn of God's grace and peace (Ephesians 6:23-24), and of His ways and love (Psalm 86:11).

Falling

However, if we fall and refuse to get up, we will never see the varying sides to God's nature. Each time we get up and start again, God becomes closer to us because we learn how much we need Him. James 4:8 says: "Come near to God and He will come near to you." Unless we are prepared to look to Him in our trials, we will never get near to Him. He wants us to know Him, and to know Him we must walk with Him and listen to Him through His Word, growing closer to Him each day. The more we rely on Him, the more we will feel his strength and sustaining power.

End of the journey

If we go to the end, we will grow more Christ-like, exhibiting the fruit of the Spirit (Galatians 5:22,23). By walking daily with Him we will grow in grace and truth (2 Peter 3:18). He will be with us every day in our hearts and lives, and not be a distant God, up in heaven, watching from far away. He will be with us, helping us and guiding us through our trials and joys. Is your God far away, in heaven, or is He with you now?

41. Who can we blame for our sins?
Sylvia Penny

Can we blame Satan?

The horrific Jeffrey Dahmer Case which came to light in Milwaukee, Wisconsin, USA in 1991 raised many questions in the minds of many people. The case was not dissimilar to one in London several years before. Both involved multiple murders, dismemberments and cannibalism. Dahmer admitted to seventeen killings and the remains of eleven bodies were found in his apartment.

Many questions have been raised as a result of the case. Should capital punishment be reintroduced for such crimes? Should the police have caught him earlier? Was he influenced by Satan? Was his upbringing partly responsible for his actions?

The first two questions are more concerned with how to deal with the results of his crimes; the last two with the cause of his crimes. It is these last two questions, and other similar ones, which have made me think again about the subject of sin and responsibility. If we sin, can the blame be attributed to Satan, to our society, to our parents, or to someone or something else? Or does the responsibility rest solely with ourselves?

Some have concluded that Dahmer's actions must have been influenced by Satan. This is because what he did was so terrible, so calculated, and so much enjoyed by him. They argue that no man could get pleasure from behaving in such a monstrous way unless he was influenced by some external, evil source. However, this opinion is unsubstantiated by Scripture which states in Matthew 15:19 that "out of the heart come evil thoughts, murder, adultery, sexual immorality, theft, false testimony, slander."

In the period covered by the Gospels, the time when our Saviour was on earth, it appears that Satan and the evil spirits caused some people to have inhuman strength (Mark 5:1-13) and to hurt their own bodies (Mark 5:5; Mark 9:17,18). Satan, himself, tried to tempt Jesus (Matthew 4:1-11), but did not harm Him physically, although he entered Judas just before Judas went off to betray Jesus to the authorities (Luke

22:3). However, there is no indication that Satan was the direct cause of violent and immoral acts by humans against others at that time.

Can we blame society?

Whenever the prevailing conditions in society have been right, and particular circumstances have reinforced it, enormous acts of physical violence by one group of human beings against another have occurred throughout history. Such acts have even been enjoyed by the perpetrators.

Nero provided entertainment for people in the form of the public torture and execution of Christians. The French Revolution provided similar spectacles for the masses when the leaders of the day initiated the public execution of thousands of aristocrats by guillotine. Hitler and the holocaust of the Jews is another example.

Today we have such entertainment enjoyed by thousands throughout the world in the simulated form of horror movies. These appeal to the baser instincts and sinful nature within all of us.

When society at large condones such actions, then individuals no longer feel inhibited and some fail to suppress this part of their make-up. Such individuals feel encouraged to follow their desires and violence can sometimes explode.

However, individuals in such societies do still have a choice. They can choose to follow their baser instincts, and go along with the society, or they can obey their conscience, and go God's way. Society cannot be blamed 100% for an individual's own weakness and any resulting violent actions, but if it permits public violence, real or simulated, then it is not totally devoid of responsibility.

Can we blame parents?

Maybe the most thought-provoking and certainly the most personal question which arises is whether parents should be blamed for an offspring's actions, whatever the age of that offspring. There is no doubt that society can influence a person either for good or for evil. If that be the case, how much more influence does a parent have? And how much more responsibility?

The answer is that parents do have both an enormous influence over their children and do carry a tremendous responsibility. This is particularly true when the children are young and impressionable.

Despite this, however, once a child has grown to adulthood, should the parents still be held accountable for his actions? I think not. If the child becomes a murderer, a thief, or a slanderer, should the parents feel guilty? I do not think they should, although nearly all will and that it is a very natural feeling to have.

Even if a child does none of these things, but is merely a failure in society, at work, or in his relationships, many parents feel that in some way they are to blame. However, it is important to remember that since Adam every human is born a sinner (Romans 5:12-14) and parents can do nothing to change this fact. They can endeavour to bring out the good in their children, but if when adulthood is reached the children choose to reject their parent's standards and follow their own free will, the results cannot be blamed on the parents.

The corollary of this argument is that if children turn out to be particularly successful or are delightful individuals, should parents then pat themselves on the back and take all the praise? Again the natural feeling is one of pride in bringing up the children well and having successfully completed a difficult job. Whether this is the case, however, is dubious.

There are plenty of examples in Scripture to illustrate some of the above points. Many good and upright characters are shown to have had wicked and violent children, and some evil people gave birth to good and God-loving children. Adam's son Cain became a murderer (Genesis 4:8). Eli's two sons were wicked and disobeyed the Lord (1 Samuel 2:12-36). David's son Solomon started off extremely well (1 Kings 3), but ended up as an idolater (1 Kings 11). David was certainly in no way responsible for Solomon's slipping into idolatry. Solomon himself chose to disobey the Lord and marry foreign idolatrous women, who eventually turned his head after other gods (1 Kings 11:1-4).

On the other hand, Ahaz was a wicked king (2 Kings 16:2-4) who sacrificed one son by fire. However, another of his sons was Hezekiah, who trusted in the Lord and reversed many of his father's evil practices (2 Kings 18:1-8). Again, King Manasseh was wicked (2 Kings 21:1-6), and so was his son, Amon (2 Kings 21:19-22), but his son Josiah "did what was right in the eyes of the Lord" (2 Kings 22:1-7).

It may be possible to argue intellectually that the good and upright characters could have done a better job in bringing up their evil children, but how is it possible to explain why the evil characters managed to produce such good and well motivated offspring?

Should we blame ourselves?

The only possible explanation is that each of us is responsible for our own sins and the evil deeds that we do. They are a result of our personal choices. Maybe the society in which we live, and the parents we have, influence our actions to a greater or lesser extent, but we, personally, always have the final say as to whether we take a particular course of action. It is up to us whether we walk in light or in darkness.

Thus we, personally, must accept the responsibility for our sins. Thankfully, however, the Lord has provided forgiveness and it is up to each of us as individuals to accept that forgiveness by accepting the Lord Jesus as our own Saviour. No-one else can do this for us and this is the only way we can avoid the consequences of sin, which is eternal death, and instead receive the gift of God which is forgiveness and eternal life (Romans 6:23).

42. Looking-Glasses
Vicky Wilkinson

I work as a typist for a glass traders and mirror specialists. Attached to our office is a large showroom, full of the most beautiful mirrors of every shape and size. When I wander round this showroom, I can view myself from almost every angle; not always the prettiest of sights!

Ladies, how often in a day do you use a mirror? The Scriptures tell us that our adorning should not be the outward adorning of the plaiting of hair, and the wearing of gold, and the putting on of apparel. Rather, it should be the hidden person of the heart, or the adornment of a meek and quiet spirit which is in the sight of God a great price (1 Peter 3:3-4). Even so, if we are truthful, there is vanity in all of us.

Lavers: washing basins

Did you know that on one occasion, the Lord called upon the serving women, to give up their looking glasses. Their mirrors were not made of glass, but of polished brass. When the Lord was giving instructions to Moses for the building of the Tabernacle, which was to be God's dwelling place (Exodus 29:42-46), He instructed Moses to make from these looking glasses a laver of brass, (Exodus 38:8). This laver, made of polished brass, was to be situated inside the Tabernacle courtyard, in between the Great Altar of Burnt Offering and the entrance to the Sanctuary (Exodus 40:7), and was probably basin-like in shape, as it was full of water, (Exodus 30:17-21). These verses tell us how the priests of the Lord, who were the descendants of Aaron, washed their hands and their feet in the laver before they could enter the Sanctuary. The Lord said they must do this or they would die.

Why was it necessary for them to wash their hands and their feet in the laver when, at their consecration to office, they had already received a ceremonial cleansing, by the washing of water, (Exodus 29:4-9)? As well as a ceremonial cleansing, and an anointing with oil, the priests at their consecration were also given special garments, which were holy garments, to minister to the Lord in the priest's office. These garments, which were symbolic of God's clothing of righteousness and salvation (Psalm 132:9,16), covered all the priest's body, except his hands and feet. His hands and feet, which were typical of activity, were particularly exposed to the dust and defilement of desert life. Therefore, before he could enter God's Sanctuary, the priest had to wash his hands and his feet in order that no impurities were taken into God's holy dwelling.

Redemption and righteousness

The Tabernacle, as well as being typical of the presence of the Most Holy God, was, along with its sacrifices, a shadow of good things to come (Hebrews 10:1) namely the redemptive work of Jesus Christ. For example, the sacrifices offered at the Great Altar of Burnt Offering were typical of the one offering of Christ, who, by His shed blood, washed us from all our sins, (Revelation 1:5). God had to cleanse us in preparation for His presence in us through His Holy Spirit, who gave us life, (Romans 8:10-11). The presence of God's Spirit in us means His righteousness, (Romans 3:22). Therefore, like the priests, at our conversion, we received the covering of God's righteousness that enabled us to stand before Him as a new creation.

Daily cleansing

Thus at the altar we found a Saviour. But what about the laver? Can we, like the priest, wash in it? Should we? We received an initial cleansing at our conversion, but whilst we remain in this corruptible body we are still open to the dirt and grime of everyday living and, therefore, we need a daily cleansing. The Lord Himself showed this to be so when, at the last supper, He washed the feet of His disciples. Washing the feet of guests, whose sandalled feet had trod the dusty roads, was the custom in the east, but was usually performed by the servant. When therefore Peter objected, the Lord said to him:

> "If I wash thee not, thou hast no part with me ..... He that is washed, needeth not save to wash his feet, but is clean every whit, and ye are clean." (John 13:8,10 *KJV*)

The disciples, by their faith, were already washed in the blood that Christ was about to shed. Therefore, as well as a lesson in humility, the Lord was showing how a daily cleansing was also necessary if they were to have part with Him. Likewise, we received Christ at the altar, but if we are to continue with Him in daily fellowship then the laver is also very important to us. In fact our visit to it should be our daily concern. How though, like the priest, can we wash in the laver? Ephesians 5:26 is the scripture that will help us here: "That He might sanctify it and cleanse it with the washing of water, by the word". This scripture is speaking of the Church of the One Body, of which Christ is the Head; "That He might present it to Himself as a Glorious Church, holy and without blemish', (Ephesians 5:27). The assembly who make up this church are purified by the washing of water, by the word. It is the Word of God, along with His enlightening Spirit, that purifies. Therefore, the laver about which we must make our daily concern is God's Word.

Our daily mirror

The Lord Jesus, who is God's Living Word, and who indwells us, works with us in conjunction with God's written word. It is He who serves us by the washing of our feet. That the laver was made from the mirrors of the women is very appropriate because mirrors are used for self-examination. By looking into a mirror we can immediately see any blemishes, or anything that is out of order, or if anything needs re-arranging, and put it aright. In the same way God's word of truth reflects back to us any disorders in our lives that need correcting. We will never be perfect whilst in this corruptible body of flesh, and God knows this, but all the same, He wants us to pursue righteousness, godliness, faith, love, patience and meekness, (1 Timothy 6:11). These are the fruits of God's Holy Spirit, who is in us. Therefore our walk should not be a fleshly walk, marked with the fruits of the flesh (Galatians 5:19-21), but rather a walk in the Spirit, followed by the fruits of God's Spirit, (Galatians 5:22-23). Says verse 25: "If we live in the Spirit, let us also walk in the Spirit" (*KJV*).

It is God's word that is the sanctifier, as the Lord Himself showed when He said of His disciples to His Father: "Sanctify them through thy truth: thy word is truth', (John 17:17 *KJV*). Even so, there will be many times when we will stumble, or we may even take a serious fall, but if we do, the situation will not be hopeless, because Christ is with us as an advocate with the Father (1 John 2:1). From His word of truth, He will convict us of our sin, and when we return to Him and acknowledge our wrongdoing, He will wash our feet and wash away our sin. We are God's children, and when we do wrong, He does not cast us out, but our fellowship with Him becomes marred, and we lose our peace with our Heavenly Father. What joy for both Father and Son when the sinner who has fallen is raised up to a renewed peace and fellowship with God, through Jesus Christ, our Advocate.

Atonement

The shed blood of Christ made atonement for our sin and saved us. It brought us to an at-one-ment with the Father. If this close at-one-ment with the Father is to be maintained in our daily walk, then we need the cleansing effect of God's Word. After the death of Christ a soldier pierced His side with a spear and there came out blood and water, i.e. blood for atonement and water for cleansing.

There is no size given for this laver. To me, this says that the grace available at the laver for the purpose of cleansing has no limit. God is always prepared to forgive our sins. The laver, therefore, gives us peace with Jesus, as it works out in practice, our daily walk. Says Hebrews 4:12-13:

> For the word of God is quick and powerful, and sharper than any two-edged sword, piercing even to the dividing asunder of soul and spirit and of the joints and marrow, and is a discerner of the thoughts and intents of the heart. Neither is there any creature that is not manifest in His sight: but all things are naked and open unto the eyes of Him with whom we have to do. (*KJV*)

God's word has power and searches our innermost being, and has a cutting effect, when it convicts us of any wrong-doing. We cannot hide anything from the One with whom we have to do, and He, of course, is the Lord Jesus, who is the discerner of our thoughts and intents of the heart.

Conclusion

The laver is, therefore, a shadow of Christ's daily cleansing, as the Word of God. Let us therefore, make it our daily concern, and allow Jesus to serve us at the laver, by washing our feet, by the washing of water by the word (Ephesians 5:26), in order that our peace with God will be unhindered. Let the Word of Christ dwell in us richly, that it may teach and admonish us, and the result will he that the peace of God will rule our heart, (Colossians 3:15-16).

43. Why pray?
God already knows our needs!
Sylvia Penny

This question was asked at a recent Bible Study, as an opener for discussion and comment. It certainly makes you stop and think, and perhaps all of us would come up with slightly differing answers. As Christians undoubtedly we all pray, so the question centres around the reasons for which we do so.

My first reaction was that if we accept that the Bible is the inspired word of God, then as it tells us in numerous places to pray, that should be good enough reason in itself. However, for the thinking person, blind obedience is not necessarily good enough. There should be tangible reasons for God wanting us to do the things He wants us to do.

God's will

One of the most basic reasons for prayer is that it is God's will. Therefore, for us to please God, it should be part of our daily walk. It is a basic assumption that if we have accepted Christ as our personal Saviour then, as a result of that, our main desire and wish is to please God in any way we can. This includes a prayerful life. 1 Thessalonians 5:16-18 says, "Be joyful always; pray continually; give thanks in all circumstances, for this is God's will for you in Christ Jesus."

If we love someone, we naturally want to communicate with them. As God loves us, He desires to communicate with us, and He wishes us to do likewise. One way we can do this is through prayer. Even though people we love and are close to may already know how we feel and what our needs are, there still remains a desire to communicate these things despite the fact it may be intellectually unnecessary. I wonder whether God is like this. After all, He has made it very clear throughout Scripture that He wants a relationship with people, not just that we should intellectually acknowledge that He exists.

A privilege

In addition, it is a privilege for us to be able to pray whenever we like. Deuteronomy 4:7 states, "What other nation is so great as to have their gods near them the way the Lord our God is near us whenever we pray to him?" Although this statement was made by the nation of Israel thousands of years ago, the fact remains as true today as it was then. We should feel it a privilege to have access to God (Ephesians 3:12), to be able to pray to God freely whenever we want to. He is always near us (Philippians 4:5). He always hears us. He wants to hear us. It is His will, after all.

Gives us peace

Not only is prayer God's will for us and a privilege, we also benefit from prayer. Philippians 4:6-7 says:

> Do not be anxious about anything, but in everything, by prayer and petition, with thanksgiving, present your requests to God. And the peace of God, which transcends all understanding, will guard your hearts and your minds in Christ Jesus.

If we share our problems and anxieties with close friends and loved ones, do we not feel better, even if those problems and anxieties are not actually solved in the process? In this verse God seems to be saying that such comfort and peace will also come from Him. And as it comes from God Himself, the level of comfort and peace should be greater than that from our fellow human beings. However, this may not necessarily be true. It depends on our relationship with God. If we are not close to a person, we derive little comfort from them in times of difficulty. Unbelievers derive no comfort from God, as they have no relationship with Him. Conversely it must be true that mature believers will receive the greatest feeling of peace as a result of their deeper relationship with God. We are all at different stages in our walk with God, and so I feel this verse will have a different level of meaning to each individual believer.

Jesus said we should pray

I have already said that blind obedience is not good enough for most people, but perhaps encouragement to do a thing by someone we love, may be a good enough reason, particularly when that Someone is our Lord Jesus Christ. In Luke 18:1-8 the parable of the persistent widow is recorded. Verse 1 says, "Then Jesus told his disciples a parable to show them that they should always pray and not give up." It seems our Lord was well aware that His disciples, and we, were liable to give up praying, and so He encourages them, and us, to carry on. It does not tell us why they may have given up, but perhaps one of the reasons was to do with the question asked at the beginning of this article.

Jesus also seems to link the question of continuing in prayer with faith. At the end of verse 8 He says, "However, when the Son of Man comes, will he find faith on the earth?" implying there will be a lack of faith, and thus a lack of prayer. Of course, the main thrust of this parable is that the disciples should be persistent in prayer, just like the widow was persistent in demanding justice from the judge. However, does this not contradict the passage preceding the Lord's prayer in Matthew 6:5-8? Here, the Lord says in verses 7 and 8, "And when you pray, do not keep on babbling like pagans, for they think they will be heard because of their many words. Do not be like them, for your Father knows what you need before you ask him."

It was not praying many prayers that was condemned by the Lord, but the many empty words that were used by the pagans when they prayed. They liked the sound of their own voices, and needlessly repeated phrases over and over again. Christ Himself prayed in the garden of Gethsemane using the same words three times, (Matthew 26:44) so even repetition is acceptable if it is part of a real and heart-felt prayer. What Christ was condemning was a vain and empty ritualistic type of prayer, in which the same words were said over and over again by rote. The tongue was active but the heart and mind was not.

If we pray from our heart about subjects which mean a lot to us, God will respect and accept such prayers, just as in the case of the persistent widow, even if such prayers are repeated and the same or similar words used. It is empty repetition which is condemned.

And it is in this very passage that Christ mentions the question originally asked, "Why pray, when God already knows our needs?"

However, His advice is not that the disciples should not pray, but that they should pray in a meaningful way. He then gives the now very well-known Lord's Prayer as a model. He did not intend that these exact words should be repeated by rote *ad nauseam*, but that they should structure their prayers like that one, including the things they wished to say, succinctly and without pomp and ceremony. We should follow suit, and do the same.

Jesus often prayed - even though the Father knew His needs

If we wonder why we need to pray, as God already knows our needs, then it should be even more difficult for us to understand why Jesus Himself prayed to the Father when surely He knew all that His Son was going to say! Jesus often went to the hills to pray. He stayed up all night sometimes to pray. John 17 records the words of a prayer for Himself, His disciples, and for all believers. In Luke 22:32 Jesus tells Peter that He has specifically prayed for him, that his faith would not fail. And I have already mentioned His prayers for Himself in the garden of Gethsemane recorded in Matthew 26, Mark 14 and Luke 22.

How can we make sense of the Lord Jesus' desire to pray? The answer must surely come back to one of relationships. If we have a relationship with someone, naturally we want to communicate with them. If we love someone and want to know them better, then we do what they would like us to do. So it should be between ourselves and God. Jesus Christ gave us an example of what a perfect man would do, and this included prayer.

Paul often prayed

Paul is a great example of someone who often prayed, for both others and himself. He often encouraged believers to continue in prayer, both for themselves and others. In Ephesians 6:18 Paul said, "And pray in the Spirit on all occasions with all kinds of prayers and requests. With this in mind, be alert and always keep on praying for all the saints." There was no doubt in Paul's mind that we should pray, and keep on praying. In Colossians 4:2 he said, "Devote yourselves to prayer, being watchful and thankful."

Not only did he encourage other believers to do this, but he modelled a prayerful life himself. In Philippians 1:4 he said "In all my prayers for all of you, I always pray with joy because of your partnership in the gospel." Paul continually refers to himself as praying all the time, and in all circumstances.

He also makes it clear that prayer is not just a shopping list. Our prayers should not be composed only of our needs, requests and desires - but should include an element of thankfulness and praise. Colossians 1:3 says, "We always thank God, the Father of our Lord Jesus Christ, when we pray for you." So it seems that despite the fact God already knows what we want and need, and that He knows we are thankful for everything we already have, He still likes us to express this to Him. And as a result we can know the peace of God in our lives.

We may not know what to pray for

Lastly, coming at the question from a different angle, it may be that God knows our needs, but that we do not! In this case it is possible we may discover through prayer what our real needs are. Romans 8:26-27 says:

> In the same way, the Spirit helps us in our weakness. We do not know what we ought to pray for, but the Spirit himself intercedes for us with groans that words cannot express. And he who searches our hearts knows the mind of the Spirit, because the Spirit intercedes for the saints in accordance with God's will.

It is clear from this passage that the Holy Spirit plays an important role in our prayers. Each of us, when we become a believer, is sealed by the Holy Spirit (2 Corinthians 1:22; Ephesians 1:13) and He dwells in our hearts. One of His roles in our lives appears to be interceding between ourselves and the Father when we pray. In this way we may discover which needs of ours are in accordance with God's will.

Conclusion

To sum up, it seems the main reason we pray is because God wants us to. For many people the feeling is mutual and so there is no problem! For those who are a little more analytical, perhaps some of the reasons given in this article will add something more tangible to the argument, and will encourage us all to pray on all occasions.

44. Who will get eternal life?
Sylvia Penny

For those of us living in countries where Christianity is the accepted religion it is easy and comfortable for us to talk of being saved through the gospel of Christ. We know we have righteousness and eternal life through Him Who died for our sins. We also know equally well that those who do not believe in Jesus Christ as their Saviour, those who reject Him and His message, remain dead in their sins and will not receive eternal life. There are many Scriptures we can look at to verify these very basic facts of our faith.

John 3:36 says "Whoever believes in the Son has eternal life, but whoever rejects the Son will not see life, for God's wrath remains on him." John 3:18 says "Whoever believes in him is not condemned, but whoever does not believe stands condemned already because he has not believed in the name of God's one and only Son." Romans 8:1 says "Therefore, there is now no condemnation for those who are in Christ Jesus, because through Christ Jesus the law of the Spirit of life set me free from the law of sin and death."

In addition we know that it is faith alone that gives us righteousness and eternal life. Any good works we may do, do not earn us salvation. Salvation is a gift; good works may earn us a reward in addition to our salvation, but not our salvation. Scripture again is very clear on this point. Romans 6:23 refers to the gift of God being eternal life, and Ephesians 2:8-9 says "For it is by grace you have been saved, through faith - and this not from yourselves, it is the gift of God - not by works, so that no-one can boast."

Millions have never heard of Jesus

However, how do we reconcile these beliefs with the obvious fact that many millions, if not billions of people, have lived on earth, or are now living, or will live, without ever having heard of the gospel of Christ, nor met anyone who has? This enormous group of people includes many today who are living in China, Africa and parts of Asia. From the time of Christ to the present day it includes all those many nations who were never reached by missionaries for hundreds of years - the Americas, parts of India, Malaysia, Indonesia, Australia and New Zealand to name but a few.

When we consider this vast proportion of humanity, what do we think their eternal destiny is? Do we write them all off in one big lump as doomed to eternal death, simply for the misfortune of having been born in the wrong place at the wrong time!

God is a little more loving and gracious than we are!

I would suggest that God is a little more loving and gracious towards the creatures He made than we are. There are a few Scriptures which appear to touch on this subject, the main two being Romans 2:1-16 and Revelation 20:11-15. The passage in Romans refers to God's righteous judgement. Verses 14 and 15 mention Gentiles who obey the law of their conscience, and verse 13 says that "it is those who obey the law who will be declared righteous." By application it appears that Gentiles who have no other law to follow than that of their own consciences will be judged by their actions. This follows on from verses 6-8 which say:

> God will give to each person according to what he has done. To those who by persistence in doing good seek glory, honour and immortality, he will give eternal life. But for those who are self-seeking and reject the truth and follow evil, there will be wrath and anger.

Romans 10:14 refers to those who have never heard the gospel preached to them and asks, "how can they believe in the one of whom they have not heard." The answer is clearly, they cannot - and so Romans 2:7 gives an alternative by which they may attain eternal life. It is also, however, quite clear from Scripture, that those who *have* heard the gospel have no such alternative available to them.

But it is also true that God knows what people would have done if their circumstances had been different. In Luke 10:13 the Lord says,

> "Woe to you, Korazin! Woe to you, Bethsaida! For if the miracles that were performed in you had been performed in Tyre and Sidon, they would have repented long ago, sitting in sackcloth and ashes."

He knows what people's responses would have been if they had been given the opportunity to hear the gospel. There is surely no doubt that God is the perfect Judge. It is we who are not! It was Abraham who said, "Will not the Judge of all the earth do right" (Genesis 18:25).

The dead were judged according to ...

Turning to the passage in Revelation 20:11-15 this refers to the last resurrection, the one that takes place after the thousand years when the millennium is over. Here, the dead that are raised and judged are all those who never heard the gospel, or those that did hear, but didn't believe it. Verse 12 tells us that "The dead were judged according to what they had done as recorded in the books." Verse 15 says "If anyone's name was not found written in the book of life, he was thrown into the lake of fire."

This is in accordance with what we have already seen in Romans 2:7, and also with John 5:28-29 where the Lord says:

> "Do not be amazed at this, for a time is coming when all who are in their graves will hear his voice and come out - those who have done good will rise to live, and those who have done evil will rise to be condemned."

This message is in total opposition to the message for those who have heard the gospel, and it is very important that the two are not confused. However, it does explain how God will deal justly with the many millions, or maybe billions, of people who have lived and died without ever having heard of Him, or of the Lord Jesus Christ.

Apart from such people, there are also a few other categories of people who, again, through no fault of their own, have never heard or understood the message of salvation by grace through faith.

Babies and toddlers

I am sure many of us have wondered about, and have had conversations about, what is to happen to babies or toddlers who die. Even if you believe, as some do, that very young children are capable of understanding the message of salvation and accepting it, there are few who would disagree that a child who has not yet learned to talk could accept Christ as his or her Saviour.

That being the case, how do we know whether or not they will have eternal life? The short answer is that unfortunately we will never know. Only God knows what sort of person that baby would have grown into, if circumstances had allowed it. As mentioned above, only God knows how a person would respond to the gospel message if they had heard it. One thing is certain however, and that is a baby does not get automatic entry into everlasting life simply as a result of dying young. Each one of us, when we are born, is a sinner and in need of a Saviour. Romans 3:23 states that "all have sinned and fall short of the glory of God" and Romans 5:12 says "sin entered the world through one man, and death through sin, and in this way death came to all men, because all sinned".

When a person is prevented from making a response to the gospel, for whatever reason, then we have to leave their eternal destiny in the hands of our Lord Jesus Christ: " The Father judges no-one, but has entrusted all judgement to the Son" (John 5:22).

Mentally handicapped

Another group of people are the mentally handicapped, usually through no fault of their own. The same questions apply to this group as to the previous one. As their brain is incapable of understanding the message of salvation, again we have to leave their eternal destiny in the hands of our heavenly Father. He is the only one Who knows how that person would have responded to Christ had their brain been in good working order.

People who lived before Abraham

A very different group of people to be considered are all those who lived prior to the time of Abraham. In the Bible these people are swiftly dealt with in the first eleven chapters of Genesis. From a biblical standpoint we know very little about them, except that they had populated the earth for at least 2000 years, if not longer, before Abraham came on the scene. When we realise that this period of time is longer than that which has intervened between the time of Christ and today, it is difficult to ignore the fact that here is a large group of people who could never have heard the message of salvation and eternal life through faith in our Lord and Saviour, Jesus Christ. Neither could they have heard of the "God of Abraham, of Isaac, and of Jacob", as these people had not yet been born! Thus neither could they have been saved by being blessed through the people of Israel, as the people of Israel did not yet exist.

There are very few hints given as to how God dealt with these people. We have a record of His speaking directly to Adam, to Eve, to Cain and to Noah. We are also told that Enoch "walked with God" (Genesis 5:24) until God "took him away". It is not clear whether every person was made individually aware of God, or whether knowledge of God was passed down from generation to generation through written records, or word of mouth, from the time of Adam.

However, in Hebrews 11, such people as Abel, Enoch and Noah are included with many others as having a great faith in God. Obviously God had made it clear to these people what He wanted them to understand about Him and if they believed that, they were commended for their faith, and would receive the gift of eternal life, just as we who are Christians in this age will receive the gift of eternal life through belief in Christ's death and resurrection. We have to acknowledge the fact that what these people had to have faith in, was quite different from what people today have to believe.

People who lived from the time of Abraham to the time of Christ

The last section of people I would like to consider are those who lived from the time of Abraham to the time of Christ. These people can be divided into three separate categories. The first are those who never came into contact with the people of Israel at any time. These I covered above.

The second group are the people of Israel themselves - those descended from Abraham, Isaac and Jacob. And the third category are those Gentiles who came into contact with the people of Israel and learned something about the One True God.

The people of Israel

How did the people of Israel themselves receive eternal life? What did they have to believe? From the time of Abraham, to the time of Moses giving the Law, God continued to deal directly with certain individuals, who then influenced those around them. Hebrews 7 mentions Melchizedek the Priest who lived in Abraham's time and to whom Abraham gave a tenth of his possessions. Hebrews 11 talks about Isaac, Jacob and Joseph and their faith through which they were commended to God (Hebrews 11:39). There was, as yet, no formalised system of Law to which the people had to adhere.

Genesis 15:6 says "Abram believed the Lord, and he credited it to him as righteousness", and this is the basis for righteousness throughout the Bible. Romans 4 explains exactly what Abraham believed. He believed all that God had told him about having a son and being the father of many nations. Hebrews 11 gives further details as to what Abraham had faith in.

Then, continuing in Romans 4, Paul goes on to say that just as Abraham was credited with righteousness for his faith so we also can be credited with righteousness "for us who believe in him who raised Jesus our Lord from the dead" (Romans 4:24). It is made clear that what Abraham had to have faith in was very different from what we have to have faith in. What is important to God is the faith itself, being willing to believe what it is God wants us to believe.

However, from the time of Moses onwards, God instigated a very strict and detailed Law for the people of Israel. Any Jew who believed what the Law taught would receive eternal life. Romans 3:20 says "...no-one will be declared righteous in his sight by observing the law; rather, through the law we become conscious of sin". So it is clear that righteousness and eternal life were achieved by faith and belief - not by observation of the Law. But the faith and belief required at that time was in believing what the Law of Moses said about God.

Gentiles who had contact with Israel

Lastly, there is the third category of people - Gentiles who did come into contact with the people of Israel. What did they have to believe to receive eternal life?

In Genesis 12:2-3 God, speaking to Abraham, says:

"I will make you into a great nation and I will bless you; I will make your name great, and you will be a blessing. I will bless those who bless you and whoever curses you I will curse; and all peoples on earth will be blessed through you."

From Abraham's time on, God's blessing fell on anyone who treated his descendants, the people of Israel, well. If these Gentiles treated God's people well, they were blessed by Him. Did this include the blessing of eternal life?

There are examples of Gentile nations coming into contact with Israel in the Old Testament and who subsequently put their faith in the God of Israel. The Babylonians, under Nebuchadnezzar, were instructed to follow the God of Daniel when his three friends - Shadrach, Meshach and Abednego - emerged unharmed from the fiery furnace into which they had been thrown.

The Ninevites, under their king, repented of their wicked ways in sackcloth and ashes after Jonah told them his message from God. The Persians, during Esther's time, accepted the people of Israel and their God.

Earlier, we know that the Egyptians, during the time of Joseph, treated the people of Israel well, until a foreign king came to the throne. From archaeology we know that around this time the Egyptians turned to monotheism.

We also have the example of Ruth, a Moabitess (Ruth 3:3-4), who treated her mother-in-law Naomi well. Naomi was an Israelite and Ruth was finally blessed for her faithfulness. And Rahab is another example of a Gentile treating the people of Israel well, and who accepted their God.

From this variety of examples we find many Gentiles who came into contact with the people of Israel who were blessed through them in this life, and those who put their faith in the God of Israel also received eternal life.

Conclusion

So, who will get eternal life? It seems that many more people than we may think at first will receive this wonderful gift. We have seen that faith is a crucial element at all times, and in all places, We have also seen that what people may be required to have faith in, and believe, may be different at different times, for different people. The message of salvation through Christ's sacrifice on the cross as atonement for our sins has been of utmost importance for the last 2000 years for those who have been privileged enough to hear it. But we have to recognise that this may not be the case for those who have never heard the message, nor for those people who lived during the 4000 years or so before Christ came to earth.

In addition, God's omnipotence also comes into play for those people who we, as limited humans, are not able to judge as either having or not having the ability to believe and so receive eternal life. One thing we may be sure of, however, is that God is the righteous judge and every person will be judged fairly and every judgement will be correct.

45. The Race of a Lifetime
Vicky Wilkinson

In New Testament Scripture, the Apostle Paul uses several analogies to describe a Christian, to help us to comprehend the Christian life more fully; for example a builder (1 Corinthians 3:10-15), a soldier at war, a farmer (2 Timothy 2:4,6), and a runner in a race (1 Corinthians 9:24-27). It is the last we are now to consider, a runner.

The entrance requirement

The Christian race is a race of a lifetime and the greatest race ever opened up to mankind for entry. In all major races preliminary races must be run first in order for the entrant to qualify to run in the major event. However, in the Christian's race things are different in that the candidate doesn't need to qualify in preliminary heats first. The reason for this is because someone else has run the preliminary race on his/her behalf. Hebrews 6:20 speaks of Christ as the forerunner. He is the One who came down from His heaven's glory to run the race for us in the man Jesus Christ. Despite all the hurdles along the way, Christ completed the race when at His death He took all our sins upon Himself and died in our stead. His last word before He took His final breath was, "It is finished". He completed the course God sent Him on, and because of this God raised Him up to His own right hand, far above all, crowned with honour and glory (Hebrews 2:9). Because of this He has become the author of salvation to all who believe in Him.

On your marks!

Thus, it is faith in Christ's work of redemption which He accomplished at Calvary that sets us up on the starting line and secures a lane for us to run in. We do not need to earn this place by our own good works because this is God's gift to us by His grace and love, and Romans 6:23 tells us that this gift is eternal life through Jesus Christ our Lord. Therefore, when we set our feet on the starting line by our faith, then we are set on the foundation of Christ, which is a sure foundation, and the result is that we are now "in Christ" and He in us. This is because at this moment, the moment of our salvation, God sealed us with His Holy Spirit of promise which makes sure our hope in Him. Once we are sealed, nothing or no one can undo this, for this is as a deposit or guarantee of our inheritance until the day that we are actually with Christ in the glory (Ephesians 1:13-14). Therefore, even before we take one step in God's race we have life; we are saved forever.

The race

When an athlete runs he wears the minimum amount of clothing and carries nothing with him because such would only hinder him. When we run as Christians we also have an advantage, because when Christ completed His race He took a great burden from us in order that when we run we won't be hindered by this load, which is sin. Hebrews 12:1 - 2, tells us to lay aside every weight and sin which so easily ensnares us and run with endurance the race that is set before us. Sin therefore no longer has dominance over our lives, for our run is now with the Spirit, (read Romans 8). Even so it would be quite easy for us to lapse back into sinful ways and therefore become hindered by such an entanglement. That is why Hebrews 12:2 adds, "looking to Jesus the author... of our faith". In most major races the top athletes have a pace-maker. This is a runner who is not really in the race to win, but to set the pace for the competitor. We likewise have a pacemaker who is Jesus our Lord. If we keep our eyes on Jesus and how He overcame such temptations, this will keep us at the right place in the race of a lifetime

Fellow competitors

In Hebrews 12, we are also pointed to a great cloud of witnesses (v.1) who have already run the race before us as examples to be encouraged by. The previous chapter (11), reminds us of great men and women of faith who have run this race and because of this they look forward to a reward as well as the gift of life that God gave them because of their initial faith (v.6). This is because they, like Jesus, completed the course with merits, enduring all the problems and suffering along the way. God has provided something better for such men and women of faith (v.35,40). They will receive the reward of their inheritance (Colossians

3:24) which in their case is a place in the Heavenly City, Jerusalem, as co-rulers with Christ (Hebrews 12:22).

The prize

I say this because Paul shows that the prize for those who run to win is a crown, an incorruptible one (1 Corinthians 9:25). Paul, when writing his letter to the Philippians was still running the race and was forgetting the things behind him, which could have so easily entangled him in his past, and was pressing towards the goal for the prize of the upward call of God. In Paul's valedictory, when he knew his time was at hand, he could say:

> I have fought a good fight, I have finished my course, I have kept the faith: Henceforth there is laid up for me a crown of righteousness which the Lord, the righteous Judge, shalll give me on that day. (2 Timothy 4:7,8 *KJV*).

Paul had overcome by his faith despite all the ordeals along the way (2 Corinthians 11:24-28), therefore he looked for his reward.

The agony ...

The Christian race is not like a flat race or sprint but more like an obstacle race or even a marathon. Once we begin to run it won't be long before we encounter obstacles along the way. Also, like a marathon runner, we will not complete the race without enduring much suffering and pain. But the comforting aspect of this is that we are not on our own for the Lord is with us. Even if everyone else leaves us in the time of need, the Lord will not, as Paul could say when his brothers forsook him at a critical time, "the Lord stood with me and strengthened me" (2 Timothy 4:17). He will carry us over the hurdles that appear too difficult for us and set us down on firm ground again. Each obstacle we overcome will strengthen and refine us and re-affirm our faith because we have allowed the Lord to work in our lives, as Paul could say, "When I am weak, then I am strong" (2 Corinthians 12:10).

... and the ecstasy

Another aspect of the Christian race that is so very different from a secular race, is that those who are running in the lanes alongside us, who are brothers and sisters in Christ, will take the time to stop and help us if we stumble or even take a fall. They will help us back on our feet again in order that we can run again.

Discipline's reward

What if we do stumble or even take a serious fall? What if we begin to take on luggage that will slow us down and hinder us? Will such disqualify us and cause us to lose out? Well, we cannot lose out on life, for even if we never take one step in God's race, this was secured for us at the starting line. But no athlete ever gets this far and fails to run even if he falls at the first hurdle. Whilst we cannot lose out on the gift of life, what the Scriptures do indicate is that we could lose out on the prize (see Colossians 2:18). That is why Paul says, "run that you may obtain the prize", which in this case is a crown (1 Corinthians 9:24-27). These verses show that this won't be easy. Like Paul we need to train and discipline our minds and strive to keep our eyes on the goal, the prize. The Lord said to the Church at Smyrna, "be faithful until death and I will give you the crown of life", and to the Church at Philadelphia, "Hold fast what you have that no man take your crown" (Revelation 2:10, 3:11). The salvation that was secured for us at the starting line needs to be worked on in order that we grow spiritually.

Therefore we are told to work out our own salvation with fear and trembling (Philippians 2:12), so that on the day of God's testing of Christian service our work will endure the fire (See 1 Corinthians 3:10-15). Paul uses the analogy of builders, whose work is burned because they used only flimsy materials. Thus, while they suffer loss of reward, even so they will be saved (v.15), because Christ is not only the author, but is also the finisher of our faith (Hebrews 12:2). For He who began a good work in us will complete it (Philippians 1:6).

Part 6
A Christian Perspective on Modern-Day Issues

46. *Abortion*
Carolyn Mansell

In England and Wales alone, from the introduction of the 1967 Abortion Act until the early 1980s, over two million unborn babies were aborted.

The Bible

There is no specific reference to abortion in the Bible. Therefore, some may feel that Christians should avoid this controversial issue, as it appears that we can have no firm Biblical conclusion, but shouldn't we, as concerned Christians, have an opinion on this issue? I believe we cannot afford to ignore the moral issues of our day, and our caring attitude will be noticed by our family and friends to whom we witness.

There are several relevant Scriptural passages which we must take into consideration. In the Bible the value of human life is stressed and the commandment not to murder is given in Exodus 20:13. We are also told that God made man in the image of Himself and that every man shall be accountable to God for the life of his fellow man, (Genesis 9:5-6).

In certain passages the Bible does indicate that life exists before birth. For example, David states that God knit him together when he was still in his mother's womb and it was while he was there that he was fearfully and wonderfully made, (Psalm 139:13-14). We know that John the Baptist leaped for joy in his mother's womb as Mary greeted Elizabeth with the news of the coming birth of Christ, (Luke 1:44). Some commentators suggest that John was filled with the Holy Spirit inside his mother's womb, (Luke 1:15; see *NIV* footnote). This is obviously a special case and we cannot generalise from this one incident but it does show personality before birth.

Handicapped

Some people feel strongly that where unborn babies are diagnosed as being handicapped, the pregnancy should be terminated. This is a very difficult decision for the parents, especially the mother. After working with brain-damaged children I know that they can create a tremendous strain and pressure on a marriage and upon other children in the family. This may be particularly true in our society where people are selfish and some parents tend to think of themselves rather than their children.

However, the handicapped can bring much joy and happiness if they are cared for and loved. I am greatly encouraged by having known a thalidomide young man who has recently become a Christian and whose life is full of praise and thankfulness to the Lord Jesus Christ, His Saviour. What a wonderful witness and how sad if he had never been given the chance to live because society said he must die, simply because he wasn't a normal baby! In such a situation the responsibility is the mother's who has the right, under British law, to choose if her baby's life is terminated or not. The Christian woman, however, is told that her body belongs to God and that it is a temple of the Holy Spirit, (1 Corinthians 6:19,20). Is an abortion, then, an option?

We are accountable to God in all we do

There is much disagreement and debate amongst scientists and doctors as to the precise point in time when a human life begins. Personally I feel abortion is wrong. However it is up to each individual. Our conscience has been given to us to guide us where we have no Scriptural authority, but we must be careful that our conscience is not seared by society. All of us will be held accountable to God in all that we do, but in all this uncertainty it is a great comfort to know that the lives of all of us, including mothers and unborn babies, are ultimately in the hands of an all knowing and loving God and Father.

47. The Place of the Single Woman in the Scriptures
Ruth Harman (née Stoneman)

Women's rights and their equality with men have been debated since the beginning of this century, and since then this equality has been seen to be of paramount importance to many women. Hardly a week passes without some aspect of these issues being mentioned in the media. The views of various people are sought but what does God, as Creator of both male and female, have to say on these important subjects? How do the Scriptures portray the life-style of the single woman? Is it different from that of a married woman or single man? It is important that we know what God has to say on these subjects so that we can be faithful to His standards rather than to what we think the standards are or should be.

Old Testament

There are few passages in the Bible where it is clear that the woman is single. In the Old Testament there is a law relating to single women in Numbers 27:1-8. If they had no brothers, then the daughters were to inherit their father's property. Another law in connection with this is given in Numbers 36:1-12. This stated that if the daughters subsequently wished to get married, they should marry within the tribal clan of their father so that the property inherited by them would remain in that tribe.

New Testament

In the New Testament possible examples of single women are Mary, sister of Lazarus (Luke 10:38-42; John 11:1-44; 12:1-8); Dorcas (Acts 9:36-41); Lydia (Acts 16:13-15) and the unmarried daughters of Philip the evangelist (Acts 21:8-9). However, few of these shine much light on how a single woman should live.

There are so few examples because the general rule was for women to get married. Arranged marriages were the custom and the daughter was the responsibility of her father until she married. Then she was supported by her husband.

The Principle of Marriage

The principle of marriage is found to be the case throughout Scripture. God's order is seen to be the family orientated society.

> The Lord God said, "It is not good for man to be alone. I will make a helper suitable for him." (Genesis 2:18)

> "Haven't you read," he replied, "that at the beginning the Creator 'made them male and female' and said, 'For this reason a man will leave his father and mother and be united to his wife and the two will become one flesh?' So they are no longer two, but one. Therefore what God has joined together, let man not separate." (Matthew 19:4-6)

So the general rule was for women to get married, but there were exceptions and it is therefore necessary to see if there are any Scriptures which shed more light on this subject.

Those who are not Married

First of all it is important to note that there is no difference in God's eyes between men and women as far as sin and salvation are concerned, for there is "neither male nor female, for you are all one in Christ Jesus" (Galatians 3:28).

There is one main passage in the New Testament which has something specific to say to those who are unmarried:

> Now to the unmarried and widows I say: It is good for them to stay unmarried, as I am. (1 Corinthians 7:8)

This advice appears to go against God's natural order of marriage and so we must take into account the wider context of this passage. The return of the Lord Jesus Christ was an imminent possibility at that time, but it required the repentance of the nation of Israel.

Repent, then, and turn to God, so that your sins may be wiped out, that times of refreshing may come from the Lord, and that he may send the Christ, who has been appointed for you - even Jesus. (Acts 3:19-20)

Paul knew that if the Lord had returned there would first have to be the great tribulation during which it would be far better to be single than to have the responsibilities of marriage and parenthood, (see Matthew 24:19). Thus in 1 Corinthians 7:29 Paul states that "the time is short" and in verse 26 mentions "the present crisis" during which it is better not to marry. However, in verse 34 he goes on to say:

An unmarried woman or virgin is concerned about the Lord's affairs: Her aim is to be devoted to the Lord in both body and spirit. But a married woman is concerned about the affairs of this world - how she can please her husband.

This principle holds good today, that the concern of a single person, both male and female, should be the Lord's affairs. The aim of the unmarried person is given in verse 35. It is to "live in a right way in undivided devotion to the Lord " This then, is the key for the single person. We can give our undivided attention to the Lord.

General Rules

Other passages in the New Testament give us further information as to how we should live, but these may be applied to both married and unmarried.

Whatever you do, work at it with all your heart, as working for the Lord, not for men ..... it is the Lord Christ you are serving. (Colossians 3:23-24)

Specific examples of this principle are given in this chapter for the family orientated society; wives, husbands and children (vs 18-20). Other general principles indicating how we should walk, whatever our status, are given in Ephesians 5. Verses 1 and 2 state we should be "imitators of God and live a life of love." Verse 8 states "live as children of light" and verse 15 be "very careful, then, how you live - not as unwise but as wise."

Conclusion

Let us, then, if we are single, give our undivided devotion to the Lord and realise that we have the freedom to serve the Lord without the responsibilities that go with marriage and parenthood. Thus the Lord reveals a different standard for those without such worldly duties; an awesome responsibility and a sobering thought!

However, whatever our status, we should be thankful and content (Philippians 4:11,12), for our loving heavenly Father knows what is best for us. As we are told to live lives honouring to Him and to give the Lord Jesus Christ first place in all things, we should do everything for Him, and not for Man.

48. Suffering
Sylvia Penny

Suffering in New Testament times

Mary flung herself onto her bed, sobbing bitterly. It was all over at last. Her husband was dead and life for her would never be the same again. It had been a terrible way to die and she could hardly think about it without shivering and folding her arms about herself.

How he must have suffered, and how she was suffering now. No one alive could know the pain of being torn apart, gnawed and eaten by lions and other wild beasts in a public arena, least of all the bloodthirsty crowd with their insatiable appetite for human flesh. The roar of their approval was still ringing in her ears. Their total lack of respect for human life, their degradation, their bestiality left her bemused. She could not begin to comprehend it.

It had all begun just one short week ago, when she was talking to a couple of friends in the market place. She had mentioned the change there had been in her and her life and how wonderful it had been to hear the Apostle Paul speaking about the Lord Jesus Christ. She had said how much they enjoyed fellowship with other Christians, despite having to meet in secret and in fear of the Roman authorities. The message of forgiveness, of salvation, of resurrection life and of the many blessings they had in Christ Jesus was too wonderful to miss.

Someone must have overheard their conversation and reported it to the authorities, for everything had happened all too quickly after that. The Roman soldiers had arrived and arrested her husband while she had been out visiting a sick friend. Many others had been rounded up as the Emperor wanted plenty of victims for the feast day spectacular he was providing for his foreign guests and for his ever-appreciative Roman populace. Christians were their favourites and they were being arrested and herded together along with the scum of Roman society - thieves, swindlers, extortionists and murderers.

They had been set loose into the arena one by one, or sometimes in small groups to vary the entertainment, and then the animals were let out. One by one they had suffered their terrible deaths, and Mary's husband had been among them. Her grief, the sense of uselessness and futility overwhelmed her until, at last, worn out with crying she became calm and lay limply on the bed.

It was then that she remembered something that Paul had said at their last meeting, the last meeting she would ever attend with her husband. Paul had said that he considered that our present sufferings were not worth comparing with the glory that is to be revealed in us. How wonderful that glory must be to make up for all the suffering that Paul had been through - and how wonderful it must be to make up for all the misery that she was now experiencing.

Paul had also taught them that the Father of our Lord Jesus Christ was the God of all comfort and that anyone could share in that comfort. He had said that anyone who suffered for Christ would also share in the comfort He experienced. Mary felt she needed this and wanted it more than anything else in the world.

As she lay there, she felt desperately lonely.

Suffering here and now

Jane locked herself into the toilet and let the tears flow freely down her cheeks. She felt ostracised, an outsider and she sobbed as she dabbed at her face with a crumpled tissue. It was a terrible thing always to be the butt of everyone's jokes in the office, to find that people stopped talking when she entered the room as if they had been talking about her, ridiculing her. The people surrounding her, day in and day out, had a total lack of respect for her in particular and for what she held to be the most important thing in life. It used to be all right in the office, but now, since she had owned up to being a Christian, she was suffering.

It had all begun one long week ago when she had overheard a conversation between two of her fellow-employees, about how fed up they were with life in general and their jobs in particular. What was the point of it all if they couldn't do what they wanted to do and enjoy themselves when they wanted to and how they liked? What was the purpose of living?

Somehow Jane had found herself drawn into the discussion and her opinion was asked. She found herself admitting to a belief in Christ, and doing this for the first time to unbelievers. A barrage of questions followed, most of which she could not answer. Then came the comments and criticisms with which she was unable to cope.

The word spread quickly, as by the next day it seemed everyone looked at her and treated her differently. Some seemed to be guarded in her presence but others were more blunt; "Call yourself a Christian? I saw what you did the other Thursday!" "You're a fine one to be a Christian. I remember what you said about ..."

She felt totally inadequate and very depressed. Christians were supposed to have an inner joy, a contentment which was supposed to surpass anything an unbeliever might experience, so why did she feel only a sense of failure and rejection? As her tears were drying on her cheeks she remembered some words she had heard at last week's Bible Study. "I consider that our present sufferings are not worth comparing with the glory that will be revealed in us."

How wonderful that glory must be to make up for all the misery that she was now going through. Could she really believe the words of Paul to the Corinthians, that the Father of the Lord Jesus Christ was the God of all comfort and that anyone could share in that comfort? Jane felt she needed this comfort and wanted it more than anything else in the world. As she opened the door she felt desperately lonely.

Questions

1) Can Jane's sufferings really be compared with those of Mary?
2) In Romans 8:18, and elsewhere, does Paul include feelings of rejection in what he means by suffering or does the word refer only to physical suffering and, possibly, ultimately martyrdom?

49. Swearing
Sylvia Penny

A while ago I was asked, as a mother of two small children, what I thought of the increasing practice by some people of taking the Lord's name in vain or using it as a swear word in front of children. I was shown a clipping from a local newspaper which asked why we are content to sit back and allow the names "Jesus" and "Christ" to be used commonly as swear words. It is unimaginable that Muslim countries would tolerate such usage of "Allah" and "Mohammed".

In the newspaper an example was given of a boy who thought that "Jesus" was a swear word and nothing more. This is a sad reflection of our society. How can a child reach the age of seven or eight and have never heard of God or the Lord Jesus Christ, other than in the context of swearing?

Not only does this mean that the child's education is sadly lacking, but that adults no longer curtail their swearing in front of children.

How things used to be

A compulsory part of the school day in Britain is assembly, and all schools used to observe this. However, this is no longer the situation. Children were required to be present for prayers, hymns/choruses and Bible readings or plays. It would be rather difficult for a child to remain ignorant of the Lord Jesus in such a school. The child would know the details of at least His birth and also of His death and resurrection.

And it used to be that men never swore in front of women, let alone children. Now some men and women think nothing about swearing in the presence of their own children. The crudest language trips off their tongues and abusive usage of "Jesus" and "Christ" is common. How can Christians cope with this situation? How should we react in such situations to protect our children?

Definition of terms

Firstly, it is important to define what we are talking about. Is there a difference between blasphemy, taking the Lord's name in vain, and bad language? If so, what does the Bible have to say on these subjects?

Blasphemy in the Bible

Leviticus 24:10-16 tells of a person who "blasphemed the Name with a curse".

> The Lord spoke to Moses and said, "If anyone curses His God, he will be held responsible; anyone who blasphemes the name of the Lord must be put to death. The entire assembly must stone him."

Blasphemy was so serious that the punishment was death. Hundreds of years later this was still the case. In John 10:33 the Jews picked up stones to stone Jesus, accusing Him of blasphemy:

> "We are not stoning you for any of these (miracles)," replied the Jews, "but for blasphemy, because you, a mere man, claim to be God."

It appears that blasphemy involves more than bursting out with an exclamation of a name. It involves cursing God, being purposely profane about Him and claiming to be equal with Him. The Oxford Illustrated Dictionary defines to blaspheme as to "talk impiously; utter profanity about, revile." Although exclamations and expletives involving our Lord's name are distasteful and unnecessary, it would appear that these do not come into the category of blasphemy.

Taking the Lord's name in vain

This well-known phrase comes from the *KJV* of the Ten Commandments:

> Thou shalt not take the name of the Lord thy God in vain; for the Lord will not hold him guiltless that taketh His name in vain (Exodus 20:7).

This is translated in the *NIV* by:

> You shall not misuse the name of the Lord your God, for the Lord will not hold anyone guiltless who misuses His name.

The issue is whether this commandment is broken every time someone habitually exclaims "God', "Jesus", "Christ" or whether this commandment refers to a more serious misuse of His Name. Passages where the word misuse, or taking something in vain, is used, involve the idea of falsity. For example, in Exodus 23:1 we read, "Do not spread false reports. Do not help a wicked man by being a malicious witness," and in Hosea 10:4, "They make many promises, take false oaths and make agreements; therefore lawsuits spring up like poisonous weeds in a ploughed field." The word translated false in these verses is the word translated misuse in Exodus 20:7. Consider also Psalm 139:19-20. "If only you would slay the wicked, O God! Away from me, you bloodthirsty men! They speak of you with evil intent; your adversaries misuse your name."

The tone of these passages is that people are aware that they are making false oaths, false reports and misusing God's name to give authority to their lies. It would seem, therefore, that "taking the Lord's name in vain" involved the more serious intent of being false on purpose, rather than using it as an expletive.

Bad language in the Bible

Bad language is referred to, for example, in Colossians 3:8:

> But now you must rid yourself of all such things as these: anger, rage, malice, slander and filthy language from your lips.

Ephesians 4:29 refers to unwholesome talk and Ephesians 5:4 to obscenity. Such "filthy language" referred to would be all forms of swear words and obscenities, including words and phrases with double meanings and talk with innuendoes, such as are rife today. Also "God', "Jesus" and "Christ" are commonly used as swear words nowadays and I would categorise them as forms of bad language.

However, it must be noted that Christians have come to accept certain expressions which in the past would have been condemned. "Damn', "hell" and "blimey" are, perhaps, the most common three. The question is, are such expressions as these acceptable? Or does this prove that the gradual decline in the values of society eventually permeates Christian standards?

Whatever the answer to this question, we know that the speech of Christians should be wholesome and pure. We should endeavour to make sure it is like that throughout our lives, all day, every day. But what about people who do not claim to be Christians? Should we admonish such people for using what we, as Christians, deem bad language?

Certainly we have a good case for admonishing fellow Christians if they use such language, as there is plenty of advice in the epistles telling us to admonish one another. In this way we keep each other on the straight and narrow; for example see Colossians 1:28 and 3:16.

What about non-Christians?

However, what about those who do not claim to be Christians? Should we try to enforce biblical values and standards on them? Should we, politely, tell them that their use of certain words offends us and we would prefer not to hear them, to say nothing of our children? Or should we keep quiet? If we do keep quiet, are we letting down the Christian cause? These questions are not easy to answer.

There seems little point nowadays in trying to enforce Christian standards upon those people who do not accept them. Little is achieved by such attempts except, possibly, putting their backs up and ensuring they are less likely to listen to Christians in the future. What may be more helpful is to ensure that those with whom we have contact know that we are Christians, by our actions as well as our words, and letting them moderate their own behaviour in our presence accordingly.

I have found sometimes, though not always, that people who do know my beliefs do actually try and control their language when I am around. Considering that swearing is a habit, and like any habit it is difficult to break let alone curtail, then such attempts should be applauded and encouraged and the people respected, even if the odd word does slip out.

What about our children?

However, more important is the affect of such slips upon our children who notice and pick up unusual words used forcefully. As an adult Christian it is possible to cope with, understand or merely ignore bad language. But how do we deal with the situation when our children are present?

With young children it would seem that avoidance is the best route. It is fairly easy to steer a pre-school child clear of undesirable adult influences. Even when at school most teachers are sensitive and caring and it is possible to control who they mix with outside of school hours. However, in the playground they may learn new words from their peers. To counteract this, there needs to be positive input from more than just the family. The children can be taken to Sunday School regularly and encouraged to make friends with the others they meet there.

Personal faith

It is also especially important for us, as Christian parents, to ensure that our children have a good grounding in Christian values, and an understanding of how much the name of the Lord Jesus Christ means to us. However, it is impossible and undesirable for us to keep them closeted at home, and we cannot keep them away from external influences as they get older. Under such circumstances it is even more important that Christian parents give their children a sure foundation for their lives. It will not come from society.

Christian parents

Christian parents need to teach their children from an early age what is right and what is wrong. Then, when they come into contact with other children in school, or adults in the world at large, they will know how a Christian should talk and behave.

I have a suspicion that this is easier said than done. Young children may follow the standards of their parents. However, as the teenage years advance youngsters without a personal faith in the Lord Jesus Christ are likely to lack both the desire and motivation to live a life pleasing to the Lord.

Television

There is one other factor: television! It used to be that programmes were censored and that very rarely, if ever, would any bad language have been used. When it first became permissible to use it, it would certainly not have been at a time when children would have been watching.

However, today the picture is quite different. What people class as mild bad language is used frequently and with videos available at all hours of the day, even strong bad language may be heard by children.

The only answer for Christian parents is to have no such videos at home and to strictly censor the programmes watched by the children. However, this gets increasingly difficult as the child gets older and spends more time out of the house and away from parental influence.

The direction in which society seems to be going is one away from Christian views and values. We are becoming more and more of a minority as we struggle to swim against the tide. We must bring up our children "in the training and instruction of the Lord" (Ephesians 6:4) for the only answer for our children is that they will come to know the grace of God and accept the Lord Jesus as their Saviour. Without doing so they are not likely to accept the standards, morals and values that should be part and parcel of the Christian life.

50. Giving
Sylvia Penny

The subject of giving is never a popular one, particularly in today's society. Become treasurer of any organisation you may care to think of and you suddenly realise how reluctantly many people part with their money, even when there is a legitimate debt.

And when it comes to freewill offerings, donations, and money given for nothing in return, then quite often you are up against a brick wall!

However, as Christians, do we know better? And more importantly, do we *do* better? The answer to the first may be "Yes!', but the answer to the second may be "No!".

The Church of England has revealed that the average weekly contribution from church members is a mere £2. That wouldn't get you into a cinema!

On the subject of giving there appears to be two main questions to ask: how much should we give and who, or what, should we give to?

How much should we give?

The answer to the first question that springs to mind is that we should give a tenth, based on the tithing system detailed in the Old Testament. However, the salaries received nowadays from work done are a far cry from the system in operation when tithing was recommended.

The Israelites had to give a tenth of certain items, such as grain, oil, herds and flocks. These were used to support the Levites, the priestly tribe, who had no lands to work and who ministered to the remaining eleven tribes. This was a fairly cut-and-dried system. Everyone knew how much to give and who to give it to.

The New Testament, however, is totally silent on the subject of tithing. It gives little or no indication as to how much people should give. It seems to be more concerned with people's attitude and motivation for giving, rather than stating any particular amount or percentage.

1 Timothy 6:18, referring to rich people, says, "Command them to do good, to be rich in good deeds, and to be generous and willing to

share". It connects the command to give generously with an attitude of willingness.

Tithing and the married woman

How can the Old Testament principle of tithing be applied today? To start with, not only do we have the problem as to whether we should give ten percent of our earnings before or after tax, but if we are married do we pool our earnings before calculating our ten percent, or do we calculate (and give) separately?

Then what if the wife does not work? Does this mean she has no say in how much is given, as the family income is all earned by the husband? There is no guidance for this situation set out in the Bible. The societies of its day were so totally different from ours. Then women had no say in many such matters. The tithing would have been carried out by the men. The women would not have been involved.

However, it would be difficult in this day and age to take the line that women have no responsibility towards giving if their husbands are the sole wage-earners.

In our marriage ceremonies we promise to share our worldly goods with one another, and this surely includes our respective incomes. Therefore in a Christian marriage it would seem sensible that either we decide together where our ten percent should be given, or that each should decide where his and her five percent should go.

Non-Christian husband

Of course, if a Christian woman is married to a non-Christian man the problems are increased. It would be difficult, if not impossible, for her to insist that he gives ten percent of his salary away, however worthy she feels the cause may be. He is not likely to be sympathetic to her insisting that she has her five percent. He may not be averse to her putting a pound or two in the collection each Sunday morning (which may partially explain the Church of England statistics quoted earlier), but he would object to her embarking on a consistent planned approach to giving.

However, the Lord understands all our individual circumstances and difficulties, and judges accordingly. The example of the widow offering two copper coins in Luke 21:1-4 shows this to be the case. He considered she had given more than all the wealthy because "she out of her poverty put in all she had to live on". Two pounds out of the weekly housekeeping would be considered more than twenty pounds from a millionaire's wallet.

How much do we keep?

In this day and age, rather than considering the percentage we give, perhaps it is more helpful to consider what we should keep for ourselves. If we are already able to live quite comfortably on our family income, what should we do when a pay-rise comes along? Instead of giving just ten percent of it, perhaps we should consider giving all of it to the Lord's work. After all, if it is in excess of our needs, why should we spend more on ourselves? We either end up with a clutter of material possessions, buy larger and more prestigious houses, go on more expensive and exotic holidays, or accumulate a portfolio of investments.

Each of these involves making time consuming decisions, and each brings its own worries and needless pressures. Instead we could spend the time deciding where to give the money, and that has none of the accompanying worries and pressures! How true are the Lord's words, "It is more blessed to give than to receive" (Acts 20:35).

Who do we give to?

This brings us to the second main question of to whom or where do we give our money? The situation in the Old Testament has already been referred to. The Israelites gave their tithes to the Levites in order to support them. Thus the answer for the Israelites was, again, cut-and-dried.

An application can be made from their situation to ours today. The Levites acted as priests for their nation. They carried out the spiritual duties while being supported by the other eleven tribes who worked in their lands.

If we attend church and support various Christian organisations to which we are committed, then first and foremost perhaps our support should be given to these. We need to decide how much to give to each and make a long-term commitment to do so, so that our gifts can be anticipated by the recipients and proper planning can be made for their use. Such was the case in the Old Testament where the Levites were enabled to carry out their priestly duties as they could rely on the long-term and continuous commitment of the rest of the nation. In the New Testament Paul encouraged regular giving in all the churches, and in the church at Corinth.

> Now about the collection for God's people: Do what I told the Galatian churches to do. On the first day of every week, each one of you should set aside a sum of money in keeping with his income, saving it up, so that when I come no collections will have to be made. Then, when I arrive, I will give letters of introduction to the men you approve and send them with your gift to Jerusalem. (1 Corinthians 16:1-3)

Today, we should follow these scriptural examples and set aside a predetermined proportion of our income to help and support others.

The poor and the needy

In addition to the church and Christian organisations there is one other group we need to consider. Deuteronomy 15:11 states, "There will always be poor people in the land. Therefore I command you to be open-handed towards your brothers and towards the poor and needy in your land". Such giving was on top of their regular commitment to tithing. It was to be made when a particular need came to their attention and, as such, was not a regular commitment.

Today we all receive very regular requests from different charities for gifts to go to various needy causes. As Christians it may be impossible for us to support all of these. However, it would be wrong for us to refuse to help any on the grounds that we already support the church and other Christian organisations.

There are few of us who are unable to find an extra pound or two on top of what we regularly contribute. The Israelites were requested to be "open-handed" to their brothers, the poor and the needy. We, too, should be "open-handed', willing to give that extra when a special need arises.

Motivation for giving

Lastly, we need to consider our motivation for giving. It is no good giving with an attitude of either pride or reluctance, or of thinking of what we can get out of it for ourselves. There have to be no strings attached

Deuteronomy 8:18 says, "But remember the Lord your God, for it is he who gives you the ability to produce wealth". Everything we have or own belongs to him. We are His stewards and we should use and care for His resources wisely.

2 Corinthians 8 and 9 have much to say about giving and attitudes. 2 Corinthians 9:7 says, "Each man should give what he has decided in his heart to give, not reluctantly or under compulsion, for God loves a cheerful giver". And 2 Corinthians 8:12 has, "For if the willingness is there, the gift is acceptable according to what one has, not according to what he does not have".

Thus the spirit in which we give is of utmost importance. We must be willing, cheerful and generous. However, we should not be flamboyant, making a show of what we give and ensuring everyone realises just what generous people we are! The Lord will take note of how much we give and with what attitude we give, just as He noted the widow's two copper coins.

51. Punctuality,
and meaning what we say
Sylvia Penny

When my son was five years old he was told by an adult that he could "come at any time". We had to explain to him that they didn't actually mean this. He was surprised, for as parents we have always tried to ensure that we do mean what we say.

Soon after, an adult said they would visit us for coffee with their children. They did not turn up. Again, my five-year-old son was surprised. In his mind adults always do what they say - don't they?

On other occasions he wanted to know at what time visitors would arrive. Five minutes before the appointed time he would place himself by the window to greet them. Sometimes he was kept waiting over an hour. He was always disappointed if they were late, and kept asking why they hadn't come. Did they *really* say they would come at such-and-such a time?

Does it matter?

I suppose it started me wondering whether such things matter or not. From my son's point of view they mattered a lot. If people didn't do what they said they would, he was confused and let-down. From a parent's point of view, either it can be considered a good experience, setting them up to expect and cope with the disappointments of later life, or it can be considered the very beginning of when they learn to distrust and disbelieve what other people say.

But do such things matter to us as adults? Or have we, after twenty years or so, come to expect this as the norm? Maybe as Christians we have learned to tolerate and accommodate such behaviour? Or perhaps it's something that never bothered us in the first place? But maybe the most important point is whether we reciprocate such behaviour, and whether we consider it important to carry out what we say we will do.

What does the Bible say?

The Bible has very little, if anything, to say on punctuality - for an obvious reason. They had no clocks then and they were not dominated by time as is the westernised, industrialised world today. Their society was organised in a very different way. Keeping an appointment at a precise time would have been unusual, and it is doubtful that this was an every day necessity.

Even today this is more of a westernised phenomenon, rather than a world-wide institution. Some years ago we visited the Philippines and we had to catch a little boat to travel up a river to get to a village in the middle of nowhere. When we asked at what time the boat left, we were met with blank looks. The boat went when there were enough people in it. So we just sat and sat, looking at our watches. But most people in the boat didn't have a watch! Time meant something different to them, than it did to us.

However, Paul does refer to the importance of keeping arrangements. He contrasts the way the world does not always honour commitments made with the way Christians should do so; (see 2 Corinthians 1:15-24). In today's modernised, high-tech, time-orientated society, should we as Christians be punctual, turn up when we say we will, and generally mean and do what we say? The answer is obviously "Yes!"

It is considered courteous and efficient in the business world to be on time for appointments. It could mean the difference between getting a job at an interview or losing it to someone else, between obtaining new business or losing it to a competitor. Perhaps the same philosophy should apply to our social engagements.

A good Christian witness?

It is a good witness to non-Christians if we are punctual and carry out what we say we will do when we say we will do it. If we are found to be reliable, people are more likely to be receptive to what we have to say about the Lord when the opportunity arises. It can build up people's confidence in their relationship with us, and also help to reinforce their children's trust in what adults say. It is a good habit to get into.

On the other hand, if we are often late, break appointments, and don't do what we promise, we can waste other people's time and give a bad impression. It can confuse their children and hamper our social relationships, making people wonder what our true intentions are. It can be construed as discourteous and inconsiderate.

Of course, when we are on the receiving end of such actions, we should be sympathetic and understanding, and willing to give the benefit of the doubt to the other person.

One of the most difficult things to do is to control what we say. Perhaps the next time we find ourselves saying "come any time" or "our house is always open" we should stop to think whether we do actually mean what we say.

52. *Teenage Marriage*
Sylvia Penny

Today's society is so different from any that has ever existed in the past. What was sensible for past generations may not be so today. That is why on some issues it is difficult for Christians to extrapolate from what happened in Biblical times to today's society. When certain moral behaviours are detailed in the Bible, it is very simple to know what they mean, and to know as Christians that we should put them into practice as best we can. But what about all those many subjects that the Bible remains silent upon? With those we have to reach our own conclusions based on the information we have around us, and the wisdom that we have gained through knowing our Lord Jesus Christ over the years. One such subject is teenage marriage.

My husband is a pastor and performs many weddings throughout the year, and so the prevailing attitudes towards marriage by many different sorts of people have become very clear. When people in their twenties or thirties wish to get married it is assumed that they are mature enough, and are well prepared to take such a step. When two teenagers wish to be married, without fail there are doubts and reservations expressed. Statistically, many teenage marriages end in divorce, and so these doubts and fears are well justified. But how is it that we have come so far from what, throughout the centuries, had always been considered normal?

Age of marriage in the Old Testament

Right from early times it was the normal and expected course of events for persons in their teens to get married. A few mathematical calculations made from the information supplied in 2 Kings make it very clear that many of the kings fathered their first son in their mid-teen years. Jehoram fathered Ahaziah at 17 years old (8:16); Amon fathered Josiah at 15 years old (21:19); Josiah fathered Jehoiakim at 15 years old (22:1); Jehoiakim fathered Jehoiachin at 17 years old (23:36); and it appears that Ahaz may have fathered his son Hezekiah when he was a mere ten years old (16:2; 18:2). There were more worries for parents in the past if their children were not married by the time they were twenty than if they were.

Arranged marriages

Until relatively recently, many marriages were arranged by the parents and romantic love had very little to do with it. The monetary considerations were far more important. In addition, it would not be unusual for the bride to be more mature than the groom - as may have been the case with Ahaz mentioned above. Later the rabbis worked out some practical rules regarding marriage, including a minimum age for marriage of twelve for girls and thirteen for boys.

Life expectancy has increased

Also relevant is the fact that female life expectancy in the Roman Empire was 23 years, rising to 33 years in the 14th century and 48 years by the end of the 19th century. It would therefore be only sensible to be married young. However, since modern medicine and sanitation were introduced earlier this century longevity has shot up, meaning that today there is no longer any need for people to get married at a young age. There is no danger of most people dying before they reach thirty, and there is no possibility of the population dying out if women wait until their late twenties or thirties to have their first child.

Earlier sexual maturity

However, this vastly superior technological society has produced other problems of its own. Teenagers are considered too young, too immature to get married. But they are still sexually mature at the same age, if not younger, than those that lived a thousand or two years before them. It has been proved that with modern diets, with plentiful varieties of foods, girls mature earlier than in the past. The age of first menstruation has been linked to the percentage of fat cells existing in a girl's body - and with everyone in the Western world so well-nourished, many girls are sexually mature earlier than ever before. This, of course, causes problems.

As Christians we want ourselves and our families to live within the code of morals acceptable to God. However, the society we live in makes this increasingly difficult for many reasons. We want the best for our children, which includes a good education. So, contrary to previous generations and civilisations we require our teenagers not to get married, have children and start working for their living - but to remain in school, college or university until the late teens or early twenties. Of course, as we are likely to live beyond seventy years nowadays, this is only a small percentage of their lives. However, teenagers still have the same thoughts, feelings, urges and desires that teenagers have always had. Our society, however, requires that either they suppress such feelings for ten or more years until they are considered "mature enough" to be married, or they indulge in such feelings to the contrary of Christian morals and to the possible detriment of their physical, mental and emotional health.

Encourage high-energy activities

What is the solution? Should we encourage teenage marriage, when we know that divorce rates point against it? Or should we channel teenage energies into healthy pursuits such as sports, dance, child-care and other activities demanding high energy levels, and trust that this will occupy their time, their minds and their physical stamina enough to keep at bay their sexual urges? There is no simple answer.

Too much leisure time?

It has been said that there is a basic list of instincts that humans need to satisfy, and that once the first has been satisfied you go on to the next. First comes thirst, then hunger, then warmth, clothing and shelter. Afterwards comes sex, and then various other needs or wants. In previous societies, a large proportion of time was spent satisfying the first few items on the list, which left less time for the pursuit of sexual fulfilment. Again, because of the unusual society we live in (compared to all past societies) there is now much more time for people to pursue their pleasures. And which section of our society has the most time available, and the fewest responsibilities, if not our teenagers? It is no wonder that it is considered the hardest part of parenthood to guide a child through their teens and bring them through safely into their twenties. And should it surprise us that many teens rebel, and want to "do their own thing" when, after all, in previous societies that is precisely what they were encouraged and allowed to do?

AIDS

A last thought on the subject. Maybe today the tide is turning - albeit slowly. With AIDS becoming more widespread and the resurgence of sexually transmitted diseases, many teenagers are aware that sexual activity before marriage bears a terrible cost later on. As more and more youngsters realise that people they know personally are dying of AIDS, they are beginning to realise the importance of the Biblical moral guidelines. Much more is being heard of "abstinence" and "purity" than just a few years ago and, more importantly, it is being championed by the teenagers for themselves. For that reason, it is more likely to catch on. Maybe in this lies the best hope for the solution to one of the greatest problems of today's society.

53. Stopping Shopping!
Sylvia Penny

Shopping can be a lot of fun, whatever men may say! But even the occasional man will admit to enjoying a shopping trip, as long as it's to the DIY store, the hardware store or a store stocked with the latest technological equipment – anything but a ladies fashion boutique!

The most popular American pastime is shopping, and we in Britain are fast catching on. Children and teenagers are caught at an early and vulnerable age, and seemingly hooked for life.

But have we ever stopped to think whether there is anything wrong with this seemingly harmless activity? Have we unwittingly got caught up in the modern trend of materialism and consumerism? There is so much advertising today for all sorts of products and services, cleverly aimed at just the right targets, that we may be blissfully unaware that we are one of those targets, and that we have succumbed.

One man who had wealth enough to buy whatever he liked, whenever he liked, was Solomon, and three thousand years ago he wrote:

> Whoever loves money never has money enough;
> Whoever loves wealth is never satisfied with his income.
> As goods increase, so do those who consume them.
> And what benefit are they to the owner,
> except to feast his eyes on them? (Ecclesiastes 5:10,11).

He, more than anyone, realised the futility of loving money and material possessions. Having experienced everything that money could buy, he realised that it could never bring satisfaction or contentment. For however much you have, you will always want more. So in that case, why do we continue to buy things which are not really necessary?

Should we stop buying unnecessary things?

Have we ever considered whether we *should* stop buying unnecessary things? After all, the Bible does not condemn shopping! Not in so many words, but it does have a lot to say about our wise use of time and money, and having our priorities right.

Have we ever found ourselves explaining that we cannot do something for someone, go somewhere to help out, or support some activity, because we haven't got enough time/money? If so, then it may be that we need to rethink our priorities. Of course, we all need to spend time/money on leisure activities, but maybe we need to reconsider just how much we need to spend on ourselves. In previous generations there was no such thing as a 'leisure industry' – which is an oxymoron if ever there was one! We now live in a society which continually tells us we need to take care of ourselves and our own needs first, otherwise we will be of no use to others. As Christians do we accept this philosophy of life, or do we reject it as unbiblical?

Although nothing about shopping is mentioned in the Bible, the principles for Christian living are clear. If we decide to stop shopping for unnecessary items today, then it would make more time for other activities, including helping others. It would give us more money to donate to Christian causes, and it would cure us of a shopping 'mindset' where our satisfaction comes from buying and possessing things.

Could we stop buying unnecessary things?

Having decided that perhaps we *should*, the next issue is whether we *could*. This may be easier said than done. We can make an analogy with other activities which people find hard to give up e.g. overeating, smoking and excess drinking. We may be persuaded fairly easily that we should stop each of these, but putting it into practise is another matter. However, although there are many organisations set up to assist people in stopping each of these activities, I have yet to come across one designed to curtail the shopping urge! The problem with excessive shopping is that it is so easy to excuse, it is seen as harmless, and no one else thinks there is anything wrong with it!

Christian excuses for materialism

It is the easiest thing in the world for people to justify something they want to do, and something they enjoy doing. Christians are no exception. There are plenty of plausible sounding reasons for buying unnecessary items.

1. It is good stewardship. If you see a bargain today, you should buy it, as it saves money in the long run, and then you can give away the money you save!
2. If you give away more of your money to good causes than most other people do, then you should be able to spend the rest on yourself without feeling guilty.
3. We have to live like those around us. If we don't, then people will think we are strange and then we won't be able to witness effectively.
4. We, and our homes, should look smart and fashionable, so we are a good witness. No one would want to be a Christian if they thought it meant being out-of-date, threadbare, old-fashioned, etc.

However, if we can get beyond the stage of self-justification, and start to examine the real reasons that we buy more and more things, we may start to feel a little uncomfortable

What are our real reasons for buying more things?

Do we need more clothes, or do we just want them? Do we need more ornaments, or do we just want to add to our collection? Do we need new furniture, or is it just to keep up with our neighbours? Do we need a new car, or is it just to impress? Do we need more "labour saving" gadgets, or are they just toys to amuse? When we answer these questions honestly, it is unlikely that much of our shopping has anything to do with necessity, but much more to do with enjoyment, pleasure, status, competition, etc. It satisfies our worldly nature. So we may continue to buy such things because:

1. We like shopping. It makes us feel good!
2. We have excess money to spend.
3. We like to collect beautiful, attractive things to look at.
4. There is something missing in our lives. A hole we need to fill.

5   Things cannot hurt us. People can. So we collect things rather than people.

You cannot serve both God and money (Luke 16:13)

When speaking to the disciples Jesus told them "You cannot serve both God and money." When the Pharisees, who loved money, heard this and sneered at Jesus He said to them "You are the ones who justify yourselves in the eyes of men, but God knows your hearts" (Luke 16:13-15).

We will know in our hearts whether this is a problem area for us or not. Do we feel happy with our attitude towards money and possessions, or do we secretly feel a little guilty about the amount of money (and time) we spend on ourselves? It will probably depend upon whether we think we are spending excessively or not. Everyone has a different yardstick where money is concerned. What some people regard as thrift, others regard as stinginess. And what some people regard as normal spending, others regard as wastefulness.

We do not have to try to convince other people that our levels of spending are acceptable. We do not have to justify our lifestyle to other Christians. That is what the Pharisees did. We just have to ensure that our hearts and consciences are clear before God. No one else can do this for us.

What gives us happiness?

Does our happiness depend upon frequent and excessive eating, drinking or spending money, or does it depend upon our relationships with others and with God? The way in which we spend our time and money will give the answer away.

> Keep your lives free from the love of money and be content with what you have, because God has said, "Never will I leave you; never will I forsake you." (Hebrews 13:5)

Part 7
The Apostle Paul
and Women

54. Childbirth
Sylvia Penny

There is little said in the Scriptures about either children or childbirth. Even the birth of our Lord and Saviour is covered in a mere two or three chapters. However, there is one verse in Paul's first letter to Timothy which does refer to childbirth:

> But women will be saved (kept safe) through childbearing, if they continue in faith, love and holiness with propriety. (1 Timothy 2:15)

This is a puzzling verse as, at face value, it seems to be saying that as long as women displayed these three qualities, then they would be rewarded by the safe delivery of their children. Yet this verse was written nearly two thousand years ago, and certainly it cannot be said categorically that every believing woman who has been faithful, loving and holy, has been saved from death in childbirth since that time. Although it is very unlikely that *any* woman, believing or otherwise, will die in the process of childbirth today, this has only recently become the case. So what did Paul mean when he wrote these words to Timothy?

Five interpretations

Many suggestions have been made by different people and five of these are listed below together with comments on their validity.

(1) Women will be kept safely through bearing children if they have continued in faith, love and holiness.

The drawback with this straightforward interpretation is that it is simply not true.

(2) Women will be saved if their children continue in the faith.

The word *saved* here is understood in the spiritual sense, but the gospel of salvation throughout the Scriptures is based upon a person's *own* faith, not on anyone else's.

> For God so loved the world that he gave his one and only Son, that whoever believes in Him shall not perish but have eternal life. (John 3:16)

To make a woman's salvation dependent upon her children's faith is contrary to all other Scripture and so this cannot be the correct interpretation.

(3) Women will be saved by means of the child-bearing; (i.e. the birth of Christ).

This interpretation has the merit of being true in itself but it is unlikely that this is what Paul meant here, simply because it is such an ambiguous way of saying it! If this were what he wished to say, he would surely have expressed himself far more clearly.

(4) Women will be saved, even though they must bear children.

To a certain extent this interpretation follows on from the previous verse which refers to Eve's deception and fall. The result of the fall of Eve was that the Lord said:

> I will greatly increase your pains in childbearing; with pain you will give birth to children. (Genesis 3:16)

1 Timothy 2:15 is therefore taken to mean that women can still be saved, spiritually, despite the effects of the fall on her bearing children. However, according to Mary Evans in *Woman in the Bible*, the problem

with this interpretation is that the Greek word *dia,* usually translated *through,* has to be translated *even though,* which is an unnatural meaning for it to take.

(5) Women will be saved completely through the process of bearing children and bringing them up.

In this interpretation the word *save* is used in the same sense as it is in Hebrews 7:25 where it says:

> Therefore He is able to *save completely* those who came to God through Him, because He always lives to intercede for them.

In the *KJV* it is translated as *saved to the uttermost.* It includes not only initial salvation, but also a going on to maturity, which is constantly dependent upon the Lord's present intercession, as indicated in the latter half of the verse.

The idea of being saved here is the same as that in Matthew 16:24-28 where it is not linked with the free gift of eternal life but with reward, indicating again a going on to maturity.

The Greek word for "childbirth" is *teknogonia* and is defined as follows by Bullinger in his *Critical Lexicon and Concordance*:

> The begetting or bearing of children, and so by implication including all the duties of the maternal relation.

Thus this interpretation suggests that a woman may be helped from salvation to Christian maturity by coping with the problems and difficulties she encounters through bearing children and bringing them up in the knowledge of the Lord. This continues the theme of her learning which is mentioned earlier in the chapter:

> A woman should learn in quietness and full submission. (1 Timothy 2:11)

In verse 15 she is to continue this learning process through the practicalities of bringing up her children.

Which interpretation?

In the absence of a more plausible explanation for this verse, I tend to favour the fifth explanation. It still presents problems, but less in my opinion than the other four.

One problem, for instance, is that the verse does not include men. Will not their Christian maturity also be deepened by the experience of fathering children and bringing them up? The obvious answer to that question must be *yes*! However, the fact that this passage does not point this out, does not invalidate its meaning for women.

Also, what about single women? How can they achieve Christian maturity as childbearing cannot be the method for them? The answer to this is that there are many ways by which Christians may deepen their faith and relationship with the Lord and the example given in 1 Timothy 2:15 is only one of them.

Practical application

There are many lessons, both spiritual and practical, which can be learned through having children, and attempting to bring them up in the knowledge and love of the Lord.

First, we learn something of the magnitude of God's love for us. It is humbling to know that, no matter how much we love our children, God's love for us far exceeds that love. Then, through our children, we begin to learn the meaning of showing true, unselfish love. When they are young, they demand our time and attention, giving little in return, and yet we love them regardless, simply because we helped to make them. Our love for our children is unconditional. They do not do anything to earn it. God's love for us is like that, and even more so. There are so many analogies which can be made between the relationship with our own children, and God's relationship with us.

On the practical side, as we deal with the difficulties and heartaches of bringing up children, we can use the experiences to help us grow in the qualities which the Lord desires from mature Christians. We can learn about joy, patience, kindness, gentleness, self-control, selflessness, and gradually learn to put them into practice in our daily lives. These are just some of the fruits of the Spirit mentioned in Galatians 5:22,23 which the Lord would have us display in our Christian lives.

Let us thank the Lord for our children, and learn to love them, and love God, a little more, and a little better, day-by-day.

55. The Lord Jesus, the Apostle Paul, and Women
Sylvia Penny

The Apostle Paul, because of certain comments he made in his letters regarding women and their role, is thought by some to have had a bias against women. What he wrote, however, must be looked at in its context and considered in the light of his overall attitude towards women as exhibited throughout *Acts* and all his letters.

On the other hand, the attitude towards women displayed by the Lord Jesus Christ is seen as being fairly radical at a time when Jewish men hardly spoke to women, let alone discussed or explained the Scriptures to them. Some see Paul as going back from Christ's position to a more orthodox Jewish one, but is this perception a correct one?

It is interesting to compare their attitudes towards women in order to see whether there are any major differences. To do this, the subject matter has been divided into the following sections: faith, teaching, help, widows, family, celibacy, and sexual equality.

Faith

The Apostle Paul

> I have been reminded of your sincere faith, which first lived in your grandmother Lois and in your mother Eunice and, I am persuaded now lives in you also. (2 Timothy 1:5)

The Lord Jesus

> Then Jesus answered, "Woman, you have great faith! Your request is granted." And her daughter was healed from that very hour. (Matthew 15:28)

In 2 Timothy Paul referred to Timothy's faith, and went on to remind him that this was first found in his grandmother and mother. Not only did he know of and recognise their faith, but he felt it important enough to mention in his letter, and to describe it as being sincere.

The Lord, in Matthew 15, was talking to a Canaanite woman, a Gentile. When she displayed her knowledge of scripture to the Lord He commended her for her "great faith', and granted her the healing of her daughter

Both the Lord and Paul recognised faith in these women, and in both cases considered it important enough to mention to others. The Lord did so in front of His disciples, and Paul did so to whoever read his letter.

Teaching

The Apostle Paul

> On the Sabbath we went outside the city gate to the river, where we expected to find a place of prayer. We sat down and began to speak to the women who had gathered there. One of those listening was a woman named Lydia, a dealer in purple cloth from the city of Thyatira, who was a worshipper of God. The Lord opened her heart to respond to Paul's message. When she and the members of her household were baptised, she invited us to her home. "If you consider me a believer in the Lord," she said, "come and stay at my house." And she persuaded us. (Acts 16:13-15)

The Lord Jesus

> As Jesus and his disciples were on their way, he came to a village where a woman named Martha opened her home to him. She had a sister called Mary, who sat at the Lord's feet listening to what he said. But Martha was distracted by all the preparations that had to be made. She came to him and asked, "Lord, don't you care that my sister has left me to do the work by myself? Tell her to help me!" "Martha, Martha," the Lord answered, "you are worried and upset about many things, but only one thing is needed. Mary has chosen what is better, and it will not be taken away from her." (Luke 10:38-41)

Jesus answered, (the Samaritan woman) "Every one who drinks this water will be thirsty again, but whoever drinks the water I give him will never thirst. Indeed, the water I give him will become in him a spring of water welling up to eternal life." The woman said to him, "Sir, give me this water so that I won't get thirsty and have to keep coming here to draw water." (John 4:13-15)

Jesus declared, "Believe me, woman, a time is coming when you will worship the Father neither on this mountain nor in Jerusalem. You Samaritans worship what you do not know; we worship what we do know, for salvation is from the Jews. Yet a time is coming and has now come when the true worshippers will worship the Father in spirit and in truth, for they are the kind of worshippers the Father seeks. God is spirit, and his worshippers must worship in spirit and in truth." The woman said, "I know that Messiah" (called Christ) "is coming. When he comes, he will explain everything to us." Then Jesus declared, "I who speak to you am he." (John 4:21-26)

In Acts 16:9 Paul is recorded as having a vision:

During the night Paul had a vision of a man of Macedonia standing and begging him, "Come over to Macedonia and help us."

So he immediately sailed to Macedonia, and finally arrived at Philippi which was a Roman colony, where he stayed with his companions for a few days.

There must have been no synagogue in Philippi, as Paul went to the river on the Sabbath day to find a place of prayer. He found a group of women there, and so he spoke to them of the gospel, and as a result Lydia and her household were converted.

Paul obviously considered it was worthwhile speaking to a group of women and was not deterred by the fact that there were no men present. Thus, as a direct result of his vision, Paul was moved to spread the gospel to Europe, and his first recorded message was to women, and his first recorded convert was a woman, together with her household. Paul, in this incident, shows not the least inclination towards the orthodox Jewish thinking that it was not worth teaching women spiritual things. His attitude appears to be one of complete impartiality.

His attitude is comparable with that of the Lord, shown in the two instances quoted above. The Lord considered it worthwhile teaching Mary, and told Martha that Mary had chosen a better course of action in listening to Him.

In the second instance, the Lord approached a Samaritan woman, and although it appeared she had neither an intellectual nor a moral inclination to understand His words, the Lord continued to explain some deep spiritual truths to her. Just as Christ was not averse to speaking to a Samaritan woman, Paul was not averse to speaking to a group of women at Philippi. The attitude shown here by both is the same. Neither were over-concerned with the customs of the day, and neither thought it unnecessary or wasteful to spend their time in teaching women.

Help

The Apostle Paul

> I commend to you our sister Phoebe, a servant of the church in Cenchrea. I ask you to receive her in the Lord in a way worthy of the saints and to give her any help she may need from you, for she has been a great help to many people, including me. (Romans 16.1,2)

The Lord Jesus

> After this, Jesus travelled about from one town and village to another, proclaiming the good news of the kingdom of God. The Twelve were with him, and also some women who had been cured of evil spirits and diseases: Mary (called Magdalene) from whom seven demons had come out; Joanna the wife of Chuza, the manager of Herod's household; Susanna; and many others. These women were helping to support them out of their own means. (Luke 8:1-3)

Although it is not altogether clear from the verses in Romans 16 exactly what sort of help Phoebe gave to the people in the church at Cenchrea or to Paul, what is clear is that Paul greatly valued her service and told others so, and commended her to the believers in Rome.

He accepted her help, just as the Lord and His disciples accepted the help of the women who had been cured of evil spirits and diseases.

Both Paul and the Lord were quite happy to let these women help and support them.

Widows

The Apostle Paul

> Give proper recognition to those widows who are really in need. (1 Timothy 5:3)

> No widow may be put on the list of widows unless she is over sixty ... as for younger widows, do not put them on such a list ... I counsel younger widows to marry ... If any woman who is a believer has widows in her family, she should help them and not let the church be burdened with them, so that the church can help those widows who are really in need. (1 Timothy 5:9-16)

The Lord Jesus

> Soon afterwards, Jesus went to a town called Nain, and his disciples and a large crowd went along with him. As he approached the town gate, a dead person was being carried out - the only son of his mother, and she was a widow. And a large crowd from the town was with her. When the Lord saw her, his heart went out to her and he said, "Don't cry." Then he went up and touched the coffin, and those carrying it stood still. He said, "Young man, I say to you, get up!" The dead man sat up and began to talk, and Jesus gave him back to his mother. (Luke 7:11-15)

> When Jesus saw his mother there, (near the cross) and the disciple whom he loved standing near by, he said to his mother, "Dear woman, here is your son," and to the disciple, "Here is your mother." From that time on, this disciple took her into his home. (John 19:26,27)

> As he taught, Jesus said, "Watch out for the teachers of the Law. They like to walk around in flowing robes and be greeted in the market-places, and have the most important seats in the synagogues and the places of honour at banquets. They devour widows' houses

and for a show make lengthy prayers. Such men will be punished most severely." (Mark 12:38-40)

In 1 Timothy 5 Paul is concerned about the needs of the widows, and how they should be looked after. He is very practical in his outlook and said that first and foremost they were the responsibility of their immediate family. However, any widow over sixty who was really in need and who had showed herself to be a true member of the group of believers, was entitled to be put on the list of those to be cared for by the church.

His attitude is one of practical care and concern, rather than one of sentimentality. The resources of the church must have been limited, and Paul's concern was that the most deserving cases should be rewarded with the benefits which the church could afford.

Funds were not to be wasted on undeserving women, or those that would remarry and thus be supported by their new husbands.

The Lord's attitude both to the widow of Nain, and to His own mother was also one of practical care and concern. We are told "his heart went out to" the widow of Nain, and He brought her son back to life

Apart from this widow's grief at her son's death, it was likely that he was also her source of support, and in bringing him back to life the Lord ensured her continued daily provision. In the case of His own mother, while He was dying on the cross, His thoughts were for her, and He was concerned for her provision after His death. So John, the disciple who Jesus loved, was picked by Him to look after her, as if she were his own mother. In this way He provided for her future.

His comments in Mark 12 regarding the "devouring of widow's houses" and the subsequent severe punishment to be expected also indicated His caring attitude towards widows.

Both Paul and the Lord showed a practical care and concern for widows, which was of far more benefit than any sentimental or transitory emotion would have been.

Family

The Apostle Paul

> Children, obey your parents in the Lord, for this is right. "Honour your father and mother" - which is the first commandment with a promise. (Ephesians 6:1,2)

> Children, obey your parents in everything, for this pleases the Lord. (Colossians 3:20)

> If anyone does not provide for his relatives, and especially for his immediate family, he has denied the faith and is worse than an unbeliever. (1 Timothy 5:8)

The Lord Jesus

> "You know the commandments: 'Do not murder, do not commit adultery, do not steal, do not give false testimony, do not defraud, honour your father and mother'" (Mark 10:19: similar in Matthew 19:18,19 and Luke 18:20)

> For God said, "Honour your father and mother" and "Anyone who curses his father or mother must be put to death." (Matthew 15:4; similar in Mark 7:10)

> When Jesus saw his mother there, (at the cross) and the disciple whom he loved standing near by, he said to his mother, "Dear woman, here is your son," and to the disciple, "Here is your mother." From that time on, this disciple took her into his home. (John 19:26,27)

Paul upheld the Old Testament commandment that children should honour their fathers and mothers. He repeats this advice twice, once in Ephesians and once in Colossians. The Lord also upheld this Mosaic law and emphasised its importance.

Paul was also concerned that people should care for their immediate family just as the Lord showed concern for His mother, and provided for her by placing her under the care of John, His disciple.

Thus both Paul and the Lord showed an equal attitude towards family life. Parents were to be honoured and obeyed, and any family member was to be looked after in times of need.

Celibacy

The Apostle Paul

> It is good for a man not to marry. (1 Corinthians 7:1)

> Now to the unmarried and the widows I say: It is good for them to stay unmarried, as I am. (1 Corinthians 7:8)

> Now about virgins: I have no command from the Lord, but give a judgment as one who by the Lord's mercy is trustworthy. Because of the present crisis, I think that it is good for you to remain as you are. Are you married? Do not seek a divorce. Are you unmarried? Do not look for a wife. (1 Corinthians 7:25-27)

> So then, he who marries the virgin does right, but he who does not marry her does even better. (1 Corinthians 7:38)

> A woman is bound to her husband as long as he lives. But if her husband dies, she is free to marry anyone she wishes, but he must belong to the Lord. In my judgment, she is happier if she stays as she is - and I think that I too have the Spirit of God. (1 Corinthians 7:39-40)

The Lord Jesus

> The disciples said to him, "If this is the situation between a husband and wife, it is better not to marry." Jesus replied, "Not everyone can accept this word, but only those to whom it has been given. For some are eunuchs because they were born that way; others were made that way by men; and others have renounced marriage because of the kingdom of heaven. The one who can accept this should accept it." (Matthew 19:10-12)

The verses quoted from 1 Corinthians 7 above have been picked out as the main ones which seem to indicate that Paul considered celibacy preferable to marriage. However, when referring to this subject, he stated that it was good to remain unmarried, but he only said that this was preferable to the married state "because of the present crisis." In 1 Corinthians 7:29 he said that "the time is short" and as it was possible that the last days with the great tribulation could have happened at that time, his advice was to be understood in that context. His suggestion that celibacy was a good state to maintain and his preference for that state for all believers was limited to that particular point in time. In fact, he expressly advised younger widows to go out and get married in 1 Timothy 5:14, as by then "the present crisis" had passed.

His attitude towards celibacy is comparable with that shown by the Lord in the quotation given above. The Lord recognised that not everyone could remain in this state, but those that could accept it should do so "because of the kingdom of heaven". The Lord agrees with Paul's attitude that celibacy was a good state to maintain, indeed He Himself was celibate, but this was to be understood in the context of the situation at that particular time.

Sexual Equality

The Apostle Paul

> The husband should fulfil his marital duty to his wife, and likewise the wife to her husband. The wife's body does not belong to her alone but also to her husband. In the same way, the husband's body does not belong to him alone but also to his wife. Do not deprive each other except by mutual consent and for a time, so that you may devote yourselves to prayer. Then come together again so that Satan will not tempt you because of your lack of selfcontrol. (1 Corinthians 7:3-5)

The Lord Jesus

> The teachers of the law and the Pharisees brought in a woman caught in adultery. They made her stand before the group and said to Jesus, "Teacher, this woman was caught in the act of adultery. In the

Law Moses commanded us to stone such women. Now what do you say?" . . . (Jesus) said to them, "If any one of you is without sin, let him be the first to throw a stone at her" . . . Jesus straightened up and asked her, "Woman, where are they? Has no-one condemned you?" "No-one, sir," she said. "Then neither do I condemn you," Jesus declared. "Go now and leave your life of sin." (John 8:3-11)

Although these two passages relate to very different circumstances, the attitude of both Paul and the Lord towards the equality there should be in sexual matters was the same. The Lord dealt with a point laid down in the Law of Moses concerning adultery, whereas Paul dealt with sexual relations within marriage and did not refer to the law of Moses. Paul's concern was that both husband and wife were to give and receive equally within their relationship. The man was to have no advantage or superiority over his wife in sexual matters.

In the case of the adulterous woman, the Lord was concerned that the man had not been brought to him for stoning also. Due to the unfair advantages men had in their society, the teachers of the law and the Pharisees had not brought him to the Lord, despite the fact they had been "caught in the act', but had probably let him go for a price. According to the law, both should have been stoned for adultery. However, the Lord was concerned that men should not have such an unfair advantage over women. And would not have the penalty carried out on only one of the guilty parties. He therefore let her go, after telling her to leave her life of sin, thus giving her equal treatment with the man.

Other passages

There are several other passages in the New Testament where Paul gives advice to and comments upon women and which indicate further his attitude towards them, but they touch on subjects upon which the Lord remained silent or where His advice has not been recorded for us in the Scriptures. These, therefore, have not been included here.

They relate to various subjects such as the role of women in general, their role as wives in particular, their dress and conduct. There are also a number of references where he expresses gratitude for the work of various women.

However, from the seven subjects we have considered - faith, teaching, help, widows, family, celibacy, sexual equality - it is clear that there is little difference, if any, between the attitudes towards women by the Lord Jesus Christ and the Apostle Paul.

The Lord's words, behaviour and actions towards women were quite often matched by Paul and there are no clear or obvious differences between them. Paul was very much in harmony with his Saviour in praising the faith of women, teaching women, accepting their help, caring about widows. His teaching concerning their role in the family, the place of celibacy and of sexual equality for them mirrors that of the Lord Jesus and shows the truth of Paul's words in 1 Corinthians 11:1, "Follow my example, as I follow the example of Christ."

56. *Head coverings and long hair*
Sylvia Penny

"I praise you for remembering me in everything and for holding to the teachings, just as I passed them on to you. Now I want you to realise that the head of every man is Christ, and the head of the woman is man, and the head of Christ is God.

Every man who prays or prophesies with his head covered dishonours his head. And every woman who prays or prophesies with her head uncovered dishonours her head - it is just as though her head were shaved. If a woman does not cover her head, she should have her hair cut off; and if it is a disgrace for a woman to have her hair cut or shaved off, she should cover her head. A man ought not to cover his head, since he is the image and glory of God; but the woman is the glory of man. For man did not come from woman, but woman from man; neither was man created for woman, but woman for man. For this reason, and because of the angels, the woman ought to have a sign of authority on her head. In the Lord, however, woman is not independent of man, nor is man independent of woman.

But everything comes from God. Judge for yourselves: Is it proper for a woman to pray with her head uncovered? Does not the very nature of things teach you that if a man has long hair, it is a disgrace to him, but if a woman has long hair, it is her glory? For long hair is given to her as a covering. If anyone wants to be contentious about this, we have no other practice - nor do the churches of God." (1 Corinthians 11:2-16)

To whom are these verses addressed?

This is the only passage in the Bible which tells us that women should cover their heads and have long hair. We need, therefore, to ascertain whether Jews or Gentiles, or both, are addressed in these verse.

Many of the believers in the Church at Corinth would have been Gentiles, but there would also have been a large Jewish section. In Corinthians, Paul sometimes addressed both groups together, but at other times addressed them separately.

1 Corinthians 10:1 refers to "our forefathers" and being "baptised into Moses", both of which are Jewish terms. However, 12:2 addresses different people by saying "when you were pagans" and "led astray to mute idols", indicating the Gentiles in the church were now in the writer's mind.

Chapters 10 and 11, then, appear to form a particularly Jewish section and if it is assumed that Jewish men and women are the subject of this passage, it is easier to understand why Paul was so insistent that these outward signs should be adhered to.

The Jewish nation was used to signs and symbols, outward tokens with a spiritual meaning, and the Jews at Corinth would be no exception. Gentiles, on the other hand, were not used to such symbols and their significance would be lost upon them. Thus it is most unlikely that Paul was enforcing new rules upon Gentile men and women.

However, with part of the congregation being Jewish, it was necessary for him to reaffirm among them the accepted customs, as they may have felt they no longer needed to observe them as the Gentiles did not have to.

Was the head covering a veil?

What, exactly, is meant by covering the head? Many suggestions have been made by various commentators and it is difficult to choose between them. The most obvious one is that it refers to the oriental veil worn by Jewish women at that time. However, it was also the custom for married Jewish men to wear a *tallith* or veil over their heads, as a sign of their guilt and condemnation. Therefore if veiling were meant, Paul appears to uphold one Jewish custom (by requiring women to veil themselves) but disregard another (by requiring men not to veil themselves).

Also, although most agree this passage is ambiguous as to whether it refers to a physical veil or not, Paul is clear in 2 Corinthians 3:12-18 when he refers to physical veils. If the veiling of women and the unveiling of men was so important, then it is strange that the teaching is not expressed as clearly in this passage.

Another objection to this view is that in both 1 Timothy 2:9 and 1 Peter 3:3, women are exhorted not to wear braided hair. If women were to be veiled, then the style of hair beneath the veil would seem to be irrelevant. Therefore, it seems unlikely that Paul was referring to the custom of veiling.

Was the head covering the length or style of hair?

Some suggest that the answer lies in verse 15 which states that "long hair is given to her as a covering". Thus the covering is having long hair and does not refer to a material veil.

Another variation on this is that Paul was referring to hair styles. Men should have short hair, not arranged in effeminate styles, and women should have long hair and wear it in a feminine way. In either case it is the actual hair which is referred to, rather than a physical covering. However, this is not obvious from the text.

If it is accepted that the covering refers to the length and style of hair, it is still difficult to understand verses 4 and 5, which refer to a man dishonouring his head if he prays or prophesies with his head covered, and to a woman dishonouring her head if she prays or prophesies without her head covered. This, wrote Paul, is just as bad as if she were shorn, which in that society was a punishment for a prostitute.

Is the head figurative or literal?

The head can be understood either figuratively, as in verse 3, or literally. If figuratively, it is difficult to see how a man dishonours the Lord by "covering" his head; or how a woman dishonours her husband by "uncovering" her head, especially if the covering does not mean veiling.

If the covering were a veil, it might be possible to say that a man should no longer wear his *tallith* as it signified guilt and condemnation which, for the Christian, had been removed by Christ's death on the cross. Thus if a man continued to wear his tallith it could be interpreted as dishonouring to the Lord.

Similarly, if a woman did not wear her veil, which signified her submission to her husband, then this may be interpreted as dishonouring him.

However, if the head is understood literally, then possibly either a man or a woman could be said to dishonour themselves by dressing their hair in an effeminate manner (for a man) or cropping it short (for a woman).

What does the "sign of authority" refer to and who are "the angels"?

The remaining problem with this passage is in verses 8-10:

> For man did not come from woman, but woman from man; neither was man created for woman, but woman for man. For this reason, and because of the angels, the woman ought to have a sign of authority on her head.'

Ronald Knox says on this verse:

> The word translated "authority" may mean authority or power to do things, or (commonly in this epistle) liberty of choice. If we understand that the wife ought to wear on her head a symbol of her husband's authority over her, we satisfy the sense, but give a very strained interpretation of the Greek. If we understand that the wife has power over her own head, liberty to dispose it as she likes, the Greek is satisfied, but the whole sense of the context is ignored.

One interpretation of verses 8 to 10

Whichever interpretation we wish to accept for this verse, there are difficulties. The majority of commentators say that the husband's authority is referred to here, and that this is symbolised by his wife wearing a veil on her head. The *RSV* even translates this verse "That is why a woman ought to have a veil on her head," interpreting the Greek for "authority" as being a veil.

However, why should she wear a veil "because of the angels?" One possible explanation of this recognises that Corinthians was written at a time when the nation of Israel was being called to repent and if they had done so the Lord would have returned (Acts 3:19-20), but the days leading up to that return hold many dangers.

At certain times in the past angels have visited the earth and have formed relationships with women resulting in children. For example, see Genesis 6:1-5 where we read of the sons of God who saw the daughters of men and married any of them they chose. The result was the

Nephilim, men of renown, who filled the earth with wickedness and evil.

The parable of the weeds (Matthew 13:24-30 and explained in verses 36-43) deals with a time just prior to Christ's return and has the good seed, sown by man, and weeds, sown by an enemy. Both the good seed and the weeds are allowed to "grow together until the harvest." If the Jewish nation had repented in the years following Christ's ascension, then before the Lord returned the unfulfilled prophecies relating to the last days would have taken place. These include the weeds sown by an enemy or, as Matthew 13:38 puts it, "sons of the evil one" which are to be sown into the nation of Israel, "the sons of the kingdom". This could come about as it did in the days of Noah, with angels taking women in marriage.

Therefore in Corinthians, Paul may be suggesting that if a Jewish woman was veiled, showing she was under the authority of her husband, this would ensure her protection from being influenced by such angels. Although this may sound far-fetched to some today, it has to be remembered that the Jews accepted, and were used to, such signs for protection. Hundreds of years earlier, their firstborn had been protected from slaughter by painting the blood of a sacrificed lamb on the door-posts and lintels as a sign (Exodus 12:21-23).

However, at the end of Acts the nation of Israel had become blind and deaf (Acts 28:26-27) and Christ's return ceased to be near, the possibility of the end times also lapsed, as did the danger to women from such angels. Thus the need to wear the veil for protection was no longer valid.

Tertullian, a Christian theologian who lived in the second century, considered this to be the correct explanation of this verse, although few modern scholars would agree.

Another interpretation of verses 8 to 10

As we have seen above, it is uncertain if veils are being referred to in verses 8-10 and as none of the surrounding verses refer to veils, then it is unlikely that verse 10 does, for as Knox said, this gives a strained interpretation of the Greek.

Being literal then, this verse states that a woman should exhibit a sign of her own authority because of the angels. However, this is as equally difficult to understand, although it does make sense of verse 11, which says "However, woman is not independent of man". This appears to qualify the statement of verse 10 that she is able to exert her own authority.

However, the way in which she should give a sign of her authority is not made clear, except that it has something to do with her head. Perhaps the answer lies in the suggestion that the covering refers to a woman's hair, that it should remain long, and be arranged in a feminine way and that only if she complied with this should she pray and prophesy in public. That is, her authority to pray and prophesy in public would depend upon her doing so in accordance with Paul's instruction. Thus the authority referred to in this verse is that which allows her to pray and prophesy in public which, after all, seems to be the main reason why Paul included this passage in his letter.

An alternative understanding of the phrase "because of the angels", and one upon which most commentators are agreed, is that the angels referred to are those who are present at public worship and who expect it to be carried out decently and in order. In 1 Timothy 5:21 Paul refers to these angels: "I charge you, in the sight of God and Christ Jesus and the elect angels, to keep these instructions without partiality, and to do nothing out of favouritism."

This would indicate that certain angels were watching how believers conducted themselves. Perhaps, then, this passage means that women had to indicate to the angels their authority to pray and prophesy in public by wearing their hair in the correct way. Again, this explanation seems hard to accept as the true interpretation, but the importance of signs, symbols and the manner of dress adopted by Jews in public worship at that time has to be kept in mind.

Conclusion

Having considered the various interpretations of these verses, it is important to realise that this is the only passage in the New Testament which deals with the subject, and that this passage is ambiguous. It is therefore unwise to base any major doctrine or make any binding application to people today, as both could turn out to be wrong.

Additionally, as we have seen, the passage is peculiarly Jewish and addressed to that section of the Corinthian church. To apply the conditions set out there to Gentiles today would seem to be very unwise, especially as we cannot be sure exactly what those conditions were.

57. "I do not permit a woman to teach"
Sylvia Penny

In Christian circles there are many different opinions as to whether women should be allowed to teach others. They vary from not allowing women to speak at all, allowing them to teach children or a group of other women, to allowing them to teach and speak to a full congregation of men and women.

Should women remain silent at all times?

1 Corinthians 14:33-36 appears to teach that women should never speak in any meetings of the church:

> For God is not a God of disorder but of peace. As in all the congregations of the saints, women should remain silent in the churches. They are not allowed to speak, but must be in submission, as the Law says. If they want to inquire about something, they should ask their own husbands at home; for it is disgraceful for a woman to speak in the church. Did the word of God originate with you? Or are you the only people it has reached?

However, an interpretation which insists that women remain silent at all times would be in direct contradiction to 1 Corinthians 11:5 where Paul referred to women both praying and prophesying in public meetings. Therefore, there must be another explanation of the above passage.

Some suggest that these verses are not Paul's own opinion, but that he is quoting the Corinthians' own views. He then follows it up with a sharp rebuke, saying, "Did the word of God originate with you? Or are you the only people it has reached?" In other words, Paul strongly disagrees with them, as he has already shown in 11:5.

In *Woman in the Bible*, Mary Evans confirms that "The transposition of verses 34-35 in the Western texts shows that they were linked together and makes feasible the possibility that they are a separate quote." Paul does on other occasions quote from the Corinthians' own views and then follows it up by condemning them; see 1 Corinthians 6:12-13; 10:23.

However, if 1 Corinthians 14:34-35 is a quotation, it is certainly the longest one Paul uses. Also, if this explanation is correct, it seems strange that the passage has been consistently misunderstood from very early Christian times.

Women should remain silent sometimes

A more popular view is that this is Paul's own advice, but that the exhortation to remain silent and not speak was limited in its scope.

In order not to contradict 1 Corinthians 11:5, it must at least allow for praying and prophesying by women. It appears quite possible that what was meant in chapter 14 was that wives should not call out questions to their husbands in a public meeting. Rather they should wait until they were at home and ask them in private.

Verse 35 is then taken as a further explanation of the sort of silence Paul refers to in verse 34. A wife should submit to her husband and it would be disgraceful for her to question her husband in public. J. Keir Howard has the following to say on this passage:

> The implication is that during the formal teaching session of the church, probably conducted in the form of orderly discussion and argument, the women were interrupting noisily. Consequently they are told to be silent (*sigao*). The whole statement itself is unusual. There is no mention of unmarried women or widows, indicating that only one group of women is in view, namely certain wives who were apparently publicly arguing with their husbands over matters of teaching and interpretation. If there were points that were unclear or matters of disagreement then the proper course of action was for them to ask their husbands at home rather than disrupt the proceedings of the congregation. The fact that such a course of action was unavailable to single women or widows indicates the limited applicability of this statement

The Student's Commentary states that "Women in the East at that time, as still today disturbed the congregation by conversing among themselves or by asking questions."

Women should not chatter through services

The word used for "speak" in these verses is *laleo* which the *Companion Bible* (Appendix 121.7)defines as meaning "to talk or to use the voice, without reference to the words spoken." It is therefore possible that Paul was condemning the women for chattering to each other through the services, as well as calling out questions. This would have been against the Lord's wishes, as He is "not a God of disorder but of peace".

Whichever explanation of 1 Corinthians 14:33-36 is accepted, it is clear that these verses cannot support the view that women should never take an active part in a meeting of believers, nor that they should be condemned unconditionally to keeping completely silent.

Women should learn in quietness

The only other passage in the New Testament which refers to a woman keeping silent is 1 Timothy 2:11-14:

> A woman should learn in quietness and full submission. I do not permit a woman to teach or have authority over a man; she must be silent. For Adam was formed first, then Eve. And Adam was not the one deceived; it was the woman who was deceived and became a sinner.

The *Companion Bible* notes on the word "woman" that "the whole context shows that wives are in the apostle's mind". This is clear from references to submission, to Adam and Eve, and, in verse 15, to the bearing of children. Mary Evans, on verse 11, says:

> There is certainly no indication here that there is a particular submission required from all women to all men, other than that which is generally required from every Christian to every other.

The "quietness" required here refers to when a woman is learning, and is a sensible piece of advice so that maximum benefit can be obtained from the teaching being given. It does not restrict the woman to silence at all times, but indicates the manner in which it is best for her to learn. The fact that Paul emphasises she should learn at all was fairly radical at that time. In the Jewish community it was not considered worthwhile to teach women anything regarding the Law or the Scriptures.

Should women teach others?

1 Timothy 2:12 then says, "I do not permit a woman to teach or to have authority over a man; she must be silent." Some people take this to be the absolute prohibition of any woman ever teaching any man for all time. However, it must be borne in mind that this is the only verse in the whole of Scripture which seems to suggest this. As such, care should be taken to ensure that this view is in harmony with other scriptural principles.

Acts 18:26 refers to Priscilla and Aquila who together instructed Apollos in their own home:

> He (Apollos) began to speak boldly in the synagogue. When Priscilla and Aquila heard him, they invited him to their home and explained to him the way of God more adequately.

Here is an example of a woman, together with her husband, teaching a man who was a capable speaker in his own right. Paul obviously thinks highly of both her and her husband and greets them at the end of his letter to the Romans (16:3-4). There is no condemnation of this woman who he calls in Romans 16:3 "my fellow-worker in Christ Jesus". She played her role in teaching a man "the way of God more adequately" (Acts 18:26). Therefore, it seems that 1 Timothy 2:12 cannot be taken as a complete prohibition of women ever teaching men.

Don Williams, in *The Apostle Paul and Women in the Church*, refers to this verse and says:

> In the Greek it is a present active indicative verb which can be translated "I am not presently permitting a woman to teach or to have authority over men . . ." This in contrast to the extremists demanding full women's liberation in Ephesus. Paul prohibits the teaching of those not properly instructed.

The suggestion made here is that because of the tense of the verb used in the Greek, Paul was only prohibiting the women of that particular time and place and he did not intend it to be taken as a timeless prohibition.

1 Timothy 1:7 refers to a group of people who were teaching others erroneously: "They want to be teachers of the law, but they do not know what they are talking about or what they so confidently affirm." It is possible that some of the women at Ephesus formed part of the group referred to here and, because of this, Paul included his exhortation in 1 Timothy 2:12.

A wife should not teach her own husband

However, returning to the note in The Companion Bible which suggests that the whole context of this passage shows that wives and husbands are in mind: it is possible that this verse merely prohibits a wife from teaching her own husband. The singular form of both "woman" and "man" is used which suggests that this may be so, for the words can equally well be translated "wife" and "husband". This appears quite likely when the context is taken into consideration. The previous verse refers to submission which is due by a wife to her husband. The following verse refers to Adam and Eve, the first example of a husband and wife in Scripture.

The analogy which Paul uses here may imply that wives should not presume to teach their husbands in public, especially if they, like Eve, had misunderstood or misinterpreted God's word as a result of being deceived.

This Interpretation of 1 Timothy 2:12 is in accordance with Peter's advice in 1 Peter 3:1-2:

> Wives, in the same way be submissive to your husbands so that, if any of them do not believe the word, they may be won over without words by the behaviour of their wives, when they see the purity and reverence of your lives.

Here Peter suggests that the practical outworking of a believing wife's Christianity would be more effective in converting her husband than any amount of teaching. In both passages the attitude of submission is important, whereas talking and teaching is advised against.

A wife should not domineer her husband, or teach others to do so

A last suggestion as to the meaning of 1 Timothy 2:12 is given in *The Students Commentary*: "What God says here is that a wife is not to govern her husband nor to teach other women to govern their husbands." This, again, agrees with the view that husbands and wives are being referred to, and that the teaching merely refers to women attempting to domineer their husbands and telling others to do likewise. Don Williams states that "The meaning of the infinitive "to have authority" is literally "to domineer"", so 1 Timothy 2:12 could be paraphrased. "I do not permit a wife to domineer over her husband, or to teach others to do so." This explanation fits in very well with the context, which is nothing to do with teaching, but deals with the attitude which a woman should adopt towards her own husband.

The example of Adam and Eve

The understanding of the example of Adam and Eve given in 1 Timothy 2:13,14 depends upon which interpretation of verse 12 is favoured.

(1) Those who prefer the explanation that women should never teach men under any circumstances, feel that the example of Adam and Eve is given to show that, as it was a woman who was deceived and not a man, it is sensible that women should never be allowed to teach men. They say that this verse is used by Paul to illustrate that women, by nature, are more easily deceived than men. However this is questionable as Paul uses the same analogy in 2 Corinthians 11:3 where both male and female believers are likened to Eve in their liability to deception:

> But I am afraid that just as Eve was deceived by the serpent's cunning, your minds may somehow be led astray from your sincere and pure devotion to Christ.

Paul was well aware that both men and women are capable of being deceived and was not averse to likening either sex to Eve where necessary. However, generally Adam and Eve are examples of the husband and wife situation, not of men and women (Matthew 19:3-9).

Also, if it were true that women are more easily deceived than men and so more likely to teach error, then not only should the prohibition have applied to women teaching men, it should have included teaching other women and children, which it did not. Children are far less likely to be able to detect error in the teaching of a woman than a man would be. If this was what Paul had in mind, he would have been more concerned about preventing women from teaching children, rather than from teaching men who, are capable of thinking and questioning for themselves.

(2) If 1 Timothy 2:12 was intended to prohibit only certain groups of women at Ephesus at that time, then the analogy used by Paul may be between the deception of Eve and the deception of these particular women. Neither should presume to teach when in such a condition. Just as Eve had been deceived by Satan, these women may have been deceived by "certain men" (1 Timothy 1:3-4).

(3) If 1 Timothy 2:12 refers to husband and wife, then the meaning of the next two verses has already been considered above.

(4) Lastly, if it refers to women domineering their husbands, then Paul uses the example of Adam and Eve to show that she has no grounds to claim any superiority over her husband.

Conclusions

Based on the discussion above, it seems there is no good scriptural basis for excluding women from teaching others about the Scriptures. Priscilla is a good example of a woman who successfully helped to teach a man, and women clearly prayed and prophesied in meetings.

However, women were told not to chatter during meetings, and certain wives in the Corinthian church were also told that if they had any questions, they were to ask their husbands privately at home. As a general rule, it also seems that women were not to teach their own husbands. If their husbands did not believe, they were to be won over by their wives' pure and reverent behaviour, and not by their teaching or talking (1 Peter 3:1,2).

Part 8
Bible Background

58. *Jewish Women in the First Century*
Sylvia Penny

When we begin to read the Bible, we have little knowledge of its background and of the societies about which we are reading. We understand little about the customs, the culture, and the accepted norms. In order to bring the people to life we need to know a little about their society and this will also enable us to read the Bible more meaningfully and understand it better.

One problem is that the Scriptures span thousands of years and a variety of cultures, but to us the New Testament is the most important part. And perhaps it would be most helpful to concentrate on how women were regarded during this period.

There were two very distinct societies at that time which had completely different customs and lifestyles. The ways in which they conducted their business and their domestic affairs also contrasted greatly. One society was that of the Jews who were governed by the Torah and the teachings of the Rabbis. The other was the Gentile world, dominated by Greek and Roman influences, and even the customs of the Greeks and the Romans differed slightly and formed two separate sub-cultures in the non-Jewish world.

Looking at women in the New Testament, then, requires us to have some knowledge of these three groups. In this article we will look at Jewish women, and in the next one we will look at Greek and Roman women.

Jewish women and men

In general it was accepted that women were second-class citizens, that they were inferior to men, and consequently they had a very low status in society. Various rabbinical sayings at that time showed that women were almost despised; e.g. "Happy is he whose children are males and woe to him whose children are females" and "He who teaches his daughter the law, teaches her extravagance." Women were also restricted in public life, education and religious gatherings. They were not permitted to take part in public affairs and Jewish schools were open only to boys and men. It was considered irrelevant and unnecessary to teach girls and women, apart from the finer arts of spinning, cooking and other household duties.

As can be seen from the rabbinical sayings quoted above, it was considered an extravagance to teach a daughter the Law. A woman was considered to be frivolous and undiscerning by nature and unable to learn anything.

Women and Slaves

A woman in Judaism was considered to be more of a possession than a person. In fact a wife was considered essentially to be her husband's property, rather than a person who had her own rights and opinions.

Repeatedly in the writings of that time, women were linked with children and slaves, the acquisition of a wife being compared to the acquisition of a Gentile slave. In the law courts, a woman's testimony bore little weight and where a woman's evidence was acceptable so, too, was that of a Gentile slave.

The wife's duties were to do the household tasks and to wash her husband's feet, a task even the slaves could not be compelled to do. This shows what an incredible act of condescension it was when the Lord Jesus stooped to wash the feet of each disciple in turn. What great humility!

Women and Mothers

So, in Jewish society, the wife was totally dominated and controlled by her husband's will. She had few rights, if any, and was not valued as a person. If valued at all, it was solely in her capacity for bearing children, particularly male children. In some cases women were valued by their husbands for being both a wife and a mother. Society had a high regard for marriage as an institution, but possibly only in the light of a woman's capabilities of producing a male heir.

The sect of the Essenes went as far as to suggest that women were totally irrelevant apart from procreation. They emphatically protested against the practice of polygamy in the Damascus Document, which suggests that polygamy may have been fairly widespread at the time. However, it was probably only the richer members of the Jewish community who could afford to indulge in this practice.

Failure to produce children could be cited as a reason for divorce and men could obtain a divorce from their wives for trifling reasons. On the other hand it was impossible for a woman to divorce her husband, as legally she was his property.

Restrictions on women

In Palestine, and especially in the towns, women were kept in seclusion as much as possible. In the country it was more lax as it was necessary for women to go to the wells and help their husbands at work on the land. To that extent they had more freedom of movement.

In the towns women were, as a rule, confined to their homes and the society of other women and children as far as possible. If they ventured out they were not expected to speak to anyone in the street. It was certainly not proper for a man to address a woman who was a stranger to him and, in this respect, this makes the incident of the Lord Jesus speaking to the woman at the well even more unusual. No wonder the disciples were surprised when they returned to find him talking to her.

As far as religious life was concerned, women were severely limited. They were permitted to enter the Temple at Jerusalem only as far as *The Court of Women and Gentiles* and were not allowed to go any further. They appear to have been treated as second-class citizens.

Where there was a quorum of three or more women present, one of them was allowed to say grace at a meal table, but if only one man were there, he was the one to take precedence.

Women did not count in the quorum of ten needed to hold a synagogue service. If there were not the appropriate number of men present, then the service would not be held.

To sum up

So in all spheres of life, Jewish women were totally dominated by their men and they had few, if any rights of their own. Women living in the country, however, had more freedom than those dwelling in towns. The one redeeming feature of all women appeared to be their capacity for bearing male heirs to their husbands.

Understanding the background of the life of Jewish women in New Testament times may help us to appreciate a little more the significance of what is being said or done when we read the Scriptures. We can also appreciate more the impact which Christ's teachings and actions had on such a male orientated society.

59. Greek and Roman Women in the First Century
Sylvia Penny

There were two very different societies during New Testament times, which had completely different customs and lifestyles. One was that of the Jews, which we looked at in the previous article, and the other was that of the Gentile world, dominated by Greek and Roman influences. In this article we will look at the Gentile society, and see that even the customs of the Greeks and Romans within it differed from one another.

Greek Society

In Greek society women had a higher status than in Judaism, but they were still considered to be inferior to men. The Greek philosophers affirmed equality between the sexes in principle, but this ideal was seldom seen in practice except with the Epicureans, who were a small group.

There was less polygamy than amongst the Jews and a good wife had the rule of her husband's household. The laws on divorce were more equitable in that either could divorce the other. Maybe as a result, divorce was more common in Greek society. When a couple divorced it was necessary to divide the property equally between the husband and the wife. It was accepted that a woman had a right to own things and to hold property.

It was not the custom for Greek women to wear veils, nor were they restricted in business or confined to the home. They were allowed to organise their own businesses and, if capable, they could attain influential roles in society. Therefore, on the whole, they had far more freedom than Jewish women and were considered to be people in their own right, rather than being little more than a slave.

Hand in hand with this more relaxed attitude went a greater degree of moral laxity. There was little regard for sexual purity, and there was widespread prostitution, homosexuality and sexual immorality. Whether this was a result of the greater freedom given to women or just an unrelated phenomenon is not clear. It seems unlikely to be related, as

Roman society gave an even higher status to women yet they considered sexual purity a virtue, something to be sought after.

Roman Society

In Roman society women enjoyed an even higher status than in Greece. Men and women were virtually on an equality with one another, and although a woman was under the authority of her own husband she was none-the-less treated with dignity and had freedom.

The Roman view of marriage was higher than that of the Greeks and sexual purity was considered to be a virtue and something worth maintaining. The Romans were also strictly monogamous and their divorce laws were similar to the Greeks; either the husband or the wife could instigate divorce proceedings.

There was increasing emancipation for women in the first century under Rome. They could become involved in such areas as politics, organisation of town life and even the administration of provinces. However, after the first century there began a gradual moral decline in the Roman Empire and in its later years divorce became so common that it was said that women counted the years by their husbands rather than by consuls.

Like Greek women, it was not necessary for Roman women to be veiled and they could move freely in public to meet and converse with men if they so wished. Roman women were also educated as it was not considered an extravagance to do so.

Conclusion

From this brief look at the different societies of New Testament times it is obvious that there were considerable differences in the ways the Jewish and Gentile women were regarded and treated.

Certainly the Jewish women living in Jerusalem and the towns of Palestine were very subordinate and had little freedom, although those in the country had more.

It is not easy to ascertain what life was like for the Jewish women living in the dispersed Jewish communities which were scattered around the eastern half of the Roman Empire. No doubt many of them and their families had been influenced by either the Roman or Greek culture in which they lived and thus their relationship with their husbands would be very different from those resident in the land.

For example, Aquila and Priscilla in Acts 18:2,18,26 seem to act as a pair on almost equal terms, perhaps reflecting the Roman society from which they came. When we come to various passages in the New Testament, we need to consider who is being addressed and to take into account the background of the people. If we do this we may appreciate a little more the significance of what is being said or done.

60. *A Woman's Uncleanness*
Sylvia Penny

Genesis 1:28 says: "God blessed them (men and women) and said to them, 'Be fruitful and increase in number.'" Originally the ability to reproduce was a blessing from God, with no strings attached. However, the fall of Genesis 3 changed all that for ever. Subsequently, everything to do with a woman's reproductive cycle is marked out as "unclean".

The Curse

God delivered three curses - one each to Satan, the woman, and Adam. Genesis 3:16; "To the woman he said, 'I will greatly increase your pains in childbearing; with pain you will give birth to children.'" The gift of reproduction remained, but after the fall it was to be for evermore a painful experience for all women. One wonders what things would have been like if Adam and Eve had never succumbed to the temptation.

Childbirth

Not only do women suffer from what is quite often the worst pain in their lives at childbirth, but also many suffer from regular monthly pains and mood swings, not to mention the many problems experienced both at puberty and menopause. Could all of this also have resulted from the fall? Surely God did not originally intend women to suffer in this way when He created them.

Childbirth is often used as a simile to indicate excessive pain, for example in Isaiah 42:14 "But now, like a woman in childbirth, I cry out, I gasp and pant." Such pain, many times in the past, led to death:

> Rachel began to give birth and had great difficulty. And as she was having great difficulty in childbirth, the midwife said to her, "Don't be afraid, for you have another son." As she breathed her last - for she was dying - she named her son Ben-Oni. But his father named him Benjamin. (Genesis 35:16-18)

However, despite knowing all this, the vast majority of women throughout history have always considered having children a blessing, such is the maternal instinct placed deep within.

Uncleanness after childbirth

Not only is pain and inconvenience associated with the whole process, but also Jewish women under the Law were rendered ceremonially unclean for long periods of time. Leviticus, one of the main books in the Old Testament to give us the details of the Jewish law, sets out exactly when a woman was to be considered unclean after she had given birth.

Leviticus 12:1-8 tells how a woman was to be "purified from her bleeding." Interestingly she was unclean for twice the length of time if she gave birth to a daughter, rather than to a son. For a son she had to wait forty days, but for a daughter it was eighty! There is no reason given for this disparity, and it seems unlikely it was for purely physical or biological reasons, as the actual flow of blood usually stops after thirty days or so, regardless of the sex of the baby.

The period of forty (or eighty) days was divided into two distinct periods. Firstly a woman was ceremonially unclean for seven (or fourteen) days after the birth, so that she would be separate from her husband, family and friends. Those that had to attend to her would also be ceremonially unclean during that period. The following thirty-three (or sixty-six) days she was regarded as unclean in respect of performance of religious duties. This meant she would be separated from the sanctuary, forbidden to eat the Passover or peace-offerings, and excluded from any other such religious occasions.

Matthew Henry notes on this passage:

> The exclusion of the woman for so many days from the sanctuary, and all participation of holy things, signified that our initial corruption would have excluded us for ever from the enjoyment of God and his favours if he had not graciously provided for our purifying.

A well-known example of this law being carried out is given in Luke 2:21-23 where Mary and Joseph waited until her time of purification was over before they went to Jerusalem to offer a sacrifice.

Uncleanness during and after a period

A woman was also rendered unclean during her monthly period, and for seven days afterwards. Anyone who touched her, laid on her bed, or touched anything she sat on, would also be rendered unclean until that evening, and would also have to bathe in water (Leviticus 15:19-30). There is an interesting verse in Genesis 31:35:

> Rachel said to her father, "Don't be angry, my lord, that I cannot stand up in your presence; I'm having my period."

This little family scene took place hundreds of years before the law was given to Moses as detailed in Leviticus, and yet it appears some rudiments of the same custom existed even then. Jacob, Rachel's father, was searching for his household gods, and she had hidden them, and sat on them. It seems that, even then, a woman had to be separate during her monthly period, and that whatever she sat upon was not to be touched by anyone else.

A later example of this law being carried out is in 2 Samuel 11:4. David sent for Bathsheba and slept with her, but in parentheses it is noted that "she had purified herself from her uncleanness." She was bathing herself when David first saw her from the roof, and perhaps this was part of her purification ritual. It seems rather ironic that the niceties of the ceremonial law were complied with, and yet two of the most important moral laws were broken, when David indulged first in adultery and then in murder.

Effect on sexual relations

The practical effect of this law would seem to be that a husband and wife would have to remain separate for two weeks out of every four, due to the wife's uncleanness. Leviticus 18:19 and 20:18 both prohibit sexual relations during the "uncleanness of her monthly period", and Leviticus 15:24 says that if such relations did take place the man would be unclean for seven days afterwards in exactly the same way as the woman. Ezekiel 18:6 refers to a righteous man who does not "lie with a woman during her period".

However, this may not have necessarily been as prohibitive as it seems at first sight. As we have already seen, bearing children was considered a great blessing and the women usually had large families. Bearing in mind that breast-feeding often suppresses periods, many women may not have had many periods at all throughout their child-bearing years. Therefore the only time they would have been unclean would be just after the birth of each child.

Uncleanness at other times

The verses in Leviticus 15:19-30 refer to a further time of uncleanness for women. Verse 25 says:

> When a woman has a discharge of blood for many days at a time other than her monthly period or has a discharge that continues beyond her period, she will be unclean as long as she has the discharge, just as in the days of her period.

Also once the flow stopped she was still ceremonially unclean for seven days. Just such a woman is described in the gospels, and Mark 5:24-34 gives the fullest account. She had been "subject to bleeding for twelve years", and despite spending all her money, she had suffered under the hands of many doctors and had got worse, not better. According to the Levitical law she would have been permanently unclean and not much better off than a leper. No-one would be able to touch her, nor her them, for they would become unclean too. Imagine her relief at being finally "freed from her suffering." Not only did her bleeding stop, but, after seven days she would be free to live a normal life at last. How she managed to reach Jesus in the crowd, and touch His cloak, without having contact with anyone else is not dealt with in the passage. It is clear she only touched His clothing and not His person, and presumably this was acceptable and did not render the Lord ceremonially unclean, otherwise He would not have been able to go on and heal Jairus' daughter. If ever we think we are suffering unduly from "women's problems" let us think again about what this poor woman had to endure.

Today's way of life

The concept of being "unclean" due to monthly periods and childbirth is alien to the modern Gentile woman's mind, and would render today's westernised way of life impossible. It is difficult to even imagine the sort of restrictive life these women must have lived, and yet even today women in Moslem countries continue to live restricted lives similar to theirs.

It is also difficult for us to understand the way in which the Lord looked on a woman's uncleanness. Ezekiel 36:16,17 says:

> Again the word of the Lord came to me: "Son of man, when the people of Israel were living in their own land, they defiled it by their conduct and their actions. Their conduct was like a woman's monthly uncleanness in my sight."

How fortunate we are to live today, when we know Christ's blood has made atonement for all our sins, and so we know the Lord does not look on us as unclean at any time during the month, or after the birth of a child.

Index of Quoted Scripture References

Index of Books Quoted and Referred to

Index of Hebrew and Greek Words

Kent Women

Famous Infamous Unsung

Written and Compiled
by
Bowen Pearse

JAK Books

ISBN: 0 95234 911 6

JAK Books
PO Box 275, Tunbridge Wells, Kent, TN4 0YH
Tel: 01892-529228   Fax: 01892-542798

Printed by Staples Printers
Neptune Close, Medway City Estate,
Frindsbury, Rochester, Kent, ME2 4LT.
Tel: 01634-712200   Fax: 01634-724242

Front Cover Illustrations:
Left: Edith Nesbit   Main: Gladys Cooper   Right: Octavia Hill

Back Cover Illustrations:
Main: Mary Tourtel   Right: Pocahontas

"Kent, sir - Everybody knows Kent. Apples, cherries, hops and women",

Charles Dickens, From The Pickwick Papers

To Janice,
an Aussie by birth, a Kent Woman by adoption

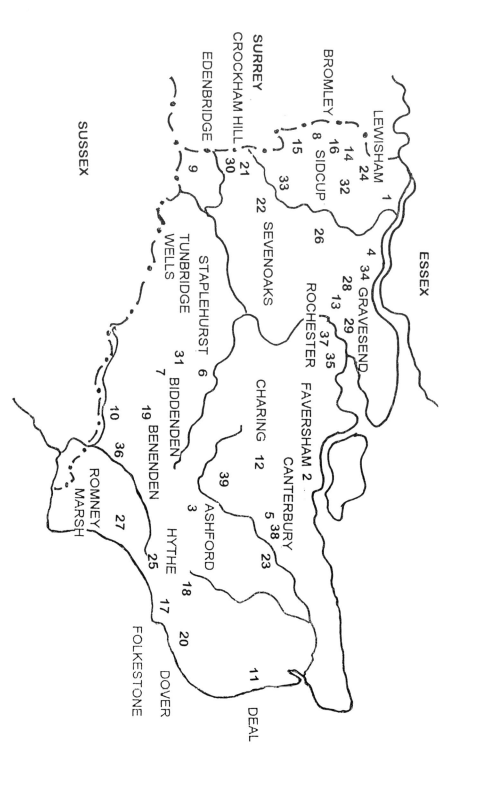

ACKNOWLEDGEMENTS

M any people helped put this book together. My special thanks go to Kent librarians. Not only did they winkle out likely names but went to great lengths to get me books, cuttings and archival material. Of particular note is Miss Spencer of Maidstone Reference Library; David Cousins, Heritage Services Officer, at Canterbury Library; Mrs Saunders of the Centre for Kentish Studies; Amber Baylis, Arts and Heritage Officer, at Sevenoaks Library; Miss Stevens of Dartford Library; Mrs Myers of Rochester upon Medway Studies Centre; Hilary Streeter of Tonbridge Library; and the staff of my local library at Cranbrook. Outside the present Kent borders (but inside prior to 1965), my thanks to Loraine Budge, of Bromley Library; and Richard Martin of Lewisham Library.

William Allen threw additional light on the lives of Susannah Lott and the Holy Maid of Kent; my thanks also to Carson Richie for loaning me the artwork for the entry on Eleanor Cobham.

I am grateful to Ann Thwaite and Maureen Duffy for allowing me to use illustrative material from their biographies of Frances Hodgson Burnett and Aphra Behn. My thanks also to Jane Jones for letting me use the results of her recent research into the life of Aphra Behn.

My thanks to Jasper Ridley, Kathleen Strange and Sharon Searle for reading the typescript. They made many useful comments and suggestions. A final thanks to Bryan Darby for preparing the copy for the printer.

INTRODUCTION
BY JASPER RIDLEY

This is a book about 39 women who are connected in one way or another with Kent. They are a varied bunch. They cover a period of 1,400 years from the beginning of the seventh century to the end of the 20th. Several of them died before they were 30, and two lived beyond the age of 90.

Some, like Elizabeth Carter and Enid Blyton, lived most of their lives in Kent. Others like Aphra Behn in 1640 and Gladys Cooper in 1888, were born in Kent but left at an early age and never returned. Frances Hodgson Burnett was born in Manchester and died in the United States, but lived for 13 years in Kent. The American Indian Princess Pocahontas in 1617, and the French philosopher Simone Weil in 1943, came to Kent for the first time and died there shortly after their arrival.

Of the 39, 16 were writers, six were actresses, six were queens or princesses, two died for their religious beliefs, and two were executed for murdering their husbands. Eanswythe was a saint and Kitty Fisher was a courtesan. Hester Stanhope was an eccentric aristocratic traveller and Octavia Hill was a philanthropist. Elizabeth Carter was an 18th century translator and classical scholar; Marie Stopes was a 20th century pioneer in sexual liberation; Anne Pratt was a botanist; Ethel Smyth was a musician and a champion of the Suffragettes; Eleanor Cobham was a 15th-century duchess who was accused of being a witch; and Eliza and Mary Chulkhurst of Biddenden were Siamese twins who are still remembered there today, though we do not know if they lived in the 12th or the 16th century.

Some of these women excite our admiration, others our pity, and some both our admiration and our pity. They have one thing in common: they were all unusual and remarkable women, whose life stories will interest many readers, and especially those who live in Kent.

CONTENTS

ANNA OF CLEVES
(1515-1557)
FOR THE TEMPORARY QUEEN, RETIREMENT IN KENT

It was all a matter of sex. Good down-to-earth sex. When Thomas Cromwell, one of the king's chief ministers, advised Henry VIII that his marriage with the Protestant Anna of Cleves would be politically expedient, Henry not unnaturally wanted to know what the girl looked like. Anna was the sister of the Duke of Cleves (in present day Germany) and brought up in the Lutheran church. Protestant England wanted all the Protestant allies it could get. This was all well and good as far as Henry was concerned, but was the girl pretty? Was she beddable?

Henry sent his favourite painter, Hans Holbein, to paint a portrait of the lady who was to be so prematurely forced into early 'retirement' in Kent. To Henry, she couldn't have looked too bad - for on the strength of this painting, he agreed to the marriage. The officials who had already met Anna were reported to be enthusiastic.

Something, however, was very wrong. The king was anything but enthusiastic. For when he met his future Queen in the flesh, she was a colossal disappointment to him. Why was this? It was something that Holbein's painting didn't reveal - perhaps it could really only be experienced in a meeting. Today we would call it sex appeal. To the king, Anna had none.

There were other drawbacks, chief of which may have been that Anna spoke no English. Henry found communication painful. But she also lacked other skills almost obligatory in the Tudor court. She had none of the expected courtly manners. And in contrast to Henry's love of music, she could neither sing nor play an instrument.

But politics is politics. In 1533, Anna's father was the most powerful supporter of Protestantism in western Europe. So, before any meeting had officially taken place between Henry and Anna, the marriage contract had to be signed and this was done at Windsor on September 24th 1539. Anna was 24, Henry was exactly twice that age.

Anna arrived at Calais, then English territory, on December 11th, where she was met with great ceremony by a number of lords and ladies and a loud firing of cannons. She waited there until the winds were favourable and set out across the Channel on December 27th.

The royal party arrived at Deal and from there proceeded to Dover, Canterbury and Sittingbourne, then to Rochester, where she was again received by a goodly number of lords and knights, presided over by the Duke of Norfolk. It was by now New Year's Eve.

On New Year's Day, she had a mystery caller who met her when she was looking out of the window at a bull baiting. The mystery man was really the king in disguise - who had come, he said, to 'nourish love'. According to the records, she 'showed him commonplace civility and continued looking out of the window'. This was too much for Henry. He went to another room and returned, identifying himself in royal purple velvet.

The king spent the evening with Anna and came again to her next morning when he stayed till past noon. Henry then returned to Greenwich. He reported to Cromwell that although Anna was 'well and seemly', she was 'nothing so fair as had been reported'. The king asked, 'is there no remedy then but that I must need put my neck in the yoke"?

The following Tuesday, Twelfth Night, was to be their wedding day. The king said to Cromwell, 'My lord, if it were not to satisfy the world and my realm, I would not do that which I must do this day for none earthly thing'.

Archbishop Cranmer, however, performed the rite and there was much pageantry with jousts and a procession down the river. The musicians had come specially from Venice and they brought with them an instrument never before played in Britain. This was the violin.

But at some time the party had to stop - and the newly weds were faced with their wedding night. Perhaps the most revealing account of their sexual relations comes from Anna, made to her ladies some months later. 'When he comes to bed', Anna said referring to the king, 'he kisses me and taketh me by the hand and biddeth me, "good night sweet heart" and in the morning, kisses me, and biddeth me, "Farewell, darling." Is not this enough'?

Anna may have been protected from humiliation by ignorance but her husband wanted none of it. When, after the wedding night, Cromwell asked the king how he liked the queen, Henry replied, 'I liked her before not well, but now I like her much worse'.

It seems in truth, then, that the marriage was never consummated. The king told Sir Anthony Denny, a member of the Privy Chamber, that Anna was 'not as she was reported, but had breasts so slack and other parts of body in such sort...'. In conclusion, Henry said that 'he could never in her company be provoked and steered to know her carnally'.

When, on June 25th, the king sent a deputation to the queen to tell her of the planned dissolution of the marriage, Anna at first fainted. However, it seems that after discussing matters with the clergy, she accepted it as a *fait accompli*. From now on, she was to be the king's 'sister'. And as one of the conditions, she could never again travel abroad.

Henry and Anna were divorced after a hearing before convocation on July 9th, which was afterwards confirmed by Act of Parliament. This declared the marriage null and void. Not long after this, Henry married one of the ladies in waiting, Katherine Howard, niece of the Duke of Norfolk.

In the terms of settlement, Anna was awarded an annual pension of £4000. She was given over 100 manors. Among her favourites were Dartford Manor and Hever (which had been the home of Anne Boleyn) both in Kent. She also spent a good deal of her time at her house in Chelsea. She struck up friendly relations with the two princesses, Elizabeth and Mary, who often came to visit her. At the coronation of Queen Mary, Anna rode in the procession with Princess Elizabeth. Anna died in Chelsea on July 16th 1557. On Queen Mary's instructions, she was buried in Westminster Abbey with great ceremony.□

ALICE ARDEN

(d 1551)

FOR FOUR CENTURIES, A CELEBRATION OF MURDER.

Just after seven o'clock on the dark, snowy Sunday evening of February 15th 1551, the former Mayor of Faversham, Thomas Arden, was murdered in his own parlour - at the instigation of his wife, Alice. One of his assailants crept up on him from behind and placed a cloth over his mouth and nose. Another man, a tailor, brained him with a heavy tailor's iron, and a third cut his throat with a long dagger.

The murder is recorded in the Holinshed Chronicles and in the play, *Arden of Feversham*. Described as 'one of the greatest of pre-Shakespearean tragedies', the play is probably the earliest domestic drama extant. It was entered in the Stationers' Register in April 1552, a year after the murder took place. The authorship is unknown.

Thomas Arden was a capable but not a popular man. His post was that of Commissioner of the Customs of the Port of Faversham (in those days, spelled Feversham). It was the time of the dissolution of the monasteries and he was given a grant of nearby Abbey lands. He made good money but caused bitterness for dispossessing other land owners. A member of the Common Council, he was made mayor in 1547, but he betrayed the trust of this position.

It had been common practice for the annual fairs to be held in the town or on the Abbey Green, on alternate years. The revenue from the fair went to the town or the Abbey, depending on the venue. In 1549, when it was the town's turn, Mayor Arden ignored precedent and secured the fair for the Abbey Green. By doing this, Arden was not only going against an established custom, he was also accused of breaking his oath to uphold the rights of the people of the town.

Arden's actions caused fury among the jurats and the Common Council. They acted immediately to depose Arden and also to disfranchise him.

Arden's wife, Alice, seems to have more than shared the general antipathy towards her husband. At some point in her marriage she became infatuated with her father's steward, Thomas Mosby, a tailor by profession. So great was her passion that it drove out everything else from her mind. Love for Mosby turned into hate for her husband. If she was to have Mosby, she would have to be rid of her husband.

Alice and Mosby planned the murder. They first tried poisoning but failed in the attempt. They then recruited two professional assassins, Black Will and George Loosebag, plus a man called Greene and another called Michael. Greene considered himself wronged by Arden and bore a grudge. Michael, a serving man in the household, was bribed by the offer of the hand of Mosby's sister in marriage - Susan, a comely wench, who was also a servant in Arden's house. It has never been explained why Alice needed quite so many accomplices.

Another plan was to dispatch Arden while he was away in London on business. However, despite careful preparations and professional killers who should have known what they were doing, the plot failed.

The conspirators then decided to kill Arden in Rainham. They would waylay him along the road. They waited for their victim but instead of finding him alone, Arden was accompanied by a Lord Cheney and a number of his men. There were too many people on the road to take on, So their mission was thwarted again.

Alice and her merry men then learned of Arden's planned journey from Faversham to the Isle of Sheppey the next day. The plotters lay in wait. But did they get their man? Indeed they did not. This plot also miscarried.

The next scheme was to slay Arden near his house, during the St Valentine's Fair. Mosby would provoke Arden. There would then be an ensuing tumult during which Arden would be dealt the fatal blow. But Arden would not be provoked.

In desperation, Alice urged her accomplices to kill Arden at his house. They must destroy the barrier to Alice's happiness, come what may. The hired assassins would earn their kill fee. Mosby, however, was worried. He was aware of the greater risk this plan would entail. But he put up little resistance. Alice persuaded everyone to act exactly as she instructed. How did she manage this? It is necessary to look at the way in which the dramatist, writing soon after the event, depicted Alice.

The atmosphere of the play itself is one of horror and savagery, primitive hatred, and sheer relentless doom. Alice is portrayed as thorough and cold-blooded. She was demented by passion and a hatred of her husband. It was her enormous inner strength that drove on the conspirators, even to their own destruction.

In all the annals of dastardly murders, there must be few that were more inept. With all of the plotters together, they finally carried out the deed. And what did they do with the body? Hide it so that nobody would ever find it? Not a bit of it. They dragged the corpse through the snow to a neighbouring field, leaving a helpful trail of footprints in the snow. And it had been a messy death with blood everywhere, just waiting for inspection.

Discovery was thus quick and clear. The body was found in the neighbouring field and the footprints followed nicely back to the house. At first, Alice denied all knowledge of the murder. But then the servants implicated her and later, when he was captured, so did Mosby.

The hired killers, however, moved rapidly. William Blackbourne (Black Will) had received his reward of £8 and bolted but was later caught. George Loosebag vanished. All the rest of those involved, including Alice, Michael, and Mosby, were arrested.

Sentences were about as harsh as the time permitted. Alice - a husband killer - was thereby guilty of petty treason and sentenced to be burned at the stake, in Canterbury; Mosby and his sister were hanged at Smithfield in London. Michael, the servants and helpers were hanged in chains in Faversham and left to rot. Greene was picked up in Cornwall the following July, tried and hanged in Faversham. Black Will was caught and burnt at the scaffold at Flushing, though it is not certain whether this was for the Arden murder or another. Black Will spread his villainy far and wide. Only George Loosebag seems to have escaped capture.

The murder caused a sensation. The small town of Faversham had never seen anything like it. The play of the murder, *Arden of Feversham* , became a continuing success. A second edition was published in 1599. It was reprinted in 1633 and again in 1770, this time by Edward Jacob who claimed Shakespeare's authorship.

There are in fact several claims to authorship. One theory is that the original 1552 manuscript was lost and that another version was written in the 1590s by Shakespeare, Marlowe or a writer named Thomas Kyd.

Scholars have closely compared the Arden play with others written by Kyd. They say the writing uses Kyd's phrasing, vocabulary, diction and mannerisms. The script assumes a knowledge of legal documents and legal procedure, both of which Kyd had. And that further, the style has similarities to a number of Kyd's works - and like them, *Arden of Feversham* was published anonymously by Edward White.

Revivals of *Arden of Feversham* took place during the 18th century with many more during the 19th century. Some were straight from the original, others were adapted and reduced in length. In the 20th century, the play had a two night stand at the Renaissance Theatre in 1925 and Joan Littlewood produced it the Theatre Royal, Stratford, London , in 1954. It ran for a season at the Lyric Hammersmith in repertory with two other plays, in January 1963.

At various times, critics have taken different sides. In 1963, they were not kind. An example from *The Times* of February 7th 1963, says, 'it is difficult to understand why *Arden of Feversham* should have received three professional performances on stage and radio during the past year...the play is not by any standards a good play...'

Joan Littlewood, an outstanding theatrical director, notes that 'the play was created by a writer of no mean calibre'. It is unlikely *Arden of Feversham* would have been produced so many times without a good portion of merit. One way or another, the theatre has been play-acting Alice Arden's nasty, bloody murder for a very long time.

Was Alice evil? Was she a minor Delilah or Messalina? Certainly, the playwright seemed to think so. Alice is the chief persuader, egging everyone on. Mosby takes the initiative only once, in the manner of poisoning. Then when Alice objects (in case she is poisoned herself in error) Mosby leaves everything else to her.

What Alice says goes. At a time when women were in many respects, treated as second class citizens, Alice manages to persuade everyone to carry out her wishes even when it is pointed out that murdering Arden at home is too risky. To accomplish what she does, Alice used sheer willpower which was born of hate and love. And it eventually destroys them all.

This then is the conventional story. However, recent research by Lena Orlin, an America academic, and Patricia Hyde, Vice President of the Faversham Society, who is at present working on a biography of Thomas Arden, has shown that a different account of the main events of the story should be considered. Ms Hyde points out that the author of *Arden of*

Feversham used Holinshed's printed sources; she obtained her version of the events from a manuscript by a John Stowe.

Alice's mother married three times, Alice was probably the daughter of the first marriage. The first two husbands were merchants, the third was Sir Edward North, a great nobleman and Privy Councillor. Alice would therefore have grown up in a great aristocratic house.

Around 1537, Alice married Thomas Arden, who then joined North's household as assistant clerk of parliament. She fell in love with Thomas Mosby, North's steward. The affair between Alice and Mosby went on for years, and - according to Patricia Hyde - Arden was quite content to leave matters as they stood. It seems he would put up with most things as long as he could retain his position.

Lena Orlin points to another flaw in the conventional story. She is suspicious of any narrative which attempts to impose a moral. The author of *Arden of Feversham* writes into the play a number of attempts at murder. This, Ms Orlin maintains, is to demonstrate that murder isn't easy - just in case any of the audience were thinking of trying it!

Another important element in the new approach is Arden's will. At his marriage with Alice, Arden agreed to leave his widow £40 a year in the event of his death. He didn't get around to writing his will until December 20th 1550. In the event, this proved to be his death warrant. He was murdered by the will's beneficiary less than two months later.

The recent research also points to two other things. These concern the punishment of Alice. It seems that between the trial and the death penalty being carried out, Alice was 'made available' to any men of the town who wanted her. In effect, she was gang-raped - considered an appropriate sexual punishment for her sexual crime with Mosby. There is also slight evidence that she may have been disembowelled. If this was the case, it would have been a most unusual punishment for a woman.

But only a severe punishment would nevertheless have satisfied society's outrage. In the social tumult created by the Reformation, scapegoats were needed and women became the ideal victims. Looked at through the eyes of the prevailing patriarchal world, women were treacherous, deceitful, lecherous, and dangerous.

The researchers' view is that Alice was none of these things. Why did she commit the crime in the first place? Like many a modern woman in an unhappy marriage - she was desperate to be free. She was neither loose nor evil - just determined and in love.□

ELIZABETH BARTON
(1506?-1534)
THE HOLY MAID OF KENT - SAINT OR TRICKSTER?

Most will have heard of Joan of Arc, the Holy Maid of Orleans, but few Kentish people know much about Elizabeth Barton, their own Holy Maid of Kent. Yet historians have pointed out a number of similarities. Both girls came from peasant stock, both heard voices, saw visions, made prophecies. And in the end both died for their beliefs - as martyrs.

The Holy Maid of Kent, as she came to be called, was born at Court-at-Street, about a mile from Aldington and some four miles south of Ashford. In about 1525, she was a domestic servant on a farm, Cobb's Hall. Her boss was Thomas Cobb, a bailiff to the Archbishop of Canterbury, who owned vast estates in the vicinity.

Elizabeth Barton was illiterate and sickly - and this was where the trouble started. At Easter of that year, she was attacked by a severe illness which lasted throughout spring and summer. It probably wasn't epilepsy (as some have suggested) because she had continuous high temperatures.

9

She would lapse into long periods of ecstasy when she 'babbled o'green fields'. She also began to predict the future.

Then came the first 'miracle' that carried her name to all parts of the county and beyond. In November, one of the Cobb children, sharing a room with Elizabeth, lay sick in its cot. Elizabeth announced that the child would soon die. That night the child was dead and the word was out.

For several days, the Holy Maid lay in a trance, telling 'wondrous things done in other places'. Her hysterical cries were 'of marvellous holiness in rebuke of sin and vice' or were about 'the seven deadly sins and the ten commandments'.

In the village, they whispered that Elizabeth was possessed - by the Devil or the Holy Ghost. Her master, Thomas Cobb, summoned the parish priest, Richard Masters, who pronounced that she was inspired by the Holy Ghost. At this stage, Elizabeth ceased to be a domestic servant and was invited to share Cobb's household as one of the family.

More important people had to be told and the matter was referred to Warham, Archbishop of Canterbury, then in his dotage. The Archbishop sent a message to the girl, saying that she was 'not to hide the goodness and the works of God'.

Elizabeth took the advice to heart. In a few months the illness left her but once having been in the limelight, she was loath to lose it. So - as she later confessed - she proceeded to feign trances and prophecies.

In about 1526, Archbishop Warham found her reputation still growing and instructed the prior at Christ Church, of Canterbury, to send two monks, Edward Bocking and William Hadley, to observe her more closely.

Bocking saw the girl as a means of restoring popular belief in the old church to the detriment of the Protestants. He taught Elizabeth the Catholic legends of the saints and persuaded her to claim her utterances came from the Virgin Mary.

She learned to anathematise the opponents of the Catholic church and cogently dispose of the Protestant arguments. Such a display of learning from an ignorant village girl provided further testimony that she was divinely inspired. She was even tutored to perform 'miracles', for which she went into more trances. The monks saw to it that the results were spread far and wide. Elizabeth Barton was becoming more of a name to be reckoned with.

At the command of the Virgin, she left Aldington for a cell at the priory of St Sepulchre, Canterbury. Bocking was her confessor. Here her prophetic abilities further developed and she became known as the Nun of Kent.

As her fame spread, she was consulted by many people, for personal matters and things affecting the kingdom. This continued throughout 1527 and 1528. The monks secretly supplied her with sufficient information to ensure that she didn't make a complete fool of herself.

She added to her reputation by long fasting. It was claimed that she had the gift of *inedia* - the ability to go for long periods without food or drink. She suffered self-inflicted wounds ('combats with the devil'). She even told stories of ascents to heaven by way of the priory roof! And it was said that she could 'light candles without fire' and 'moisten women's breasts that wanted milk'.

The Nun's oracles were set down and in 1528, Archbishop Warham showed the collection to Henry VIII, who refused to accept their veracity. Sir Thomas More at first said they were as 'such as any simple woman might speak of her own wit'. But later when More examined her, his notes indicate that he gave considerable credence to her utterings.

But then the Holy Maid of Kent went too far. 'In the name and by the authority of God', she took open opposition to the King's plans to divorce Catherine and marry Anne Boleyn. If Henry went along with his plans, he should 'no longer be king of this realm and die'.

She met Wolsey who 'was confirmed by the girl in his repugnance to the divorce'. At Wolsey's death in 1531, the Nun said that it was by her intercession that the Cardinal would be admitted to heaven. All over the kingdom, the Kentish Maid became known as the champion of Catherine and the Catholic church. Alan Neame, in his *The Holy Maid of Kent*, called her, 'a one-woman Catholic Revival'.

The great and the unknown trooped to see her. Bishop Fisher wept with joy over her revelations. The monks of the Charterhouse, the Friar Observance of Richmond, Greenwich and Canterbury publicly avowed the veracity of her prophecies. Peeresses frequently invited her into their homes. Copies of her prophecies were sent to Queen Catherine and Princess Mary. She even went so far as to threaten the Pope and his agents with certain destruction unless they prevented the divorce.

Henry VIII and the Boleyns tried in vain to bribe her into silence. And when Henry passed through Canterbury on his return from France, Elizabeth thrust herself into his presence and tried to terrify him into changing his plans.

Henry married Anne on about January 25th 1533. The populace waited in vain for the heavenly thunderbolts. None came. The Nun changed her prophecy. Henry would not die but, like Saul in the Bible, he would no longer be king in the sight of God. The newly appointed Archbishop of Canterbury, Cranmer, saw this as high treason - that it was tantamount to inciting people to kill the king.

Elizabeth was summoned to his presence. After repeated examinations, Elizabeth Barton confessed that her whole reign had been a sham. She had never had visions, all had come from her own imagination. In the end, her examiners concluded that, 'her inspiration and ecstasies were merely juggle and deceit'. She was charged with high treason.

There was little the Maid could do in the way of a defence. There was no free press in Tudor England. Records were set down - for the present and for the future - by the king's men. The king's word was law.

On September 25th, Elizabeth and her chief counsellors, Bocking and Hadley, were arrested. Bocking made a full confession. Those who had helped and directed her were rounded up and all threw themselves on the mercy of the court.

The prisoners were made to recite a full public confession, at St Paul's Cross and at Canterbury. Others were implicated but Sir Thomas More's pleadings of having merely examined Elizabeth were accepted.

The terrifying sentences were read out. All were to be drawn through the streets to the place of execution, at Tyburn. There the worst punishments were reserved for the men. They were to be hung, cut down while still alive, then revived. They were then to be castrated, disembowled, beheaded and cut into quarters. The head would be set up where ever the king decided - partially cooked to reduce the smell. The equivalent sentence for a woman was that she be burned alive.

April 20th was the date on which the sentences were to be carried out. Elizabeth made a final speech from the scaffold. She was responsible for her own death and that of the others. But she was only 'a poor wench without learning', puffed up by learned men who made her a source of profit for themselves.

Confessions from the scaffold were common practice but it is questionable as to how sincere they really were. A bargain was often made with the condemned. Provided the prisoner said what he was told to say, his family, friends and dependants would not be harmed. In the Maid's case this would probably have meant the Benedictine Community of St Sepulchre's, Canterbury, would not be touched. Such bargains could also influence the way that the condemned died.

Joan and her accomplices benefited from a late act of mercy. All the sentences were commuted to death by hanging - a painful but nevertheless a more humane end.▢

MRS BEETON
(1836-1865)
FIRST CATCH YOUR REINDEER

Rise early, bath daily (in cold or tepid water), form friendships slowly, invite guests who are amusing, never speak an unrefined word, keep your servants discreet, see your nurse dispenses no dangerous drugs and pay rigorous attention to the right way of frying a cow's heel.

These are some of the Victorian virtues extolled by Isabella Beeton in her best-seller, *Beeton's Book of Household Management.* - the result, she said, of "four years' incessant labour." The book is over a thousand tightly packed pages and contains everything a middle class housewife would need to know. But the most remarkable thing of all is that the book was written by a young woman under 25, who before starting had almost a total ignorance of her subject and was equally inexperienced as an author.

She did, however, have a good teacher. In many respects, Isabella's output was the result of a happy partnership between her and her husband, Sam. Isabella had married Samuel Orchart Beeton on July 10th 1856, when she was 20. He was a journalist and a publisher with an entrepreneurial flair. He had done very well for himself with the English publication of *Uncle Tom's Cabin*. And this had provided finance for other publishing ventures, the most successful of which was the monthly *English Woman's Domestic Magazine*. This was launched in 1852 as a pioneer magazine for the middle classes.

Within a year of her marriage, Isabella was contributing to the magazine and helping to run the business. Like the contents of the *Book of Household Management*, her writings in the magazines covered a wide range of housekeeping subjects: cookery, household management, bringing up children and - after she had established a Paris connection - women's fashions.

The central tenet of all Isabella's writing - at least that aimed at the middle classes - is that the reader is mistress of at least a cook and a kitchen maid and probably more. Isabella and Sam Beeton began their own marriage with a cook, kitchen maid, housemaid and gardener - a little better than average. The *Book of Household Management* gives some interesting figures as to what you would be expected to pay for your staff. A housekeeper was the best paid at £18-£45 a year; a cook £12-£30; a housemaid £10-£20; and a scullery-maid, the worst paid of all, £4-£9. On average, the total wages would total about one-eighth of the family income.

With no 20th century labour saving devices, the servants had plenty to do. Few things were pre-wrapped and pre-bottled. Most had to be made up. Isabella included a section on cleaners and polishes, some not for the squeamish. A mixture for restoring whiteness to scorched linen includes vinegar, fuller's earth, dried fowls' dung, soap and onion juice. (An edition brought out recently advises that 'dried fowls' dung is not obtainable today unless you specifically prepare it, which is hardly advisable...')

Isabella's great tome included medical tips and even a section written by a lawyer. But the greater part of the book was devoted to the cookery section - some 40 chapters. Each recipe had been researched and tested in Mrs Beeton's own modern kitchen. They were on the whole simple recipes - nothing that would tax a barely literate cook.

The information given was more detailed - and therefore of more use - than in any previous recipe book. Earlier writers had only given the method of preparation. Isabella included the time of year when the ingredients would be available, the cooking time, the number of people served, the cost, and all the ingredients with exact weights and measures.

Publication made Mrs Beeton a household name. Part of the book's success can also be attributed to clever marketing. There were part-issues sold between 1859 and 1861, the illustrated edition of 1861 and later cheap issues for "the working classes".

Isabella's family never approved of Sam and they blamed him for working his wife "unlike a lady." But it is doubtful if Isabella needed much urging. She remembered much of her single life as consisting of hour upon hour of being "a lady" and experiencing nothing but boredom. She wouldn't have thrown herself into publishing quite so enthusiastically if it had not greatly appealed to her.

A number of other publications evolved from the Beeton stable. An upmarket weekly, the *Queen,* was launched in 1861. This included accounts of the latest fashions from Paris, high-quality colour fashion-plates and a pattern service for readers - things which later were to become 20th century standards. Another good seller was the *Boys Own Paper,* a magazine which was followed in due course by a similar one for girls.

Isabella Mary was born on March 12th or 13th 1836, in Milk Street, in the City of London. She was the eldest in the family of three daughters and a son, of Benjamin Mayson, linen factor of Milk Street, London, and his wife Elizabeth Jerram. Isabella's father died when she was four and in 1843, her mother married Henry Dorling of Epsom. Like all good Victorians, they went in for big families and in 20 years, Isabella had 20 younger brothers and sisters.

Isabella's schooling began in Islington, then for a short time in Heidelberg - where she did well in both music and languages. She also learned pastry-making and she continued with this when she returned home to Epsom in 1854 - at a local confectioner's. Her family thought this was "ultra modern and not quite nice".

After Sam and Isabella's marriage the couple settled into a rented house in Pinner and commuted from there to Sam's offices in the Strand. But after the success of their publishing ventures, the couple wanted a house of their own and bought an inexpensive low, rambling farm house at Greenhithe. They moved there in the spring of 1863. Greenhithe was then a small Kent village, set amid undulating hills - just right for a bit of country life, conveniently connected to London by train.

Isabella gave birth to four children during her marriage, two of whom died - one as a baby, the other as a toddler. But it was the fourth birth which killed her. In those days, puerperal fever, infection of the birth canal, was fairly common, likely to have been caused by the doctor's (unsterilised) hands. Isabella died eight days after the birth on February 6th 1865. She was only 28. Sam outlived her by only 12 years. He died of tuberculosis on June 6th 1877, at the age of 46.◻

APHRA BEHN
(1640-1689)
THE FIRST PROFESSIONAL.

On a small slab of black marble in Westminster Abbey, there is an inscription to one of the most remarkable women of Restoration England - the first English woman to earn her living with her pen. Her name is Aphra Behn, née Johnson. This much is certain. Equally well known are her bawdy theatrical romps, her novels and her poetry. But parts of her fascinating and adventurous life are still a mystery and the subject of much debate.

Aphra was not an uncommon name in the 17th century. According to E G Withycombe's *Oxford Dictionary of English Christian Names*, it derives from a misunderstanding of a verse of the Book of Micah: 'In the house of Aphrah roll thyself in the dust', where Aphra is in fact a word meaning dust.

It was once thought that Aphra's birth place was in Wye but subsequent research indicates that it was more likely to have been Canterbury, perhaps the area of Harbledown, a village to the west, half a mile outside the city walls. It also seems likely that her father was a barber.

In 1663, when she was about 20, Aphra and her family sailed to Surinam, a British possession on the north coast of South America. Her father had been nominated by Lord Willoughby to take up the post of Lieutenant-Governor. Why a country barber (if that indeed was what he was) would be considered for such an elevated post is something of a mystery.

One explanation may be that around the time of the Civil War, there was a good deal of uncertainty, and favours done and debts owed may have been resolved in this way. Whatever the reason, the barber cum Lieutenant-Governor died on board ship and was buried at sea. The family, however, continued on to Surinam and rented a residence called St John's Hill, reputedly the best house in the colony. In those days, Surinam was a wilderness, populated by convicts and dubious colonialists in search of a quick fortune - a good background for a potential writer.

It seems that the family stayed in Surinam until the following year. Various sources say that Aphra made the acquaintance of a famous slave there called Oroonoko (or Oroonoco). She described him as a heroic prince among his own countrymen. And from him, Aphra learned of the cruelties of the slave trade.

She subsequently wrote what is probably her best known work, *Oroonoko, or the History of the Royal Slave*. In it she castigates the slave trade and Christian hypocrisy. Later in London, Aphra was accused of having a love affair with Oroonoko but this seems to have been nothing more than rumour.

When Aphra Johnson (as she then was) returned to England, she met and married a man named Behn. He was probably Dutch (one description calls him 'Deutsch'). He seems to have been very wealthy and may have been a city business man. Some say he might also have been connected with the slave trade. (So much of Aphra's life is still conjecture). The marriage, however, was short lived; Mr Behn died within about two years, possibly of the plague, then ravaging Europe.

Her husband's death left Aphra very poor, although she does appear to have had rich and powerful contacts. She also seems to have been well educated with a good knowledge of foreign languages. As a girl, she would have had plenty of opportunity to learn. In Aphra's day, her birthplace Canterbury was full of French-speaking Huguenot refugees and nearby Sandwich had a large number of Dutch who had fled from the Low Countries. So there must have been a good supply of tutors.

Both languages would have been useful in the next episode of her life. She now moved into a cloak-and-dagger world: Charles II commissioned

17

her to spy for Britain against the Dutch. She was in Flanders in or about 1666, the year that war broke out against Holland.

From all accounts Aphra seems to have been very beautiful and in Antwerp she was besieged by would-be suitors (she has left us a very lively account of her experiences). One of these young men was sufficiently indiscreet to inform Aphra of Holland's planned war moves. According to a Cornelius de Witt, the enemy was to sail up the Thames and the Medway. She immediately got a message back to Charles.

Expecting warm congratulations from her sovereign, Aphra was mortified when the king treated the suggestion with incredulity. She resolved to have nothing more to do with politics and to spend the rest of her continental stay in search of pleasure.

She became engaged to a Dutchman named Van der Aalbert. It was planned that the two lovers were to travel separately to London and meet again there. It seems however, that once again, fate had other plans for her - her fiancé died of a fever in Amsterdam. Aphra sailed home alone from Dunkirk, but her ship was wrecked in sight of land and she narrowly escaped drowning.

When she finally arrived back in London, King Charles neglected to pay her for her spying services and for a while she actually had to languish in a debtors' prison.

But Aphra Behn was not easily defeated. She was now a widow approaching 30 with no money and no family to support her. In the 17th century there was little such a woman could do - except perhaps acting or prostitution or going into service. So quite simply, Aphra sat down and did a Jeffrey Archer. She wrote herself into a good income, becoming the first professional woman writer in English history.

Her first attempts met the fate of most first manuscripts, but rejection only made her more determined. Gradually, she began to make friends with other (male) writers of the day. One of the first to come to her aid was Edward Ravenscroft. He was supposed to have written many of her early epilogues. In 1671, her tragi-comedy *Forc'd Marriage* was produced at the Duke's Theatre. This was followed by a comedy called *The Amorous Prince*. More and more of her plays found their way onto the stage.

Soon her fame was reckoned alongside writers like her friend John Dryden. Her most popular play was probably *The Rover* (in two parts, 1677-81). One of the characters was supposedly based on a new lover, John Hoyle, lawyer and son of Thomas Hoyle.

Aphra sized up the market and, like any pragmatist with an empty purse, she supplied what the market wanted. Restoration London was a coarse, bawdy place and the theatre followed the fashion. Aphra thus

18

made her plays robust and licentious and the punters flocked to pay their entrance money. Later generations, living in more puritan times, have criticised her writing for just those qualities that sold theatre seats.

Even in her own day, there was much criticism - simply because she was a woman. She was accused of both plagiarism and lewdness. In response, Aphra retorted angrily: 'Bawdiness is the least and most excusable fault in the men writers, to whose plays they all crowd - but for a woman it is unnatural'! But as late as 1905, Ernest Baker said her work was 'false, lurid and depraved'. It took another woman writer, Virginia Woolf, to spring to her defence. She describes Aphra's writing as having 'all the plebeian virtues of humour, vitality and courage'.

Altogether Aphra created some 18 plays and 15 novels. She also wrote pamphlets and poems, and published translations. It is as a dramatist, however, that she should be best remembered.

In the freezing winter of 1688, Aphra injured her hand when her coach overturned on the ice. The incident seems to have led to a series of ailments and, in the last years of her life, she suffered a great deal. Money problems and accumulating doctors' bills didn't help. Her spirits seem to have been very low and she described herself as 'dying'. When the end finally came on April 16th 1689, she was 49. It is said that she may well have lived but for the lack of skill of her physician.

Even in death, Aphra played second fiddle to the men. Virginia Woolf said she was buried 'scandalously'. The male poets are in Poets Corner of Westminster Abbey - Aphra was consigned to the cloisters. It is not known who wrote the epitaph inscribed on her tomb. But Aphra would probably have approved. And it may even have brought comfort to her critics. It read simply:

'Here lies proof that wit can never be
Defence enough against mortality'.□

ALICE BENDEN

(d 1557)

MARTYRED FOR HER FAITH.

In Memory of
FORTY-ONE KENTISH MARTYRS
WHO WERE
BURNT AT THE STAKE ON THIS SPOT
IN THE REIGN OF QUEEN MARY
A.D. 1555 - 1558.

FOR THEMSELVES THEY EARNED THE MARTYR'S CROWN
BY THEIR HEROIC FIDELITY THEY HELPED TO SECURE
FOR SUCCEEDING GENERATIONS THE PRICELESS BLESSING
OF RELIGIOUS FREEDOM.

PRECIOUS IN THE SIGHT OF THE LORD IS THE DEATH OF HIS S*

On the outskirts of Canterbury, at Wincheap, is a place called Martyrs' Field or Martyrs' Hollow. It was here, in 1896, that workmen came across the common grave of 41 Kentish martyrs, victims of the Protestant persecutions of Bloody Mary. The bodies were lying where they had been dumped, showing all the signs of violent death. It was said burnt flesh and hair still adhered to the skulls. They had died because they wouldn't renounce their Protestant faith, when a Catholic queen was on the throne.

Between the reigns of Henry VIII and Elizabeth I, persecutions had taken place on one side or the other. In the Protestant reigns of Henry VIII and Edward VI, the target had been the Catholics. Then under Queen Mary, it was the Protestants who were terrorised. This is the account of one Kentish martyr, a woman called Alice Benden.

On March 23rd 1556, Cardinal Reginald Pole became Archbishop of Canterbury and one of his first jobs was to discover the faith of the clergy and lay-people in the diocese. The upper classes on the whole kept their heads down, but many peasants and clergy felt it their duty to loudly declaim their beliefs. To them, it was more important than life itself.

On October 14th 1556, a Staplehurst girl, Alice Benden, was arrested and brought before Justice Roberts at Cranbrook. Her crime? Not going to church. Alice replied that her faith would not permit her to endure the idolatry of the Catholic mass. She was sentenced to jail but at the end of 14 days, by the intercession of her husband, Edward, and friends, she was freed.

The following Sunday, Edward invited Alice to go to church with him. She refused. In anger, her husband told the neighbours what she had done. His words reached the ears of Sir John Guildford, a magistrate, who again made out an order for her imprisonment. Edward even offered to escort his wife to the prison; he in fact accepted money to do so. Scornful of this, Alice gave herself up to a constable. It was agreed that her young son, rather than her husband, would take her to Canterbury Castle, where she was held.

The ever-vacillating husband then went to the Bishop, pleading for his wife's release. But this time, the Bishop refused, calling Alice a determined heretic who refused to reform herself. Edward then warned the Bishop that Alice's brother, Roger Hall, must be stopped from visiting Alice as he was advising her not to relent. The Bishop gave orders that the brother was to be arrested if found visiting Alice. It was also arranged for Alice to be transferred to a more secure prison - an underground vault beneath the Canterbury Cathedral precincts (called Monday's Hole).

This hell hole was surrounded by a paling fence some four-and-a-half feet high and three feet from the window, thus excluding any outlook. There was a little straw on the floor of the cell to rest on but nothing else, and the place was riddled with vermin. Alice was there for nine weeks. Her ration of food and drink was three farthings worth a day. She wasn't even able to wash or change her clothes.

Her brother finally found her one morning, by hearing her chant the Psalms of David. It was very early and the keeper was away ringing the church bell. At the risk of his own life, her brother attached some bread and money to the end of a long pole and managed to get it to his half starved sister.

On March 25th, Alice was again called before the Catholic Bishop of Dover. He promised her great favour if only she would return home and conform. She replied that by her experiences, she knew he was not of God and that he sought her utter destruction. She showed him that lack of food, cold and harsh conditions had made her lame. She could not move without pain.

The Bishop gave instructions for her to be moved to a prison at Westgate where she was allowed to wash and change her clothes. The physical reaction made her skin peel, just as though she had been poisoned.

At the end of April, Alice, with others, was condemned to death by burning and committed to the Castle 'until the slaughter day' - which was to be June 19th 1557.

On the day of her execution, Alice emerged with six others, all due to share the same fate. On arriving at Martyrs' Field, they discarded their outer garments and "stood in the pure white robe of martyrdom." From her waist, Alice took a piece of white lace and gave it to her keeper, begging him to pass it on to her brother. She had borrowed a shilling from her father when she was first imprisoned. She now returned it with "obedient salutations...as a token of God's goodness to her in all her sufferings, that he might understand that she had never lacked money while she was in prison."

The prisoners all bent their knees in prayer before being tied to the stake and the fire lit. It is likely that Alice's bones were among those recovered by the workmen in 1896.

All over the country, 227 men and 56 women Protestants were burnt at the stake during the reign of Queen Mary I - known afterwards as Bloody Mary. Apparently, Canterbury has the dubious honour of carrying out more burnings than any other provincial borough. From 1555 to 1558, 41 Kent martyrs perished in the flames, in the area outside the city walls. But none of these poor wretches came from Canterbury itself. Other Kent burnings took place at Wye, Ashford, Maidstone and Tonbridge.

All this information is recorded in the celebrated compilation, Foxe's *Acts and Monuments,* popularly known as *The Book of Martyrs.* It is said that at one time, it was treasured in people's homes, second only to the Bible.

A year after Alice's execution, Elizabeth I came to the throne. Two years after that, a memorial was erected on the site, a stone obelisk some 25 feet high, surmounted by a Canterbury Cross. Alice's name is inscribed there, with 40 other Kentish Martyrs. The memorial can still be seen today, rising above the back streets of Wincheap.▫

THE BIDDENDEN MAIDS
(d 1134?)
THEIR LEGACY LIVES ON.

No book on Kent women would be complete without Biddenden's famous Siamese Twins although really very little is known about them. Eliza (or Elizabeth) and Mary Chulkhurst were born joined at the hip and shoulder. But even their century is disputed. It was either the 12th or the 16th.

One noted historian points out that people living in the 16th century were fascinated by monstrous births and that letters and diaries frequently refer to the such occurances as the birth of a calf with two heads. They took it as proof that God disapproved of Henry divorcing Catherine of Aragon. But no such accounts refer to the Biddenden Maids. Those who favour the 16th century say that illustration of the Maids shows them in 16th century dress. But of course this could only go so far as indicating that the illustration itself was made in the 16th century, showing them in 'modern dress', That is all.

The twins lived for 34 years until 1534 (or then again it may have been 1134!) when one of them died. The other was offered the chance of surgical separation but it is highly unlikely that such could have been attempted at that time. According to the story, the one still alive said, 'as we came together, we will go together'. And she was also dead within six hours - as they were being carried on a litter, in the care of the monks at Battle Abbey.

There is no trace of their grave at Biddenden. It is thought they were probably buried at Battle Abbey or Hastings, away from prying eyes of the morbidly curious.

The sisters left a more permanent memorial in the form of a charity. This was the income from the 20-acre 'Bread and Cheese Lands', located to the west of the church. Every Easter, cheese and two 4lb loaves were distributed to the poor of Biddenden. At one time, beer was also included.

The doling-out ceremony was held inside the church on Easter Sunday until, in 1682, the Rector, Giles Hinton, reported to Archbishop Sancroft, that '...which custom even to this time is with much disorder and indecency observed and needs a regulation by His Grace's Authority'.

Subsequent distribution was made in the church porch until the end of the 19th century. Then it was carried out from the Old Workhouse - now called the White House (and reputedly haunted). It is situated to the west of the church and nowadays the distribution takes place on the Easter Monday. (The agreement of the tenant that this can be carried out is always assured every time the house is let.)

Another gift associated with the Maids is a small hard biscuit with their image embossed on it. It is made from flour and water, is barely edible and will keep for years. The biscuit tradition dates from the 18th century and was previously distributed on the Tuesday following Easter.□

ENID BLYTON
(1897-1968)

THE MOST SUCCESSFUL BRITISH CHILDREN'S AUTHOR OF THE 20TH CENTURY.

Despite strong opposition from librarians, more Enid Blyton books are loaned from public libraries than books by any other children's author. In 1994, she was still one of only five children's authors whose books have been on loan more than one million times annually. And this in the face of a common library policy of 'stocking but not encouraging' books by Enid Blyton.

The antis say that the books are racist, sexist, and politically incorrect. And the vocabulary is 'drained of all difficulty until it achieves a kind of aesthetic anaemia'. The fans simply reply that Enid Blyton writes what children like and getting young kids to read one book will lead on to them borrowing other authors.

Critics say that the story in which Noddy is set upon by three golliwogs, is really about a racial mugging. Similarly racist is the story of the little black doll whose blackness is washed off by magic rain. Against this, adherents simply say that racism is in the eye of the beholder and that if Enid Blyton is banned, then - far more seriously - so should most of Shakespeare.

Enid Mary Blyton was born on August 11th 1897 in Dulwich, East London, and moved to Beckenham, then in Kent, a few months later. She was the oldest child in a family of one girl and two boys. She was very close to her father, a businessman of modest means, and it was his wish that she become a concert pianist. She studied hard and took her LRAM (Licentiate of the Royal Academy of Music) at an early age.

When Enid was 13, her father left home for another woman, which must have affected her badly. She played the piano less and less after this and eventually stopped altogether and began writing stories and poems.

Enid was educated at St Christopher's School for Girls in Beckenham, where she became head girl and captain of games. She later trained as a teacher in Ipswich. After completing the course in December 1918, she taught at Bickley Park School in Kent. The following year she left to become a nursery governess in Surbiton.

Writing success began when at the age of 14, she had a poem published in one of Arthur Mee's children's papers. Other stories and poems followed. Her first book, a collection of poems called *Child Whispers* , came out in 1922. Her earnings began to expand. In the following year, she earned £300. In 1924, she was well enough known for Newnes to commission *The Enid Blyton Book of Fairies.* That year she earned over £500 and by 1925 it was well above £1200 - a very considerable income. She also began to write and edit a new magazine, *Sunny Stories.* By this time she was devoting herself entirely to writing.

Her publishers, Newnes, had an added attraction for Enid. Her editor there was Major Hugh Pollock, a war hero. Although married, his wife had left him and Enid was immensely attracted to him. She made a note in her diary: 'I want him for mine'. She had her wish. The couple married in August 1924. They had a new house in Beckenham in Kent, which Enid called Elfin Cottage. Then, from 1926 to 1929, they lived at 83 (then 31) Shortlands Road, Bromley.

The writing continued apace with *Sunny Stories for Little Folk,* editing of such part-works as the *Teachers' Treasury* and *Modern Teaching: practical suggestions for senior and junior schools* and the re-working of some of the standard nursery stories.

For a feature in *Teachers' World,* Hugh Pollock interviewed his wife. It is interesting to read his description of her:

'Imagine a slim, graceful, childish, figure with a head of closely cropped hair framing a face over which smiles and mischief seem to play an endless game. A pair of merry brown eyes peep out at you'.

Enid Blyton had intense personal ambition. She was stubborn to the point of ruthlessness and would do practically anything to avoid being thwarted. But she always made the most of what talent she had.

Enid often found personal relationships difficult. She had little small talk but given the chance to air her views on her favourite subjects, like children or her work, she was prepared to expound at length.

But perhaps the most difficult personal relationships existed between Enid Blyton and her children. The younger of the two children, Imogen Smallwood, has given a very different picture of life in the Blyton household in her autobiographical *A Childhood at Green Hedges*, published in 1989.

There was no granny or grandpa, as mother Enid had cut all ties with her family. And because she was so busy at her work, Enid had little enough time for her own children. Imogen is bitter at the memory of her mother entertaining child fans to tea and making good copy out of her two daughters - while at least one of the daughters was growing up lonely and bewildered. Amongst all the riches, Imogen felt emotionally deprived and un-cared for.

During the 1930s, Enid Blyton kept in touch with her innumerable readers through the Children's Page in *Teachers' World*. This contained a letter chatting about the doings of her life, another letter from her dog, Bobs, and a story, poem, or puzzle. Correspondence from hundreds of delighted child readers poured in. Charitable appeals had enormous response.

Although she had been producing several short children's books a year, it was not until 1937 that she brought out her first full-length fiction. *The Adventurers of the Wishing Chair* initially appeared in serial form in *Sunny Stories*, (which consisted entirely of Enid's own work). In 1938, she published *The Secret Island* and also *Mr Galiano's Circus* - which spawned a 'Circus' series. The *Famous Five* series was launched in 1942 and the first of the *Secret Seven* a few years later.

Enid's output was prodigious. There were rumours - quite baseless - that she had a team of ghost writers working for her. Not a bit of it! An average day would produce 10,000 words - on a portable typewriter balanced on her knees. She was known to write an entire book from Monday to Friday. She used to say she would get the first line right and the rest of the story simply poured out with the writer in an almost trance-like state. Critics would counter with the remark that the writing seemed as though it had indeed been written in a trance!

Because of the paper rationing during the Second World War, her output was too great for one publisher, so she began to spread her manuscripts around. By the early 1950s, she had almost 40 British publishers. Her total output amounted to some 400 different titles. And many of these had been published in translation - in 20 or more different languages. The writing was targeted at differing age groups so that a child could discover Enid when he or she first began to read and continue his diet of Enid Blyton until aged 15 or so.

It is said she based her characters on a series of drawings of puppets, by a Dutch artist called Harmsen van der Beck. There was Big Ears, Mr Plod and her most successful creation, Noddy. Noddy was everywhere - not just in millions of books, but also on cereal packets, dolls, pyjamas, and toothpaste. There was a 'Noddy in Toyland' Christmas pantomime and 52 Noddy puppet films on television.

Rather than employ a literary agent, Enid dealt personally with all her different British and foreign publishers. She had a reputation for striking a good bargain. She wouldn't accept an advance on royalties, but insisted on a minimum print run of 25,000 copies. She also demanded control of the artist and art-work for the covers.

Although best known for her children's fiction, Enid was really ready to turn her hand to almost anything. The 1940s saw an abridgement of T A Coward's *Birds of the British Isles and their eggs,* a children's life of Christ, other bible stories, a version of *Pilgrim's Progress,* various poetry and books on botany.

Her marriage had been in trouble for some years. Her husband, Hugh, began to drink heavily and became ill in the process. Then, during the war, his constant absences on military duties didn't help. They were divorced in 1942. Some six months later, she married a middle aged surgeon, Kenneth Fraser Darrell Waters. Imogen, who was eight at the time, remembers her mother telling her coldly that her Daddy was never coming back and that there would be a new stepfather. Their new father had the children's surnames changed by deed poll.

By the 1950s, Enid Blyton had become a household name with an income in excess of £100,000 a year. Despite this immense wealth, she lived quietly and tried to give help to younger writers. She would even write to literary editors, asking them not to review her books but rather, to give newcomers a chance instead.

Enid Blyton started to suffer from ill health in the 1960s and began to lose her memory. In her last years, she wrote very little except for her Noddy books. Her second husband died in 1967 and Enid followed him a year later.

It seems that there will always be controversy surrounding Enid Blyton and her work. In her *Times Literary Supplement* review of April 7th 1989, Rosemary Dinnage cruelly sums up the picture of Enid Blyton that emerges from Barbara Stoney's biography. 'This one-woman production line', she writes, 'whose record number of translated books comes third only to Lenin's and Simenon's, was a tiresome, insecure, pretentious, Thatcheresque woman whose only interesting feature - shared with Barbara Cartland and Agatha Christie - was the ability to pour out unlimited quantities of harmless drivel'.

It is nevertheless true to say that Enid Blyton did what she did extremely well. Her writing might not have been great literature. But it was rollicking, good, enjoyable fun for kids. Millions of them.□

ANNE BOLEYN
(1507-1536)
'NO ACQUITTAL FROM A COURT OF SLAVES'

Anne Boleyn was no great beauty although men caught in her charms seldom noticed. She seemed to exude a sexual fascination, experienced by almost everyone she met, none more so than Henry VIII.

So what was she like, this 'fresh young damsel' - the woman who indirectly caused the Church of England to be founded, Roman Catholicism to be rooted out and the dissolution of the monasteries?

Anne's best feature was probably her eyes - black and sparkling, with dark, silky and well-marked eyebrows. Her neck was long and slender; this gave her a special grace in the ballroom. A courtier spoke of her 'passing excellent' skill at the dance. But she also had verbal charms. Another observer referred to her 'very good wit'.

In contrast to the fair-haired, blue-eyed ideal of the day, she had an olive complexion and thick, dark, lustrous hair . The few moles on her face could have passed for beauty spots. She was of 'middling stature', quite slight or at least not full-breasted - the Venetian ambassador remarked that her bosom was 'not much raised' (fashion dictated the 'trussing' of breasts). It is also possible that she had a sixth finger on her left hand - something she would obviously be at pains to conceal.

Anne was born in 1500 or 1501, at Blickling in Norfolk. She may have spent the early part of her childhood there; later the family lived at Hever in Kent. Her father was Sir Thomas Boleyn, afterwards Earl of Wiltshire and Ormond. Her brother was called George, later Viscount Rochford, and she also had an elder sister, Mary.

At the age of 12 or 13, Anne's father took her to the court of Archduchess Margaret of Austria, the Regent of the Netherlands, at Brussels. Then from 1514-1521, she was at the court of King Louis XII and King Francis I of France. Here she learnt to speak fluent French and to excel in courtly pleasures such as the dance. She also learnt the art of pleasing - sophisticated conversation, rallying remarks, flirtatious allusions. Anne was much praised for her skill in music and her singing voice. She was being primed for the English court, where she would excel more than her wildest dreams. She was called home at the end of 1521 or the beginning of 1522, owing to 'England's hostile intentions towards France.'

After her return from France, Anne became involved with the young Lord Percy. The romance had progressed to the stage when they were bound together with a promise of marriage. But the king had already noticed Anne and he had Wolsey put an end to the affair.

The king began calling at Hever and at the same time gave more and greater honours to Anne's father. Anne and Henry began exchanging love letters in which the king is seen to pursue his suit with vigour and passion. During the courtship, which seems to have begun around 1526, it is uncertain as to how long Anne held on to her virginity. In Antonia Fraser's excellent study of all six queens, she is of the opinion that there was plenty of foreplay between the two lovers and that things may well have developed as far as *coitus interruptus*.

It is thought that Henry VIII made proper love to Anne before the end of 1532, as, around the first week of December, Anne was pregnant. Despite Henry's efforts to have his first marriage to Catherine annulled and their child declared illegitimate, this had not yet taken place. Notwithstanding, a secret marriage was held between Henry and Anne in January 1533. At Easter, the union was made public and on May 23rd, the king's first marriage was nullified. Nine days later, on Whit Sunday, June 1st 1533, Anne's coronation took place in Westminster Abbey.

Having been crowned queen, Anne now acted with the arrogance and vindictiveness that in the end were to be her downfall She was already unpopular with the general population and by her actions created more enemies. She openly sought the deaths of Queen Catherine and her daughter, Mary, and asked the king to bring them to trial under the statute that made her children the legitimate heirs to the throne. Henry refused. Anne had hated Wolsey from the time he separated her from her first love and was delighted by his downfall.

The king's ardour for Anne began to cool. There was much 'coldness and grumbling' between the king and queen. In answer to her repeated fits of jealousy and when she used 'certain words' that he particularly disliked, Henry told Anne that she must shut her eyes as her betters had done. Just as he had raised her up, he threatened, he could equally bring her down.

It was shortly after this, on September 7th 1533, that Anne gave birth to the Princess Elizabeth. The birth of a girl went against all court predictions for a son and did nothing to improve relations between Anne and her husband. She ignored warnings by her father and her uncle, both now in powerful positions. Becoming alarmed, they too turned against her. In fact, she so infuriated her uncle Norfolk that he called her 'the great whore'.

In January 1536, Queen Catherine died. When the messenger brought her the news, Anne was washing her hands in a bowl made of precious metal. So pleased was she that she immediately gave the bowl to the messenger.

Two days after Catherine's funeral, on January 30th 1536, Anne gave birth to a stillborn son. It was an enormous disappointment to her and one of the final straws which turned the king against her. Henry's latest attraction was the young, pretty Jane Seymour, one of Anne's ladies. When Anne discovered her on Henry's knee, the king cut short any criticism, upbraided Anne and left the room in a fury.

Anne had now lost the king's love, most of her friends and the good regard of her relations. There were rumours about the court that Anne had been unfaithful. On May Day, the king and queen attended a tournament at Greenwich. Anne - by accident or on purpose - dropped her handkerchief. It was caught by one of the men in the lists, thought to have been one of her supposed lovers. He wiped his brow on it. At this, the king's face coloured and he abruptly left his place with six attendants, one of whom was a man called Norris, whom the king suspected of adultery with his wife. On the ride back to Whitehall, Henry urged him to confess. Norris refused, and on his arrival at Westminster, was committed to the Tower.

Anne followed him back to London the next day. She was charged with adultery with four men and incest with her brother and put on trial before a court of 26 peers. The court was presided over by her uncle. Her

32

father had been excused but he had already declared his opinion that she was guilty.

It is believed that at least two of the men accused with her, under torture, admitted something incriminating. Anne was given no opportunity to refute the so-called evidence. It was said, however, that she conducted herself with the true dignity of a queen. Her brother, too, put up a spirited defence.

But whatever passed for a trial, they were doomed before they spoke a word. As one commentator put it, 'it was neither wisdom, wit, truth, innocence, eloquence, nor all the powers and virtues which could draw an acquittal from the court of slaves bound by selfish terror to the yoke of the most blood-thirsty despot who ever disgraced a throne..

Anne's uncle passed sentence that she was to be burnt or beheaded as the king might decide. Anne heard it without fear and prayed to a higher authority. 'O, Father, O Creator! Thou, the Way, the Life and the Truth, knows whether I have deserved this death!'

The king signed the death warrant the same day but commuted the sentence to death by beheading. Anne was advised by the Lieutenant of the Tower that 'the pain will be very little'. The king had arranged for a swordsman from Calais to be specially brought over. When this news reached her, Anne put her hands around her throat and said, laughing, 'And I have a little neck'.

The execution took place not in public on Tower Hill but within the Tower, on the Tower green, with only a few officials present. Anne was 36 when she died; she was buried in the chapel of the Tower, beside her brother.

Henry, who had been impatient for Anne's death, waited no longer than the following day to become engaged to the girl set to be the next queen of England - Jane Seymour. They were married on May 30th.◻

FRANCES HODGSON BURNETT
(1849-1924)
THE OBJECT WAS REMUNERATION.

'When I enter its gates, I feel as if I had belonged here always', Frances Hodgson Burnett wrote of Maytham Hall, Rolvenden, in 1898, the year she took up the lease. The Rose Garden there was the basis for her finest and best remembered book, *The Secret Garden*.

At this time of her life, Frances was already a successful novelist with a string of novels (adult and children's), short stories and plays to her credit. And there were plenty more to come. Many of the Rolvenden folk would have already enjoyed *Little Lord Fauntleroy*, her most successful work to date - meant to be a children's novel but read by adults as well. She was already a divorcee - which carried something of a stigma at that time. But it is likely that the townspeople would have seen her simply as a writer and not worried too much about her marital status.

At Maytham Hall, she loved playing the role of Lady of the Manor, trotting through the town in her carriage, with two coachmen in top hats.

But she was also extremely generous. Come Christmas time and she was the lady bountiful - distributing bundles of baby clothes, little frocks and petticoats, and filling stockings with marbles and dolls for the village children. She would take an enthusiastic part in the annual dinner given by the 'gentry' to the 'old villagers' at the Bull. And often when her carriage passed by around the town, she would pick up ragged kids along the way and give them lifts.

Frances Eliza Hodgson was born on November 24th 1849, in Cheetham Hill, Manchester. She was the eldest daughter of a family of two sons and three daughters. Her father, Edwin Hodgson, was a wholesaler of decorative ironmongery, who died in 1854, aged only 38.

Frances' mother, Eliza Boond, attempted to keep the business going but abandoned the struggle when her brother, writing from America, suggested she emigrate with the children to Tennessee. They made the move in 1865; the early years were hard and they were often hungry.

The young Frances was determined to bring in some money and decided to try submitting stories to magazines. But she had no knowledge of how much was paid or what requirements were demanded of contributors. In response to a tentative enquiry, she heard from one publisher that manuscripts would not be accepted without return postage.

So to raise the money for paper and postage, Frances picked and sold wild grapes. She sent her first two stories to *Godey's Lady's Book*. Her object, she wrote in a covering letter, was remuneration. The stories were published in June and October 1868 - for which she received a fee of $35. It was a significant sum for a poor household and this was just the beginning. At 18, Frances was now a published writer and from then until her marriage, she supported her family with a stream of stories.

In 1873, she married an up-and-coming eye and ear specialist, Swan Moses Burnett. They had a son in their first year of marriage. Knoxville, where they lived, was really too small for Swan to establish a profitable business and he dearly wanted to further his studies in Paris. They had a little money saved up and once again Frances had to become the provider. Her publisher agreed to a sufficient advance to allow them to live in France - but they were still very poor.

On their return, they moved to Washington where Swan's businesses went from strength to strength. Frances also continued to have more and more success with her writing. Her first novel, *That Lass o' Lowrie's*, won high critical acclaim. Published in 1877, it was an authentic tale of a Yorkshire mining village. According to some critics, it was not equalled by any of her subsequent books.

Other novels and short stories followed. Her husband took a great interest in her writing. Swan would push her on to complete this chapter or finish that book. There must have been times when Frances wished he was more of a typical 19th century husband, urging her to do less!

In 1886, she published her first children's book, *Little Lord Fauntleroy,* based on her second son, Vivian. It was a tremendous success with stage and - later - film versions appearing. It started a new fashion for boys. Mothers followed the book illustrations in and dressed their children in black velvet and lace suits. In Ann Thwaite's well documented biography, *Waiting for the Party* , she suggests that Frances may have got some idea of this style from her meeting with the flamboyant Oscar Wilde.

Despite her great fondness for her two sons, Frances seems to have treated marriage responsibilities fairly casually. She was frequently away, in America and Europe, often staying in England for months at a time. Here she moved in high society, counting Henry James and Israel Zangwill among her friends. In 1890, she suffered an enormous blow with the loss of her elder son, Lionel, from tuberculosis. She had once said 'the one perfect thing in my life was the childhood of my boys'.

During the 1890s, she continued to pour out a string of novels and stories as well as her autobiographical *The One I knew Best of All.* By now she was commanding advances of $5,000 and royalties of 20 per cent! Again her life style demanded ever more money. In the 1890s, as well as Maytham Hall, she also rented a fine house in Portland Place, which needed servants, carriages and horses.

But, despite the financial success, her marriage was not going well. In 1898, she divorced Swan Burnett for desertion and failure to support - grounds that would not have been accepted in an English court at the time. In 1900, when Frances was 50, she married her secretary, Stephen Townsend, aged 40. It was an ill-matched affair, both seeming to have married for the wrong reason.

Frances had never been particularly attractive and she was now fat, rouged and unhealthy. She found Stephen efficient and probably felt she needed him. She may also have been flattered to be wanted by a man ten years her junior. Stephen, however, simply wanted the money and the contacts that Frances could give him. The marriage lasted one year.

Frances renewed her love with Maytham Hall and Kent; she visited here in 1901, 1904, 1905 and 1906. But in 1908, she bought a large piece of land at Plandome, Long Island. It was a magnificent site, on which she built an Italian-style villa. Her last years were mainly spent on Long Island and in Bermuda - although she made several more journeys to Europe and elsewhere. She died at Plandome on October 29th 1924.□

ELIZABETH CARTER
(1717-1806)
THE 'BLUE STOCKING' LINGUIST

Elizabeth Carter is known for two remarkable things. She won the whole hearted commendation of Dr Samuel Johnson; and once earned nearly £1000 - a fortune in 18th century England - for her translation of the Greek Epictetus. She was famous at 21 and world famous at 41.

But learning didn't come easily to Elizabeth Carter. Her father began teaching her Greek, Latin and Hebrew but became exasperated with her slow learning. Angrily, he suggested she confine her studies to simple household tasks. She replied that she would gladly make herself a proficient housekeeper but would also excel in languages. Of that she was determined. She begged her father to let her continue and she would surprise them all.

Well, surprise them all she did. The 'dullard' studied hard and long, by flickering candlelight, staying awake deep into the night, 'when everyone else was asleep'. She worked an eight to 12 hour day - keeping awake by

37

chewing green tea, taking snuff, wrapping a wet towel around her head and drinking copious cups of coffee.

Her achievements were extraordinary. She became fluent in Latin, Greek and Hebrew. She was even able to put the bishops right on the translation of two verses from the New Testament. She acquired French by staying in the house of a refugee Huguenot Minister of Religion, in Canterbury, for a year. She taught herself Italian, Spanish, German and Portuguese. She even acquired sufficient skill in Arabic to compile an English-Arabic Dictionary.

Elizabeth took a great interest in astronomy, ancient and modern history, and ancient geography. She played both the spinet and German flute and was good at needlework. But for all this brilliant learning, she paid a terrible price. For the rest of her life, she suffered from constant and severe headaches.

Elizabeth Carter was born in Deal, in Kent, on December 16th 1717. Her father was the perpetual curate of Deal Chapel and one of six preachers at Canterbury Cathedral. Elizabeth's mother was heiress to a large fortune, most of which seems to have been invested in the South Sea Bubble disaster. Like most of the other investors in this highly speculative deal, she lost everything. It was said that her death, when Elizabeth was only ten, was directly related to her decline over her lost fortune.

When she was 22, Elizabeth consulted a physician about her headaches. The doctor offered no hope of a cure 'this side of the grave' but suggested early rising and walking or riding. The ever provident Elizabeth invented her own alarm clock to ensure she didn't sleep in. A heavy weight was suspended by a piece of string. Then she devised that a candle burn through the string at the precise time she wanted to be woken. The weight crashed down 'with a strong, sudden noise.' Elizabeth was awake!

After studying from five to six, she pinned on her hat against the strong Kentish winds and set off on her morning constitutional - in all weathers. Soon she became a familiar figure striding through the countryside around Deal. She claimed to be one of the best walkers in England. As a result of all this healthy exercise, she had, she said, 'the impolite colouring of a milkmaid'.

On other outings, she would often walk in preference to taking the coach. From one of her notes, when she was 25, she describes 'playing the rake enormously these last two days'. She 'sat up till near three in the morning...walked three miles in a wind that I thought would have blown me out of this planet, danced nine hours and then walked back.'

The publisher of the *Gentleman's Magazine*, Edward Cave, was a friend of Elizabeth's father. He invited her to contribute. Her first poem, written when she was 16, was a riddle - something very popular with Georgian readers. In 1738, Cave published a 24-page pamphlet containing eight of Elizabeth's poems. The work was called *Poems Upon Particular Occasions.*

It was through Cave that Elizabeth met Dr Samuel Johnson - lionised in literary quarters but unknown in others. In 1738, her father wrote to Elizabeth saying that [Johnson's] 'is a name with which I am utterly unacquainted'. Johnson's great *Dictionary of the English Language,* came out in 1755.

Elizabeth's own master work, Epictetus' *Discourses,* was published three years later in 1758. Epictetus was a first century 'heathen' philosopher who professed a stoic's answer to the time honoured question of all mankind - how to achieve happiness.

Elizabeth began the work as a favour to her friend, Catherine Talbot, and she sent pages and pages to her over a period of seven years. Then, on the advice of the Archbishop of Canterbury, Elizabeth was persuaded to publish on a one-guinea subscription basis. Elizabeth had worked hard on the book. But now the great and the famous flocked to pay their guinea, the Prince of Wales and Catherine the Great of Russia among them. Altogether 1250 copies were published with fine leather bindings.

Publication brought in almost £1000 - a considerable fortune in 18th century England. It was enough to keep Elizabeth comfortable for life. One of the first things she did with a small portion of the money was to convert four cottages near Deal's sea front into one fine dwelling called Carter House. Elizabeth had a large garden where she loved working in the summer months. She planted an acorn which grew into what she claimed to be the most easterly oak in England. In the house, she entertained royally. The Princess of Wales and the Duke of Cumberland were among her many guests.

But if her Deal garden was for the summer, winter was for the inner woman - the intellectual. Elizabeth took a house for the London winter season. In Clarges Street, Piccadilly, neighbours included Lady Hamilton (No 11), Edmund Kean (No 12) and Admiral Lord St Vincent. Elizabeth became a member of the 'Blue Stocking' circle.

Today, the term 'Blue Stocking' describes a pedantic, earnest woman. In the second half of the 18th century, 'blue stockings' was the term used for an informal group of intelligent, learned women - among whom was Elizabeth - who attended the fashionable, intellectual evenings. There were no playing cards permitted as these killed conversation and refreshments were kept to tea, coffee, and lemonade. The evenings became so popular that men joined the circle, with figures like Sir Joshua Reynolds, Dr Johnson, Boswell, Garrick, and Walpole.

The origin of the term 'Blue Stocking' is from the stockings of Benjamin Stillingfleet, who was too poor to have fine evening dress and came to the evening receptions in his daytime stockings of blue worsted. But the man was such a wit and conversationalist that, according to Boswell, in his absence, it was said, 'We can do nothing without the Blue Stockings!'

Elizabeth Carter never married, though - as was the custom - at a mature age she took the title Mrs Carter. She had several offers of marriage Among her suitors were both the Archbishop of Canterbury (Dr Secker) and the Bishop of London. For one reason or another all the offers were unsuitable. One suitor was a 'gentleman in every way unexceptional'. Her father advised her to accept him. Elizabeth, however, refused him along with the rest. Her reason was that some light verse of his showed a 'licentious' turn of mind.

It was among her father's dearest wishes that she marry. But on this one point at least, Elizabeth would not do her father's bidding. She once said: 'If I have suffered from the troubles of others, who have more sense, more understanding and more virtues...what might I not have suffered from a husband? Perhaps be needlessly thwarted and contradicted in every innocent enjoyment of life, involved in all his schemes, right or wrong and perhaps not allowed the liberty of even silently seeming to disprove them'.

On Christmas Eve, 1805, Mrs Carter arrived at Clarges Street for her usual winter season. In the following February, she became ill and died in her 89th year. She had left instructions that she was to be buried 'with as little expense as possible.' Her funeral nevertheless was attended 'by a vast concourse.' Her body was interred not in Deal, but in the burial ground of Grosvenor Chapel, St George's, Hanover Square, London.

Samuel Johnson was a friend of this remarkable woman for almost half a century and it is Dr Johnson who should be left with (almost) the last word. 'My old friend, Mrs Carter,' the great lexicographer wrote,' could make a pudding as well as translate Epictetus from the Greek and work a handkerchief as well as compose a poem'.

And that, from an 18th century man, was saying a very, very great deal.□

JULIA CARTWRIGHT
(1851-1924)
A CELEBRATION OF ART AND WOMEN.

On March 18th 1896, after the funeral of Sir Frederick Leighton, the former president of the Royal Academy, Julia Cartwright made a note in the diary she kept all her adult life. 'Seated amongst the writers but close to the artists'.

In a way, this summed up her whole professional career. As a writer, she had a prodigious output - non-fiction books, novels and articles by the score. But it was as an art critic that she made her name.

Her biographies of artists and historical figures made her famous and produced a substantial income. Her novels, which also brought in a tidy sum, were something else entirely that she would give up if her other writing made demands. The novels, as was the custom, were all written anonymously.

Julia Cartwright was born in 1851, one of nine children - five girls and four boys. The family home, Edgcote, was an 18th century country house, on the Oxfordshire/Northamptonshire border. She called it 'the earthly paradise'. In the first diary of 1868, she wrote, 'we go home to dear Edgcote, Hurray'!

Her brothers went to Eton; Julia was educated at home. She was denied Latin studies but determined that this wouldn't stop her; she borrowed her brothers' books and learnt enough of the language to read manuscripts in the British Museum. She also learnt French, German and Italian.

In 1868, the family went on a grand tour of Europe and, most of all, she loved Italy. She had studied Roman history, read the classics, and had the benefit of an Italian tutor. She sketched and took copious notes of everything Italian. Italy was to feature large in her writing and she made subsequent visits in 1874 and 1875.

She began contributing to art magazines at the time of their enormous expansion. When she started writing around 1868, there were perhaps a dozen published. By the 1890s, there were over 60. She also began writing for the *Manchester Guardian* and other papers. By the late 1880s, she was earning several hundred pounds a year from her writing, no mean sum in the late 19th century.

She met the rich and the famous, and the diaries give us well observed vignettes of such people as John Ruskin, George Bernard Shaw, and Winston Churchill. She had to add extra pages. Other names appear, public life intermingled with private - men like Gladstone, Disraeli, Bismarck and Dreyfus, all written about within their contemporary context.

She had married Henry Ady, a clergyman, in 1880, when she was 29. Her mother - with whom she never seemed to reach agreement on anything - disapproved of Ady. He had little money and no title to bestow on Julia. However, the marriage does seem to have been a happy one. At the end of the first year, Julia confided to her diary that 'a year of married life has made us feel how impossible it is to be happy apart.'

On June 13th 1888, the couple moved from Edgcote to Charing in Kent. Throughout the diaries, Henry is referred to as the 'Rector' of Charing. However, his name appears among the 'vicars' displayed in the Church of St Peter and St Paul. The Adys lived in the Vicarage and not the Rectory so the term seems to have had kudos rather than pecuniary benefit. She loved the house which their friend, Scott-Holland, a fellow cleric, said was one 'which had slipped out of heaven'.

She writes: 'The garden will delight Cecily (their one child), I am thankful the whole house is turned south and there are plenty of woods and birds'. She enjoyed the Kentish countryside around Charing and when she wasn't writing, spent as much time as possible with her daughter exploring by bicycle.

Julia was now earning enough to send Cecily to boarding school. She later won a scholarship to Oxford.

Very prominent in Julia's work were her biographies of famous women. These heroines shared common qualities, which, as she wrote in *Madame,* published in 1894, was 'a love of culture and refined taste in art and literature.' Before being published, some of these books, like *Sacharissa,* were serialised in *Macmillan's Magazine,* printed alongside articles by Henry James, Thomas Hardy and Kipling. In 1899, the editor wrote to Julia that 'anything from your pen is acceptable.'

She enjoyed good sales in the US as well as Britain. Her biography of Beatrice d'Este, was reprinted 17 times in London and New York, between 1899 and 1928.

Her own success made her aware that not all women were so lucky and she applauded the triumph of women's suffrage. However, this was not to say she always approved of the methods used. She spoke disparagingly of 'those silly suffragettes'.

Julia was shocked by the suffering of the poor but was wary of reforming bodies like the Fabians. She wrote: 'The saddest thing about the Fabian Socialists is their agnosticism and utter disbelief in a higher Power.' It was comfortable for her to retreat into the world of art where such problems of conscience never arose.

Julia continued to write her diaries after she left Charing in 1903; she displays real grief as she notes the deaths of some of her friends. In 1907, she quotes from W B Yeates:

'Outworn heart in a time outworn...'
and
'But I being poor have only my dreams;
I have spread my dreams under your feet
Tread softly because you tread on my dreams'.

Henry Ady died of cancer in 1914 and their friend and mentor, Scott-Holland, in 1918. In 1919, Julia become too ill to write and she died in Oxford, in 1924. Cecily Ady became Reader of Renaissance History at Oxford University and the dedication of her book, *Pius II,* published in 1913, is to 'My mother, in memory of happy days in Italy'. □

ELEANOR COBHAM
(d 1446?)
THE CRUSHED 'FLOWER OF KENT'.

Of all Shakespeare's female characters, only one - in *Henry VI* - has a strong Kentish connection. And this is Eleanor of Cobham, in real life a lady charged with dabbling in the black arts.

Eleanor, one of the most beautiful women in the kingdom, was the daughter of Reginald Cobham of Sterborough in Kent, commonly called Lord Cobham. Eleanor had become lady-in-waiting to Jacqueline of Hainault, first wife of Humphrey, Duke of Gloucester. Humphrey had been appointed Protector of the Realm with the dying wish of his brother, Henry V, until the young Henry VI came of age.

In 1425, Eleanor became Humphrey's mistress. She bore Humphrey two children and when, in 1428, a papal decree freed Humphrey from his marriage to Jacqueline, they married.

Humphrey and Eleanor had many enemies. A deputation of women appealed to the House of Lords. 'It was a shame', they protested, 'that the Duke should abandon his first wife in her distress and then console himself with a harlot'. They said Eleanor had used cosmetics to enhance her appearance and thus lure Humphrey away from his first wife. Eleanor was described as 'a handsome, greedy, sensual woman with doubtful antecedents'.

Rumours were rife. It was believed that heretics and witches were planning the death of the young Henry VI. The Vicar of Dartford and his servant were charged with the heresy of Lollardism (Lollards were followers of the English reformer, Wycliffe. By this time the movement had gone underground). The men were burnt amidst scenes of hysteria. Weeping crowds collected the ashes and made offerings of burning wax candles before the stake.

By this time, Humphrey's period of power had come to an end. He was offered no more public appointments. And the charges against his wife made the situation that much more serious. It was alleged that Eleanor had been flirting with the devil and his works.

Roger Bolingbroke, 'a great and cunning man in astronomy', encouraged Eleanor to believe that her husband would become king. He and Thomas Southwell, canon of St Stephen's, exposed a wax doll, in the image of King Henry, to a slow fire in the belief that the health of the King would likewise dwindle away. Bolingbroke and Southwell were arrested.

On July 19th 1440, in panic, Eleanor attempted to obtain sanctuary at Westminster. But there was no sanctuary against witchcraft and heresy and she too was arrested. Later, she tried running away but was again captured and brought back. It was said that the two attempted escapes 'proved' her guilty.

On Sunday July 23rd, Roger Bolingbroke abjured his black art on a high stage at Paul's Cross during sermon time and accused Eleanor of being his instigator to treason and magic.

Two archbishops, Cardinal Beaufort and Ayscough , held court in St Stephen's Chapel, before which the Duchess was called upon to answer charges of necromancy, witchcraft, heresy and treason. She was found guilty and on August 11th, imprisoned at Leeds Castle in Kent.

She was to be tried by an ecclesiastical court, from which her husband's friend, the Archbishop, now withdrew - a bad sign for Eleanor. An additional accomplice was brought forward. This was Margery Jourdemain - also accused of being a witch - from whom the Duchess had bought drugs and cosmetics.

A search was made for further evidence, including a search of Humphrey's library. Two books on astronomy were found, one owned personally by the Duchess.

In October, a special commission was formed. Bolingbroke and Southwell were accused as principals and Eleanor as an accessory. There was a further hearing on October 21st. Eleanor admitted some of the charges and denied others. Yes, she had dabbled in fortune-telling but no, she had not attempted treason.

On November 13th, she was found guilty and sentenced to walk bare-headed (and probably bare-footed too) through the streets of London, carrying a wax candle weighing some two lbs - which she 'offered at various churches'. The remainder of her sentence was perpetual imprisonment.

Eleanor was at first held at Chester Castle. In October 1443, she was transferred to Kenilworth and in July 1446, to the Isle of Man. Bolingbroke was hung and quartered. Another of Eleanor's allies, the witch of Eye, was burnt at the stake. Southwell died in the Tower.

Eleanor - by some called 'the flower of Kent' - is thought to have died around 1446, but it is unknown how she spent her last years. She could have moulded away in a dark damp dungeon. Or was she - as some think - imprisoned in comfort, surrounded by her own servants?

Humphrey doesn't come out well in these proceedings. He knew full well that the charges had been trumped up. And according to a prose chronicle written by a Canterbury monk, there was a method by which he could have disposed of both his enemies and Eleanor's.

Accusations of treason against the king were becoming commonplace. Eleanor had a right to a champion and nobody could have denied her this. It is believed that if Humphrey had issued a challenge to defend Eleanor by ordeal, it is unlikely that his enemies would have been eager to meet him in the lists. But Humphrey, it is stated, chose another way. Humphrey 'took all these things patiently and said little'. Well, it did him little good. In due course, Humphrey too was arrested.

In *Henry VI, Part 2,* Eleanor tries to warn Humphrey of his general unpopularity. Shakespeare catches the mood of the crowd: 'See! how the giddy multitude do point, And nod their heads, and throw their eyes on thee'.□

GLADYS COOPER
(1888-1971)
MOST BEAUTIFUL GIRL ON THE ENGLISH STAGE.

Sheridan Morley, biographer and grandson of the actress, Gladys Cooper, once summed her up in one word - unafraid. In an autobiographical article in a 1914 edition of *The Strand Magazine,* she wrote: 'I look upon opportunity in much the same way as Peter Pan looked upon death - as a great adventure'. She had no formal training and described her success both on the stage and in films as 'doing a job'. What led to her acting success? What was her secret? She said simply : 'One just goes on and *is'*.

Gladys Constance Cooper (afterwards Dame) was born on December 18th 1888, at 23 Ennersdale Road, Hither Green, Lewisham, then in Kent. She was the eldest of three daughters of Charles William Frederick Cooper, journalist and editor of the magazine he founded, *Epicure.*

Her education began at home with a French governess; she then went briefly to a school in Fulham. From seven, she took up modelling for the studio of Downey's in Ebury Street, London. Even then it could be seen that she was going to be one of the great beauties of her generation.

But the pull to be an actress also came early. She wrote: 'I can never remember the time when I did not cherish a secret desire to go on the stage...In my teens, I used to lie awake hour after hour, longing for the days to come when I should be considered old enough really to *know* what I wanted to do in life'.

Her big chance came in 1905, when a school friend took her to an open audition at the Vaudeville Theatre and she was offered the leading role in *Bluebell in Fairyland.* She was told she 'looked the part'. The play opened in Colchester on her 17th birthday. Within another year, she had joined George Edwardes' company at the Gaiety, signing a contract for £3 (increasing to £5) a week. She was engaged in small dancing and singing roles in musical comedy. She was a Gaiety Girl.

One night when she was 19, a 26-year-old Boer War soldier, then working for Ladbrokes, Herbert John Buckmaster (known as Buck), saw her from the audience and was transfixed. He was determined to meet her and within a couple of days had arranged an introduction. They were married in December 1908. In 1910, she gave birth to her first child, Joan.

Gladys Cooper was already a picture postcard beauty but had grave doubts that she could obtain a starring role in musical comedy. Her first role in the 'legitimate' theatre was as Cecily in *The Importance of Being Earnest*. This was followed by parts in the works of Shaw, Galsworthy, Arnold Bennett and others. In 1913, Gerald Du Maurier gave her a leading role in a revival of Sardou's *Diplomacy.*

By now she was earning the considerable sum of £40 a week, twice as much as her husband. But there were more important things happening in the world. With the outbreak of war, Buck joined the cavalry and they both found themselves at the front - he fighting the Germans, Gladys entertaining the troops. Then, in June 1915, her second child, John, was born.

After playing in two comedies at the Playhouse, in 1916, she was invited to go into partnership in the theatre with Frank Curzon, which she accepted. Her continuing success put great strains on the marriage and she and Buck were divorced in 1921.

Her next great triumph was the revival, in 1922, of *The Second Mrs Tanqueray,* with Du Maurier directing. *The Times* notes that this was a great night for an ex-Gaiety girl. 'She proved that it was possible to be the most beautiful actress in the theatre and also to carry guns enough for the most famous of Pinero's dramatic heroines.'

Gladys had appeared in her first Somerset Maugham play in 1919, and over the following decade played in three more; she became Maugham's favourite actress. She appeared regularly at the Playhouse where most of her plays had good runs. It was said that she was at her best in modern plays but disappointing in the classics.

Gladys Cooper spent the 1920s bringing up her two children and managing the Playhouse. She took over full management of the theatre in 1926. She worked hard, drove herself relentlessly and expected everybody else to keep pace. In 1928, she married Sir Neville Arthur Pearson, a wealthy publisher; by him she had her third and last child, Sally.

In the 1930s, the Depression, increasing labour costs and competition from the Talkies brought financial ruin to the Playhouse. In 1933, Gladys paid out a large sum of money to cover her debts and buy herself out of the remainder of the lease. It was a blow. But it had happened and now it was over. She didn't sit and brood.

In 1934, she made her American debut in *The Shining Hour.* It played to good houses in the States and was followed by a successful run in Britain. In 1935, she was back in New York to play Desdemona and Lady Macbeth, both of which were flops. Gladys simply was not a Shakespearean actress. She had more luck in her leading man. He was the English born actor Philip Merivale whom she married in Chicago in May 1937 - her previous marriage to Sir Neville Pearson having been dissolved. For the next 30 years, America was to be her home.

Both Gladys and Philip had had some bad runs and were in serious financial straits when she received her first offer from Hollywood - Alfred Hitchcock wanted her to play a part in *Rebecca.* Other films followed, in which she played minor roles. Then in 1942, she was nominated for an Academy Award for her playing of Bette Davis' mother in *Now Voyager.* Another nomination followed in 1943 for her role as the Mother Superior in *The Song of Bernadette.* MGM then put her under contract. There was also much grief at this time. In 1946, Philip Merivale died and in the following year, her son, John, became mentally ill.

In 1945, she came back to England to make a film, *Beware of Pity.* In 1948, on three months leave from MGM, she was on the London stage, in Peter Ustinov's *The Indifferent Shepherd.* From about this time onwards, she divided her time between America and England, and bought a house in Henley-on-Thames.

After several more plays in London, Gladys was appearing in *The Chalk Garden* in New York, when she answered a cry for help from the London production of the same play. There, Edith Evans had had to abandon the leading role because of sickness. Gladys Cooper was invited to replace her - immediately! Now almost 70, Gladys left Long Island within hours, arrived in London the following morning and played at the Haymarket that same night.

Successes continued with *A Passage to India* in New York in 1962 (she played Mrs Moore) and in the film, *My Fair Lady*, in 1963, in which she was Mrs Higgins. There was various other work including a popular television series, *The Rogues*, with David Niven. In 1966, Gladys Cooper sold her house in California and returned to England for good. The following year, she was created a Dame of the British Empire.

December 18th 1968 was her 80th birthday. Gladys was working as usual - in Ira Wallach's *Out of the Question*, at St Martin's. But there was a surprise in store. The management had bought out all the tickets for the evening performance and filled the stalls with her family and friends. At a point in the play when her stage grandson should have appeared, Robert Morley, her son-in-law in real life, made an unscheduled appearance with a tray of clinking glasses and champagne.

Gladys was determined never to retire and in fact she acted until the end. In 1971, on a tour of a revival of *The Chalk Garden*, she became ill with lung cancer and died on November 16th.

The acting spirit remained in the family. Her daughter, Joan, as mentioned, married Robert Morley. Her son, John, began his stage career in 1934. Her other daughter - from her marriage with Sir Neville - went on the stage as Sally Cooper and in 1961 married Robert Hardy. And of course her grandson, Sheridan Morley, became a leading theatre critic.◻

MRS DINAH CRAIK
(1826-1887)
REMEMBERED FOR HER 'GENTLEMAN'.

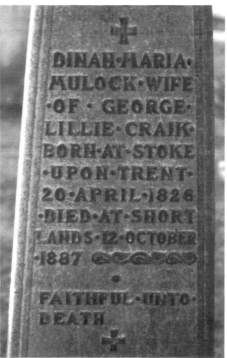

A lthough the author of numerous novels, children's stories, essays and poems, Mrs Craik is remembered for one book. *John Halifax, Gentleman,* a best-seller on both sides of the Atlantic. It had already sold more than a quarter of a million copies - a fabulous figure for its day - before she died in Bromley, Kent, in 1887. And years after this, visiting Americans were still visiting the 'Halifax country of Tewkesbury' - where the novel is set.

Mrs Craik was born Dinah Maria Mulock on April 20th 1826, at Stoke-upon-Trent, Staffordshire. After a sound education, she came to London about 1846, determined to be a writer. Her early stories were strictly for the young. The best known of these was *Cola Monti* in 1849. In the same year, her three-volume novel. *The Ogilvies* came out to great success. Others followed. In fact, her output was prodigious. Altogether, she published nearly 50 volumes of various works.

She was now living at Wildwood, North End, Hampstead. It was in 1857 that she wrote *John Halifax, Gentleman,* a story depicting the highest ideals of English middle class life. Other works followed, some very popular but never again would she achieve the success of *John Halifax*.

In 1864, Miss Mulock married George Lillie Craik, a partner in the publishing firm, Macmillan. Soon afterwards, the newly-weds moved into Shortlands Road, near Bromley. She remained here until her death. There is as yet no house plaque in her memory. When this was mooted after the last war, it was refused on the grounds that her best-seller was not written at Shortlands. It seems that even the local council is determined to judge her on that one book.

But Kentish neighbours also remembered Mrs Craik for her many kindnesses and one story, often retold, illustrates this well. It was a freezing winter's morning in January 1868 (or it could have been 1869). A man on his way to work, at the junction of St George's Road and Bromley Road, heard a baby's cry. He found the baby near some bricks and carried her to Beckenham Police Station. Mrs Craik heard about this, saw the baby and went through the legal procedures of adoption. She brought up the girl as her own child.

It was the sort of story that might easily have come out of Mrs Craik's own fiction. And sure enough, in 1880, the book, *Little Sunshine* was published, roughly based on the foundling.

Mrs Craik died suddenly on October 12th 1887, from heart failure. She was buried in the churchyard of Keston Parish Church, near the Beckenham border. There is a plaque to her memory in St Mary's Church, Shortlands, near where she lived. It gives her name, dates of birth and death and the simple inscription, 'She Wrote John Halifax, Gentleman.' There is another memorial to her in Tewkesbury Abbey. Why? Because it was the scene of *John Halifax, Gentleman* - why else?❑

RICHMAL CROMPTON
(1890-1969)
THE 'WILLIAM' PHENOMENON.

When, in later years, Richmal Crompton's niece sympathised with her aunt for having polio, Richmal replied that she had had 'a much more interesting life because of it'. The reason for this, of course, was her masterful creation, that scruffy, rebellious, perennially-11-year-old, William Brown.

Richmal had an attack of poliomyelitis in 1923, when she was teaching at a school in Kent, in her early thirties. The illness lost her the use of her right leg. She was still able to walk with a stick but her doctor advised her nevertheless to give up her teaching job. She was therefore forced to devote herself entirely to writing. From then until the end of her life, she was to write some 37 William adventures and a number of other novels.

There never was a model William on which Richmal based her character. He might have been something like her brother, something like her nephews, something like boys in the choir or a composite of 'all the boys I've ever known', as Richmal once admitted.

In 1969, a correspondent to the *Kentish Times*, who signed himself 'Elviri,' described how the first William story was discovered. Working in

53

the editorial department of the monthly magazine, *Home,* in the 1920s, he found William in the slush pile and recognised its worth.

'Elviri' remembered all the battles that the magazine then had with William's creator. The main problem seemed to be getting Richmal to turn out sufficient William stories to satisfy reader demand. Apparently, Miss Crompton fancied herself more as a romantic writer so the solution had to be blackmail. The magazine would publish one of her romances *after* she had written another William story! In this way, *Home* seldom came out without our badly-behaved hero.

Another periodical in which William appeared at that time was the *Happy Magazine* . Richmal confesses that she tried to get rid of the scruffy schoolboy rebel after writing *William and the Outlaws,* but found that William simply seemed to take over. Her first William book, *Just William,* appeared in the spring of 1922 and since then the sales of William books in the English language alone, have topped an estimated 9,000,000.

In each succeeding generation, Richmal kept pace with the world about her. When Al Capone was gunning down rivals in Chicago, out came *William the Gangster.* In the Second World War, there was *William and the ARP,* followed by *William & the Evacuees.* After the war, *William and the Brains Trust.* Then, in the 1950s, came *William & the Moon Rocket* and *William's Television Show. William & the Pop Singers* was published in 1965.

There were other changes to reflect the changing times. In the 1920s, the Browns lived in a large house with a library, pantry, cook and maids. The servants addressed the young rebel as 'Master William'. By the 1960s, the house is rather more modest with only a daily woman to do the chores.

Richmal Crompton produced a number of light novels, not intended for children. But few will be remembered today. In 1949, she attempted to launch the first of a new series on a younger child character. These were to be the Jimmy books but alas, they never caught on. William books, on the other hand, have been adapted into films and plays and for radio and television. The books have also been translated into a number of other languages.

Richmal Crompton Lamburn was born on November 15th 1890, in Bury, Lancashire. Her father was the Rev Edward John Sewell Lamburn, curate and schoolmaster and her mother was Clara Crompton. She had an elder sister and a younger brother.

She went to the Clergy Daughters' School in Warrington and later in Darley Dale, Derbyshire. A bright child, she was awarded a founder's scholarship to the Royal Holloway College, London University, in 1911.

54

She gained a university scholarship in 1912 and the college's Driver scholarship in classics in 1914. She left London University in 1914 with second class honours in the classics.

From 1915 to 1917, she taught at her old school, Darley Dale. She then moved to Kent to become classics mistress at Bromley High School for Girls, from 1917 to 1924. It was around this time that she first began sending stories to magazines.

Bromley and its surrounds became the background to all her stories. In 1927, her income had risen to £2,336 11s 5d, a substantial sum for that time. Of this, the William stories accounted for £1,300. These earnings enabled her to move to a larger house, still in the vicinity of the Common. She stayed here until February 1954, when she moved again to a bungalow in Chislehurst. She died in 1969, aged 78.

But William, of course, goes marching on. Having survived the last 70 years or so, there seems every reason to think that William and the outlaws will still be up to their imaginative pranks for the enjoyment of readers in another 70 years and more. ❏

ST EANSWYTHE
(614-640)
FOLKESTONE'S PATRON SAINT

In June 1885, during the installation of a sanctuary in Folkestone's parish church, St Mary and St Eanswythe, the workmen found a small cavity in the north wall containing an ancient lead coffer. The coffer was found to contain the remains of a young woman who had died in the 7th century. From the place of burial near the high altar, the position of greatest honour and distinction in the church, it was concluded that here were the long lost relics of St Eanswythe, which, tradition had it, had been hidden in the church during the Reformation. Suddenly, here was a tangible link with the Saxon world of 12 centuries earlier.

The remains were reverently re-interred in the place where they had been discovered, still in the Saxon coffer and enclosed behind an elaborate brass grill and engraved door. This bestowed a rare distinction upon the church, and it is now one of the few remaining churches in the country where the bones of its patron saint are buried within its walls.

Imagine a very different England - in the dark days of the Anglo-Saxons. Christianity had first been introduced about the 2nd century but was in danger of dying out with the worship of pagan gods. The efforts of one young woman were now to introduce a revolution of faith.

St Eanswythe (also spelled Eanswith and Eanswide) was a Saxon princess, born around 614. She was the daughter of Eadbald, King of Kent and his Queen, Emma, daughter of the King of the Franks.

St Eanswythe's grandfather (Eadbald's father) Ethelbert had been converted to Christianity by St Augustine in 597. It is thought that her mother was also a Christian and that she herself had been baptised. However, her father, Eadbald, was pagan.

When Ethelbert died in 616, there were fears for the survival of Christianity. Eadbald practised idolatry. This had been dying out but was now practised openly.

A church Council was held. This was attended by Laurence, Archbishop of Canterbury, Mellitus, first Bishop of London, and Justus, first Bishop of Rochester. It was decided to cease preaching to the barbarous infidels of England and Mellitus and Justus retired to Gaul. Laurence was about to follow when a miracle occurred to change his mind.

He was reluctant to leave and had his bed carried into the church of St Peter and St Paul (the earlier Folkestone parish church), where he prayed hard and long, then dropped off to sleep. While he slept, St Peter appeared and upbraided him for thinking of deserting his flock. The apostle reinforced his words with hard blows, the marks of which Laurence showed to Eadbald in the morning. This 'miracle' was apparently sufficient to convert King Eadbald to Christianity.

According to M Woodward's *The Past and Present of the Parish Church of Folkestone,* the King's daughter, Eanswythe, is supposed to have 'from infancy renounced worldly pomp, studied to serve God, trod under foot all the treasures of this world'. She 'embraced the holy doctrine' and 'longed with constant desire for the heavenly kingdom'.

Eadbald embarked on a programme of church building. For his daughter, he 'selected a suitable place, remote and unfrequented, called Folkestone'. And it was here that Eadbald built St Peter's and St Paul's church and gave it to Eanswythe. The first nunnery in England was also built in Folkestone. In 630, Eanswythe became Abbess of a religious community of sisters. Under the King's instructions, other churches rose up here and there throughout Kent.

However, when Eanswythe reached a marriageable age, her father began to look for a suitable match and to persuade his daughter to co-operate. But Eanswythe had already made up her mind to remain a virgin. She gave a very shrewd rebuttal:

'Dearest Father, if you are able to bring to my virginity an unending duration of delight, a perpetual enjoyment of marriage, an immortal spouse and infinite joy in offspring, I will gladly acquiesce in your design. But if you are thinking of bringing me friendship mingled with hate, sterile nuptials, a transitory enjoyment of them, a mortal husband, the distressing loss of children and the corruption of everything that appertains to virginity, then even the counsel of my father, unless he desires to throw off a father's qualities, will advise adherence to the better part.

'...I long for the embrace of a heavenly and immortal Spouse: for Him I reserve the flower of my virginity: for when loving Him I shall be chaste, when touching Him, I shall be pure, when accepting Him I shall be a virgin still...I beg, O father to be allowed to build an Oratory for myself.

Moved by her prayers, Eadbald began to build an Oratory for her. Work had already begun when the King of the Northumbrians arrived with a large following, to ask for her hand in marriage.

The king of the Northumbrians was a heathen and Eanswythe proposed a bargain. One of the beams for her Oratory was three feet too short. If the king's gods could by his prayers, lengthen the beam by the wanted three feet, then she would marry him.

The King took her at her word and spent much time praying to his gods, without any success '...and in the sight of all present he went away filled with shame'.

Eanswythe, however, approached the beam, made a prayer, and the beam obediently lengthened to the required size. This was the first miracle.

The nearest water to the Oratory was a long distance away and had to be brought by hand. Eanswythe therefore, went to the spring a mile or more away in the village of Sweeton. Using a stick, she made the water follow her, up and down, over cliffs and rocky summits, to her Oratory, where it delivered abundant water for men and animals.

In miracle number three, the young virgin placed an 'interdict' that the birds should stop settling on the nearby fields and consuming the produce. And so it was - the birds obeyed. She performed still further miracles. She restored a blind woman's sight, made a madman sane and restored health in others from various diseases. St Eanswythe is thought to have died at the young age of about 26, in 640.

Today, you can see several pictures of the saint inside the church. There is also a large stained glass window in St Eanswythe's chapel. The modern church continues to do her reverence. Flowers and lighted candles are usually placed before the brass grill and engraved door which guard her relics. And parishioners pray to her memory.◻

QUEEN ETHELBURGA
(590-647)
SAXON ENGLAND'S EVANGELIST FOR CHRIST

PARISH CHURCH OF
ST MARY & ST ETHELBURGA
LYMINGE

FOUNDED AS AN ABBEY IN A.D. 633

Times of Sunday and weekday services
can be found in the porch.

Open daily for Meditation & Prayer.

This early Saxon queen is best remembered in the church named after her in Lyminge in Kent - St Mary and St Ethelburga. She came here in 633 and built a place of worship, most likely upon Roman ruins, then some 250 years old. It was a Double Minster - a convent for men and women. The queen herself became the first abbess.

Lyminge is thought to have been the birth place of Ethelburga, in about 590. She was the daughter of King Ethelbert, and the sister of Eadbald, who became the next king of Kent in succession to Ethelbert. Ethelburga's mother was Bertha, daughter of the king of Paris.

In about 624, seven years after her brother began his reign, Princess Ethelburga married Edwin, the King of Northumbria. (Northumbria was one of the seven kingdoms of the Saxon Heptarchy). It seems likely that Lyminge was the place where the wedding ceremony took place. Their personal beliefs must have been a problem from the beginning. The princess was a devout Christian, the king a pagan.

Edwin, however, was a very understanding man. He was happy for Ethelburga and her attendants to practise their religion and he even permitted the missionary, Paulinus, to accompany them to Northumbria. Edwin further promised to adopt Christianity himself if he found it offered more than his present faith. Ethelburga thus set about doing all she could to convert her husband to Christianity and very soon succeeded.

In 626, Paulinus was made Bishop of York. At his suggestion, Edwin called a Council of the *Witan* or wise men so that they could discuss the new faith. The Council resolved to destroy their heathen temples. King Edwin agreed he and his court should receive religious instruction. They were all baptised on Easter Eve, 627, in a small wooden church on the site of the present York Minster. This was a significant step, linking the two great Christian houses of Anglo-Saxon England.

Christianity spread rapidly in Northumbria, but the happy times were not to last. According to the Venerable Bede, 'the king and queen had to take up the cross in a time of persecution'. An attempt was made to assassinate King Edwin. A rebellion broke out, assisted by Penda, King of Mercia. There was a battle at Heathfield in Yorkshire. Edwin was killed in April 633. A terrible persecution of the church followed.

Ethelburga realised she would have to flee with her followers. The journey over land was considered far too dangerous, so the queen resolved to return to Kent by sea. She and Paulinus gathered the queen's children and their possessions together and set sail. They arrived in Kent without mishap and were greeted warmly by the Archbishop of Canterbury and by King Eadbald, Ethelburga's brother. It was Eadbald who helped her found the monastery at her birthplace, Lyminge.

In 634, Northumbria was regained for Christianity by Edwin's nephew, Oswald, a Christian educated at Iona.

Ethelburga died in 647. She was regarded as a Saint and her remains placed in the northern porticos of her church; this made Lyminge a pilgrimage shrine. In the ninth century, the abbey is thought to have been overrun by marauding Danes. However, Ethelburga's relics seem to have remained unmolested and were moved to St Gregory's Priory in Canterbury in 1085. Sadly, they were lost in the dissolution of the monasteries.

Today, small links with the Saxon queen still exist. The visible remains of the original church erected by Queen Ethelburga soon after she came here in 633, are to the east of the porch. The eastern apse where the altar stood and the beginnings of the rectangular nave (the north wall of which is continued under the present porch) can be seen clearly.

A shrine of St Ethelburga is thought to have been housed in a recess near the pulpit. Two of the figures on the alabaster reredos show St Ethelburga and St Paulinus - Ethelburga's chaplain and the first Archbishop of York - and St Dunstan.□

KITTY FISHER
(C. 1738-1767)
THE NOTORIOUS COURTESAN

'All that we know of her
Is this - she was a milliner
Her parentage so low and mean
Is hardly to be trac'd, I ween;
Say, has she wit - or has she sense?
No! nothing but impertinence'.

There were many satirical verses composed about the 'notorious Kitty Fisher' and this was one of them. As to its veracity, certainly she came from humble beginnings and worked in a milliner's shop. But many people gave a far better account of her fine wit and very good sense.

The first part of the story of Catherine 'Kitty' Fisher - buried in Benenden Cemetery - is all too familiar. Pretty, young and vivacious, she worked as a shop girl in London. (She may have had German origins as her name is sometimes spelt Fischer). To her London shop came the rich, good looking, well placed Ensign (afterwards Lieutenant-General)

Anthony George Martin, nicknamed the 'Military Cupid'. Kitty succumbed to his charms but if she was hoping for a long term arrangement, she was disappointed. According to C F Hardy's *Benenden Letters,* the Ensign was 'unable' to maintain her as his mistress'. But apparently Kitty was always fond enough of him to 'return to his protection at odd times'.

For most girls, such an experience would have led to their ruin. Kitty turned it into a triumph! That one seduction seems to have been enough to launch Kitty into a career as a courtesan. And very successful she seems to have been. After the 'Military Cupid' she progressed through the ranks until she was - simultaneously - the lover of both Field Marshal Lord Ligonier and Admiral Augustus Keppel.

By the mid-1750s, she was the most famous courtesan in London. She was known to the court itself and the upper classes (with whom she dallied); even the man in the street could have picked her out of a crowd. She was the companion of princes and lords. She was full of good spirits, skilful in small talk, and fluent in French. She dressed expensively in the very latest gowns and was followed by crowds whenever she ventured out of her splendid coach, drawn by four fine greys. Kitty was becoming rich. Very rich.

There was another reason why she became so well known. Her beauty and style were sought not only by fashionable beaux, but also by the leading artists of the day. As a play on her name, Nathaniel Hone painted her sitting beside a kitten fishing in a goldfish bowl - as you can see with this entry. She sat many times for Sir Joshua Reynolds. He also asked her to sit in for other grander ladies. He used Kitty as a model for their hands, arms, and neck. This saved the time of the real subject. According to Leslie's *Life of Reynolds,* the great painter was much amused by Kitty's small talk.

Reynolds' notebooks tell us she sat for him many times from 1759 to 1766. The most famous painting is one at Petworth, several times engraved, in which she leans across the table in a pensive attitude, facing the viewer. This was painted in 1759 when Kitty was about 20. In the picture, a letter is on the table and we can see it is addressed to Kitty.

In 1760, Kitty was painted as Cleopatra in the wanton act of dissolving a pearl in a cup of wine. The face is round and full, with finely-pencilled eyebrows and a pretty nose. Her brown hair is gracefully gathered on to the top of her head, secured by a ribbon.

There is a third Reynolds, at Lansdowne House. This shows Kitty in profile, leaning back with arms outstretched, her fingers teasing a parrot perched on her left hand. Her expression is attractive and coquettish.

A lesser artist, a portrait painter called Francis Cotes, also drew Kitty's likeness. This painting was apparently 'in the character of Danae, the lady who could not resist Jupiter when he took the shape of a shower of gold.'

In fact, the shower of gold arrived in the guise of John Norris, a Kentish land owner and 12 years MP for Rye. He owned Hempstead Manor, Benenden. It is thought that Kitty was already his mistress when he proposed marriage. After some ten years as London's most famous courtesan, Kitty was ready to settle down - particularly in the circumstances John Norris was able to provide for her. They were married at St George's, Hanover Square, London, on December 4th 1766. Kitty was John Norris' second wife. The records say nothing of his first wife or what happened to her.

From all accounts, Kitty was an excellent and attentive wife and made a good beginning with her tenants - treating them with kindness and generosity. She even set about building up her husband's dilapidated fortune. Country life suited her and she took to it with a relish, riding to hounds with the best of them. Even in London she had been known as a superb horsewoman and now she was able to show off her prowess. It was said she allowed no gate to be opened for her. Looking splendid on her jet black, high spirited, thoroughbred mare, she cleared the fences with ease and grace.

But, alas and alas, Kitty had little time to enjoy her position as mistress of Hemstead Manor. After only four months of marriage, on March 10th 1767, she died while taking the waters at fashionable Bath. Accounts vary as to the cause of death. It might have been smallpox. Or did she ingest the poisonous white lead used in her make-up? Whatever it was, it was a young death. Her age must have been no more than 29. According to her wishes, she was placed in her coffin in her best ball gown; she was buried at Benenden on March 23rd 1767.

John Norris mourned in his Kent estate - but not for long. Soon he had married his third wife, a French actress.

There had been rhymes and stories written about Kitty while she was still alive - some extremely rude. There was 'My eye, Kitty Fisher'. and 'Lucy Locket lost her pocket, Kitty Fisher found it'. There was even 'An Elegy of Kitty Fisher lying in State in Bath'. And finally, the obituary:

'She wedded to live honest - but, when tried
The experiment she liked not - and so died'.□

FANNY ELIZABETH FITZWILLIAM
(1801-1854)
A LIFE IN THE THEATRE

Attitudes to the theatre changed greatly during the 19th century, and the Dover Theatre - with which the actress, Fanny Fitzwilliam is closely associated - clearly reflects these changes. At the time of Fanny's birth in 1801, next door to the theatre, patronage by royalty had encouraged the theatre's manager, Fanny's father, Robert Copeland, to call it the Theatre Royal.

But almost half a century later, a local guide from circa 1844, quoted the town's 'sectarians' and 'puritans' condemning the theatre as 'the devil's temple'. And it wasn't just Dover that was affected but 'every other country town in the kingdom'. The guide goes on to say that 'in lieu of crowded audiences receiving a moral lesson *veluti in speculum* (as beheld), we have now...a beggarly account of empty boxes'. By the end of the century, however, the popularity of the Dover Theatre returned - so much so that by 1896, it was rebuilt on a grander, more extensive scale.

Like the children of most theatrical families in the 19th century England, Fanny Fitzwilliam first trod the boards when she was an infant of two or three years old. She was one of the children in a play called *Stranger*. Fanny and the Dover Theatre both prospered. She sang professionally at ten, in *Savourneen Deelish*. At 12, she was expert enough to play the piano at a concert in Margate. Her first significant role was in *The Poor Soldier*, at the Dover Theatre, a year later. At 14, she had singing lessons which qualified her as a ballad singer as well as an actress.

But - as for all performers - London beckoned then as it does now. In 1817, she opened at the Haymarket as Lucy in the *Review*. Other important roles followed and she was soon getting star billing. On December 2nd 1822, Fanny married Edward Fitzwilliam. He had been a popular actor of Irish characters but his success was now about to wane and Mrs Fitzwilliam seems to have been left to carve out her own fortune.

Fanny played in Dublin, in the provinces, and at the Adelphi in London, and continued to attract popular support in a variety of roles. In 1832, she became manager of Sadlers Wells and in 1837, left for an American tour. She appeared in New York and Boston, and on a later trip, in New Orleans and Havana. After Fanny Kemble, she became the second best paid actress in the United States.

Back in England, Mrs Fitzwilliam played in many provincial theatres before returning to the Adelphi. She continued to command leading parts until her sudden death from cholera on September 11th 1854. *The Times* wasn't the only paper to comment on 'the unexpected death of this excellent actress'.

The Era, of September 16th 1854, and the entry in the Dictionary of National Biography, both report that, had she lived, Fanny was to marry a Mr Buckstone, manager of the Haymarket Theatre, 'within a month'. Neither source, however, explains what happened to her first husband. Mrs Fitzwilliam was buried at Kensal Green in London.

Critics called Fanny 'one of the liveliest and most genuine actresses that ever trod the boards'. Her acting, they said was 'sweet and womanly'. She was a little on the short side with blue eyes, a light complexion and a lovely face and was much praised for her excellent singing voice. She left two children. Her son, Edward Francis, was a composer and her daughter, Kathleen, became a popular actress. Her brother was also on the stage.◻

OCTAVIA HILL
(1838-1912)
'OPEN AIR SITTING ROOMS' FOR YOU AND ME.

This was how Octavia Hill described the aims of the National Trust, the organisation she helped to found. Some couple her name with Florence Nightingale as one of the two greatest women of the 19th century; Octavia Hill was determined that the green open spaces of Britain - as well as our historic buildings - should be saved for everyone to enjoy.

The success of the National Trust today is a direct result of her initial efforts. And what a success. The Trust now owns some 600,000 acres, over 200 buildings of outstanding architectural or historic importance and holds covenants protecting development of further beautiful countryside of around 80,000 acres and many other buildings. And all this started with one little Victorian lady with the determination and capacity for hard work that would make her dream come true.

Octavia Hill inherited no great privileges. She was born in 1838, the daughter of two social reformers of modest means, living near to the green open spaces of Hampstead Heath. But in 1840, the Hills' bank collapsed and the family were forced to move to Fitzroy Square where, as Octavia later wrote, 'the first knowledge of misery and poverty came to me'. And it was this realisation that became the reason for her life's work.

Her mother was the manager of a Christian Socialist inspired Ladies' Guild, employing poor women to paint on glass. Octavia came to realise something of the desperate need of the London poor. She was put in charge of poor children making toys; she had a natural talent for managing both the workers and the business. At this time, she also fell under the influence of Rev Frederick Maurice, a pioneer of Christian socialism.

When Octavia was about 17, she came into contact with the great art historian and critic, John Ruskin. Ruskin was heir to a large fortune and wanted to spend his money on social reform. He agreed to teach Octavia drawing and offered her work as a copy illustrator for his books.

In 1864, Octavia persuaded Ruskin to lend her the enormous figure of £1500 to renovate three slum houses in St Marylebone Court. Octavia was convinced that a good landlord could produce good tenants. Ruskin's only condition was that the rents must be fair and firmly collected. The houses were in a dreadful state but Octavia quickly set about stopping leaks, repairing, scrubbing, re-glazing and replastering.

Confronted with drunkenness, brawling and filth, Octavia triumphed. Her philosophy was simple and almost Christ-like. She treated her tenants as she treated her friends. In return, rents were paid and self-respect returned. But bringing decent housing to the poor was only the first step. She remembered the wide open spaces of her Hampstead childhood and knew she had to preserve green fields, trees and fresh air for the poor and enable them to experience it.

During the 1860s, London expanded rapidly and developers were pouncing on every spare piece of land. In 1864, the Commons Preservation Society was founded and Octavia was later invited to join. In 1875, her sister, Miranda, also concerned about social welfare, formed the Kyrle Society. The aim was 'to bring beauty to the homes of the poor'. Octavia extended this vision to people being able to get out of their homes and enjoy the beauty of the open spaces. It was at this time that she invented her term, 'open air sitting rooms'.

By 1878, Octavia was a woman of influence. She had given evidence to the Royal Commission on housing and had heard a letter of hers read in parliament. She had expanded her housing management to other parts of England and also to Europe, America and Russia. She was briefly engaged to one of her helpers then broke it off. She quarrelled with Ruskin. It was suddenly all too much for her and she broke down.

She was out of the public eye for some three years. But the task for which she is best remembered hadn't yet begun. In 1884, she was involved in a major appeal to save 310 acres of land adjoining Hampstead Heath (which was much smaller than it is now). A sum of £50,000 was raised by the co-operation of the Kyrle Society, the Commons

Preservation Society and the Metropolitan Board. Further 'open air sitting rooms' were secured at Vauxhall, Wandsworth and Tooting Common.

Octavia was chiefly responsible for the formation of the Kent and Surrey Committee of the Commons Preservation Society, which was particularly concerned with footpaths. Another reformer, Sir Robert Hunter, particularly impressed Octavia with his vision. It was Sir Robert who, in 1884, first had the idea of forming a national organisation for the protection of open spaces. The aim was not only to preserve them for the public's enjoyment. He also wanted to control private speculators.

In the same year, 1884, a Mr Evelyn had attempted to give his Deptford estate, Sayes Court, to the nation. He asked Sir Robert to see how this could be done. Sir Robert found that there was no legal provision for such a gift and he immediately looked around for a solution.

In February 1885, Sir Robert had a meeting at his house, which Octavia attended. It was thought that 'company' was too commercial a term to describe the sort of organisation they had in mind. Octavia later wrote to Sir Robert that 'trust' would be preferable. He scribbled across the top of the letter: '? National Trust'.

Ruskin introduced Octavia to Canon Hardwick Rawnsley. Another reformer, he was working in the slums of the notorious Seven Dials district of London. He also saw potential in Sir Robert's ideas and he became the third member of the trio.

Nothing more was done until 1893, when Canon Rawnsley wrote endorsing the ideas of Octavia and Sir Robert and urging the need for a body to implement them. In 1894, an inaugural meeting took place at the offices of the Commons Preservation Society, arranged by Sir Robert. Canon Rawnsley and Octavia Hill were both present. Octavia set out the aims of the Trust, the philosophy of which has stood to this day. In January 1895, The National Trust was registered by the Board of Trade.

Octavia herself would not accept a post with the new organisation. However, a friend with whom she shared a house at Crockham Hill, Harriet Yorke, became treasurer. Octavia died in 1912 and was buried in Crockham Hill churchyard, directly beneath a yew tree, to the right of the gate. Inside the church, there is an effigy. The inscription reads:

'Noble in aim, wise in method, unswerving in faith and courage, she devoted her life to raising the bodily condition of her fellow citizens.'

Additional honour was paid to Octavia in 1981, when Sevenoaks District Council gave the National Trust 103 acres, called Octavia Hill Woodlands. The new land adjoins Toys Hill, already owned by the Trust, and which features Octavia Hill's Well, sunk by Octavia for the use of the villagers and given to the Trust in 1898.◻

GERALDINE JEWSBURY
(1812-1880)
THE RUSH FOR LOVE.

'I think of you as Catholics think of their saints, to keep them out of evil...You know I love you as nobody else can, and everything you do is right in my eyes'.

This was written by Geraldine Jewsbury, not to a man, but to Jane Carlyle, shortly after they had met in March 1841. Jane, and less so, Thomas Carlyle, became central to Geraldine's life. And in fact, when Susanne Howe was preparing her biography, *Geraldine Jewsbury, Her Life and Errors* (1935), she received a letter saying: 'You had much better not write a life of Geraldine Jewsbury. She would be quite forgotten today but for her friendship with the Carlyles. Mrs Ireland's (1892) edition of her letters does all that needs be done to preserve the memory of this entirely unimportant person'.

We don't know what particular axe the letter writer had to grind but there are a number of reasons why Geraldine Jewsbury - who spent the last 18 years of her life in Sevenoaks - should be remembered. In fact,

Thomas Carlyle himself noted that this talented, temperamental and impetuous women was one of the most interesting he had seen for years. He described her 'clear, delicate sense and courage looking out of her small sylph-like figure...the flimsy tatter of a creature...seeking passionately for some paradise to be gained by battle'.

Geraldine suffered from frail health and this prevented her from entering the rough and tumble of journalism, although, as a freelance, she did contribute to magazines on such subjects as the servant problem and the condition of the lower classes. She was for many years a contributor to the *Athenaeum* and was also a publisher's reader for Bentley's, exercising considerable influence over the choice of books for Mudie's circulating library.

Geraldine wrote six novels, which her biographer describes as 'tempestuous and over-heated circulating-library novels'. These concerned working-class life in northern England or were historical. Her first novel, *Zoe, the History of Two Lives,* was published in 1845. Her second, *The Half-Sisters,* which came out in 1848, would have contained a dedication to Jane Carlyle, had Jane not feared it might offend her husband. In addition to her novels, Geraldine wrote stories for *Juvenile Budget* and *Household Words*.

She had a clear idea of what her books should be and what they should contain. They were to have a clear moral tone with 'nothing unpleasant.' For the success of a novel, she stressed the need for the 'eternal importance of love'.

Geraldine Endsor Jewsbury was born at Measham, Derbyshire, in 1812, the daughter of Thomas Jewsbury. The family went to live in Manchester about 1818, where the father was a merchant and insurance agent. Her mother died shortly after the move and Geraldine was brought up by her elder sister, Maria.

Maria was already a successful writer. She contributed to various magazines and had had four books published. She provided the stimulus for Geraldine's education and introduced her to the Wordsworths and other celebrities. In 1832, Maria married, went to India with her husband but died there of cholera the following year.

After Maria's marriage, Geraldine had taken responsibility for the household. At this time she was aged 20 and was already corresponding with the Wordsworth family and also with the Carlyles. She was a good housekeeper and a good hostess and was generally much liked by her own growing circle of friends. Jane Carlyle wrote of her: she 'possessed the gift of fascinating young and old, learned and unlearned, servants included'. Geraldine continued her correspondence with the Carlyles; her letters evidently made such an impression that she was invited to stay at the Carlyles' house in Cheyne Row, Chelsea.

During the 1840s, Geraldine's friendship with Jane Carlyle deepened, but generally the sources leave the physical part of the relationship unanswered. It is probably safe to assume that Geraldine was bi-sexual. She had a number of other affairs and was wont to declare undying love to both men and women.

Geraldine was a brilliant conversationalist as well as having winning manners, a kindly disposition and a good sense of humour. These personal qualities made her a firm favourite, first in Manchester and then in London. Thus, when an application was made for her to secure a Civil List pension, she was supported by a number of famous writers, artists, statesmen and scientists. These included Thomas Hardy, Thomas Huxley (she was god-mother to his youngest daughter), Charles Kingsley, John Ruskin and Alfred Tennyson. She was also a friend of the Brownings, Charlotte Bronte, Thackeray and Jenny Lind.

Following the publication of *Zoe*, her first pulsatingly romantic novel, a man known only as Q, pursued her. We are indebted to Jane Carlyle for the information but apparently this man believed that Geraldine had modelled the passionate Zoe in every respect upon herself.

Flattered at first, Geraldine soon found the approach of Q emotionally more than she could cope with. Her biographer writes: 'Accustomed as she was to being tossed hither and yon on waves of emotion, Geraldine found this crisis a little more violent than most'. She finally refused his offer of marriage.

Another man with whom she had a romantic fling was Charles Lambert, an English official in the service of Sulaiman Pacha of Egypt. He arrived at her house in Manchester, in oriental costume and Geraldine sat at his feet while he held forth on solving the problems of the world.

Yet another beau was Walter Mantell, a scientist, explorer and administrator, from New Zealand. She met him in 1856 when she was 44 and he was 38. She saw much of him during his three year stay in England but he then returned to New Zealand - resisting her pleas to take her with him. Over the next 23 years, they corresponded, while he went about his own affairs and married twice. During this time, she wrote him more than 500 letters.

Her father died in 1853. Then, because of her friendship with the Carlyles, she moved to Chelsea in 1854, to be near them.

In 1866 (or it may have been 1872 - sources differ) Geraldine moved to Sevenoaks in Kent. Here she lived at Walnut Tree-House, an old-fashioned house on the London Road, where her back windows looked out on a shady, secluded garden. She continued to write her *Athenaeum* reviews, correct proofs, read manuscripts, supervise translations, and write long gossipy letters. She often visited London - to see friends, conduct business and hear readings.

Her biographer quotes a Sevenoaks resident who remembered Geraldine at that time. 'Her hair was quite grey and she always wore black-tinted spectacles. I do not think I ever saw her without them. She generally dressed in quiet colours, black or grey, and wore a large black hat with an ostrich feather, and draped at the back with a black veil which was brought round her face and fastened beneath the chin with a little brooch'.

Geraldine died on September 28th 1880, aged 68, of cancer, in a private hospital in Edgware Road, London. Among her last visitors were Carlyle, Professor Huxley and J A Froude. She was buried at Brompton Cemetery.

At the end of Howe's biography, the author quotes words written to Thomas Carlyle by John Sterling just before his death. Howe thought it might be applied to Geraldine:

'I tread the common road into the great darkness, without any thought of fear, and with very much of hope. Certainty, indeed, I have none...It is all very strange, but not a hundredth part so sad as it seems to the standers-by'.□

JOAN, THE FAIR MAID OF KENT
(1328-1385)
'THE MOST BEAUTIFUL GIRL IN THE KINGDOM OF ENGLAND.'

That was what the Norman historian, Froissart, called her. And he added 'the most loving'. His appellation, 'cette jeune demoiselle de Kent,' has made her immortal. But it wasn't just her beauty that makes Joan, the Fair Maid of Kent, important. She occupied the stage in one of the more tumultuous periods of our history, shared it with some of the most interesting characters and - through her marriages - exerted power behind the throne. Her third husband was Edward, prince of Wales, the Black Prince; one of her sons became Richard II.

Joan was born in 1328, probably the younger daughter and third child of Edmund of Woodstock, Earl of Kent, sixth son of Edward I. Even at the age of two, Joan was never spared political reality. Her father, Edmund of Woodstock, was beheaded in 1330, after a failed plot on behalf of Edward III.

Joan married three times, all believed to be love matches. She first attracted the adoration of both the young William de Montacute, second Earl of Salisbury, and - at the same time - the earl's steward, Sir Thomas

73

Holland. Holland was the faster mover and secured a marriage contract. In those days, a betrothal was a bond that included cohabitation. And this was *before* the actual wedding ceremony.

Before wedlock had been solemnised, however, Holland was called away to war and Salisbury stepped in with another contract of marriage. When Holland returned, a war hero from the battle of Cressy, he enlisted papal intervention which finally came down on his side. Joan's marriage with Salisbury was dissolved.

In 1348, while still the Countess of Salisbury, Joan helped create a custom which survives to the day. It took place at a ball in Calais, held to celebrate the fall of the town. During the dance, Joan dropped her garter. King Edward III - thought to be in love with Joan - picked up the garter and bound it to his knee. He rebuked the jests of the bystanders with words that were to become famous in the history of England: *'honi soit qui mal y pense'* Prophetically, the king declared that the garter 'would soon be most highly honoured.'

Following the deaths of both her brothers in 1352, Joan assumed the title of Countess of Kent and Lady Wake of Liddell, in her own right. The king granted her an annual income of 100 marks, a considerable sum. In 1358, Joan accompanied her husband to Normandy, where he was governor of the fort of Creyk. Two years later, Holland assumed the title Earl of Kent from his wife. He had little time to enjoy it however; he died in the December of that year.

The Fair Maid of Kent seems to have wasted little time in mourning for within a few months, she was apparently head over heels in love with her cousin, Edward, Prince of Wales, the Black Prince. A match was concluded but without the knowledge of the king. Later, however, the king accepted the arrangements and a papal dispensation was obtained. The couple were married by the Archbishop of Canterbury, Simon Islip, at Lambeth Palace, on October 6th 1361. The joyous celebrations lasted five days.

In the following spring, in 1362, the newly weds were sent to Aquitaine, where they reigned as viceroys for Edward III. Here there was plenty of opportunity for the Black Prince to demonstrate the superiority of the English longbow against the heavily armoured knights on horseback. The most dramatic illustration of this took place at the Battle of Poitiers when the Black Prince with only 8,000 men defeated the elite French army of over 60,000.

The couple stayed in Aquitaine for nine years during which time the Black Prince was chiefly concerned with destroying the armies of the several princes of central France. Joan gave birth to two sons, one of whom was the future Richard II. The family returned to England in 1371.

The Black Prince died on June 8th 1376 and on November 20th, Richard was created Prince of Wales. One third of the revenues went to Joan as dower.

The remaining family stayed in the royal manor of Kennington, where the Fair Maid gave another demonstration of her popularity. John of Gaunt and Henry Percy, who had been identified by an infuriated London mob, asked Joan for protection. Joan sent three of her knights to make peace with the populace. The crowd replied that, because of their love for the Maid, they would honour her request.

In June 1381, on the outbreak of the Peasants' Revolt, Joan was 53 and according to contemporary reports, clearly a lady not accustomed to weight watching. Despite her corpulence, however, she still had enough beauty to win over a crowd of rebels.

Wat Tyler and his Kentish men stormed and captured the Tower of London. They beheaded the hated Archbishop of Canterbury on Tower Hill and went looking for more sport. They entered Joan's bedroom and found her in bed. But it wasn't to be a fate worse than death. The historians record that the aging Fair Maid 'escaped with a few kisses'.

But some things were beyond her persuasion. Her son by her first marriage, John Holland, was accused of the murder of the son of Ralph Stafford, one of the king's favourites. Joan appealed to King Richard for a pardon but was refused. The grief caused by this was apparently Joan's undoing for she died a few days later. The final irony was that the king, when his anger had cooled, pardoned her son after all.

In Canterbury Cathedral you can see the small chapel in the crypt, built by the Black Prince to commemorate his marriage. A quaint stone above the organ is supposed to be a 'portrait' of Joan of Kent.

Joan, who owned land in Lincolnshire, was - at her request - buried with her first husband, Sir Thomas Holland, in the Franciscan Grey Friars Church in Stamford, in 1385. The records state that their tomb was a 'sumptuous chapel' adjacent to the choir. Today, nothing remains but the ruins of the gateway.

But finally we are left with a mystery. The portrait reproduced with this entry comes from a medieval manuscript, supposed to have been taken from a statue of Joan, which once stood in a church in Stamford. The picture is clearly not of a maid fair! So could history have got it all wrong? It's rather more comforting to think that the picture is really of somebody else. Or is this *really* what Joan looked like in her more mature years? If it is, perhaps it's not surprising that Wat Tyler let her go 'with a few kisses'.□

MARIE LLOYD
(1870-1922)
THE GREATEST MUSIC HALL ARTISTE OF THEM ALL

It wasn't what Marie Lloyd said that had audiences rolling in the aisles and the critics cheering. It was the *way* she said it, the you-know-what-I-mean kind of pause, the huge wink, the body language. Her hesitations created more merriment than most other people's words.

She was the mistress of the *double entendre*. Her Cockney humour was as natural as the earthiness of Shakespeare's Falstaff. It was said that when she came on the stage, the entire theatre was instantly aware of her, subdued and obedient. She did what she liked with the audience. And they adored her for it.

Marie - who later lived in Lewisham, then part of Kent - was born Matilda Alice Victoria Wood, at 36 Plumber Street, Hoxton, on February 12th 1870. She was the eldest of the 11 children of John Wood, an artificial flower maker and his wife, Matilda Mary Caroline Archer. In such a large family, there was seldom any money to spare.

Marie was a natural entertainer. While still a child, she formed a troupe of little girls, the Fairy Bell Minstrels, who sang and acted in schoolrooms and mission halls.

She made her first proper public appearance on May 9th 1885, when she was 14. It was on the stage of the Grecian Music Hall, attached to the Eagle public house in London's City Road. She went by the stage name of Bella Delmare; before very long she changed this to Marie Lloyd. By August, she was fourth on the bill in a music hall in Bermondsey, earning fifteen shillings a week. At the beginning of 1886, she went to Ireland at £10 a week and by the end of the year she was playing at several halls for the fabulous sum of £100 a week. At this stage of her career, she quite naturally slipped into the part of a child or young girl.

In 1891, and for the two succeeding years, she was in pantomimes at Drury Lane and also in some suburban and provincial theatres. She was less successful as a straight actress. In a play, she had to stick to the script. Her real talent was for improvisation.

She came into her own in the music hall, then enjoying an increasing boom of popularity. Her songs were all written for her but it was her interpretation and the appropriate actions that brought the cheers and the laughter. Mostly, she made them joyfully improper.

Her eyes were full of fun, big laughing eyes, and she had dazzling teeth and lovely legs. But despite her pretty face, blue eyes and golden hair, she never made a display of herself, she was never a sex object. She was as popular with the women as she was with the men.

Marie had a gift for language - particularly vulgar English and Cockney, which she used to full advantage. And she attracted praise from people like Bernard Shaw, Ellen Terry and Sarah Bernhardt. She also travelled abroad - to Australia, South Africa and the United States, where she was greeted by the same cheers and laughter wherever she went.

Max Beerbohm, the famous painter and graphic artist, said of her: 'she has an exquisitely sensitive ear, impeccable phrasing and timing. But sheer joy of living was always her strongest point'. Some of her most popular songs were 'Oh Mr Porter!', 'My Old Man Said Follow the Van', and 'A Little of What You Fancy does You Good'.

At home, however, her risqué songs brought her into confrontation with the licensing authorities and an organisation called the Purity Party. But they don't seem to have cramped her style too much or lessened her success.

She married for the first time in 1887 - Percy Courtenay was a race-course tout. The couple set up house at 196 Lewisham High Road, Lewisham, then in Kent. They had a daughter, also named Marie, but never really got on as a married couple. Percy turned out to be unreliable, violent and a womaniser. They were in court in January 1892, Percy charged with throwing champagne in Marie's face and threatening her. They were legally separated on January 23rd but not divorced until 1905.

The following year, 1906, Marie married again - Alec Hurley was another music hall artiste. She had lived with him for some time and travelled to Australia with him. He was a decent man but Marie - never a good judge of husbands - threw him over for Bernard Dillon, an Irish jockey, 18 years her junior. He won the Derby in 1910 but lost his jockey's licence the following year and took to drink.

After the outbreak of the First World War, Marie toured the hospitals and munitions factories, singing patriotic songs. But, not for the first time, things were going badly wrong at home. Dillon was unfaithful and violent and Marie also began drinking too much. In 1920, she sued Dillon for assault and shortly after this, they separated.

Marie was now in her fifties. She had lost her youth, her looks, her good health and even the strength of her voice. She no longer played at the top theatres and the music hall itself was slipping in popularity. Marie began playing roles that were sadly appropriate - that of broken-down old women. One of her songs most characteristic of this time was 'I'm one of the ruins that Cromwell knocked about a bit.'

Marie was loved not only for her work but also because of her generosity - both of money and time. She spent lavishly on the poor and the unhappy. In 1907, there was a music-hall strike on behalf of the minor performers. Like everybody else, Marie the great star took her turn on the picket line.

Like the true professional she was, Marie died in harness. She collapsed on the stage of the Alhambra - the audience clapped loudly at what they took to be a brilliantly realistic piece of acting. But for once this wasn't theatre. She died at her home in Golders Green on October 7th 1922. She was only 52.

They said of her that nobody had been loved like Marie. She could do whatever she liked. Her real secret - in spite of an often difficult personal life - was the ability to forget everything but her audience. She would stand on the stage and produce a kind of magic that won fans for her - again and again and again. That's why they called her the greatest music hall artiste that ever lived.□

SUSANNAH LOTT
(d 1769)
THE LAST SENTENCE

At about 11.40 on the morning of July 21st 1769, a young woman, Susannah Lott, dressed in mourning black, was taken from Maidstone gaol in a cart the two miles to Penenden Heath - 'the usual place of execution'. A seven-foot stake was driven into the ground. Susannah was made to stand on a stool and a rope was placed round her neck and tied to a peg on the top of the stake. The stool was then taken away, leaving Susannah to hang.

Although it took some 15 minutes for her to die, this was an act of mercy - she had not been burned alive as had been her sentence. Actually those found guilty of murder would usually have been hanged but the person Susannah had murdered was her husband and in 1769, this was petty treason - punishable by burning. (Men were burned alive for heresy and buggery but women met their end in this way for heresy, witchcraft, high treason and petty treason).

But the formalities were still carried out. Susannah's dead body was fastened to the stake with a chain and a large quantity of faggots piled around it. These were set on fire and kept burning until her body was reduced to ashes.

Details of the events leading up to the murder include all the usual ingredients of a grisly story - passion, violence and greed. The murdered man, John Lott, was a grazier and butcher, who lived in Hythe. He was a man of 'considerable substance'. About two years prior to the murder, he hired the comely Susannah as a maid servant. He was strongly attracted to the girl and in due course, asked for her hand in marriage. Susannah refused not once but again and again and finally felt it prudent to leave his employment. She went to live with her sister and her brother-in-law, Thomas Buss.

Thomas' brother, who also lived there, was a smuggler called Benjamin Buss. Benjamin was young and good looking and soon he and Susannah became very close. On at least one occasion, they spent five days together in London.

John Lott continued to shower Susannah with his proposals of marriage and she continued to refuse him. Then Benjamin Buss intervened. He urged Susannah to accept Lott. Lott, being older, would die first, Benjamin said. Then she would get her hands on his considerable wealth. It's clear that from the start that it was Benjamin's intention to murder Lott, but it is not known whether Susannah was yet aware of this.

After further prompting, Susannah agreed to marry John Lott. The wedding took place at Rolvenden on Monday, August 15th 1768.

The marriage was barely solemnised before the smuggler called round to see Susannah and was hardly in the room before he proposed poisoning the affluent groom. Susannah refused - 'in horror' as noted by the *Gentleman's Magazine*. But Benjamin was both persistent and persuasive. On a number of occasions, Benjamin brought her the poison. And each time - according to the full confession she later gave to the court - Susannah disposed of it down the 'necessary' or other places.

Benjamin bought two ounces of corrosive sublimate from a Hythe apothecary, Mr Gipps. A few days after the wedding, John Lott, Susannah, and Benjamin set out on a ride. In Burmarsh, they stopped at a pub and ordered a pint of Milk Bumbo (milk and rum). Susannah and Benjamin drank about half of it. Benjamin then managed to lace the remainder with the sublimate and offered it to John Lott. Unaware, Lott drank the poison and complained that the drink was 'bitter' and 'hot' and had 'a bad taste'.

John mentioned this to the woman of the public house. After the party had left, she and her daughter both tasted the doctored drink. They were disgusted by the taste and said the sediment at the bottom of the glass looked like paint. The daughter was later sick.

In the meantime, Mr Lott, who'd taken a liberal amount of the poison, had stomach pains and vomiting. The three of them stopped at another pub at Eastbridge. John Lott had two 'dishes' of tea, some brandy and water and a glass of gin'. Not surprisingly, he was very sick and vomited several times.

Over the next several days and weeks, Benjamin came and went, continually pressing more poison onto Susannah. Eventually, however, despite Susannah's professed efforts to prevent the murder, it was all too much for John Lott's constitution. Benjamin was in the house on the night that he died. Apparently, Lott never mentioned any suspicion that he was being poisoned.

Enquiries made by the authorities, including an interview with the woman at the pub, led to the immediate arrest of both Benjamin and Susannah. Mr Gipps, the Hythe apothecary, was subpoenaed as a vital witness but he died before the summer assizes.

Susannah and Benjamin were sent to different prisons. Susannah spent seven months at Canterbury gaol and another four months at Maidstone. Her behaviour was noted to be 'modest and penitent'. She gave birth to a baby in prison, which she apparently 'suckled with great tenderness'. She claimed that the child was John Lott's. There are no records as to the sex of the child nor its eventual fate.

Benjamin had likewise been in prison eleven months, all the while protesting his innocence -'impudent and obdurate.' However, after coming down with gaol fever, he called for a clergyman and made a full confession. Then, after he had recovered from his sickness, he retracted everything he had said!

The case finally came to trial and the jury found both Susannah and Benjamin guilty. Benjamin's various testimonies proved to be lies. He even attempted to prove that he had had no relationship with Susannah. He brought in a woman who swore that there was a contract of marriage between her and Benjamin.

The court records testify that Benjamin 'frequently and suddenly changed posture, lifted up his eyes, listened with eager attention and had a wild confusion in his look'. Later, just before he was hanged, he was asked if he acknowledged the justice of the sentence and he replied hastily, 'I do, I do!'.

Susannah's behaviour during the trial was quite different. According to eye-witnesses, 'she looked humble and dejected'. Her eyes were red with weeping. Her baby was brought to her to be suckled on several occasions during the trial, 'which was a very affecting circumstance and her behaviour and lamentations over it after sentence had been passed upon her, would have forced tears from the most obdurate and insensible'.

But all this didn't sway the jury. To all outward appearances, Susannah Lott died the death of someone who had committed petty treason, in front of a crowd of some 5,000 people. But she was the last to be sentenced to burn in Kent. A woman (in another county) was sentenced to be burned for petty treason in 1789. But by this time, the sentence as was always automatically commuted into death by hanging. The punishment of burning alive was finally abolished by Act of Parliament in 1790. There were other methods of judicial killing.□

KATHARINE MOORE
(1898-)
LIVING PROOF THAT YOU'RE NEVER TOO OLD TO WRITE

By Leigh Eduardo

K atharine Moore, now well into her nineties, recalls with vigour and enthusiasm her Edwardian upbringing and early life.

She has lived in Kent for more than 30 years, but she was born in Hampstead, London, on April 25th 1898. Then, Victoria was on the throne and she ruled over the glorious British Empire, with over 400 million subjects across the world. It was a time of foreign possessions, national wealth and unquestioned security.

It was also a time of marked class distinction. Fortunately for Katharine, she was born, one of four children, into a comfortable middle class family, a much cherished child. She both admired and resented her domineering father but loved her mother - seeing no wrong in this pretty, charming and witty creature. Her father had a mercurial temper and strong overbearing religious beliefs. He wasn't alone; contrary to the attitudes of today, one fought for God and Country, in that order. As good Presbyterians, he and his wife reared their children with strict adherence to the teachings of the Bible.

Although it was fashionable to have a nanny, Katharine had instead, a maiden aunt. The aunt was devoted to the image - the *idea* - of her brother (Katharine's father), she never married, giving herself instead to the early education of his children. Years later, Katharine would write a best-selling exploration of the subject called *Cordial Relations: The Maiden Aunt in Fact and Fiction*, Heinemann, 1966.

Life in the family was agreeable, both domestically and socially. Katharine's father was not a wealthy man but before the First World War, he was able to supply his family with three servants and a gardener.

Her nonconformist parents wanted Katharine's first school to have a strong religious atmosphere. Edwardians liked their children to know the Bible, believing it to have a strong influence on character development.

From an early age, Katharine had total access to the many books in her parents' house. Through her father, she discovered Homer, Dickens, Scott, Browning and other literary giants. Her mother's preference was for books in lighter vein, including those by E F Benson, and G K Chesterton. By reading widely, the child became acquainted with a large variety of style and content.

At the age of eight, Katharine kept a diary for a time which recorded some of her early impressions. It was later useful as a starting point for her book, *Queen Victoria is Very Ill,* 1988, a fascinating memoir of her early life.

The success of the book led to a second set of memoirs: *A Family Life, 1939-1945.* This is presented as a straightforward diary and tells simply the moving story of the Moore family during the Second World War, when they were living in Sevenoaks. (At one point, Sevenoaks and the surrounding district was the most bombed area in the country after the capital). Her son, Christopher, then at Sevenoaks School, prepared Molotov Cocktails to throw at the Germans should they ever march through the town.

The book is also a celebration of disciplined living under violent stress...the importance of holding on to normalities, of camaraderie, of unlikely friendships made under a common fear, and ultimately of the strength of the human spirit. Well received, both books went on to become minor social histories of the two periods.

Family prayers were the centre of her father's day. He begged Katharine to make them the centre of *her* day when she married. She deferred an answer. Such pressure makes it understandable that in her twenties she went through a period of agnosticism. She finally discovered spiritual stability in the Quaker faith, embracing it wholeheartedly. She thought increasingly of God as the great creative power of love, which includes but transcends personality.

At boarding school, Katharine discovered the pain of rejection, loneliness and being a misfit. But things were very different when she went up to Oxford to read English. She had many obstacles to overcome before she was finally accepted as a student - not the least of which was having to learn Greek and Latin just to take the Oxford entrance exam, called Responsions. But arrival at university began one of the happiest periods of her life, not least because of the splendid opportunities student life offered to make wonderful friends.

Curiously, her most remarkable friendship was brought about by an indirect connection with her university days. This was with the actress/*diseuse* Joyce Grenfell. It was remarkable because, by mutual agreement, the two women never met throughout their friendship. It began in 1957 when, on the radio, the actress was somewhat disparaging about a poem written by Professor Walter Raleigh, whom Katharine had revered at Oxford. Remembering his true worth, she defended him in a letter to Miss Grenfell, thus beginning a correspondence between them which only ceased on the actress' death, 22 years later. They were friends almost immediately, with an uncanny sense of each other's worth. The combined letters have been collected and published under the title, *An Invisible Friendship.* Another best-seller, it has been reprinted four times.

Today, in an age where violence, rape and very explicit sex are the norm on television, it is difficult to comprehend that Katharine and her friends had grown up with virtually no knowledge of sex. The period was pre-Freud; many parents felt unable to speak freely and without embarrassment to their daughters on the subject.

But at least 1919 saw the end of the chaperone system - one could now, for example, play tennis with the opposite sex without being 'supervised' by a companion! Hair was cut short (bobbed) and clothes were less restrictive.

The university's rules changed at the end of the year. Katharine went down for the summer vacation as a woman student and returned in the autumn as one of the first women undergraduates at Oxford.

Katharine had first met Harold Moore in 1916; she married him in 1922. A noted metallurgist working largely in research, he eventually became Director of The British Non-Ferrous Research Association; he was also awarded the CBE. Katharine and Harold Moore took up residence in Kent in 1929 - living in Otford, Sevenoaks and finally in Shoreham in 1960, where Katharine still resides and works. She inherited three step-daughters from Mr Moore's first marriage; soon she presented her husband with twins - Christopher and Jane. Sadly, Christopher was drowned during a holiday in Devon in 1947. He was in his early twenties. As a tribute to their son, the couple adopted a war orphan, aged two - not as their son, but as their grandson, respecting the difference in their ages.

The Moores were happily married for 50 years. When Harold died suddenly at the age of 92, he had been healthy and active to the end of his life. Katharine, 20 years younger, called him her anchor in life. It was after her husband's passing that Katharine, discovering the difference between loneliness and solitude, turned more and more to writing.

She had come a long way since her first acceptance in 1936 - a children's book called *Moog*. Reprinted in 1982, time seemed only to have enhanced it, for the reviews were excellent. *The Times Literary Supplement* said '...it has the true enchanter's touch...belongs to the best writers of children's tales'. Her only other children's book, *The Little Stolen Sweep*, 1982, garnered equally pleasing reviews. 'Marvellously done!' raved *The Daily Telegraph*.

Katharine Moore's three serious novels date from 1983, when *Summer at the Haven* won the 1984 Author's Club Silver Quill Award, for the most promising first novel, published on her 85th birthday. *The Observer* compared her most glowingly with Mrs Gaskell. Then came *The Lotus House*, 1984, followed by *Moving House*, 1986. It is significant that all three novels are centred in, or around, old houses. (Her own house in Shoreham dates back to the 1740s). The three novels proved to be so popular that they have been collected under one cover as *The Katharine Moore Omnibus*. A single volume of short stories, *Six Gentle Criminals*, appeared in 1990.

Katharine Moore always spends much time in research for her non-fiction works. Authenticity and sincerity are of paramount importance to her - as can be seen in the highly-praised anthology, *The Spirit of Tolerance*, Gollancz, 1964; in *Cordial Relations: The Maiden Aunt In Fact and Fiction*, 1966; in *Victorian Wives*, 1974; and *She For God: Aspects of Women in Christianity*, 1978. Her latest work, *A Particular Glory*, 1994, has taken two years to research and write.

It is a fitting tribute to Katharine Moore's long residence in Shoreham that this latest book is a part-history of the village in the 18th century. Appropriately, the book was launched at a reception at the Old Vicarage, Shoreham, where the Rev Perronet that Katharine wrote about lived from 1728 until his death in 1785. Everyone associated with the book's publication is from Kent, making it - to quote the Darenth Press editor - 'a total Kentish enterprise'.□

EDITH NESBIT
(1858-1924)
A BOHEMIAN LIFE

E dith Nesbit is remembered almost as much for her unusual sex life as she is for her wonderful children's stories. Married to a philanderer, sharing a house with his mistress, and bringing up his illegitimate children as her own, Edith must have felt a justifiable sense of freedom in her own extra-marital affairs, which were many and varied.

As a writer, she had over 80 works published, including novels, poetry and children's stories but it is only the children's stories that have lasted. There must be few houses that don't have a battered Nesbit Puffin or two -*The Railway Children, The Treasure Seekers, The Wouldbegoods,* or *The Story of the Amulet?* Noel Coward once said that she was 'the only children's writer of recent times who was first-rate'.

Edith Nesbit was born on August 19th 1858, at 38 Lower Kennington Lane in London - then still countryside with farms and green lanes. She was the sixth child and youngest daughter of John Collis Nesbit, an agricultural chemist and principal of an agricultural college. Her large real-life family was later to become the model for her very successful fictional Bastables and the five children which feature in her best known stories. Sadly, her father died before Edith's fourth birthday.

She was educated at an Ursuline convent in France and briefly in Germany and Brighton, and after that, settled at Halstead Hall, just north of Sevenoaks in Kent. She began to take writing seriously in 1876, when she was about 18. She first broke into print with a poem, 'The Dawn,' which appeared in *The Sunday Magazine* in the same year. She always wrote under the androgynous E Nesbit.

In the 19th century, relationships between women were often warmer and more openly expressed than is the case today. There seems to be a good reason for this. There were huge areas of conversational topics - such as functions of the body - that could never be shared with men friends. And even when young women were allowed access to men, they were seldom without their chaperone. No such restrictions applied in woman-to-woman relationships and these were therefore of great importance. Edith's extravagant affection often turned into verse. The following poem - written to a young friend, Emile Bailey, in the summer of 1879 - is typical of how she expressed herself. It began:

'Enchanting darling, love to you
Makes all old thoughts as dreams to me!
I only know you never knew
Love so entire as mine will be.'

In the later summer of 1875, Edith met Ada Breakell - described 30 years later as 'my dearest and oldest friend'. In January 1884, Ada sailed to Australia to marry her fiancé, Edith's brother, Harry. However, things didn't work out and the marriage never took place. Ada and Edith corresponded at length. Edith was passionately fond of Ada and in one letter actually proposed marriage!

But in 1880, a marriage did take place. Edith, seven months pregnant, married the child's father, the journalist, Hubert Bland, at a registry office, witnessed by two strangers. Although giving every impression of being a proper gent, Hubert was in fact pure Cockney, born and bred in Woolwich. Needless to say, the Nesbits did not approve.

It is likely that the Nesbits disapproved of the workings of the marriage even less. In today's parlance, it would probably be termed an 'open marriage'. Hubert started. Edith followed. She came to terms with Hubert's constantly roving eye and realised that his passions eventually blew themselves out. She was perhaps in this sense a realist who accepted what one of her friends concluded - that 'Hubert made love to every young woman who came near him'.

On January 22nd 1882, Edith met Alice Hoatson, a woman who was going to mean more to the Blands than any other person. Edith and Alice became close friends and at Edith's invitation, Alice moved in with the family. It wasn't long before Hubert had charmed his way into Alice's bed and not long after that, Alice was pregnant. For a variety of reasons - but mainly to save Alice from 'ruin' (a very real danger in the case of unmarried mothers in Victorian England) - Edith offered to adopt the baby. Alice, somewhat reluctantly, agreed.

In the years before Edith and Hubert both found success, financial pressure forced Edith to write whatever would sell and she produced mostly hack work, much of it published in periodicals. She did manage to have three volumes of poetry published but the general criticism of her work was that it was sincere and accomplished but nothing more.

Among the magazines to which she was a contributor was *The Bacon Journal.* She became an ardent Baconian, devoting time, money and energy to the curious belief - with ciphers, cryptograms and codes - which holds that Bacon wrote Shakespeare.

Edith became interested in socialism and was one of the founders of a Fellowship of New Life, out of which, in 1884, came the Fabian Society. Some In 1908, she had published *Ballads and Lyrics of Socialism.* About this time, she cut her long hair short and began to wear less restricting clothing. She had already taken up smoking, something that either belonged mainly in the masculine domain or was adopted by 'fast women'.

In the summer of 1888, she persuaded her Fabian colleagues to support a match girls' strike at Bryant & May. The girls worked a 14-hour day, for less than five shillings a week, in appalling conditions and suffered from phosphorous poisoning. Edith raised money and doled it out to the strikers at the factory gates, as strike pay. It is interesting that in her books for children, Edith's characters lived in another world, far away from the evils of modern industrial England.

It was through the Fabian Society that Edith met George Bernard Shaw. Shaw was a harsh critic of her poetry. She accepted the criticism and also felt herself much attracted to the young Shaw. In fact, her relationship with Shaw was the first which tempted her to be unfaithful.

But although a romance blossomed between them, the affair was unconsummated. Why is a puzzle. Edith was all too aware of Hubert's constant infidelities and may have wished to restore the balance. So why did her relationship with Shaw not end up in bed? It seems that during July and August 1886, Edith may have overcome her inhibitions about being unfaithful and to have prepared herself - believing that Shaw's preparatory caresses were a prelude to a passionate affair. But it never happened. Later, Edith reproached Shaw: 'You had no right to write the preface if you were not going to write the book.' Her biographer, Julia Briggs, suggests that it was inexperience that held them back - that Shaw was no more confident than Edith.

Both Edith and Shaw had the ability to remain friends after the romance had cooled and Shaw was a constant visitor to the Bland's house for a decade or more. Years later, after Hubert was dead, Shaw paid for Edith's son, John, to go to Cambridge.

In 1887, Hubert met a young accountant, Noel Griffith. Hubert asked him home to meet Edith. They found Edith in bed recovering from a miscarriage. However, her eyes were bright and her hair a mass of shining brown curls. The two immediately got along and Noel became one of a number of men, younger than Edith, who became her lovers. Such a relationship seemed to fit in with the family milieu and Noel accompanied the Blands on a number of outings in Kent.

Edith enjoyed surrounding herself with young men. In the same year, she met a poet by the name of Richard le Gallienne. She admired his classical profile and loved the way he showed his admiration for her poetry. For a while, she was passionately in love. At one time, after a row at home, she even announced that she was going away with him. But it was no more than a gesture. Bizarre as it seemed to outsiders, home life with Hubert seemed to suit her.

In 1886, a collection of Edith's poetry, *Lays and Legends,* was published. The poems were not highly regarded. Edith's best work was yet to come. One critic said she never really worked hard enough at her poetry.

In 1893, Edith discovered her favourite holiday spot - Dymchurch. It was just a small village on the Kent coast, remote and isolated, where the horse-bus called twice a week. Edith immediately took rooms there; the real village appeared fictionally in her books, often as Lymchurch.

After about 1902, she moved nearer to the centre of the village and in 1904 took a much larger Georgian house, which is now Dymchurch Rectory. Edith returned there often and in 1922 moved to her last home, at St Mary's Bay, between Dymchurch and New Romney. She loved Romney Marsh, with its wide skies, glowing sunsets and sense of space. A number of her stories are set in the area.

By this time, Hubert was a highly successful journalist and by the mid-1890s, Edith was receiving commissions for children's books. They came in with increasing frequency. Edith continued to write a number of stories, all hack work. But then came *The Treasure Seekers* and the other works which were to mark her as one of the greatest children's writers of the century. She refused to idealise her characters or the world they inhabited.

Critics called this her greatest strength and her most important contribution to children's fiction.

In 1898, when Edith was 40, her second baby was born dead. About this time, she fell in love with a young journalist named Oswald Barron, who in the next year, much to Edith's chagrin, married somebody else! Edith had long kept her looks and her slender figure but about this time she began to put on weight. She had always been moody, passionate and volatile. Now her moods became more extreme and less predictable.

In 1899, Edith lost another baby. Ironically, some months after this, Alice gave birth to a healthy son, which Edith again adopted. Despite their unconventional life style, in 1900, Hubert, and then Edith, were admitted into the Catholic church - though there have been some doubts as to how seriously they accepted its dogma.

By around 1907, Edith was earning a good income and enjoying a high standard of living. She ran three homes - Well Hall at Eltham, a London flat in Dean Street, as well as the house at Dymchurch, which was succeeded by a farmhouse at Crowlink, on the Downs between Seaford and Eastbourne. She had always lived above her means but by 1912 , she could no longer pay off her debts and began to borrow from Shaw. She had constant rows with her agent and publishers over money. At one time, she was dealing with about 30 different publishers.

Hubert Bland died suddenly on April 14th 1914. He had complained of feeling giddy, then collapsed on the floor. Edith had three rather miserable years after his death, prone to a lot of sickness. Then along came Thomas Terry Tucker, known as 'Skipper'. He was captain of the Woolwich ferry for the London County Council. As Edith's children and others were quick to point out, Thomas was no 'gentleman' but he did seem to make Edith happy. They were married on February 20th 1917.

But marriage didn't solve all her problems, not least of which was a shortage of cash. The war reduced her income still further and in 1915, she was given a civil list pension of £60 a year. Edith and Thomas attempted to maintain Well Hall as a guest-house. But when this didn't succeed, they retired to a bungalow at Jesson St Mary's, New Romney, Kent. A last novel, *The Lark,* was published in 1922. Edith died on May 4th 1924 and is buried in the churchyard of St Mary in the Marsh.

Her biographer wrote that E Nesbit's books were an 'escape into an arcadia that somehow epitomises the English outlook and ideal of life, a world of childhood which constitutes a permanent and precious alternative to the insistent or intractable pressures of adult life'.

She had many adult admirers. Noel Coward continued to re-read her each year. When he died, one of her books lay beside his bed. It was *The Enchanted Castle.*□

POCAHONTAS
(1595-1617)
THE PLAYFUL INDIAN PRINCESS

By Chris McCooey

Kent is the last resting place of one of the most enigmatic women who ever lived. America's first heroine and only famous princess is buried in Gravesend.

Pocahontas was one of ten daughters that Powhatan, the supreme chieftain who ruled over a number of tribes in the Chesapeake Bay area, had had by a number of different wives. (He was also reputed to have had at least 20 sons). Her real name was Matoaka - this had been given to her when she was born, probably in 1595. This birth name was regarded as magic and sacred - and to be kept secret from all but the immediate family out of a superstitious fear that if it became common knowledge, then those outside the group could do the person harm.

So as a nickname, and certainly when the outsiders with white skins came on the scene, the princess was known as Pocahontas, which derives from an adjective meaning 'playful.'

The Indians, who lived along the eastern sea board of America in the 16th century, did not know what to make of the people who began to appear over the horizon. Were they friend or foe? What were their intentions? To trade? Or to take away the Indians' sacred lands?

The first colonisers were set ashore by the Elizabethan merchant adventurer, Sir Walter Raleigh on Roanoke Island in what he called Virginia (in honour of his patron, the Virgin Queen). Whatever became of the 117 men and women who were left there in 1587 remains a mystery to this day.

The next attempt at a permanent English settlement on the American mainland was made in 1607 by the Virginia Company when three ships with about 100 colonisers on board landed in the James River area to found Jamestown (both eponymously named after the king.)

These first settlers were described by Sir Francis Bacon as 'the scum of the earth' - a motley crew including titled wasters, debtors, convicts seeking a last chance as well as merchant adventurers and ministers of the church. Their mission was evangelical as well as commercial or as a contemporary account had it: 'to sowe spirituals and reape temporals'.

The Indians spied on the new arrivals from the safety of the forest and reported back to their chief, Powhatan. It is reasonable to assume that the high-spirited Pocahontas would have had her curiosity aroused sufficiently to go and see these white skinned apparitions for herself - it proved a fateful attraction.

The ships soon left. Only four months after their original landfall in April the size of the colony had been cut by half following attacks by the Indians, privation and disease. The settlers had expected the locals to provide for their existence, a notion that the Indians fiercely rejected. It was highly debatable whether the settlement would survive the winter.

It is now that John Smith comes to the fore. An experienced and much travelled adventurer, by force of character, he became the *de facto* leader of the imperilled men. Realising that they would have to trade with the Indians to get corn to survive the winter, he led a party into Indian territory.

For what happened next we have only one source - that written by Smith himself. Much of what happened in Pocahontas's life - and certainly her near legendary status - rests on whether Smith's report is true. According to Frances Mossiker, whose biography of Pocahontas is definitive, the reader has to choose whether Smith is credible or not. Mossiker writes: 'Smith's story, as he tells it, is a compelling tale fraught with symbolism, with all the makings of a myth - if, if, if, - if it really happened as he told it. The chances are that it did.'

Smith's party was attacked. Some were killed, some escaped, Smith himself was captured. Eventually, he was brought before Powhatan and a great pow-wow was convened to decide Smith's fate. When two great stones were produced and Smith forced to kneel with his head on them - he must have thought that he was a bludgeon away from meeting his maker. The braves raised their clubs but before they could be brought down to smash his skull, Pocahontas had detached herself from the side of her father and rushed to lay her head on his - her black hair sleek, shining 'like a raven's wing' streaming across his face.

Whether it was actual death that Smith was facing or only a simulation of death is not known. Ethnologists have argued that such stories are legendary: the hero is captured, sentenced, rescued in the nick of time by the villain's daughter; they fall in love. The fact is Smith was not done to death and it appears some deal was struck.

Before being allowed to return to Jamestown, the two leaders parleyed. Powhatan wanted to know the purpose of the white man's presence on his shores, whether they came as traders or invaders. In reply, and not to put too fine a point on it, Smith lied, as he had been instructed to by his superiors in the Virginia Company. They had warned him 'not to allow the Naturals to perceive that you mean to plant among them.'

Despite returning to Jamestown with corn and venison, the colony was lurching towards disaster. More deaths occurred but out of the forest came Pocahontas with gifts of food to prevent complete starvation. The settlers tried to reciprocate - one gift destined for the chief of the confederacy was a white greyhound, a breed of dog unknown to the Indians.

Later in 1608, after reinforcements and resupplies had arrived from England, Smith was instructed by the Virginia Company to make further contact with Powhatan.

Smith and his party of four journeyed to Powhatan's capital but the ruler was not there - he was off on a hunting expedition. But Pocahontas was there and she received Smith in her father's stead. And what a reception...

Again it is Smith's account only that survives. Again its authenticity has been questioned. Was it the ultimate male fantasy made flesh? Did they actually abandon themselves to an orgy of pleasure with 30 voluptuous, bare-breasted and completely uninhibited nymphs (the word Smith himself used in his report) who danced in the firelight in front of the Englishmen deep in the forest before retiring together - but surely not to sleep?

Again Mossiker makes a plausible case that Smith was indeed entertained by Pocahontas and her female friends. He had arrived, purely by chance we assume, at the time of the great Indian festival when they

94

give thanks for the harvest of the corn - the time when the women (the cultivators) perform in an agro-fertility ritual or, if you prefer, an orgy.

Be that as it may, the story moves on.

The colonisers survived the winter of 1608/1609, again with the help of Pocahontas. In the summer of 1609, the third convoy of ships arrived from England, with supplies and recruits, including women and children, and the population doubled to 400. Smith, however, was not happy he was ordered to hand over the leadership to a new governor. He may well have stayed on in the colony but a serious leg wound caused by his musket powder bag exploding forced him to return to England for medical attention.

For whatever reason, Smith failed to tell Pocahontas that he was leaving. It is safe to assume that she loved him deeply, because once he had gone - she assumed he had died from his wound - she severed all relations with the English in Jamestown. She did not come to the colonists' aid during the next winter of 1609/1610; as a consequence many died of starvation.

The princess seems to have become completely disillusioned with the English in general and Smith in particular. She appears to have gone through a personal crisis, openly arguing with her father and then running away to a far corner of the confederacy where she married an Indian of fairly low rank (on the rebound?); in any event it upset her doting father who had indulged her from an early age but her actions were in keeping with her headstrong character.

Relations between the Indians and the English deteriorated with Smith's departure. The new arrivals displayed contempt for the pagan Indians - something Smith can never be accused of.

The conflict between the two groups was often bloody and in an attempt to force peace between them, Pocahontas was kidnapped in 1613 and held to ransom in Jamestown. Her father's concern for his daughter seems to have returned as relations between the settlers and the Indians improved albeit because of Pocahontas's enforced incarceration.

While in custody in Jamestown, the Indian princess was given Christian instruction by the colony's Church of England minister. In time and apparently without undue coercion, she exchanged her upper nakedness for a bodice, her deerskin apron for a long dress and the beliefs of her native people (as explained by the shamans) to become a baptised and Anglicised lady. She also gave up her Indian name and adopted the English name of Rebecca. The name appears to have been chosen by her mentors carefully In Genesis, Rebecca is told by the Lord: 'Two nations are in thy womb, and two manner of people shall be separated from thy bowels, and one people shall be stronger than the other people; and the older shall serve the younger'.

Finally, to complete the transformation and to begin the mixing of blood which would lead to a proud and numerous heritage, she married an Englishman, John Rolfe.

Rolfe had set sail for Virginia in June 1609 with his wife but the ship they were aboard was wrecked off an island in Bermuda. Rolfe, his wife and most of the others on board struggled ashore and they lived as castaways for eight months. During this time Rolfe's wife gave birth to a daughter who was christened Bermuda but the baby soon died.

The castaways were rescued and, some time in 1610, they made it to Jamestown. Rolfe's mission was to cultivate tobacco in the colony as a profitable commodity for export. The tobacco plant was indigenous to Virginia but it was *Nicotiana rustica*, a hardy variety with an acrid taste that burned the tongue and throat. Rolfe realised he had to get hold of some seeds of *Nicotiana tabacum* (originally from Brazil) which was cultivated in the West Indies by the Spaniards - it was mild and fragrant and was becoming fashionable to smoke in Europe.

Somehow, somewhere, and within a short time after his arrival in Virginia, Rolfe got hold of a handful of the coveted *Nicotiana tabacum* seed. He experimented with its cultivation and before two growing seasons were over, he realised that Virginia and England could compete with Spain and the West Indies in supplying tobacco to Europe. It was to become the lifeline of the colony and America's first major enterprise.

By 1613, Rolfe's wife had died, whether murdered by the Indians, from disease, or by starvation - all common enough ways to depart at this time - there is no record. In any event, he came into contact with Pocahontas.

Rolfe was completely swept off his feet by the Indian princess - her physical attractions inflamed his concupiscence almost beyond control. He wrote about the 'passions of my troubled Soule, the unbridled desire of carnal affection.' It was fortunate that Pocahontas appears to have felt the same for Rolfe - or was it that she saw in him a reincarnation of Smith, her first and true love?

But it was not plain sailing. Rolfe was a product of his time - a Puritan who had been taught to suppress carnal thoughts, to condemn beauty, to consider sex as an act of procreation - which helps to explain his letter to the governor of the colony asking for permission to marry. In it he vigorously denied his motivation was lust and even agonised about what others would think of him, a gentleman, if he married a red-skinned savage - he feared that the inspiration behind the union might have been demonic rather than divine.

The lovelorn Rolfe wrote to the governor asking him whether he should persist or desist. It was to be the latter; but the governor saw more than just true love, he also saw the opportunity to secure the well-being of the colony in a propaganda coup. A love union between the two would bring Pocahontas into submission to Christ, Powhatan into submission to James I and effect a reconciliation between the races.

Officially, Pocahontas was still being held to ransom but, by giving his blessing to the marriage, Powhatan 'desired to be included and have the benefit of the peace.' Known as the Peace of Pocahontas, although it did not last long (only during her lifetime and five years after her death), it was long enough to ensure the security of the first colony in America. Within three years, Rolfe's tobacco crop had become established and its export to England secured economic prosperity. And this was in spite of the king of England, Scotland, Ireland and Virginia personally hating the habit. He had even written a pamphlet which was a tirade against 'the vile weed and the barbarous custome' of smoking it.

The couple were married in April 1614 and the following spring a baby boy was born and christened Thomas. Their personal peace and prosperity continued when Rolfe was made secretary to the Virginia company and his wife was awarded an annual stipend by the company in recognition of her contribution to the peaceful turn of events.

Not only did the bigwigs in London decide to put her on the payroll, they wanted to put her on parade as well. What better way to further the course of evangelization and race relations - and to demonstrate the success of the beginnings of empire in the New World - than to bring the paragon princess to be presented to the king and court and shareholders of the company in London?

Pocahontas was the sensation of the social scene in London during the second half of 1616. She and her husband and child stayed, appropriately enough, at The Belle Sauvage on Ludgate Hill. She was feted and entertained where ever she went - at masks, balls and plays. A contemporary account reports: 'The whole Court were charmed and surprised, at the Decency and Grace of her Deportment; and the king himself, and queen, were pleased, honourably to receive and esteem her.'

But the sojourn in London was taking its toll on Pocahontas and her fellow Powhatans (her sister was nanny to young Thomas). One by one they fell ill and the Virginia Company, grudgingly, had to pay for medical attention or funeral expenses. The squalor of London, the stench from the open sewers, the pall of smog from the smoke of thousands of fires in winter, and the overcrowding, must have made living in the city particularly hard for the Indians from the forests of America. Half the party of 12 died and Pocahontas's health was deteriorating, probably a respiratory disease. Rolfe decided to move her nine miles up the Thames from the City to Brentford and took lodgings there hoping that the change of air would do her good.

One incident may well have set her back - her first English love, John Smith, appeared unannounced at Brentford to pay his respects to the woman to whom he owed his life. She was so upset by his belated appearance (she believed he was dead until she had arrived in England but that was six months earlier) that she had to leave the room to compose herself. When she did return, she reproached him for not carrying out his obligations to her, his neglect of her as a stranger in his land.

She certainly had a point. Maybe she suddenly realised that she had been used and abused by this white man? Maybe she realised that she had been manipulated as a pawn by the English in their geopolitical game of colonisation?

Both Smith and Pocahontas must have presented sad figures. The Englishman surely regretted that he had not seized the opportunity of marriage; the Indian woman must have been indignant that she had been scorned by the man she had loved.

Life went on. Rolfe was promoted to Recorder-General of Virginia and was keen to return to the New World (and to see how his tobacco was doing). Pocahontas, as described by one reliable source, was not keen to go back: 'her return was sore against her will.' Perhaps she knew she was desperately ill and could not face the long sea journey. Nonetheless preparations were made; a small flotilla of ships assembled in the Port of London and sometime in March 1617, it set sail.

Some sources give smallpox as the cause of Pocahontas's death but it is more likely to have been tuberculosis or pneumonia - the symptoms of smallpox were readily identifiable and no one who displayed the dread disease would have been allowed to board a crowded ship. The Rolfes were aboard the *George,* captained by Admiral Argall (the same man who had organised Pocahontas's kidnap in 1613) - when the ship had reached Gravesend, the princess was so ill that Argall ordered that she be taken ashore to get medical assistance. The ships rode at anchor awaiting the outcome.

Nobody knows where she actually died. Local legend has it that it was at the Christopher Inn, 100 yards from the main landing place; or it could have been at the Flushing, another inn used by travellers and 'run by a capital fellow, a Belgian'. Another version places her deathbed in a cottage that once stood near the waterfront on a street known today as Stone Street.

Wherever it was that she breathed her last, it was with little ceremony and considerable haste (the ships wanted to be under way and make the most of the good weather) that she was placed in a coffin and carried to the parish church of St George's. Because of her eminence, the vault below the chancel floor reserved for rectors and members of the locally prominent Robinson family was opened and her coffin lowered into it.

Not being personally known to the rector might account for the fact that the entry in the leather-bound parish register of burials reads: 'March 21 Rebecca Wrolfe wyffe of Thomas Wrolfe gent. A Virginia Lady borne was buried in the Chancel'. The family name was mis-spelt and her son's name was given instead of her husband's. It seems particularly sad that these details were recorded wrongly.

And that might have been that. No memorial chiselled into a flag stone, no relative or friend to tend her tomb or recite a prayer. The ancient church that had stood since Saxon times was burnt in the great fire of 1727 that destroyed much of old Gravesend. Another church (the present one) was erected on the same site but, again, there was no formal memorial to record the exact last resting place of Pocahontas's body.

However, the playful princess was destined not to remain unmemorialised. In 1923, with the approval of Rolfe family heirs and descendants, detailed excavations were made in and around St George's but no readily identifiable Indian bones were found. The church itself was in bad repair and was going to be demolished. But a strong tide of sentiment on both sides of the Atlantic arose and money poured in to save the church and erect a suitable memorial to America's first heroine.

Today, there are stained glass windows featuring Pocahontas's christening and the Biblical character of Rebecca surrounded by Rebecca Rolfe's native land's flowers - Virginia creeper, dogwood and redbud. In the late 1950s, the churchyard was landscaped and a stone was inscribed with the main details of her life. There is also a bronze statue - larger-than-life - a replica of one in Jamestown. It is the gift of the people of the state of Virginia to the people of Gravesend, the County of Kent 'in which soil her slight bones, her red flesh, mouldered, her New World dust forever mingled with the dust of the Old'.

Frances Mossiker again: 'Transcending history, Pocahontas had passed into American folklore…at the altar-stone - the death-defying embrace, white man and red woman aswoon with love and terror - seems fixed, frozen in time…reminding us that at least once in our history, there existed the possibility of inter-racial accommodation. For that one fleeting moment - with the blood-thirsty blades arrested in mid-air - came a flicker of hope that on this continent, at least, there would be no cause to mourn man's inhumanity to man'.

And the provider of this hope rests, and will forever rest, in Kent.□

ANNE PRATT
(1806-1893)
BOTANY FOR THE MASSES

Whether you accept the view of *The Times* Obituary ('this distinguished botanist') or that of the 1894 *Journal of Botany* ('in the strict sense of the word....*not* a botanist') Anne Pratt was an important figure in the popular culture of the late 19th century. She won a large readership and widened general interest in the plants of the British Isles.

Anne Pratt was born in Strood, Kent, on December 5th 1806, the second of three daughters of Robert Pratt, a wholesale grocer. The family moved to nearby Chatham, where Anne spent her childhood and adolescence. She was educated in neighbouring Rochester. Her school was in Eastgate House (the setting for several of Charles Dickens' novels and now the Dickens Centre).

It appears that Anne's great success began partly because she was in frail health. Her illness resulted in a stiff knee, which prevented all strenuous outdoor activity. She was nevertheless a very bright child and a

Scottish family friend, Dr Dods, offered to instruct her in botany. She excelled in her studies and was aided by her elder sister who collected the plants; they soon had a considerable herbarium.

In 1846, Anne left Chatham and stayed with friends at Brixton and other places till 1849, when she settled in Dover. Here she wrote her principal work, *The Flowering Plants, Grasses, Sedges and Ferns of Great Britain*, published in 1855, in five volumes.

On December 4th 1866, she married John Pearless from East Grinstead, Sussex, and they lived there for the next two and a half years. They then settled for some years at Redhill, Surrey. Anne died in Rylett Road, Shepherd's Bush, London, on July 27th 1893.

Anne Pratt wrote a number of books, almost all concerned with British plants. Despite professional criticism, she was painstaking and accurate in all her researches and wrote in a pleasant popular style. She also enlivened the text with exquisite drawings all done in her own hand. At one time she was rewarded for her literary efforts by a sum of money from the Civil List.

One of her most popular works, particularly among children, was *Wild Flowers*. It was published in two square volumes in 1852 and - like most of her books - was frequently reprinted. The books were also issued in sheets for hanging up in school rooms and similar places.

However, Anne's books didn't always please the scientific establishment. Critics pointed out that her descriptions were often meagre and incomplete and showed no intimate knowledge of the plants described. It is for these reasons that her name does not appear in the Royal Society's *Catalogue of Scientific Papers*.

Such criticism mattered little to her tens of thousands of readers. Altogether Anne Pratt published some 16 works, some in more than one volume and all were in great demand.□

JEAN ROOK
(1931-1991)
FIRST LADY, FIRST BITCH OF FLEET STREET

'First lady of Fleet Street', 'First Bitch of Fleet Street', 'Britain's bitchiest woman'. Even the parody Glenda Slagg, in *Private Eye*. (She rarely read it - frankly admitting it was a bit close to the bone). These were some of the sobriquets given to Jean Rook, reputedly the highest paid woman in journalism.

In all fairness, she could hardly have objected, considering the barbs she threw weekly at the celebrities she wrote about. Prince Philip was a 'hawk-nosed, slit-mouthed tetchy old devil.' The Duchess of York was 'the Duchess of Pork'. Elizabeth Taylor 'squat-bottomed and broad-beamed as an overpainted Russian doll'. Prince Edward was 'unready, unsteady, and unemployed Eddie'. She was not averse to giving gratuitous advice either. She told the Queen to pluck her eyebrows and the Archbishop of Canterbury to stop 'bleating'.

Her writing was peppered with alliteration and imaginative metaphors and there were few among the high and mighty who were not at one time the target of her venom. But she was also warm hearted and down to earth which she attributed to her Yorkshire upbringing. She was able to identify with her readers because, as she always claimed, she was 'the most ordinary person living'.

But when the copy was written and handed in and it was time to get away from the hubbub of a newspaper office, she came home to 'salvation', as she called it - she came home to Kent, to her house in Edenbridge. She had what she described as her yuppy flat in London but that wasn't really home. It was in Kent that she was able to give full vent to her magpie instincts

There was a large red telephone box in the middle of her lawn, a left-over from an interview she had had with the head of British Telecom. A wooden carousel horse dominated her study and a ship's figurehead of Neptune guarded the upstairs hall. Beside the ornate Victorian loo, there was a penny-farthing, on which Jean used to pose models in mini-skirts when she was fashion editor of the *Daily Sketch*. To be seen from her four-poster bed was a larger-than-life-size picture of Clark Gable and in the corner a collection of Victorian police truncheons. In the drawing room there was a pulpit from a redundant church, which she used as a drinks' cabinet.

Jean had photographs of herself with Ronald Reagan, with Frank Sinatra, with Basil Brush, Jeremy Thorpe, Mrs Gandhi, even with Mrs Thatcher (Jean was a tremendous fan - and interviewed her ten times during her 12 years in Downing Street). In Jean's bedroom were acres of posh clothes and drawers overflowing with jewellery. Jean Rook - tall, bejewelled, usually sun-tanned and with a mane of golden hair - was ready to meet anyone on earth and meet them face to face as equals.

It was always her boast that she earned more than any woman in the newspaper business. And as she had it so she spent it. She drove an XJ6 Jaguar with doeskin leather seats and had a son at Eton. She ate in the most exclusive restaurants, clothed herself from the finest couturiers, and travelled all over the world in her job or for relaxation and pleasure. She had giant glass jars filled with matches from every grand hotel on earth. She once said that 'before I meet the next world, I want to be sure I get to know this one.'

Jean Rook was born in Hull on November 13th 1931, the only child of a consultant engineer. She went to the Malet Lambert School in the town. She failed to get into Oxford - for which she blamed her little known school and having the wrong accent. Instead she studied at London's Bedford College, where she obtained a good second class honours degree. She hesitated about going on to do a Master's degree until her father bribed her with a second-hand car. Her thesis was *T S Eliot's*

Impact on English Drama - which showed nothing of the tabloid style that was to come.

Now in her mid-twenties, Jean talked her way into a place on the graduate training scheme run by the *Sheffield Telegraph.* She had a tough time but she later admitted that it was during this hell that she learned her professionalism. She later joined the *Yorkshire Telegraph* where she rose to become women's editor. Next came a job as fashion editor of *Flair,* then fashion editor on the pre-Murdoch *Sun.*

It was at this stage of her career that she began to adopt the outspoken style that was to make her famous. She attacked a fashion collection by Captain Molyneaux while everyone else was praising it - and was proved right. She wrote critically about the Royals at a time when nobody else did. 'Mine was the first foot on the road to realistic writing about royalty' she boasted. In this first assault, she jeered at Princess Margaret's old fashioned, diamond-patterned black stockings. In the subsequent uproar, Jean Rook was certainly getting recognition.

After the *Sun,* she wrote for the *Daily Sketch* and then the *Daily Mail.* The readers loved her and when she later joined the *Daily Express,* her readers followed her. The *Mail* did everything it could to prevent her leaving but Jean had already given her word. She said no to more salary, no to more perks and no to more everything.

What made Jean a success? It was partly her language and partly her ability to bring warm human experiences to her readers. At the Duchess of York's wedding, it was, in Jean Rook's opinion, the four-year-old 'sweet William's' day. She described how 'he stuck out his tongue at the blushing bridesmaids...He steered the little girls down the aisle like a fleet of taffeta rugs...he discovered his hat band elastic...snapped it...flipped it...rammed it in his mouth, loop by loop, like spaghetti...' It was corny but it sold newspapers. And that's how Jean stayed on top of the heap.

She was never a 'women's writer' as such and had little time for feminists (like 'whinging Germaine Greer'). She was proud to say she'd helped women writers get away from what she called 'lipstick articles - on weaving baskets and rolling pastry'. She said that her readers - 64 per cent were men - didn't think of her as a woman. They thought of her as a columnist.

On February 1st 1985, masked raiders broke into Jean Rook's house in Edenbridge. Jean was dragged down the stairs by her hair. Both she and her husband, Geoffrey Nash, were assaulted and tied up. In an interview she gave soon after that, she admitted that all the jewellery she had left was junk. The robbers took all 'the real stuff'.

But worse than the loss of personal items was the effect the break-in had on her husband. Jean was convinced that Geoffrey's illness and final breakdown were the direct results of the robbery. He died in 1988, on their 25th wedding anniversary. The following Wednesday, she told her readers all about her husband's death, just as she always shared her life with them. She buried the original typescript in the coffin with Geoffrey. Nearly a thousand readers wrote to say how sorry they were.

About a year after the robbery, Jean Rook sat in her XJ6 and confessed to her tape recorder. She had cancer and was having frightening sessions of radiotherapy. 'This is what Dante's Inferno must have felt like', she dictated. 'The heat comes from inside me, like some grim super-sunburn. I generate my own heat, so scorching I can feel it on my cheek if I bend my head. It's as if someone were putting a cigarette lighter to me - I feel flames jump the gap across my breastbone, and into the other breast'.

She wrote a full account in her autobiographical *The Cowardly Lioness*. How had cancer changed her? She recounted just how precious life was to her. She wrote about some of the simple ways her life changed. She said that once, she would never have stopped her high-powered Jag on the side of the road outside Tunbridge Wells, 'just to watch the flaming sunset'. But, she continued: 'now I do'.

She also said something that expressed her resilience and her ability to withstand almost anything the world threw at her. Essentially she was an optimist. 'When I do die,' she said, 'if I get a four-minute warning, I shall think, "My God, it was wonderful being me."

Jean Rook died on September 5th 1991.◻

VITA SACKVILLE-WEST
(1892-1962)
THE PASSIONATE POETESS

By Joan Edmonds

Vita Sackville-West

Vita Sackville-West was a child of the Kentish Weald, forever associated with Knole, one of the largest houses in England, and with Sissinghurst, where she created one of the loveliest gardens in the whole country.

A complex and gifted woman, Vita became a dedicated writer, poet, novelist, biographer, travel writer, journalist and broadcaster.

She was born and grew up in Knole, Kent, the ancestral home of the Sackvilles, Earls of Dorset. Her parents were cousins, and Vita was part Spanish on her mother's side and part English aristocrat.

Knole was her first love of her life, set in its great park, surrounded with slopes, gullies and great beeches. Against the backdrop of Sevenoaks, Knole presents a dramatic picture and has been described as not so much a house as 'a medieval village, with its square turrets, and its grey walls and its hundred chimneys sending blue threads up into the air' - words written by Vita in *The Edwardians*. It was therefore a great personal tragedy that, as a daughter, she could never inherit Knole.

Vita had many admirers, both men and women. One of these, Harold Nicolson, made a particular impression and they were married in 1913. Vita, however, carried on with her lesbian affairs - with both Rosamund Grosvenor and Violet Keppel - until she became pregnant in 1914.

Vita had two sons, Benedict and Nigel. Benedict she referred to as 'Detto,' which fuelled the first of many upsets with her mother. Lady Victoria Sackville had resented the fact that Vita's first child was not named after Vita's father, Lionel. Throughout their lives, Lady Sackville was to try to dominate her daughter and there developed between them a passion that see-sawed between love and hate.

Vita and Harold's marriage worked remarkably well. Vita often wrote that she had never known that such happiness existed. Harold, a diplomat and writer, took an important job at the Foreign Office and Vita wrote and had published several plays and poems.

In 1915, they moved into a house called Long Barn, in Weald. It was in 1917 that Harold was told by his doctor that he had contracted syphilis. Telling Vita about this depressed Harold. His letters to her on the subject are numerous and reflect his self-disappointment and depression. Vita was to be tested. They were to wait six months before they could continue marital relations.

During this period, Violet Keppel invited herself down to stay for a fortnight at Long Barn and she and Vita resumed their passionate relationship. Violet had waited patiently for a chink to appear in the so far idyllic marriage. When Vita broke down and told Violet all her problems with Harold, Violet took full advantage of the situation. The women's love affair blossomed in Polperro, Cornwall, where they stayed in a fisherman's cottage. Harold meanwhile, was still paying for his homosexual liaisons. Although Vita said that she understood and would not let it come between them, she had already taken her affections elsewhere - something he was only too aware of. Harold wrote daily to Vita about his feelings for her but Vita was beginning life anew. She had found happiness of a different kind.

Predictably, Violet's fickleness landed her in trouble. She met a Major Denys Trefusis, whom Vita apparently approved of and liked. But Vita was also jealous. Violet intended to marry the Major for reasons of security, but she stressed that there would be no sexual contact between them. Marriage, she said, would provide her with a passport to independence and freedom. Both women, being married, could pursue their own ideals and pleasures.

Harold, sensing his marriage slipping away, made an enormous effort to please Vita. She, seeing the change in him, once more transferred her affections to Harold - until Violet threatened suicide. The two women stayed in France together. Harold spent Christmas at Knole with the children. He was unhappy. Vita was unhappy. Violet was her usual spoilt self. Finally, Vita returned to the children and Violet announced her engagement to Denys Trefusis as soon as she stepped back on English soil.

Harold was delighted to have his wife back at Long Barn. He had won the battle against Violet, whom he described in one of his letters as 'an evil woman' and 'like some fierce orchid'. When he departed for France on business, he took Vita with him.

But Violet's marriage distressed Vita. She was beside herself with jealousy. She followed Violet, found her in an hotel and made love to her. This action almost destroyed both marriages. When the women eloped, the husbands followed and finally 'rescued' them. It came to light that Vita had kept Harold in touch with her whereabouts, thereby signalling her wish to be followed.

Life took on a new meaning yet again. But when Vita met Virginia Woolf, she fell under her spell. Virginia Woolf's extravagant fantasy, *Orlando*, published in 1928, was an open love-letter to Vita.

Vita also fell for a Geoffrey Scott, with whom she had an ardent love affair. Harold, on the other hand, had taken up with a colleague from the Foreign Office. There were to be many more lovers for both of them. It was a strange marriage but it seems they loved each other deeply.

It was in 1930 that they decided to move to another house, though they would still keep Long Barn. Vita had heard of a property for sale just outside Sissinghurst. The castle was a ruin, in seven acres of muddy wilderness, with no water or electricity - but they fell in love with it and bought it. Together they restored the Elizabethan buildings and Vita started to create what was to become one of the most beautiful gardens in England.

Vita excelled as a poet and a novelist. In 1922, she wrote *Knowle and the Sackvilles,* which in turn provided the setting for her novel *The Edwardians.* Other works included a pastoral poem, *The Land,* for which she won the Hawthornden Prize, *All Passion Spent, Collected Poems* and much else on travel, gardening, and literary topics. Her son, Nigel, wrote *Portrait of a Marriage* in 1973, which described his parents' unorthodox life; it was later adapted as a television play.

Vita Sackville-West was a woman who seemed to need to be constantly in love. The state of love helped her to write. She lived two distinct life-styles: wife and mother, and illicit lover. In most instances, she managed to keep the two apart. But to accomplish this, she became devious and secretive, relishing clandestine affairs. She was usually able to conduct them sensibly, rarely at the expense of her life with Harold and the children.

In 1961, Vita became gravely ill with cancer. She died at Sisinghurst on June 2nd 1962.

After Harold died in 1968, Sissinghurst Castle passed into the hands of the National Trust. Today visitors flock to see the rooms open to the public - the book-lined walls of the Tower Room, the embroideries, the many gardening and history books, and the Persian rugs. But perhaps most of all, they come to see the wonderful Sissinghurst gardens. Everything is still as Vita left it. Nigel Nicolson continues to live in part of the property.

After shopping together in Sevenoaks, Virginia Woolf wrote of Vita in her lyrical prose: 'She shines in the grocer's shop, with a candle-lit radiance. Stalking on legs like beech trees, pink glowing, grape clustered, pearl hung'. Suitable last words for an unforgettable woman.□

ETHEL SMYTH
(1858-1944)
'LISTENERS ARE INVITED TO APPLAUD WHENEVER THEY FEEL LIKE IT.'

By Anna Cerutti

Ethel Smyth was one of the most celebrated composers of her age, yet 50 years after her death, she is all but forgotten, while her contemporaries - Elgar, Delius, Mahler, Wagner - remain at the forefront of music. Her most successful compositions were written for the voice, including six operas, which were performed all over Europe. She was created an honorary Doctor of Music and a Dame.

Her achievements are all the more remarkable because she was born to a middle class family at the height of the Victorian era and had to battle to pursue her vocation. She was also a leader of the Suffragette movement, composing the anthem, *March of the Women.* More than all this, however, Ethel Smyth deserves to be remembered as a great individual.

Edward Sackville-West called her: 'a brilliantly intelligent woman who felt violently about almost everything'. Her willpower and strength of personality kept her in the public eye during a fascinating sweep of history from the mid-Victorian period to the Second World War.

Ethel Smyth was born in 1858 and raised in Sidcup, Kent, the only daughter of an Indian army general. She soon discovered a talent for music which was encouraged by a musician serving in the army corps who introduced her to Brahms and Schumann and took her to concerts and the opera. The general, who considered Ethel's music all 'damned nonsense', had the musician transferred elsewhere. But Ethel was resolved to study music at Leipzig Conservatorium and to become the first great female composer. Her ambition never altered and in 1873, having worn down her father with her own implacable will, she left for Leipzig.

To her disappointment, the tutors at the conservatorium were unmoved by what Ethel perceived as her exceptional talent. Fortunately, through her landlady, a singer, Ethel made some influential musical friends like George Henschel, who wrote: 'Our circle was brightened by the meteor-like appearance of a young, most attractive girl...None of us knew what to admire in her most - her wonderful musical talent, or her astonishing athletic prowess, jumping over fences and chairs'.

She was even introduced to Brahms but Ethel was unimpressed, finding him patronising and vulgar, although she remained a devotee of his music. She also met the tutor, Von Herzonberg, for whom she left the conservatorium, studying with him for the next seven years.

Throughout her life, Ethel was romantically attracted to women. Her most enduring relationship, however, was with a man, Harry Brewster, a married American writer. They fell in love in 1884, and, although Harry remained married, he and Ethel wrote to each other and met whenever they could. They later became lovers. He was a tremendous support to her career, collaborating on three of her operas and campaigning to have her work performed.

Although Ethel had received some positive response to her music, notably from Tchaikovsky, who complimented her on her Violin Sonata, she had yet to write anything of real significance. The inspiration for her first important work was another love affair, this time with Pauline Trevelyan. For a while, Ethel became a devout Christian. The result was her *Mass in D*, which was performed in the Queen's Hall to public acclaim, although Archbishop Benson detected Ethel's dominant personality overriding religious feeling: 'God was not so much implored as commanded to have mercy.'

Ethel had many influential friends who, bowled over by her talent and enthusiasm, supported her work. Virtually all her public performances were due to her own efforts, or those of friends. One such was the Empress Eugenie, the wife of Napoleon III. She introduced Ethel to Queen Victoria for whom Ethel played her *Mass* on the piano at Balmoral, singing all the parts and drumming her feet to extra effect. Subsequently, the *Mass* was performed at the Royal Albert Hall.

Ethel's religious conversion was short-lived and she embarked on her first opera, *Fantasia* for which Harry wrote the libretto and then *Der Wald*, which was a terrific success at Covent Garden in 1902. Their final collaboration was on *The Wreckers*, a Wagnerian style grand opera and Ethel's best work, based on the legendary 'wreckers' of Cornwall, who lured ships onto the rocks. It was put on in Leipzig and after a successful first night, was due for a run of performances. Unfortunately, Ethel objected to changes the conductor had made and confiscated the scores, refusing to allow another performance. This prompted Edward Sackville-West to comment: 'She could be exhausting and obstinate to the point of silliness. But one would have loved her less, had she been more cautious. Her passionate unity was the sign of unquestionable genius'.

The Wreckers was later performed at the Queen's Hall, conducted by Sir Thomas Beecham. It was to be Harry's last performance. He died of liver cancer in 1908. Ethel was devastated to lose him and - although they hadn't married - she remained to a great extent, Harry's widow, forever quoting his opinions and being guided by his precepts.

In 1910, Ethel was invited to support the Suffragette Movement. Surprisingly, she hadn't considered this before. Although fighting constant battles, which she attributed to male prejudice, she had not thought beyond her own situation to that of women in general. But with her usual enthusiasm, she took to the cause, becoming a great admirer of Mrs Pankhurst. To prove her commitment, she gave up composing for two years, but for her *March of the Women,* the Suffragette anthem, which was described as 'at once a hymn and a call to battle'.

She was arrested in 1912 for throwing a brick through the window of a government minister, who had upset her with his 'damnably condescending and impertinent remarks' on the suffrage question.

Sir Thomas Beecham described visiting Ethel in Holloway: 'I arrived in the courtyard to find the noble company marching round it singing their war-chant, while the composer, beaming approbation from a nearby window, beat time with a toothbrush'. After her two years with the movement, Ethel returned to composing, although she continued to support, and be devoted to, Emmeline Pankhurst. She took the opportunity, during a concert of her works in Vienna, to address the audience on women's suffrage. She found them 'lamentably ignorant' on the issue.

In her opera, *The Boatswain's Mate,* she used *March of the Women* in the overture, which has been interpreted as putting a deliberately feminist slant on the story, but may just have been an example of Ethel's habit of incorporating songs into her larger works, or taking bits from her operas and presenting them individually. This was partly due to a love of experimentation, but also because of her determination to have her work performed whatever the cost.

In the 1920s, she worked with Sir Henry Wood on his new promenade concerts. He was quick to realise that Ethel herself was a crowd pleaser and invited her to conduct her own concerts, which she did flamboyantly with her gown slung over the tweed suit she always wore. She published nine volumes of autobiography and became a well-known writer. She never took this seriously, however. She would have found it inconceivable that some people might value her writing more than her music.

Afflicted by deafness, Ethel devoted her last years to *The Prison,* an oratorio based on a philosophical treatise written by Harry Brewester, which she conducted herself at the Queen's Hall. Her final love affair was with Virginia Woolf, a stormy relationship, which lasted until Virginia's death in 1941.

Ethel's reputation remained high. There was a celebratory concert of her works and her *Mass* was revived and conducted by Sir Adrian Boult. She died in 1944, aged 86.

Why has Ethel Smyth's music not endured? Some who knew her, such as Edward Sackville-West, considered her to be more than her music. He felt that her music lacked originality, whereas Ethel was a true individualist. Certainly, the quality was uneven. She was erratic, sometimes neglecting music for a love affair or the women's movement, before returning to it with new ideas, but her technique had become rusty.

The lack of public performances, due in part to the male prejudice that she always cited, is telling. Without Ethel herself to push for recognition, her work was neglected. She was also unfortunate in writing operas in England. On the continent, *The Wreckers* alone would have ensured her continuing fame. Nevertheless, in her lifetime, she achieved great success, earning the plaudits of her fellow musicians and many other admirers. Her music was always impassioned and totally sincere. In the programmes to her concerts she wrote: 'Listeners are invited to applaud whenever they feel like it.' She deserves to be remembered as one of the most vivid characters, a boon to both the musical and literary worlds.□

LADY HESTER STANHOPE
(1776-1839)
QUEEN OF THE DESERT

By Marion Field

When eight-year-old Lady Hester met the French Ambassador, she was so impressed she decided to set out for France as soon as possible. A visit to Hastings provided the ideal opportunity. Finding an unattended boat on the shore, she loosened the rope and set off on the first of her travels. She didn't reach France on that occasion as, to her indignation, she was 'rescued' and returned in disgrace to her Chevening home. But the spirit of adventure and daring that was to lead her to travel to places never before visited by a white woman was evident in her from a very early age.

She was born on March 12th 1776 at Chevening in Kent. Her father was the son of the second Lord Stanhope and her mother was the daughter of Lord Chatham and the sister of William Pitt the Younger.

Two more sisters followed Hester, but when she was four her mother died.

Hester's father was heartbroken but this did not prevent him marrying again within six months. His second wife had no time for either her step-daughters or the three sons she bore in swift succession. Lord Stanhope became very eccentric and all his children except Hester were terrified of him. Hester was her father's favourite and he would often hold philosophical discussions with her. These early discussions in her father's study at Chevening laid the basis for her future ability to talk on an equal footing with the greatest in the land.

In 1800, Hester left Chevening to live with her grandmother, Lady Chatham, in Burton Pynsent in Somerset but sadly her grandmother died in 1803 while Hester was on her first trip to Europe. Her bachelor uncle, William Pitt, the Warden of the Cinque Ports, offered her a home in his official residence, Walmer Castle near Dover.

In 1804 he became Prime Minister for the second time and Hester moved with him to Downing Street, where she soon became a lot more to Pitt than just his hostess. He listened to her opinions and often took her advice. Even King George III considered that no man was 'a better politician than Lady Hester.'

When Pitt died in 1806, Hester was given a Government pension which enabled her to rent a house in London. In 1808, she became unofficially engaged to General Sir John Moore and when he was killed at the Battle of Corunna by a cannon ball, she was devastated. In February 1810, she left England for Gibraltar. She was never to return to her native land, although stories of her adventures were to entertain London society for years to come.

Among her travelling companions was the physician, Dr Charles Meryon, who spent the next 30 years of his life - unpaid - with her as she roamed the East. Another man who fell under her spell was the 21-year-old Michael Bruce. He was travelling abroad before planning to settle back in England, but meeting Hester changed the direction of his life.

Michael joined her party to the chagrin of Dr Meryon, who became very jealous when Lady Hester and Michael became lovers. London society was scandalised when the news reached England. Although Michael offered marriage, she declined but the three years they spent together were probably the happiest of her life.

Her party travelled to Constantinople where they remained for a year. Lady Hester eschewed the small English community and preferred the Turks whom she regarded as 'a very superior people' and they in turn respected and admired her.

In October 1811, the group moved on to Egypt but was shipwrecked off the coast of Rhodes. All on board eventually reached the shore with their lives, but few possessions. When they finally reached Rhodes, Lady Hester had to replenish her wardrobe. She bought breeches, boots, shirts and waistcoats. For the future, she decided it would be best to dress as a Turkish man. She never again donned western dress and this added spice to the gossip already circulating about her in London.

They travelled to Damascus where Muslim law dominated. Lady Hester was horrified to discover that, not only was she expected to stay in a squalid quarter of the town and always wear a veil, she was also forbidden to ride a horse. She ignored all edicts. To the apprehension of her followers, she rode, unveiled, and spectacularly dressed, into the city. The inhabitants were so startled at her appearance she was allowed to pass unharmed. Then, disgusted with her dwelling quarters, she forced the Pasha of Damascus to allow her to live in the more luxurious Muslim area.

From Damascus, she made her legendary trip to Palmyra, the mysterious derelict city, once linked with King Solomon. Her cavalcade rode into the city under the protection of the Bedouin tribe, who had lived in the desert since Biblical times and regarded it as their territory.

Her fame had gone before her, and as she rode in, the people poured out to greet her - the first European woman to set foot in their city. They danced around her and, as she reached the triumphal arch, a wreath of palm leaves was placed on her head. She was crowned 'Queen of the Desert'. It was the highlight of her life.

However, clouds loomed on the horizon. Plague was sweeping the area and already many had died. Lady Hester and her party decamped to Latakia on the coast and it was here that Michael Bruce left for England. They never met again. After his departure, Lady Hester became depressed and eventually succumbed to the plague; but with her usual resilience, she recovered.

Meanwhile, her luxurious life style, her sumptuous entertaining and her frequent travels had taken their toll of her finances. Her pension proved insufficient and she was soon in debt to moneylenders. In 1817, she moved to Djoun where she set up her home in a former monastery. Here she spent the last 18 years of her life. In spite of her financial state, a small self-contained village in which refugees and those in need could find sanctuary gradually came into being. In true English style, she even created a garden.

She became obsessed with astrology and prophecy. In her stable was a deformed horse which gave the impression it already bore a saddle. Lady Hester believed this was 'the horse born saddled' on which tradition said the Messiah would ride into Jerusalem. Also in the stable was a pure white mare on which the eccentric Englishwoman was convinced she was destined to accompany the Messiah on his triumphant journey.

Because of her obsession and eccentricity, many who visited her believed her insane, but she could still carry on a rational conversation and take an interest in local politics. When, in 1825, she heard that her beloved half brother, James, had committed suicide, she was heartbroken. She never left Djoun again and her financial affairs continued to cause concern. The final blow came in 1838. The British government decided to stop her pension until one of her outstanding debts had been paid.

Her health had deteriorated but she still summoned her resources to fight what she saw as an injustice. She wrote to friends in England in the hope they would be able to publicise her plight and persuade the government to change its mind. She even wrote to Queen Victoria. But her efforts were unsuccessful and in a fury she renounced her British citizenship and, knowing she was now near death, she threatened to shoot any English consul or 'any English of any sort' who approached her in her 'last moments'.

In June 1839, she died, alone in her dilapidated home, as her servants had all deserted her. Despite her last instructions, the British Consul in Lebanon and an American missionary went immediately to Djoun when they heard of her death.

Lady Hester's coffin, draped in a British flag was carried out to her garden and, in spite of her renunciation of the country of her birth, she was buried according to the rites of the Church of England. Her bones rest many miles from her home in Chevening in Kent - but the legend of Lady Hester Stanhope lives on.❏

MARIE STOPES
(1880-1958)
CHAMPION OF ENJOYABLE MARRIED SEX

There seems little doubt that Marie Stopes' own active libido provided the spur for her revolutionary work in family planning. Sexual love was to be enjoyed - a startling new thought when applied to women - and complete sexual enjoyment could only be had without the risk of unwanted pregnancy.

Her books on married love sold all over the world and at home she became the nation's first Agony Aunt on sexual problems. But for all that, although married twice, the tragic irony is that Marie herself never really achieved a satisfactory marriage.

Marie Charlotte Carmichael Stopes was born in Edinburgh on October 15th 1880 but her parents moved to London when she was six weeks old. Her father, a man of private means, was passionately devoted to archaeology. Her mother, Charlotte Carmichael, was a pioneer of women's university education. Marie was taught Latin and Greek when she was five but didn't show an aptitude for them; she had little formal education until the age of 12, when she went to St George's, Edinburgh. This was followed two years later by the North London Collegiate School. She was not allowed to attend afternoon school and only stayed in London from Monday morning until Friday mid-day.

Marie's father was attracted to the prehistoric archaeology of north Kent, and in 1894, he moved the family to Swanscombe. Marie was 14. They rented a house called the Mansion House, south of the High Street. (It has since been demolished.) It was located a few hundred yards to the east of St Peter and St Paul's Church. The Stopes family stayed in Swanscombe until 1899.

Marie always remembered Swanscombe, in Kent, with fondness. She later wrote of her school-girl memories of Norman Maccoll, the well known editor of the *Athenaeum* and his insistence that the children wear gloves when going into the woodlands. She also remembered Seton Karr, the famous lion hunter. She records that once the children had to form a body guard between Seton and some very ordinary cows. But she also says that 'with the exception of one annual day for their chief school friends', they had almost no contact with other children.

Marie showed great interest in her father's collection of some 85,000 flint implements - many of which she and her sister had collected. In 1902, at University College, London, she obtained first class honours in botany and third class honours in geology and physical geography.

After a year of research, she went on a scholarship to Munich, where she obtained her PhD. While there, Marie met a Japanese botanist, Professor Kenjiro Fujii. She was 23 and he was 14 years older, married with a daughter. A romance blossomed between them and in spring 1905, the Professor gave Marie her first kiss. Although Marie found the experience 'quite horrid', it was none the less a momentous event for her. She was determined to follow the professor to Japan and, in 1907, the Royal Society sponsored her to take a trip to Japan for further research in her field. At first, she saw a lot of the man who was responsible for her first kiss - then the romance simply petered out.

Before her Japan trip, Marie had become the youngest Doctor of Science in England and the first woman to be appointed a lecturer on the staff of Manchester University. As her researches yielded results, she became well known in her field. In 1906, her first book, *The Study of Plant Life for Young People*, was published. Critics praised it, saying the textbook was 'written with a breadth of knowledge not before met with in an English elementary book'. She became a fellow of University College, London, in 1910.

In 1911, when she was 31, Marie met and within weeks married Dr Reginald Gates, a 29-year-old Canadian botanist. The marriage was never consummated and Marie resorted to literature to find out what had gone wrong. After reading everything relevant that she could find in the British Museum, she sued as *virgo intacta* and had the marriage annulled in 1916. An examination by a doctor had confirmed that her hymen was unbroken.

Her husband claimed that Marie was 'super-sexed to a degree that was almost pathological'. Marie maintained that Gates was impotent. Gates said further that when Marie was his fiancée, she had insisted that he visit a doctor before their marriage to obtain advice about contraception. Gates was a timid man and found this very difficult. The doctor was opposed to contraception and only agreed to give the information on one condition: Gates must agree to stop using condoms after he obtained a post in London. As things worked out, Gates seems never to have needed them.

The sexual frustration and break-up of her marriage was to scar Marie for life. But it gave her a purpose, a mission, to prevent others going through what she had suffered. She would write a book that would enable married couples to understand each other's sexuality. She told a friend: 'I am writing something that will electrify England'.

The year 1918 was an eventful one for Marie. As well as publishing two books, in February she met and married Humphrey Roe (despite the fact that he was already engaged to somebody else). He was co-founder of the AVRO aircraft company. To Marie's delight, he was a keen supporter of birth control and a committed feminist.

Marie's first book on the subject, *Married Love*, begun in 1914, was rejected by a number of publishers until it finally came out in 1918. It was an immediate success and was translated into 13 languages including Hindi. Over 2000 copies were sold in the first fortnight. Years later, Baroness Stocks commented that 'few books have brought more happiness to more people'.

But this first book contained only the briefest reference to contraception. In response to readers' letters, *Wise Parenthood* came out later in the same year. This was a guide to contraceptive techniques and went into explicit detail. Objections were made against condoms (largely harmful), withdrawal (bad for the nervous system of both sexes), douching and the 'safe' period (unreliable) for having penetrative sex.

Within nine years, *Wise Parenthood* sold half a million copies in the original English edition alone. Like some other books of hers, it was banned in certain American states.

On March 17th 1921, Marie and Humphrey opened the first British birth control clinic in Holloway. In 1925, it moved to 108 Whitfield Street. Today, Marie Stopes International is at the same address.

From the start, there was medical opposition to the clinic because it failed to have a qualified gynaecologist on the staff. (Marie, of course, was not a medical doctor but a Doctor of Science). She was convinced that women would respond more readily to trained nurses than to doctors who were for many women associated with expense and illness. But there was in fact a doctor on the premises, when one was needed. And that doctor was a woman.

The books drew both praise and abuse. Thousands of letters poured into her publishers. Marie almost became public property as the nation besieged her for advice. Many fans suggested that the book should be given to every couple on their wedding day. And it wasn't just women who wrote in - some 40 per cent of the letters came from men. Marie became the nation's first acknowledged adviser on sexual and emotional problems.

The medical profession, however, was outraged. The *Practitioner* hit out at *Married Love:* '...medical men have found in popular handbooks written by women with no medical qualification, practical information of which they had been hitherto ignorant and a great deal of which they might legitimately disapprove'.

Slowly, however, more were coming round to Marie's way of thinking. *The Times* continued to boycott her books but other sections of the press became less critical. The *Medical Times* wrote: 'All medical men and women should read this....they can't fail to glean valuable information'. The prestigious *Lancet* described it as an 'extremely sensible little book'.

But the church was still against her. And she seemed to be personally inviting hostility when she advocated sexual intercourse as an 'act of supreme value in itself...separate and distinct from its value as a basis for the procreation of children'. It took another 40 years before the established church agreed with her. The Roman Catholic church is still strongly against her ideas. At one time, Marie even wrote to the Pope to try to convert him to her way of thinking. She waited in vain for a reply.

In 1919, when Marie was 38, she suffered the tragedy of her first baby being still born. But on March 27th 1924, a fine boy baby was born to her. This gave her another reason to become obsessed with sex education. There followed a pamphlet, *Mother, How was I Born?* Then came *The Human Body and its Functions* - the first popular book to actually show the sex organs. In 1928, *Enduring Passion* appeared - a sequel to *Married Love* .

In 1932, Marie bought Norbury Park, an 18th century mansion, set in 40 acres of Surrey hills and woodland. But for all her worldly success, there were problems in the marriage. Slowly, over the years, her husband,

Humphrey was reduced to the position of a helper - he no longer did anything that wasn't subservient to her. Poor Marie. For all her theories, her own sex life always seemed to be unsatisfactory. Humphrey announced an end to their physical relationship.

Then in the summer of 1938, Humphrey did an extraordinary thing. He sent Marie a formal notification that she was perfectly free to have as many lovers as she chose! But was it Humphrey who initiated the letter? Some observers have posed the thought that Marie herself might have dictated the note to Humphrey. And Marie did indeed look for lovers - even in her sixties and seventies. And she liked them young.

Although a celebrity throughout the world for her sex books, Marie had always produced other writing - drama, novels, travel and poetry. These were not very successful. After 1939, almost all output was in verse. Typical was her long poem, *The Bathe*, written in 1946, sensuous and rather high flown.

Marie told her friends that she planned to live to 120 but she died on October 2nd 1958, aged 78. There was a memorial service to her in St Martin-in-the Fields. All her life she had looked for lasting married love and never found it. But through her writings on family planning, she helped millions. Today her books seem old fashioned. But as pioneering texts, they changed the world.□

NELLY TERNAN
(1839-1913)
THE *VERY* SECRET LOVE OF CHARLES DICKENS.

After Charles Dickens died in 1870, the first item in his will was a gift of £1000 to someone he had strenuously tried to demonstrate didn't exist! She was Claire Tomalin's 'Invisible Woman', from the book of the same name. Most of this account has been taken from that source.

When Dickens was 44, he met an actress, Nelly Ternan, aged 18, who became his mistress. But because - through his writings - he had become the nation's ideal family man, he realised that this secret dalliance must never be known. To achieve this cloak of secrecy, he went to the most extraordinary lengths. This is the story of Dickens' closet life and his closet girl from Kent.

Of course, the mere existence of the £1000 legacy simply deepens the mystery. Why, if Dickens had wanted to hide his affair, had he put Nelly's legacy first, giving it extra prominence? Or if, on the other hand, he had done it to demonstrate his affection for her, why was the legacy so small? After all, the total value of the estate - huge for the late 19th century was over £90,000.

These and other questions have been the subject of a number of books. For decades, researchers have queried this and made a guess at that. But it is only with Claire Tomalin's masterful 1990 biography that a number of answers have been given in a much firmer tone of voice.

Nelly (she was also called Ellen but was generally known as Nelly) was born to a theatrical family, in a small house in Maidstone Road, Rochester on March 3rd 1839. She had two sisters - both of whom in time would become actresses - her mother was on the stage and her father was an actor-manager. These early days were happy enough but before Nelly was six, her father developed an incurable mental illness (probably brought on by syphilis) and he was committed to an insane asylum at Bethnal Green. He died a few months later.

Deprived of the father's income, thrown back on their own wits for making a living, the Ternan family found life very hard. During Nelly's childhood and teenage years, they travelled from theatre to theatre, always on the look-out for work, which never seemed enough. They were often hungry.

In the summer of 1857, something happened to change their lives. Charles Dickens, who had always had a passion for the theatre, was helping to put on a play by his friend, Wilkie Collins. *The Frozen Deep* was an amateur production, held at the Gallery of Illustrations in Regent Street, London. The parts were taken by Dickens and his friends. Despite their amateur status the play was an enormous success, even attended and applauded by the Queen.

It was suggested that they transfer to the Manchester Free Trade Hall in August. Dickens grew concerned about the ladies in the cast. One had already suffered a sprain and could not go on. The Manchester venue was also much larger - would the voices of amateur ladies carry that far? So for one reason and another Dickens decided to do what was in fact common practice. He would keep the male amateurs but replace the ladies with professional actresses.

A friend introduced the Ternans and each of the four women - mother and three daughters - was given a role. Nelly has been described as 'fair and pretty and well developed'.

For 25 years, since before Nelly was born, Dickens had been the supreme entertainer of the nation. He was brilliant, rich and loved by everyone. So when Dickens began to pay her compliments and give her presents, Nelly accepted with pleasure. The romantic in Dickens heard with joy that Nelly had been born in Rochester - the place where Dickens had spent some of his own happiest years.

How did Dickens really feel about this 'fair, pretty' girl? Years later, a friend recalled that Nelly 'came like a breath of spring into the hard-working life of Charles Dickens - and enslaved him. She flattered him - he was ever appreciative of praise - and though she was not a good actress she had brains, which she used to educate herself, to bring her mind more on a level with his own. Who could blame her?...He had the world at his feet. She was a girl of 18, elated and proud to be noticed by him'.

According to other biographers, Dickens came upon Nelly earlier, when she was playing in *Atlanta* at the Haymarket. He is reported to have comforted her after finding her behind the scenes crying at the scantiness of her costume. We shall probably never know which meeting came first.

The kind of affair that was beginning was a situation that Dickens had written about in his novels. It made him hesitate - but he was too smitten to hold back for very long. The fictional story went like this. A rich man picks up a poor girl, gets her with child and then abandons her. Was he in danger of becoming that kind of villain?

But Dickens was no hard nosed exploiter. And there was still enough of the romantic in him to make him do unexpected things. His own marriage with Catherine had not been going well and Dickens now physically cut himself off from her. At their London home, Tavistock House, he blocked the door between his dressing room and what had been their marital bedroom - which now was left for Catherine alone. Soon after this, Catherine left the family home for good. Dickens found her a small, pretty house on the north side of Regents Park.

Dickens looked after all their children except Charley, who insisted on being with his mother. But there was now a lot less contact between the children and their father. That year, for the first time, he had them stay on at boarding school over the Christmas holidays. Where was the merry Christmas family man now?

The world began to get a whiff of scandal - but just a whiff, nothing of substance. Dickens reacted by going on the offensive. He put an announcement in both *The Times* and in his own *Household Words*, strongly denying the rumours. It is likely, however, that the population at large - Dickens' public - wanted to believe their favourite novelist. Friends of Dickens who may have alluded to an entanglement were likely to lose Dickens as a friend. It was more than just a fear of gossip. His friends had to act as if Nelly didn't exist!

But of course the affair went on. By 1858, Dickens was becoming very close to the whole Ternan family. One of Nelly's sisters, Fanny, had set her heart on singing lessons and now Dickens made this possible - he paid for her and her mother to spend a year in Florence. This left Marie and Nelly unchaperoned, in lodgings in Berners Street, London.

This however, proved difficult for the single girls returning home late at night from the theatre. Dickens then bought the Ternans a house in Mornington Crescent, close to Regents Park. By doing this, Dickens had offered Nelly her liberty if she had wanted it. But - according to Claire Tomalin - the house was 'a gift no respectable woman would have accepted and no mother who cherished her daughters' good names would have permitted.' Nelly accepted.

By August 1859, when Nelly left the theatre for the last time, it seems that the whole family was being supported by Dickens. From this time onwards, Dickens redoubled his efforts so that both of them - he and Nelly - could disappear from the limelight. In fact, if it was possible, Dickens would have liked them both to disappear without trace. Dickens had to remain 'respectable' in the eyes of his public and it is likely that the love of his public meant even more to him than the love of one woman.

By 1866, Nelly was settled into another address - Elizabeth Cottage in High Street, Slough. The Rate books show an amazing range of names that Dickens gave instead of his own. There was Mr John Tringham, Charles Tringham, later Ternan, and others. Slough was in a good position for Dickens to come and go on the expanding railway system. Later, Dickens moved Nelly to another house, this time in Peckham.

Dickens led a double life - Charles Dickens at his house at Gads Hill, near Rochester and Charles Tringham or whoever at Peckham. When he returned from his final reading tour of the US, none of his friends or family saw him until a week after he had arrived back in England. Of course, he was at Peckham with Nelly.

According to the standard account, Dickens died on June 8th 1870, at his country home, Gads Hill. But in the 1991 edition of *The Invisible Woman*, Claire Tomalin adds a final chapter. In this, she suggests an alternative account of Dickens death. He may, she points out, have died at Peckham. In this alternative version, Nelly brings the body to Gads Hill, to make it seem that - as far as the world was concerned - he died there. The story seems very plausible.

Nelly lived for another 44 years after Dickens' death, keeping the secrets of her past secret. On January 31st 1876, she married teacher and cleric, George Wharton Robinson. They bought the half share of a school at Margate and at first, things went well.

Then, in 1886, George had some kind of a breakdown. They were forced to sell the school and for the rest of their lives, were never really financially secure again. Nelly even had to sell the house Dickens had given her - in order to support her son, Geoffrey, as a proper officer in the army. Nelly died on April 25th 1913, admitting to an age over ten years younger than she really was. An actress to the end.□

ELLEN TERRY
(1847-1928)
ESCAPE TO KENT
by Amanda Hodges

George Bernard Shaw once said that the name of Ellen Terry was 'the most beautiful in the world; it rings like a chime through the last quarter of the 19th century'. Adored and feted by the public in her lifetime, Ellen Terry's legacy lives on - at her cottage in Smallhythe, maintained as a museum by the National Trust, and in her great-nephew, Sir John Gielgud.

The fourth child of Benjamin and Sarah Terry, strolling players, Ellen was born in 1847, in Coventry. In her *Memoirs*, she describes it as 'Shakespeare's own country'. All the Terry children were expected to

127

follow in their parents' footsteps. In 1856, at the age of nine, Ellen made her first appearance in Charles Kean's production of *A Winter's Tale*.

Even as a small girl, she displayed that feistiness of spirit that was later to endear her to the nation. During a performance of *A Midsummer Night's Dream*, Ellen's toe became trapped in a stage door. Despite the agonising pain, she carried on bravely until the end. As a reward for her fortitude, her salary was doubled!

When she was 16, Ellen's personal life began to encroach upon her time as an actress. She left the stage to marry the painter, G F Watts, 30 years her senior. The marriage was an unmitigated disaster and Ellen resumed her career. At this time, 1865, Ellen played second fiddle to her older sister, Kate (John Gielgud's grandmother to be). Kate was the star of the family, until her marriage in 1867.

In 1868, when she was 21, Ellen was again enticed away from the stage - she eloped with the architect, Edward Godwin. A friend of William Morris and the painter, James Whistler, Godwin was a charismatic widower who was keenly interested in the aesthetics of stage design. He is credited with influencing Ellen's highly visual acting style.

They were never legally married and although the union was to end with Edward Godwin's abrupt departure in 1875, Ellen always regarded him as the love of her life. The partnership brought her two lasting benefits - firstly her two children, Gordon and Edith Craig, who became esteemed stage and costume designers respectively. Godwin also left her with an abiding love of the countryside.

Tom Prideaux, a recent biographer, calls Ellen 'an incurable collector of cottages'. In these country retreats, Ellen could rest and recuperate. Tower Cottage at Winchelsea, near Rye, was one such haven, which she bought in 1896 and used intermittently until 1912. Although her cottage was intended as a brief respite from the acting world, Ellen could not entirely forget her roots. It is said that during these visits, she would often advise local amateur theatrical groups. Ightham Moat, near Sevenoaks, also provided Ellen with a chance to escape for a country weekend. The painter Sargeant, captured one such occasion, which depicts Ellen and the Palmer family enjoying a house party.

After the break-up of her relationship with Edward Godwin, Ellen was broke and badly in need of a job. She was recalled to the stage by her friend, Charles Reade, for the princely sum of £40.

Her first major triumph was in 1875 as Portia, in *The Merchant of Venice*. She radically changed the character's presentation, portraying Portia as a spirited, self-reliant heroine. Alice Comyns Carr describes her portrayal as 'utter naturalness of manner...which came directly from her own essential nature.' In her 1908 autobiographical *Story of my Life,* Ellen says she experienced the heady 'feelings of a conqueror'.

The young Oscar Wilde saw her performance and was so dazzled, he composed a sonnet that acclaimed:

'...In that gorgeous dress of beaten gold...

No woman...looked upon

Was half as fair as thou whom I behold'.

Tom Prideaux, in his biography, *Love or Nothing,* calls Ellen a 'century spanner, with one foot in the future and the other in the past'. Ellen lived at a time when the respectability of her profession was in the ascendant, after long being considered disreputable.

In her personal life, Ellen seems distinctly modern. After the breakdown of her early marriage, she conducted her affairs with discretion but also with an unusual degree of personal freedom for a Victorian woman. Her children were born illegitimate and it was one of Ellen's main concerns to shield them from the harsh glare of her fame. She aspired to be as much a dependable mother as an esteemed actress.

In her *Memoirs,* Ellen apologised for dwelling largely on theatrical concerns. 'I have lived very little in the world,' she wrote, 'for the life of an actress belongs to the theatre.' But by this, she did *not* mean that she was an actress first and a woman second. Unlike her beloved Irving, she did not live simply to act. Much of her appeal derived from her vivacious temperament and freshness, which was inseparable from her personal as well as her professional life.

The year 1878 was an important one in Ellen's career. It marked the beginning of her celebrated partnership at the Lyceum Theatre with the actor-manager, Henry Irving, which was to last until 1902. These years saw Ellen's greatest successes: as Ophelia (which Henry James, living in Rye, praised as 'schoolgirlish'); as Olivia in an adaptation of a Goldsmith play; and most memorably, to universal acclaim, as Beatrice in *Much Ado About Nothing,* opposite Irving's Benedict.

Although Ellen tackled a wide variety of roles, it was in Shakespeare that she found her niche. Her vivacious personality drew her to comedy which , with the enormous scope Shakespeare provided, well matched her poetic temperament. Max Beerbohm, always maintained that Ellen was ill-suited to most modern roles (such as the part J M Barrie created for her in the 1905 *Alice-Sit-by-the-Fire).* 'One longs for Shakespeare', Beerbohm intoned, 'who, alone among dramatists, can stand up to her'.

In 1899, happily fulfilled in her career, Ellen bought Smallhythe Place, near Tenterden in Kent. It was to become her favourite home. Apparently, whilst travelling through Kent some years earlier with Irving, Ellen had first glimpsed the farmhouse. In her impetuous fashion, Ellen declared to a nearby shepherd, 'This is where I should like to live and die'.

Years later, a postcard reading 'House for Sale' made the dream come true. 'The Farm,' as Ellen called it, was built in the 16th century. It struck a chord in Ellen's personality. In 1936, *The Times* critic E V Lucas noted that 'there was a wildness in her nature which assorts well with this brave old house...these rich beams...this isolation among fields.'

Smallhythe, despite its small size and seclusion, had once been a trading port. But its glory days were long gone when Ellen went to live there in 1900. Today, the charm of the house can still be felt. The low ceilings were a feature that reminded Ellen of her first childhood memory. She recalled 1908, when she watched the changing colours of the sky from the top of a bureau in the attic. Smallhythe was a return to the familiar.

During the First World War, Ellen would frequently recreate her past performances for the delight of her grandchildren, both of whom were living with her. Tom Prideaux recounts: 'a midnight wayfarer passing the Smallhythe cottage might see a dim light in an upstairs window. He would hear a woman's melodious voice mingling with a little boy's laughter as Ellen's grandson, Teddy, rolled with mirth in his blankets'.

Ellen retained a flat in London but it was to Smallhythe that she always returned. Here 'she was exactly where she wanted to be, watching the world around her'.

Ellen never officially retired. She celebrated her stage jubilee in 1906 and in 1915, played her final Shakespearean role - as the nurse in *Romeo and Juliet*. As the years went by, she charmed a new audience in America with her highly successful series of lectures on Shakespeare.

When she died, on July 21st 1928, her funeral service was held with the bells ringing joyously and with all those attending arrayed in colourful summer frocks - exactly as Ellen had instructed. The funeral procession made its way slowly to Golders Green in London where people thronged the route, paying homage to her memory. She was cremated and her ashes laid to rest in St Paul's, Covent Garden.

Edy, Ellen's daughter, bequeathed Smallhythe to the National Trust in 1939 after converting it into the Memorial Museum we find today. Each room holds a particular theatrical significance with the exception of Ellen's bedroom. This has been maintained almost as she left it, with its view over the peaceful countryside. In the grounds, the barn has become an intimate theatre. It presents annual plays, the props dating from Ellen's time at the Lyceum with Irving.

Ellen herself chose what can be considered the most fitting tribute to her memory. On the day of her funeral, visitors to the Farm would have seen the following poem by William Allingham. It was pinned to the gate.

'No funeral gloom my dears, when I am gone
Think of me as withdrawn into the dimness,
Yours still - you mine. Remember all the best
Our past moments and forget the rest.
And so to where I wait, come gently on'.□

DAME SYBIL THORNDIKE
(1882-1976)
SHE NEVER FORGOT HER KENT ORIGINS.

It was early evening and the two children had their noses pressed against the glass of their nursery window. Down below the dignitaries were heading for Rochester Cathedral, 'swooping by with their gowns flapping'. There was the Archdeacon, Canon Cheyne, with his characteristic two-steps, run-and-hop. He turned round, saw the children in the distance and waved. But he was too far away to see them act out his two-steps, run and hop. Mimicking was among the first acts carried out by the young Sybil Thorndike and her brother, Russell.

The family had settled in Rochester in 1884 when Sybil was only 18 months old (she was born on October 24th 1882 at Gainsborough, Lincolnshire). Her father's first job in Rochester was as a minor canon of Rochester Cathedral, when they had (appropriately) lived in Minor Canon Row (immortalised by Dickens in *Edward Drood*). In 1890, the minor canon became vicar of St Margaret's, Rochester and the family moved to the vicarage.

132

The young Thorndikes were regarded as friendly menaces by the cathedral vergers; the children used the crypt for their games and played hide and seek in the choir stalls.

Sybil was educated at Miss Rivett's School from age four-and-a-half to seven and then went to Rochester Grammar School. She began acting for her family at the age of four. At seven, she and her brother wrote plays and performed them for family and cathedral friends. One effort was a melodrama called *The Dentist's Cure* (subtitled *Saw their silly heads off!)* This could have been the beginning of Sybil's fascination with *Grand Guignol* - something she was to explore with such outstanding success in the 1920s. One of the first parts she played in public was as Brutus in her school's presentation of *Julius Caesar*. When she was ten, she was taken to her first professional play - *The Private Secretary* at Chatham Opera House.

Acting was Sybil's second choice for a career. Describing her childhood, she said, 'I dedicated myself to the Lord and the piano'. She continued to look to the Lord but found that in her late teens, preparation for a concert produced crippling pains in her left wrist. So when she was 20, 'feeling like a failed nun' she abandoned her musical ambitions. She took the advice of her brother Russell and joined him in training for the stage.

After three terms at acting school - which she found to be something of a doddle - Sybil joined Ben Greet's Company of Pastoral Players at Cambridge. After only a few weeks, the company set off for America; Sybil went with them, unchaperoned. She spent almost a year in the US doing mostly Shakespeare and playing a variety of roles. In fact, by 1907, she boasted that she had played 112 different parts.

She had to end her American tour after swallowing a piece of fluff - which had disastrous results. It badly affected her voice and she was prescribed six weeks of absolute silence. But even when this was over, she still had trouble with her voice for some years. It was exacerbated by overwork and overstrain - she often had to project her speech in many alfresco productions.

In 1908, she joined Miss Horniman's pioneering repertory company at the Gaiety, Manchester. Here she renewed her acquaintance with Lewis Casson, whom she married at her father's parish church at Aylesford that December. He became not only her husband and father to her children but also a lifelong manager, mentor, coach and (for much of her life) leading man.

She also met Bernard Shaw, who asked her to understudy in a revival of *Candida*. She found she shared Shaw's socialist politics and she was one of the founders of Actors' Equity in 1930.

133

Shaw, Miss Horniman's company, the Royal Court and others, were seeking a new dawn in theatrical expression, away from the purely commercial theatre. Shaw described it as 'an armoury against despair and dullness.' Casson, who had once planned to be a priest, shared this vision.

In the six productive years before the First World War, Sybil gave birth to her three children and spent two seasons with the Horniman company. She also played with the Charles Frohman company at the Duke of York's in London. She then made a short trip to America where she appeared in Somerset Maugham's *Smith.* In June 1912, she returned to Manchester.

A major turning point in Sybil's career came shortly after the outbreak of the First World War, when Ben Greet invited her to join him playing Shakespeare at the Old Vic. She remained there for four seasons, with a brief break for the birth of her second daughter, Ann. Sybil took leading roles in a dozen or more plays. To her delight, some of these were male roles as most men were with the armed forces. It was at this stage in her life - which included appearances in the commercial theatre - that Sybil began to win critical acclaim as a great actress.

She took on major roles, not only in Shakespeare but also in the Greek classics, Shaw, and modern plays. She played in *The Trojan Women,* which was tremendously successful. Her Hecuba and Medea were considered to be performances of a tragic stature that no other actress of her age in England could have achieved.

In the early 1920s, she played at the Little Theatre for two years in a series of *Grand Guignol,* mostly translated from the French. They satisfied Sybil's urge to go over the top, to pull out all the stops. In the *Old Woman,* she had her eyes gouged out with knitting needles by crazed fellow inmates of an insane asylum.

When the public had had enough of horror, Sybil acted in many other types of play. The early climax in her career came with Shaw's *St Joan,* which he had written especially for her. It opened at the New Theatre in March 1924 and enjoyed an initial run of 244 performances. According to her biographer, *St Joan* had a profound and lasting effect upon Sybil's life and her attitude to theatre. It also brought her national fame. When it was finally brought to a close by the General Strike of 1926, the play had run at three theatres and Sybil was 43. Shaw had given her permission to play it as long as she wished and, as well as the home performances, Sybil toured as Joan for eight years - in Paris, Australia and South Africa. In the intervals, she appeared in Shakespeare, modern plays, and even in silent films.

In 1929, she was given the Honorary Freedom of the City of Rochester - her old home town. Two years later, when she was nearly 50, she became a Dame of the British Empire.

134

During the Second World War, the Cassons toured the Welsh mining villages and towns, bringing *Macbeth, Medea,* and *Candida* to many for the first time. Between 1944 and 1946, Sybil worked with Olivier and Richardson with the Old Vic company at the New Theatre. Sir Lewis Casson had been knighted in 1945.

During the post war years, Sybil continued to make acclaimed appearances, both on stage and in films. She also toured Australia and South Africa again with her husband. In 1962, the Cassons joined Olivier, first at the Chichester and then the National Theatre at the Old Vic. Sybil made her final appearance at the theatre named after her, the Thorndike Theatre at Leatherhead, in October 1969, six months after the death of her husband.

In 1970, Sybil was made a Companion of Honour. She also had several honorary degrees including an Oxford D Lit awarded her in 1966. She often visited her childhood haunts in Kent. In 1961, she opened Thorndike House, a block of old people's flats. In 1969, she gave a Dickens reading in Restoration House, Rochester, where she had given her first piano recital.

After two heart attacks in two days, Dame Sybil Thorndike died in her flat in Chelsea, on June 9th 1976, at the age of 93.

According to *The Times* obituary, Sybil Thorndike achieved fame despite several acting liabilities. As a young actress, her beauty was not easily marketable. She had little erotic attraction - what Ivor Brown called the 'Cleopatra flame'. She also found it difficult to project the passion of romantic love. She said herself 'I've never really liked love parts.' Some even called her style 'masculine.'

Yet for all this, her career was an enormous success. She could be regal and have the common touch, aggressive and whisper-quiet. She could mantle herself in moral grandeur and blaze with fun. She was also a worker. Her popularity was immense and she was probably the best-loved English actress since Ellen Terry

To countless people over three generations, Dame Sybil brought not only enormous pleasure but a real sense of what great theatre is all about.□

MARY TOURTEL
(1874-1948)
THE GENIUS OF RUPERT BEAR

Little Lost Bear. By MARY TOURTEL

No. 1.—Mrs. Bear sends her little son Rupert to market.

Two jolly bears once lived in a wood;
Their little son lived there too.
One day his mother sent him off
The marketing to do.

She wanted honey, fruit, and eggs,
And told him not to stray,
For many things might happen to
Small bears who lost the way.

Since Rupert Bear first appeared on the scene in 1920, well over 100 million of his books have been sold. Such is the amazing publishing success of this delightful little cartoon character - the brain child of Canterbury-born Mary Tourtel.

The *raison d'être* for Rupert was a circulation war raging between the popular newspapers in the early 1920s. Teddy Tail was wooing the readers of the *Daily Mail* and Pip, Squeak and Wilfred were doing the same for the *Daily Mirror*. The *Daily News* had the Arkubs. But the *Daily Express* had nothing similar for its young readers.

Mary had already done some work for the *Express* and had married the night editor, Herbert Tourtel. Herbert was now asked to come up with a competing comic strip for the *Express* and not unnaturally he looked to his wife, a specialist in drawing animals. So the successful partnership began, with Mary doing the drawings and Herbert the words.

Mary Tourtel was born Mary Caldwell on January 28th 1874, at 52 Palace Street, Canterbury. She came from a very talented family. Mary's father, Samuel, designed and restored stained glass for Rochester Cathedral; his eldest son, also called Samuel, followed in his father's footsteps. Another of Mary's brothers, Edmund Caldwell, was an animal painter of distinction, who had exhibited at the Royal Academy and illustrated many children's books.

Even as a child, Mary was seldom without her sketchbook, drawing animals, which she loved. She was educated at the Simon Langton School for Girls, a new establishment which had only opened in 1881. But she was never happy there as the only thing she excelled at was art. She felt much more at home later when she moved on to Sidney Cooper's Gallery of Art, where her brother Edmund had studied. Her teacher there was Thomas Sidney Cooper, RA, then Britain's best animal painter. Mary, as one of his star pupils, studied under him for four enjoyable years. Among her many prizes was a gold medal and the much coveted Princess of Wales' Scholarship in 1894.

Mary slipped easily into a career of drawing animals for children's books. She had several sketches published by the *Express.* In 1919, the *Sunday Express* published her feature called *In Bobtail Land.* When Mary was 29, her first book. *The Little Horse,* was published, followed by *Three Little Foxes.*

But it was Rupert Bear that made Mary Tourtel a household name. During the 1920s, the little Bear established himself in the hearts of children in Britain and overseas. In the *Express,* Mary involved her characters in a series of adventures, in a world of fantasy. There were flying dragons, wicked wolves, and Rupert's own village of Nutwood. Playmates were created for Rupert. These included Algy Pug, Bill Badger, Edward Trunk, Podgy Pig, the Wise Old Goat, and many others. The stories were loved not only for the fertile imagination of their creator - they were drawn with skill and finesse.

But success also made demands. A newspaper is produced every day and there is no way of avoiding the constant, inexorable deadlines. Sometimes, Mary's backgrounds would look unfinished. On other days, she didn't manage to complete an episode at all and the editor was forced to put a notice in the paper saying Rupert was on holiday.

Mary and Herbert never had any children and it has been suggested that Rupert may have been their dream child substitute. For years, Herbert suffered from ill health. Mary, like her brother Edmund, had failing eyesight. Despite this, Mary and Herbert were both interested in aviation and often volunteered to be passengers in early flights to the continent. In

1919, they flew in a Handley-Page, on a record-breaking flight from Hounslow to Brussels.

By 1930, Mary was 56 and Herbert 57. They were devoted to each other and when Herbert developed heart trouble, Mary accompanied him, first to Italy and then to Germany, where he entered a sanatorium. On June 6th 1931, Herbert died there. Mary was devastated, not only at the loss of her partner but also the man who had been her mentor and the source of many of her ideas.

She returned to England, where her eyes continued to worsen and she found herself badly affected by bright light. The *Express* started to look for a successor. While this was being done, they tried to reduce the strain on Mary by printing some of the past Rupert series, interspersed with new ones. In 1935, Mary retired with an *Express* pension and the rights to many of her stories. A year later, in 1936, the *Express* began publication of the Rupert annuals.

Mary returned to Canterbury and settled down in Baker's Temperance Hotel, at 63 Ivy Lane (now the Chaucer Hotel). At the age of 74, Mary suddenly collapsed in Canterbury High Street. She died at the Kent and Canterbury Hospital on March 15th 1948 and was buried with Herbert's ashes in St Mary's churchyard.

In 1989, the Rupert and Canterbury Group was formed and fans have this group to thank for the various Canterbury plaques which have been put up to commemorate Mary's life.

But some say that Mary will never really die while her beloved creation lives on. The strip was continued by Alfred Bestall. His brief was that there were to be no bad characters, no magic, and no fairies. Alfred didn't always keep to this but he created a lot of new characters and took Rupert to every corner of the globe. Alfred Bestell continued until his death at the age of 93, in 1986. Today, Rupert has a new partnership - John Harold does the drawings and Ian Robinson the words.

Such longevity underlines Mary Tourtel's creative genius. Rupert Bear has been used on numerous products, songs have been written about him and he has starred on television and in the theatre. If you can find any of the early Rupert books these days, they sell for several hundred pounds in good condition. And it seems the familiar little bear with the check woollen scarf around his neck is set to go on forever.◻

SIMONE WEIL
(1909-1943)
ASHFORD'S SAINTLY FRENCH MYSTIC

On Friday July 8th 1983, the Cultural Counsellor of the French Embassy, Monsieur Giles Chouraqui, representatives of the Association for the Study of the Thoughts of Simone Weil, and local dignitaries, gathered in Ashford to pay their respects to a saint - to the woman who simply came to their town to die. Simone Weil, author, philosopher and mystic, arrived in Ashford on August 17th 1943 and died in Grosvenor Sanatorium at Kennington, Ashford (now the Police Training College) on August 22nd. She didn't have to die. She starved herself to death.

Some 40 years on, the French and English bigwigs had come to Ashford to open the new road, Simone Weil Avenue, to put flowers on her grave at Bybrook Cemetery and to honour her memory. A sign at the side of the road (at the junction with Canterbury Road) gives an account of her life.

139

Simone Weil was born and brought up in Paris, of well-to-do (non-practising) Jewish parents. She was extremely bright and attended the Lycée Henri IV, where she (and also her brother) obtained their baccalaureate at the age of 14. Simone was then one of the first women to be admitted to the august Ecole Normale Supérieure.

Some found her brilliance hard to get along with. One teacher complained: 'she aims too much for originality, even eccentricity'. Fellow students found her strange and unapproachable, even 'inhuman'. Her biographer, David McLellan, in *Simone Weil, Utopian Pessimist,* says the French intellectual world was more welcoming to *enfants terribles* than to candidates for sainthood. Simone was called 'the categorical in skirts'; for her politics she earned the sobriquet the 'Red Virgin.'

From a young age, Simone had a highly developed social conscience and wanted to be part of the poor. At the age of three, she refused the gift of a ring from one of her cousins, saying, 'I don't like luxury'.

Her family were fastidious to an extraordinary extent - this trait fostered a lifelong dread of physical contact. Kissing was forbidden for fear of germs. Mealtimes were preceded by excessive hand washing.

Self sacrifice was always part of Simone. As a child, when the family was moving house, Simone refused to budge until she was given the heaviest bundle. When she became a teacher, her qualifications entitled her to a higher salary than the general run of teaching staff - but she was determined never to spend more than those on the lower pay scale.

She admired Marx but never joined the Communist Party. However, her socialist sympathies meant that she never stayed in one job for long. Her left-wing writings and trade union activities made her unpopular with the authorities. After graduating, her first employment was teaching philosophy at a girl's school in Le Puy; she was dismissed for demonstrating with strikers outside the school.

Simone's teaching career was interrupted by her wish to experience the life of the working class. She wanted 'real work' - which in her eyes was manual. She even brought a press to class for her students to print their own compositions. But they objected to getting their hands dirty.

Simone spent a year as a power press operator at the Renault factory outside Paris. Writing of it afterwards, she said: 'I received forever the mark of a slave. Even today, when any human being speaks to me without brutality, I cannot help having the impression that there must be a mistake'. During her time in the factory, Simone refused to heat her flat 'because the poor can't afford to'. Later, she was engaged in hard manual labour on a farm near Marseilles but her constant lectures to her employers about the troubles of the world led them to say, 'so much study has driven her out of her wits'. In 1936, she served briefly with Republican forces in the Spanish Civil War.

It was during November 1938 that she had one of her most significant mystical experiences. Simone's health had always been frail and at this time she was suffering from a painful and unexplained illness. At the worst moments, she recited *Love,* a poem by a 17th-century religious poet, George Herbert. She fixed all her attention on the poem.

She later described the feeling that Christ was present. She wrote: 'A presence more personal, more certain, and more real than that of a human being...Moreover in this sudden possession of me by Christ, neither my senses nor my imagination had any part; I only felt in the midst of my suffering the presence of love, like that which one can read in the smile on a beloved face'.

Another of her biographers, Simone Pétrement, argues at length concerning this experience. He then writes: 'I believe that what permits us to distinguish the true mystic from those who often resemble him is in the quality of saintliness. A pure love, a love that does not seek egotistical satisfactions, that seeks the good of others...such a love can be believed when it declares that it has encountered a reality that goes beyond itself and is not a thing of this world'.

Such experiences brought her to the brink of conversion to Christianity. She revered the sacraments of Catholicism but she was never baptised. It seems that she preferred to identify herself with the poor and powerless outside the church.

In 1942, there was a chance to escape from German-occupied France. With deep reluctance, Simone agreed to accompany her family to America for she knew they would not go without her. However, after only a few months, she joined the Headquarters of the Provisional French Government in London. Here she began what was to lead ultimately to her death in Ashford. At work, she drove herself relentlessly, denying herself any more food than the minimal allowed in occupied France. In such a low physical state, she contracted tuberculosis which proved fatal.

Most of Simone Weil's work was published after her death. It led to her being considered one of the greatest philosophers of the 20th century.

Referring to her last days, David McLellan wondered if, in her eyes, she had become too good for this world She had rejected her Jewish heritage for a mystical Christianity. 'I have a sort of growing inner certainty', she wrote to her parents shortly before her death, 'that there is within me a deposit of pure gold which must be handed on. Only I become more and more convinced, by experience and by observing my contemporaries, that there is no one to receive it'.

Simone was only 34 when she died. The *Kent Messenger* carried this headline about the woman who had come so recently into its news-gathering area: 'Death from Starvation: French Professor's Curious Sacrifice'. Surprisingly, there was no obituary in *The Times*. □

ILLUSTRATIONS

Anna of Cleves (from the Gatehouse Exhibition, Dartford Manor).

The Murder of Thomas Arden (from wood-block print, *Arden of Feversham,* third edition 1633).

Elizabeth Barton, the Holy Maid of Kent (line drawing by Susi, from a 1796 illustration, published by R Bower, Historic Gallery, Pall Mall, London).

Mrs Isabella Beeton aged about 26 (Rodney Levick, *Isabella and Sam - the Story of Mrs Beeton,* by Sarah Freeman, Gollanz).

Aphra Behn in her 20s (The Stowe portrait in an engraving by Fittler in *Effigies Poetae,* 1824, attributed by him to Mary Beale).

The Martyrs' Memorial at Wincheap, Canterbury, where Alice Benden and 40 other men and women were burnt at the stake during the reign of Queen Mary (photograph by Bowen Pearse).

The Biddenden Maids, village sign (photograph by Bowen Pearse).

Enid Blyton's house and plaque (colour slide by C McCooey).

Anne Boleyn (from a painting by an unknown artist).

Frances Hodgson Burnett (from *Men and Women of the Day,* 1888).

Elizabeth Carter, aged 42, from the painting attributed to Joseph Highmore. In the background is a muse passing a laurel branch to somebody almost hidden in shadow. The portrait was presented to the Corporation of Deal in January 1815 by Mrs Carter's nephew. It hangs in the Council Chamber of Deal's Town Hall (by permission of Deal Council).

Julia and Henry Ady, around 1900 (photograph by permission of Joan de Smith).

Eleanor Cobham (line drawing by permission of Carson Ritchie).

Gladys Cooper (from colour postcard).

The grave of Mrs Craik in Keston Church yard (colour slide by C McCooey).

Richmal Crompton in 1929.

Statue/reliquary and stained-glass window of St Eanswythe, in St Mary and St Easnwythe church, Folkestone (colour slide by C McCooey).

Banner depicting Queen Ethelburga, in St Mary and St Ethelburga church, Lyminge, Kent (colour slide by C McCooey).

Kitty Fisher with a kitten fishing in a goldfish bowl as a pun on her name (from the original painting by Nathaniel Hone, courtesy of the National Portrait Gallery).

Fanny Fitzwilliam as a dairy maid in the 1822 play *Maid or Wife.* (line drawing by Susi from an 1822 print).

Octavia Hill (photograph by courtesy of the Octavia Hill Society).

Geraldine Jewsbury (line drawing by Susi, from a contemporary portrait).

Joan, Fair Maid of Kent (by courtesy of the British Library, from Strutt's *Regal and Ecclesiastical Antiquities,* No. XXXV ed 1793).

Marie Lloyd (photograph by courtesy of Hackney Archives Department).

Woman being burnt at the stake (drawing by Susi).

Katharine Moore (colour print by Leigh Eduardo).

Edith Nesbitt (photograph by courtesy of Greenwich Library).

Statue of Pochahontas in the garden of St George's Church, Gravesend, Kent (photograph by Bowen Pearse).

Anne Pratt (contemporary line drawing).

Jean Rook (cartoon by Susi).

Vita Sackville-West (line drawing by Joan Edmonds).

Ethel Smyth (charcoal drawing by Susi, from original drawing held in the National Portrait Gallery).

Lady Hester Stanhope (black and white print by courtesy of the British Museum).

Marie Stopes (photograph by courtesy of Marie Stopes International).

Nelly Ternan (photograph by kind permission of John Colme).

Ellen Terry (post card by courtesy of Smallhythe Place, National Trust).

Sybil Thorndike as Aunt Anna Rose in *Treasure Hunt* at the Apollo Theatre September 1949 (from an advertising poster).

Mary Tourtel (back cover - photograph by courtesy of Express Newspapers Plc).

The first Rupert cartoon to appear in the *Daily Express* (by courtesy of Express Newspapers Plc).

Simone Weil at Baden Baden 1921 (from the biography, *Simone Weil,* by Simone Petrement, translated from the French, Mowbrays, 1976).

The Publisher has tried to track down all original illustrations and to give credit. This has not been possible in every case. If those whose original material has not been credited would like to write to JAK, the Publisher will be happy to make the appropriate arrangements.

For line drawings by Susi contact:
Susi Nightingale, Box and Rose Cottage, Capton, Dartmouth, Devon, TQ6 0JE.
Tel: 01803-712579

SOURCES AND FURTHER READING

1. Anna of Cleves

Boreham, Peter W. *Dartford's Royal Manor House Rediscovered* Dartford Borough Council (1991).
Church, Richard. *Kent Contributions* Adams and Dart (1972).
Fraser, Antonia. *The Six Wives of Henry VIII* Mandarin (1993).
Keyes, S K. *Some Historical Notes* Available from Dartford Library.
Winnifrith, Rev A. *The Fair Maids of Kent* (1921).
Information Sheet prepared by Dartford Library
Anne of Cleves at Dartford. in *West Kent Advertiser* (May 5th 1922).

2. Alice Arden

Holt, Anita. *Arden of Feversham, a Study of the Play First Published in 1592* The Faversham Society (1970).
Theatre programmes from productions at the Lyric Hammersmith, the Renaissance Theatre, and the Theatre
　　　Royal.

3. Elizabeth Barton, 'Holy Maid of Kent'.

Neame, Alan. *The Holy Maid of Kent, the Life of Elizabeth Barton* Hodder and Stoughton (1971).
Winnifrith, Rev A. *The Fair Maids of Kent* (1921).
Allen, William G. Kent's Own Holy Maid in *The Criminologist*.
Tomlinson, Norma. The Predictions of the Holy Maid in *Bygone Kent* (Vol 2, No 3).

4. Mrs Beeton

Freeman, Sarah. *Isabella and Sam, The Story of Mrs Beeton* Victor Gollancz (1977).
Spain, Nancy.*The Beeton Story* Ward, Lock (1956).

5. Aphra Behn

Duffy, Maureen.*The Passionate Shepherdess* Jonathan Cape (1977).
Goreau, Angeline. *Reconstructing Aphra* Oxford University Press (1980).
Sackville-West, Victoria. *The Incomparable Astrea*.
Jones, Jane; New Light on the background and early life of Aphra Behn in *Notes and Queries*, (Vol 23 1990).

6. Alice Benden

Knight, Henry R. *Loyal to the King* D Catt (1903).
Timpson, Thomas. *Church History of Kent* Ward (1859).
Bateman, Audrey. Alice Benden, Kentish Martyr in *Bygone Kent* (Vol 8, No 10).

7. The Biddenden Maids

The Story of Biddenden Biddenden Local History Society (1989).
Winnifrith, Rev A. *The Fair Maids of Kent* (1921).

8. Enid Blyton

Carpenter, Humphrey and Pritchard, Mari, eds *Oxford Companion to Children's Literature* Oxford University
　　　Press (1991).
Smallwood, Imogen (Enid Blyton's daughter) *A Childhood at Green Hedges* Methuen (1989).
Stoney, Barbara. *Enid Blyton, the Biography* Hodder and Stoughton (1992).
Obituary in *TheTimes* (November 28th 1968).

9. Anne Boleyn

Church, Richard. *Kent Contributions;* Adams and Dart (1972).
Fraser, Antonia. *The Six Wives of Henry VIII* Mandarin (1993).
Winnifrith, Rev A. *The Fair Maids of Kent* (1921).

10. Frances Hodgson Burnett

Fisher, Lois, H *A Literary Gazetteer of England* McGraw-Hill (1980).
Thwaite, Ann.*Waiting for the Party, the Life of Frances Hodgson Burnett* Faber and Faber (1994).
Chevalier, Tracey, Ed. *Twentieth Century Children's Writers* St James Press (1989).

11. Elizabeth Carter

Gaussen, C. *A Woman of Wit and Wisdom* Smith Elder & Co (1906).
Collins, B. Parson Carter's Daughter in *Kent Seen*.
Deller, Julie. Elizabeth Carter - Deal's Blue Stocking in *Bygone Kent* (Vol 10, nos 7 and 8).

12. Julia Cartwright

Emanuel, Angela, Ed. *A Bright Remembrance, the Diaries of Julia Cartwright* Weidenfeld and Nicolson (1989).

The Europa Biographical Dictionary of British Women.

de Smith, Joan. A Victorian's View of Charing in *Kent Seen* (January and February 1990).

13. Eleanor Cobham

Hassall, William Owen. *Who's Who in History* Vol I, 55 BC-1485 Blackwell (1961).

Richie, Carson. Kent's Fatal Duchess in *Bygone Kent* (Vol 12, No 9).

14. Gladys Cooper

Concise Oxford Companion to the Theatre Oxford University Press (1992).

Kimber, Jane. *Famous Women in Lewisham* London Borough of Lewisham (1986).

Morley, Sheridan *Gladys Cooper, a Biography* Heinemann (1979).

Cooper, Gladys. Gladys Cooper Tells her Story in *The Strand Magazine* (1914).

Home from Hollywood. in *Sketch and Bystander* (September 19th 1945).

Obituary. Dame Gladys Cooper in *The Times* (November 18th 1971).

15. Mrs Dinah Craik

Todd, Janet, Ed. *Dictionary of British Women Writers* Routledge (1989)

Vinson, James, ed. *Novelists and Prose Writers* from the series *Great Writers of the English Language* McMillan (1979)

16. Richmal Crompton

Cadogan, Mary. *Richmal Crompton, the Woman Behind William* Allen and Unwin (1986).

Williams, Kay. *Just Richmal, The Life and Work of Richmal Crompton Lamburn* Genesis Publications (1987).

Obituary in *The Times* (January 13th 1969).

Watkins, A H. Richmal Crompton in *Bromleage* (September 1980).

17. Saint Eanswythe

Edwards, Dame Eanswythe. *St Eanswythe of Folkestone, Her Life, Her Relics, and Her Monastery* (1980).

St Mary & St Eanswythe, Folkestone. (The church guide).

Winnifrith, Rev A. *The Fair Maids of Kent* (1921).

Woodward, M. *The Past and Present of the Parish Church of Folkestone* (1892).

18. Queen Ethelburga

Jenkins, R C. *Pedigree of the Kentish Kings* (1867)

Winnifrith, Rev A. *The Fair Maids of Kent* (1921).

Witney, K P. *The Kingdom of Kent* Phillimore (1982)

19. Kitty Fisher

Bleackley, Horace. *Ladies Frail and Fair: Sketches of the Demi-Monde, 18 th century* John Lane (1909 and 1925).

Hardy, C F, ed. *Benenden Letters* (1901).

Haslewood, Rev F. *The Parish of Benenden, Kent* (1889).

Cooper, John. Courtesan Kitty Lives on in a Child's Ditty in *Daily Mail;* (October 25th 1994).

20. Fanny Elizabeth Fitzwilliam

Jones, J Bavington. *Dover: a Perambulation.*

21. Octavia Hill

Darley, Gillian. *Octavia Hill* Constable (1990).

Hill, William Thomson. *Octavia Hill, Pioneer of the National Trust* Hutchinson (1956).

Bradley, Ian. The Old Lady of Crockham Hill in *Kent Life* (December 1970).

Fawcett, Edward. Octavia Hill in *National Trust* (Autumn 1981).

Hiller, Caroline. Octavia Hill in *National Trust Newsletter* (1988).

Upcott, Janet. Octavia Never Looked Sideways in *National Trust Newsletter* (No 8, June 1970).

22. Geraldine Jewsbury

Howe, Susanne. *Geraldine Jewsbury, Her Life and Errors* George Allen and Unwin (1935).

Jewsbury, Geraldine. Mrs Ireland ed. *Selections from the letters of Geraldine Jewsbury to Jane Welsh Carlyle* Longmans (1892).

Geraldine and Jane in *Times Literary Supplement* (February 28th 1929).

Smithers, David Waldron. A Woman of Undying Devotion, a Brief Biography of Geraldine Jewsbury in *Kent Life* (September 1983).

Woolf, Virginia. Geraldine and Jane in *Times Literary Supplement* (February 28th 1929).

146

23. Joan, the "Fair Maid of Kent"

Tickell, S C. *Map, History, Chronology and Architectural Notes of Stamford BC 863- AD1906* Dolby Brothers, Stamford.

Walker, Henry. *Stamford with its Surroundings* The Homeland Association (1908).

Wallcott, M E C. *Memorials of Stamford: Past and Present* Henry and James Johnson, Stamford (1867).

Winnifrith, Rev A. *The Fair Maids of Kent* (1921).

Clark, Sydney. The Black Prince and Canterbury in *Bygone Kent* (Vol 6, No 9).

24. Marie Lloyd

Farson, Daniel. *Marie Lloyd and the Music Hall* Stacey (1972).

Jacob, Naomi. *Our Marie* Hutchinson.

Obituary in *The Hendon Times* (October 13th 1922, page 5).

25. Susannah Lott

Allen, William G, Susannah Lott - the Last Woman to be burnt at the Stake in this country in *Bygone Kent*.

In *Gentleman's Magazine* (September 1769).

In *Kentish Gazette* (July 1769).

Original transcript from court proceedings, by courtesy of William Allen.

26. Katharine Moore

A Family Life, 1939-45 Allison and Busby.

A Particular Glory Darenth Press

The Katharine Moore Omnibus Allison and Busby.

Victorian Wives Allison and Busby

Cordial Relations: the Maiden Aunt in Fact and Fiction. Heinemann

She for God Allison and Busby.

Moore, Katharine and Grenfell, Joyce *An Invisible Friendship* Futura.

27. Edith Nesbit

Briggs, Julia. *A Woman of Passion, the Life of E Nesbit 1858-1924* Hutchinson (1987).

28. Pocahontas

Garnett, David. *Pocahontas* Chatto (1972).

Mossiker, Frances. *Pocahontas* Gollancz (1977)

Watson, Virginia. *The Princess Pocahontas* Penn Publishing Co (1927).

29. Anne Pratt

Desmond, Ray. *Dictionary of British and Irish Botanists* (1994).

Hadfield, Miles. *British Gardeners: a Biographical Dictionary* (1980).

The Journal of Botany (1894).

Stafleau, F A and Cowan, R S. *Taxonomic Literature.*

30. Jean Rook

Rook, Jean. *The Cowardly Lioness* Sidgwick and Jackson (1989).

Grant, Georgina. Coming Home to Kent in *Kent Life;* (September 1989).

Obituary in *The Times* (September 6th 1991).

Masked Raiders Rob Jean Rook in *The Times* (February 2nd 1985).

31. Vita Sackville-West

Glendinning, Victoria. *Vita: The Life of Vita Sackville-West* Penguin (1984).

Sackville-West, Vita. *Knole and the Sackvilles* National Trust (1991).

32. Ethel Smyth

Beecham, Thomas. *A Mingled Chime* (1944).

Collis, Louise. *Impetuous Heart* Kimber (1984)

Henschel, George. *Musings and Memories of a Magician* (1918).

Pankhurst, Christabel. *Votes for Women newspaper* (1911)

Smythe, Ethel. *Female Pipings in Eden* Longmans Green (1933)

Smythe, Ethel. *Impressions that Remained* Longmans Green (1919)

Smythe, Ethel. *What Happened Next* Longmans Green (1940)

Woolf, Virginia. *Her Diary.*

Sackville West, Edward. Ethel Smythe as I Knew Her in *The New Statesman* (June 1944)

33. Lady Hester Stanhope

Childs, Virginia. *Lady Hester Stanhope* Weidenfeld & Nicolson (1990).
Haslip, Joan. *Lady Hester Stanhope* Cassell (1934).
Meryon, Dr Charles, Ed. *Memoirs of Lady Hester Stanhope* Colburn (1845)

34. Marie Stopes

Briant, Keith *Marie Stopes, a Biography* Hogarth Press (1962).
Rose, June. *Marie Stopes and the Sexual Revolution* Faber (1992).
Boreham, P W. *The Stopes Family at Swanscombe* Dartford Borough Museum. Leaflet.
Marie Stopes International. *Marie Stopes, 1880-1958.* Leaflet.
Obituary in *The Times* (October 3rd 1958).

35. Nelly Ternan

Du Can, C G L. *The Love Lives of Charles Dickens* Frederick Muller (1961). Nisbit, Ada. *Dickens and Nelly Ternan* University of California Press, and Cambridge University Press (1952).
Slater, Michael. *Dickens and Women* J M Dent (1983).
Tomalin, Claire. *The Invisible Woman* Penguin Books (1991).
Various articles in *The Dickensian.*

36. Ellen Terry

Morley, Sheridan. *The Great Stage Stars* Angus and Robertson (1986).
Prideaux, Tom *Love or Nothing* Millington (1976).
Sinden, Donald, Ed. *Theatrical Anecdotes* Dent (1987).
Terry, Ellen. *The Story of My Life* Boydell Press (1982).
St John, Chris. *A Short Biography* in *National Trust* (1947).
Woolf, Vivienne Smallhythe Place *Country Life.*

37. Sybil Thorndike

Casson, Patricia ed. *"My Dear One", a Victorian Courtship* [with the beginnings of an autobiography by Sybil Thorndike Casson] (1984).
Morley, Sheridan. *A Life in the Theatre* Weidenfeld and Nicolson (1977).
Sprigge, Elizabeth; *Sybil Thorndike Casson* [with a forward by Dame Sybil] Gollanz (1971).
Thorndike, Russell. *Sybil Thorndike* Rockcliff (1950).
Trewin, J C. *Sybil Thorndike* [Theatre World Monograph no 4] Rockcliff (1955).
Obituary in *The Times* June 10th 1976.

38. Mary Tourtel

Bailey, Ben. The Rupert Lady in *Kent Seen.*

39. Simone Weil

Encyclopaedia of Philosophy, Vol 8 Collier Macmillan (1967).
Harvey, Sir Paul, ed. *Oxford Companion to French Literature* Oxford University Press (1959).
McLellan, David. *Simone Weil - Utopian Pessimist;* Macmillan.
Raven, Susan and Weir, Alison. *Women in History* Weidenfeld and Nicolson (1981).
Petrement, Simone; translated from the French by Raymond Rosenthal. *Simone Weil* Mowbrays (1976).

Please Note.

To avoid repetition, it should be noted that the following were consulted as a matter of course: For the majority of women: *The Dictionary of National Biography,* in various dates and editions; for British women: Crawford, Anne, ed. et al *Europa Biographical Dictionary of British Women.;* for authors: Drabble, Margaret, Ed *Oxford Companion to English Literature* Oxford University Press (1985); and Eagle, Dorothy, and Carnell, Hilary, eds *Oxford Illustrated Literary Guide to Great Britain and Ireland* Oxford University Press (1981); and for actresses: *Concise Oxford Companion to the Theatre* Oxford University Press (1992).

INDEX

Bowen Pearse was born and brought up on an Australian cattle station. After completing his education in Sydney, he was employed by a local advertising agency to write copy 'in the language the countryman understands'. He later travelled extensively in Europe and Asia and worked both as a copywriter and a journalist in London, Hongkong and Tokyo. His book, *Companion to Japanese Britain and Ireland*, was first published in 1991, to great critical acclaim. He lives in a 16th-century Kentish farmhouse, surrounded by fields, with his wife, Janice, two children and a Cairn Terrier called Jacky.